# Mastering JavaServer Faces 2.2

Master the art of implementing user interfaces with JSF 2.2

**Anghel Leonard**

PUBLISHING

BIRMINGHAM - MUMBAI

# Mastering JavaServer Faces 2.2

First published: June 2014

Production reference: 1190614

Published by Packt Publishing Ltd.
Livery Place
35 Livery Street
Birmingham B3 2PB, UK.

ISBN 978-1-78217-646-6

www.packtpub.com

Cover image by Pratyush Mohanta (tysoncinematics@gmail.com)

# Credits

**Author**

Anghel Leonard

**Reviewers**

Mert Çalışkan

Michael Kurz

Thierry Leriche-Dessirier

Michael Müller

Luca Preziati

**Commissioning Editor**

Owen Roberts

**Acquisition Editor**

Owen Roberts

**Content Development Editor**

Sriram Neelakantan

**Technical Editors**

Krishnaveni Haridas

Taabish Khan

Pramod Kumavat

Mukul Pawar

Siddhi Rane

**Copy Editors**

Laxmi Subramanian

**Project Coordinator**

Akash Poojary

**Proofreaders**

Simran Bhogal

Ameesha Green

Paul Hindle

Samantha Lyon

Lucy Rowland

**Indexers**

Hemangini Bari

Mehreen Deshmukh

Tejal Soni

**Graphics**

Valentina Dsilva

**Production Coordinator**

Arvindkumar Gupta

**Cover Work**

Arvindkumar Gupta

# About the Author

**Anghel Leonard** is a senior Java developer with more than 13 years of experience in Java SE, Java EE, and related frameworks. He has written and published more than 50 articles about Java technologies and more than 500 tips and tricks for many websites that are dedicated to programming. In addition, he has written the following books:

- *Tehnologii XML XML în Java, Albastra*
- *Jboss Tools 3 Developer's Guide, Packt Publishing*
- *JSF 2.0 Cookbook, Packt Publishing*
- *JSF 2.0 Cookbook: LITE, Packt Publishing*
- *Pro Java 7 NIO.2, Apress*
- *Pro Hibernate and MongoDB, Apress*

Currently, Anghel is developing web applications using the latest Java technologies on the market (EJB 3.0, CDI, Spring, JSF, Struts, Hibernate, and so on). Over the past two years, he's focused on developing rich Internet applications for geographic information systems.

# About the Reviewers

**Mert Çalışkan** is a principal software architect living in Ankara, Turkey. He has over 10 years of expertise in software development with the architectural design of Enterprise Java web applications. He is an open source advocate for software projects such as PrimeFaces, and has also been a committer and founder to various others. He is the co-author of *PrimeFaces Cookbook*, *Packt Publishing*, which is the first book to be written on PrimeFaces. He is the co-author of *Beginning Spring*, *Wiley Publications*. He is also working as an author for RebelLabs. He shares his knowledge and ideas at local and international conferences such as JavaOne2014, JavaOne2013, JDC2010, and JSFDays2008. He is also a member of the OpenLogic Expert Community and the Apache Software Foundation.

I would like to thank my family, my beloved angel Funda, our advisers at Packt Publishing, and Anghel Leonard, the author of this great book.

**Michael Kurz** studied computer science at the Technical University of Vienna. Since then, his main professional focus has been on web development, especially in the Java EE domain. In 2007, he started working as a senior software developer for Irian Solutions in Vienna, Austria. His main focus there is to develop JSF and Java EE applications for various customers in Austria, Germany, and Switzerland. Additionally, he also does JSF trainings, talks at international conferences, and is an Apache MyFaces committer.

Besides his work as a software developer, he also likes to write about JSF-related techniques. In November 2009, his first book *JavaServer Faces 2.0, dpunkt.verlag* was published, followed by the updated edition *JavaServer Faces 2.2* in November 2013 by the same publisher.

Furthermore, he is responsible for the contents of the German online JSF tutorial at `http://jsfatwork.irian.at` provided by Irian, and he also writes about JSF-related techniques in his blog at `http://jsflive.wordpress.com`.

**Thierry Leriche-Dessirier** works as a freelance JEE consultant in Paris. He has 20 years of experience in web and Agile development domains. He teaches software engineering at ESIEA, and in between two baby bottles, he also writes for blogs and magazines.

**Michael Müller** is an IT professional with more than 30 years of experience including about 25 years in the healthcare sector. During this time, he has worked in different areas, especially project and product management, consulting, and software development. He gained international knowledge not only by targeting international markets, but also by leading external teams (from Eastern Europe and India).

Currently, he is the head of software development at the German DRG institute (`http://inek.org`). In this role, he is responsible for web, Java, and .NET projects. Web projects are preferably built with Java technologies such as JSF and JavaScript. He is a JSF professional user and a member of the JSR 344 (JSF) expert group.

He frequently reads books and writes reviews as well as technical papers, which are mostly published in German-printed magazines and on his website at `http://it-rezension.de`. Besides that, he regularly blogs about software development at `http://blog.mueller-bruehl.de`.

Michael has done technical reviewing for *Java 8 in Action, Manning Publications Co.*

> To my wife Claudia and my children: thank you for your patience during night reading and other long sessions. I love you!

**Luca Preziati** lives in Milan and has worked for six years as a Java consultant, focusing the past five years on document management systems handling massive volumes of data. In 2014, he joined GFT Italia full time. He has considerable experience with both Alfresco and Documentum, as well as Liferay and Kettle. In his free time, he enjoys swimming, biking, playing the guitar, and wine tasting with his girlfriend.

> I would like to thank all of my mentors: my parents, Ernesto and Clelia, who taught me much about work while running their own business (`www.mintel.it`); my brothers, Alessio and Stefano; and my girlfriend, Arianna.

# www.PacktPub.com

## Support files, eBooks, discount offers, and more

You might want to visit www.PacktPub.com for support files and downloads related to your book.

Did you know that Packt offers eBook versions of every book published, with PDF and ePub files available? You can upgrade to the eBook version at www.PacktPub.com and as a print book customer, you are entitled to a discount on the eBook copy. Get in touch with us at service@packtpub.com for more details.

At www.PacktPub.com, you can also read a collection of free technical articles, sign up for a range of free newsletters, and receive exclusive discounts and offers on Packt books and eBooks.

http://PacktLib.PacktPub.com

Do you need instant solutions to your IT questions? PacktLib is Packt's online digital book library. Here, you can access, read, and search across Packt's entire library of books.

## Why subscribe?

- Fully searchable across every book published by Packt
- Copy and paste, print, and bookmark content
- On demand and accessible via web browser

## Free access for Packt account holders

If you have an account with Packt at www.PacktPub.com, you can use this to access PacktLib today and view nine entirely free books. Simply use your login credentials for immediate access.

## Instant updates on new Packt books

Get notified! Find out when new books are published by following @PacktEnterprise on Twitter, or the *Packt Enterprise* Facebook page.

# Table of Contents

# Preface

This book will cover all the important aspects (Big Ticket features) involved in developing JSF 2.2 applications. It provides clear instructions for getting the most out of JSF 2.2 and offers many exercises (more than 300 complete applications) to build impressive JSF-based web applications.

We start off with a chapter about Expression Language (EL) and cover the most important aspects of EL 2.2 and EL 3.0. We continue with a comprehensive dissertation about communication in JSF, followed by an exciting chapter about JSF 2.2 scopes. At this point, we bring into discussion most of the JSF artifacts and configurations. Further, we start a suite of very interesting topics, such as HTML5 and AJAX. After that we dissect the JSF view state concept and learn how to deal with this delicate JSF topic. Furthermore, we will discuss in detail about custom components and composite components. After this, we will talk about library contracts (themes) of JSF 2.2 resources. Finally, the last chapter will fortify your knowledge about JSF 2.2 Facelets.

## What this book covers

*Chapter 1, Dynamic Access to JSF Application Data through Expression Language (EL 3.0)*, covers the main aspects of Expression Language (EL). We will cover EL 2.2 and EL 3.0, including new operators, lambda expressions, and collection object support.

*Chapter 2, Communication in JSF*, represents a dissection of JSF mechanisms used for ensuring communication between JSF artifacts. Therefore, we will cover context parameters, request parameters, JSF 2.2 actions on GET requests (view actions), and more.

*Chapter 3, JSF Scopes – Lifespan and Use in Managed Beans Communication*, teaches you to distinguish between the bad and good practices of using JSF and CDI scopes. We will discuss JSF scopes versus CDI scopes, request, session, view scope (including the new JSF 2.2 view scope), application, conversation scope, JSF 2.2 flow scope in detail (Big Ticket feature), and more.

*Chapter 4, JSF Configurations Using XML Files and Annotations – Part 1*, depicts the JSF artifact's configuration aspects in a learning-by-example fashion. Configuring JSF artifacts in the `faces-config.xml` file is pretty straightforward and boring, but if we take each artifact and exploit its potential in several use cases, then things become much more interesting.

*Chapter 5, JSF Configurations Using XML Files and Annotations – Part 2*, acts as a continuation of the previous chapter. Here, we will discuss configuring resource handlers (JSF 2.2's new `javax.faces.WEBAPP_RESOURCES_DIRECTORY` context parameter), configuring flash (JSF 2.2 `FlashFactory`, `FlashWrapper`, and flash system events), JSF 2.2 Window ID API, the injection mechanism (which, starting with JSF 2.2, is possible in most JSF artifacts), and more.

*Chapter 6, Working with Tabular Data*, pays tribute to the `<h:dataTable>` tag. Here, we will focus on the JSF 2.2 `CollectionDataModel` API (which supports the `Collection` interface in `UIData`). Moreover, we will learn about table pagination, deleting/editing/updating table rows, filtering, and styling JSF tables.

*Chapter 7, JSF and AJAX*, exploits the JSF 2.2 `delay` attribute for queue control of AJAX requests. It discusses how to reset value attributes using JSF 2.2 (input fields can be updated with AJAX after a validation error), AJAX and JSF 2.2 flow scope, how to customize AJAX script, and more. This is a classic chapter in almost any JSF book.

*Chapter 8, JSF 2.2 – HTML5 and Upload*, divides the topic into two parts. The first part is entirely dedicated to the Big Ticket feature, HTML5, and JSF 2.2 (pass-through attributes and elements). The second part is dedicated to JSF 2.2's new upload component, `<h:inputFile>`.

*Chapter 9, JSF State Management*, provides a detailed dissertation about the JSF view state. The headings of this chapter will refer to JSF's saving view state (including JSF 2.2 case insensitivity for state saving method and standardized server state serialization) and JSF 2.2 stateless view (Big Ticket feature).

*Chapter 10, JSF Custom Components*, is another example of a classic chapter in any JSF book. Obviously, the main topics are meant to shape the custom and composite components creation. We will focus on developing several kinds of components based on the new JSF 2.2 approach (Facelet's component tag can be declared via annotation).

*Chapter 11, JSF 2.2 Resource Library Contracts – Themes*, dedicates itself to the new JSF 2.2 Resource Library Contracts feature (Big Ticket feature). You will learn how to work with contracts, style JSF tables and UI components using contracts, style contracts across different kind of devices, and more.

*Chapter 12, Facelets Templating*, depicts the viral aspects of Facelets templating. We will focus on the declarative and programmatical aspects of Facelets.

*Appendix, The JSF Life Cycle*, covers a diagram of the different JSF phases.

# What you need for this book

In order to run the applications in this book, you will need the following software applications:

- NetBeans IDE (preferred version is 8.0, or later)
- GlassFish 4.0
- JSF Mojarra 2.2.6 (preferred) / MyFaces 2.2.2

# Who this book is for

This book is a perfect symbiosis between JSF 2.0 and 2.2. It is dedicated to JSF developers who have previous experience and want to upgrade their knowledge to the new JSF 2.2. By fortifying your knowledge on JSF 2.0 and adding the power of JSF 2.2, you will soon become a JSF expert.

# Conventions

In this book, you will find a number of styles of text that distinguish between different kinds of information. Here are some examples of these styles, and an explanation of their meaning.

Code words in text, database table names, folder names, filenames, file extensions, pathnames, dummy URLs, user input, and Twitter handles are shown as follows: "For example, in the following example, you call a method named `firstLambdaAction`—the lambda expression is invoked from this method."

A block of code is set as follows:

```
<ui:repeat value="#{get_sublist(myList, from, to)}" var="t">
  #{t}
</ui:repeat>
```

When we wish to draw your attention to a particular part of a code block, the relevant lines or items are set in bold:

```
<h:dataTable value="#{playersBean.dataArrayList}"
  binding="#{table}" var="t">
```

**New terms** and **important words** are shown in bold. Words that you see on the screen, in menus or dialog boxes for example, appear in the text like this: "When the **Login** button is clicked, JSF will call the `playerLogin` method."

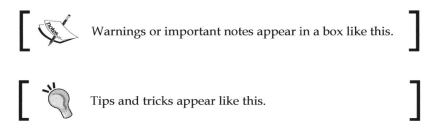

Warnings or important notes appear in a box like this.

Tips and tricks appear like this.

# Reader feedback

Feedback from our readers is always welcome. Let us know what you think about this book—what you liked or may have disliked. Reader feedback is important for us to develop titles that you really get the most out of.

To send us general feedback, simply send an e-mail to `feedback@packtpub.com`, and mention the book title via the subject of your message.

If there is a topic that you have expertise in and you are interested in either writing or contributing to a book, see our author guide on `www.packtpub.com/authors`.

# Customer support

Now that you are the proud owner of a Packt book, we have a number of things to help you to get the most from your purchase.

# Downloading the example code

You can download the example code files for all Packt books you have purchased from your account at `http://www.packtpub.com`. If you purchased this book elsewhere, you can visit `http://www.packtpub.com/support` and register to have the files e-mailed directly to you.

# Errata

Although we have taken every care to ensure the accuracy of our content, mistakes do happen. If you find a mistake in one of our books—maybe a mistake in the text or the code—we would be grateful if you would report this to us. By doing so, you can save other readers from frustration and help us improve subsequent versions of this book. If you find any errata, please report them by visiting http://www.packtpub.com/submit-errata, selecting your book, clicking on the **errata submission form** link, and entering the details of your errata. Once your errata are verified, your submission will be accepted and the errata will be uploaded on our website, or added to any list of existing errata, under the Errata section of that title. Any existing errata can be viewed by selecting your title from http://www.packtpub.com/support.

# Piracy

Piracy of copyright material on the Internet is an ongoing problem across all media. At Packt, we take the protection of our copyright and licenses very seriously. If you come across any illegal copies of our works, in any form, on the Internet, please provide us with the location address or website name immediately so that we can pursue a remedy.

Please contact us at copyright@packtpub.com with a link to the suspected pirated material.

We appreciate your help in protecting our authors, and our ability to bring you valuable content.

# Questions

You can contact us at questions@packtpub.com if you are having a problem with any aspect of the book, and we will do our best to address it.

# 1
# Dynamic Access to JSF Application Data through Expression Language (EL 3.0)

Java **Expression Language** (EL) is a compact and powerful mechanism that enables dynamic communication in JSP and JSF-based applications (including development frameworks based on JSF such as PrimeFaces, ICEfaces, and RichFaces); we embed expressions in the presentation layer to communicate with the application logic layer. EL provides bidirectional communication, which means that we can expose application logic data to the user, but we also can submit user data to be processes. Generically speaking, EL can be used to populate HTTP requests with user data, to extract and expose data from HTTP responses, to update HTML DOM, to conditionally process data, and much more.

[  Commonly, EL expressions will be present in JSP and JSF pages, but they can also appear outside, in `faces-config.xml`, for example. ]

In this chapter, you will see how to use EL in web pages to communicate with managed beans, which is the most common case in JSF applications. We will cover the following topics:

- EL syntax, operators, and reserved words
- EL immediate and deferred evaluation

- EL value and method expressions
- The conditional text in JSF
- Write a custom EL resolver

# EL syntax

In this section, you can see an overview of the main aspects of EL 2.2 and 3.0 syntax. EL supports a handful of operators and reserved words. Each of these are quickly described in the following section (more details are in the EL specification document (`http://download.oracle.com/otndocs/jcp/el-3_0-fr-eval-spec/index.html`)).

# EL operators

EL supports the following categories of operators—arithmetic, relational, logical, conditional, empty and added starting with EL 3.0, string concatenation, assignment and semicolon operators:

| Textuals | Description | Symbols |
|---|---|---|
| A + B | Addition | + |
| A - B | Subtraction | - |
| A * B | Multiplication | * |
| A {div, /} B | Arithmetic operator division | /, div |
| A {mod, %} B | Arithmetic operator modulo | %, mod |
| A {and, &&} B | Logical AND | &&, and |
| A {or, \|\|} B | Logical OR | \|\|, or |
| {not, !} A | Logical opposite | !, not |
| A {lt, <} B | Relational less than | <, lt |
| A {gt, >} B | Relational greater than | >, gt |
| A {le, <=} B | Relational less than or equal to | <=, le |
| A {ge, >=} B | Relational greater than or equal to | >=, ge |
| A {eq, ==} B | Equal to | ==, eq |
| A {ne, !=} B | Not equal to | !=, ne |
| A = B | Assignment (EL 3.0) | = |
| A ; B | Semicolon (EL 3.0) | ; |
| A += B | String concatenation (EL 3.0) | += |
| A -> B | Lambda expression (EL 3.0) | -> |

| Textuals | Description | Symbols |
|---|---|---|
| empty A | Determine whether a value is null or empty | |
| A ? B : C | Evaluates B or C, depending on the result of the evaluation of A. Known as the **ternary operator**. | ?: |
| | Used when writing EL expressions | . |
| | Used when writing EL expressions | [] |

# EL precedence of operators

Conforming to EL specification, the precedence of operators from the highest to lowest, left to right is as follows:

- [] .
- () (used to change the precedence of operators)
- - (unary) not ! empty
- * / div % mod
- + - (binary)
- +=
- < > <= >= lt gt le ge
- == != eq ne
- && and
- || or
- ? :
- -> (lambda expression)
- =
- ;

# EL reserved words

EL defines the following reserved words:

- and, or, not, eq, ne, lt, gt, le, ge, true (Boolean literal), false (Boolean literal), null, instanceof (a Java keyword to do a class comparison between objects), empty, div, and mod

# EL immediate and deferred evaluation

EL evaluates expressions as **immediate** or **deferred**.

Immediate evaluation returns the result as soon as the page is first rendered. These kinds of expressions are read-only value expressions and they can be present only in tags that accept runtime expressions. They are easy to recognize after the ${} notation. Usually, they are used for arithmetic and logical operations in JSP pages.

Deferred evaluation can return the result at different phases of a page's life cycle depending on the technology that is using the expression. JSF can evaluate the expression at different phases of the life cycle (for example, during the rendering and postback phase), depending on how the expression is being used in the page. These kind of expressions can be value and method expressions, and they are marked by the #{} notation.

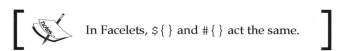 In Facelets, ${} and #{} act the same.

# EL value expressions

**Value expressions** are probably used the most, and they refer to objects and their properties and attributes. Such expressions are dynamically used to evaluate results or set bean properties at runtime. Through value expressions, you can easily access JavaBeans components, collections, and Java SE enumerated types. Moreover, EL provides a set of implicit objects that can be used to get attributes from different scopes and parameter values. Furthermore, you will see how EL deals with each of these objects.

 Value expressions that can read data, but cannot write it are known as **rvalue** (${} expressions are always rvalue), while those that can read and write data are known as **lvalue** (#{} expressions can be rvalue and/or lvalue).

# Referencing a managed bean

Referencing a managed bean is not exactly a useful example, but it is a good point to start. Most commonly, your managed bean will look like the following code (in this case, the bean's class name is PlayersBean):

```
@ManagedBean
//some scope
```

```
public class PlayersBean{
...
}
```

Or, in the CDI version, your managed bean will be as follows:

```
@Named
//some scope
public class PlayersBean{
...
}
```

Or, with an explicit name, your managed bean will be as follows:

```
@ManagedBean(name = "myPlayersBean")
//some scope
public class PlayersBean{
...
}

@Named(value = "myPlayersBean")
//some scope
public class PlayersBean{
...
}
```

Now, for the first two examples, EL refers to the `PlayersBean` managed bean, like this — the name is obtained from taking the unqualified class name portion of the fully qualified class name and converting the first character to lowercase as follows:

```
#{playersBean}
```

In addition, for the next two examples, EL uses the explicit name as follows:

```
#{myPlayersBean}
```

> You should use CDI beans whenever possible since they are more flexible than JSF managed beans, and because annotations from `javax.faces.bean` will be deprecated in a future JSF version. Therefore, the CDI ones are recommended.

When the referenced managed bean cannot be found in any scope, a `null` value will be returned.

# Referencing a managed bean's properties

As is commonly known, managed beans usually contain private fields, which are accessible through getter and setter methods as bean properties, and some public methods that exploits these properties to serve different logic tasks.

EL expressions that can access these properties contain the dot or square brackets notation, `[]`. For example, let's suppose that the `PlayersBean` managed bean contains two fields defined like the following lines:

```
private String playerName = "Rafael";
private String playerSurname = "Nadal";
```

EL can access these fields through their getter methods; therefore, you need to define them as shown in the following code:

```
public String getPlayerName() {
   return playerName;
}
public String getPlayerSurname() {
   return playerSurname;
}
```

Now, an expression that accesses the `playerName` property can use the dot notation (`.`) to refer it, as shown in the following line of code:

```
#{playersBean.playerName}
```

Alternatively, this expression can use the square brackets notation, `[]`, as shown in the following line of code:

```
#{playersBean['playerName']}
```

JSF evaluates this expression from left to right. First, it searches for `playersBean` in all available scopes (such as request, session, and application). Then, the bean is instantiated and the `getPlayerName`/`getPlayerSurname` getter methods are called (in the case of Boolean properties, the getter method will be named as is*XXX*).When you are using the `[]` notation, you can use simple or double quotes. Just remember to alternate them correctly in cases like the following quotations.

An incorrect quotation (you cannot use double quotes inside double quotes) is:

```
<h:outputText value="#{playersBean["playerName"]}"/>
```

An incorrect quotation (you cannot use simple quotes inside simple quotes) is:

```
<h:outputText value='#{playersBean['playerName']}'/>
```

A correct quotation (you can use simple quotes in double quotes) is:

```
<h:outputText value="#{playersBean['playerName']}"/>
```

A correct quotation (you can use double quotes in simple quotes) is:

```
<h:outputText value='#{playersBean["playerName"]}'/>
```

# Referencing a managed bean's nested properties

Usually, managed beans use nested properties. Such properties can be accessed by EL using the `.` and `[]` notations multiple times in the same expression.

For example, the `PlayersBean` managed bean may represent general data about tennis players, such as name, surname, titles, and finals. More detailed information, such as birthday, birthplace, height, and weight can be represented through a different class named `PlayersDetails`. Now, the `PlayersBean` managed bean contains a field of type `PlayersDetails`, which means that birthday, birthplace, and so on become nested properties of `PlayersBean`. Speaking in code lines, the relevant part of the `PlayersDetails` class is as follows:

```
public class PlayerDetails {

  private Date birthday;
  private String birthplace;
  ...

  public Date getBirthday() {
    return birthday;
```

```
    }

    public String getBirthplace() {
      return birthplace;
    }
    ...
}
```

The managed bean of the `PlayersBean` class is as follows:

```
@Named
public class PlayersBean{

    private String playerName = "Rafael";
    private String playerSurname = "Nadal";
    private PlayerDetails playerDetails;

    public String getPlayerName() {
      return playerName;
    }

    public String getPlayerSurname() {
      return playerSurname;
    }

    public PlayerDetails getPlayerDetails() {
      return playerDetails;
    }
    ...
}
```

You already know how to call the `playerName` and `playerSurname` properties using the `.` and `[]` notations. Next, you can use the same notations to access the `birthday` and `birthplace` nested properties, as shown in the following code:

```
#{playersBean.playerDetails.birthday}
#{playersBean.playerDetails.birthplace}

#{playersBean['playerDetails']['birthday']}
#{playersBean['playerDetails']['birthplace']}
```

Or, you can use both notations in the same expressions, as shown in the following code:

```
#{playersBean.playerDetails['birthday']}
#{playersBean.playerDetails['birthplace']}

#{playersBean['playerDetails'].birthday}
#{playersBean['playerDetails'].birthplace}
```

Of course, the `PlayerDetails` class can contain its own nested properties and so. In this case, just use the `.` and `[]` notations to get deeper in the hierarchy of objects until you reach the desired property.

In the preceding expressions, JSF search for `playersBean` in all the available scopes (request, session, application, and so on) and obtain an instance of it. Afterwards, it calls the `getPlayerDetails` method and the `getBirthday` method on result of the `getPlayerDetails` method (and the same for the `birthplace` property).

# Referencing Java SE enumerated types

EL can access Java SE enumerated types using a `String` literal. For example, let's have an enumerated type defined in `PlayersBean`, as shown in the following code:

```
public enum Plays {
   Left, Right
};

private Plays play;
...
play = Plays.Left;//initialization can be done in constructor
...
public Plays getPlay() {
   return play;
}
...
```

You can easily output the `play` value as shown in the following line of code:

```
#{playersBean.play}
```

To refer to the `Plays` constant, `Plays.Left`, with an expression, use the `String` literal `Left` (or `Right` for `Plays.Right`), for example, you can test whether `play` is `Left` or `Right`, as shown in the following code:

```
#{playersBean.play == 'Left'} //return true
#{playersBean.play == 'Right'}//return false
```

# Referencing collections

**Collection** items (arrays, lists, maps, sets, and so on) can be accessed from EL expressions by specifying a literal value that can be converted to an integer or the [] notation with an integer and without quotes.

For example, let's suppose that the `PlayersBean` managed bean contains an array named `titles_2013` that keeps the titles won by a player in 2013. The array is defined as shown in the following code:

```
private String[] titles_2013 = {"Sao Paulo", "Acapulco", "ATP
   World Tour Masters 1000 Indian Wells", "Barcelona", ...};
...
public String[] getTitles_2013() {
   return titles_2013;
}
```

Now, you can access the first title from the array by specifying its position in array, which is 0:

```
#{playersBean.titles_2013[0]}
```

This is equivalent in Java to getting or setting the value for `titles_2013[0]`.

However, sometimes you need to iterate over the array instead of accessing a specific item. This can be easily accomplished with the `c:forEach` JSTL tag (`http://www.oracle.com/technetwork/java/index-jsp-135995.html`). The following code snippet iterates over the `titles_2013` array and outputs each item (this is a pretty uncommon usage, so do not try it in production):

```
<c:forEach begin="0"
   end="${fn:length(playersBean.titles_2013)-1}"
   var="i">
   #{playersBean.titles_2013[i]},
</c:forEach>
```

You can simplify it as shown in the following code:

```
<c:forEach var="title" items="#{playersBean.titles_2013}">
   <i>#{title}</i>,
</c:forEach>
```

You can also use the `<ui:repeat>` tag as shown in the following code:

```
<ui:repeat var="title" value="#{playersBean.titles_2013}">
   <i>#{title}</i>,
</ui:repeat>
```

This tag is detailed in *Chapter 12, Facelets Templating*, in the *Iterating with <ui:repeat>* section.

You can use the same approach for every `List`. For example, in the case of `List`, the expression `#{playersBean.titles_2013[0]}` is equivalent in Java to `titles_2013.get(0)` and `titles_2013.set(0, some_value)`.

In the case of collections of type key-value (for example, `Map`), the EL expressions obtain items by key. For example, let's add a `Map` in `PlayersBean` that stores some match facts of a player. It can be defined as shown in the following code:

```
private Map<String, String> matchfacts = new HashMap<>();
...
matchfacts.put("Aces", "12");
matchfacts.put("Double Faults", "2");
matchfacts.put("1st Serve", "70%");
...

public Map<String, String> getMatchfacts() {
   return matchfacts;
}
```

Now, an EL expression that accesses the item with the key `Aces` can be written like the following line of code:

```
#{playersBean.matchfacts.Aces}
```

 Notice that this approach is not supported on arrays or lists. For example, `#{playersBean.titles_2013.0}` is not correct.

When the key is not an acceptable variable name (for example, `Double Faults`), you need to use brackets and quotes, as shown in the following code:

```
#{playersBean.matchfacts["Double Faults"]}
```

# EL implicit objects

JSF provides several objects related to the current request and environment. EL exposes these objects (known as **implicit objects**) that can be accessed at runtime in a Facelet, servlets, or backing bean—these objects are accessible through value expressions and are managed by the container. For each expression, EL first checks if the value of the base is one of these implicit objects, and, if it is not, then it will check beans in progressively wider scopes (from request to view, and finally to application scope).

In EL, the part of the expression before the dot or the square bracket is named **base** and it usually indicates where the bean instances should be located. The part after the first dot, or the square bracket, is called a **property** and is recursively cracked in smaller parts, which represents the bean's properties to get from the base.

You can see a short overview of these objects in the following table:

| Implicit object EL | Type | Description |
|---|---|---|
| #{application} | ServletContext or PortletContext | This is an instance of ServletContext or PortletContext. |
| #{facesContext} | FacesContext | This is an instance of FacesContext. |
| #{initParam} | Map | This is the context initialization parameter map returned by getInitParameterMap. |
| #{session} | HttpSession or PortletSession | This is an instance of HttpSession or PortletSession. |
| #{view} | UIViewRoot | This is the current UIViewRoot (the root of the UIComponent tree). |
| #{component} | UIComponent | This is the current UIComponent. |
| #{cc} | UIComponent | This is the composite component currently being processed. |
| #{request} | ServletRequest or PortletRequest | This is an instance of ServletRequest or PortletRequest. |
| #{applicationScope} | Map | This is a map to store application-scoped data returned by getApplicationMap. |
| #{sessionScope} | Map | This is a map to store session-scoped data returned by getSessionMap. |
| #{viewScope} | Map | This is a map to store current view scoped data returned by getViewMap. |
| #{requestScope} | Map | This is a map to store request-scoped data returned by getRequestMap. |
| #{flowScope} | Map | This is a map to store flow-scoped data returned by facesContext. getApplication(). getFlowHandler(). getCurrentFlowScope(). |

| Implicit object EL | Type | Description |
|---|---|---|
| #{flash} | Map | This is a map that contains values present only on the "next" request. |
| #{param} | Map | This is a map view of all the query parameters for this request. It is returned by getRequestParameterMap. |
| #{paramValues} | Map | This is the request parameter value map returned by getRequestParameterValuesMap. |
| #{header} | Map | This is a map view of all the HTTP headers for this request returned by getRequestHeaderMap. |
| #{headerValue} | Map | This is the request header values map returned by getRequestHeaderValuesMap. Each value in the map is an array of strings that contains all the values for that key. |
| #{cookie} | Map | This is a map view of values in the HTTP Set-Cookie header returned by getRequestCookieMap. |
| #{resource} | Resource | This is a JSF resource identifier to a concrete resource URL. |

# EL method expressions

With EL expressions, we can call arbitrary static and public methods that live on the server side in managed beans. Such expressions are usually present in tag's attributes (that is, inside an action or actionListener attribute) and must use the deferred evaluation syntax since a method can be called during different phases of the life cycle. Commonly, methods are called to respond with actions to different kinds of events and for autopages navigation.

Let's see some examples of calling bean methods using EL (all methods were defined in the PlayersBean managed bean):

- Calling the vamosRafa_1 void bean method with no arguments, as shown in the following code:

```
public void vamosRafa_1(){
    System.out.println("Vamos Rafa!");
}

#{playersBean.vamosRafa_1()}
```

- Calling the `vamosRafa_2` bean method with no arguments. It returns a string, as shown in the following code:

```
public String vamosRafa_2() {
  return "Vamos Rafa!";
}
```

```
#{playersBean.vamosRafa_2()}
```

The returned string, `Vamos Rafa!`, can be displayed on the web page or used for other purposes. In other words, the expression will be evaluated to this string.

- Calling the `vamosRafa_3` bean method with one argument. It returns void, as shown in the following code:

```
public void vamosRafa_3(String text) {
  System.out.println(text);
}
```

```
#{playersBean.vamosRafa_3('Vamos Rafa!')}
```

Notice that the `String` arguments are passed by using quotes.

 The `String` constants are passed between simple or double quotes!

- Calling the `vamosRafa_4` bean method with two arguments. It returns a string, as shown in the following code:

```
public String vamosRafa_4(String name, String surname) {
  return "Vamos " + name + " " + surname + "!";
}
```

```
#{playersBean.vamosRafa_4(playersBean.playerName,
  playersBean.playerSurname)}
```

The expression will be evaluated to the string, `Vamos Rafael Nadal!`.

- Calling the `vamosRafa_5` bean method for autonavigation. First, define the method in the managed bean to return a view (outcome) name (`vamos` is the view name for the `vamos.xhtml` file), as shown in the following code:

```
public String vamosRafa_5(){
 return "vamos";
}
```

Furthermore, extract the view name in the `action` attribute of any JSF UI component as shown in the following code:

```
<h:form>
  <h:commandButton action="#{playersBean.vamosRafa_5()}"
                   value="Vamos ..." />
</h:form>
```

Now, when the button labeled **Vamos...** is clicked, JSF will resolve the view name, `vamos`, to the `vamos.xhtml` file. Moreover, JSF will look for the `vamos.xhtml` file in the current directory and will navigate to it. Commonly, these navigation methods are used for conditional navigation between JSF pages.

We have used parentheses to call a method, even when the method doesn't contain arguments. A special case is represented by the methods that contain an `ActionEvent` argument. These methods should be called without parentheses, except in the case when you override the `ActionEvent` argument altogether by passing and specifying custom argument(s).

EL expressions can also be used inside JavaScript function calls. For example, when you want to pass bean properties to a JavaScript function, you need to place them between quotes, as shown in the following code:

```
<h:form>
  <h:commandButton type="button" value="Click Me!"
    onclick="infoJS('#{playersBean.playerName}',
                    '#{playersBean.playerSurname}')"/>
</h:form>
```

The JavaScript function for this is shown in the following code:

```
<script type="text/javascript">
  function infoJS(name, surname) {
    alert("Name: " + name + " Surname: " + surname);
  }
</script>
```

# The conditional text in JSF

When you need to output the conditional text (without the HTML content), you can use the EL ternary operator, which has the following syntax:

```
boolean_test ? result_for_true : result_for_false
```

For example, you can use this operator to select between two CSS classes, as shown in the following code:

```
.red { color:#cc0000; }
.blue { color: #0000cc; }
```

Now, you want to conditionally output a red or a blue text, as shown in the following code:

```
<h:outputText styleClass="#{playersBean.play == 'Left' ? 'red':
  'blue'}" value="#{playersBean.play}"/>
```

So, if the value of play is Left, the text will be displayed using the red CSS class, and if it is not Left, then the blue class will be used.

 Keep in mind that the HTML content is not recommended (for security reasons do not use escape="false"), and the else part of the condition cannot be omitted.

For better understanding, let's look at another example. Remember that you have iterated over the titles_2013 array and output each item as shown in the following code:

```
<c:forEach var="title" items="#{playersBean.titles_2013}">
  <i>#{title}</i>,
</c:forEach>
```

Well, the output of this code will be something like the following screenshot:

*Sao Paulo, Acapulco, ATP World Tour Masters 1000 Indian Wells, Barcelona, ATP World Tour Masters 1000 Madrid, ATP World Tour Masters 1000 Rome, Roland Garros, ATP World Tour Masters 1000 Canada, ATP World Tour Masters 1000 Cincinnati, US Open,*

Everything looks fine except the last comma, which should not appear since the **US Open** term is the last item to display. You can easily fix this issue with the EL ternary operator, as shown in the following code:

```
<c:forEach var="title" items="#{playersBean.titles_2013}"
  varStatus="v">
  <i>#{title}</i>
  #{v.last ? '':','}
</c:forEach>
```

Sometimes you just need to show or hide text based on a condition. For this, you can place a Boolean expression as the value of the rendered attribute (all JSF UI components have this attribute). For example, the following line of code will output a player's Facebook address only if such an address exists:

```
<h:outputText value="Facebook address: #{playersBean.facebook}"
    rendered="#{!empty playersBean.facebook}" />
```

Another common situation is to display or hide non-HTML text using two buttons of type "Show something..." and "Hide something...". For example, you can have a button labeled **Show Career Prize Money** and one labeled **Hide Career Prize Money**. Obviously, you want to display the career prize money when the first button is clicked and to hide the career prize money when the second button is clicked. For this, you can use the rendered attribute, as shown in the following code:

```
<h:form id="prizeFormId">
    <h:commandButton value="Show Career Prize Money">
    <f:ajax render="rnprizeid"
            listener="#{playersBean.showPrizeMoney()}"/>
    </h:commandButton>
    <h:panelGrid id="rnprizeid">
      <h:outputText value="#{playersBean.prize}"
                    rendered="#{playersBean.show_prize}">
        <f:convertNumber type="currency" currencySymbol="$" />
      </h:outputText>
    </h:panelGrid>
    <h:commandButton value="Hide Career Prize Money">
      <f:ajax render="rnprizeid"
              listener="#{playersBean.hidePrizeMoney()}"/>
    </h:commandButton>
</h:form>
```

Both the buttons use AJAX mechanism and an EL method expression to call the showPrizeMoney and hidePrizeMoney methods. These methods just modify the value of a boolean property, named show_prize, as shown in the following code:

```
private boolean show_prize = false;
...
public boolean isShow_prize() {
  return show_prize;
}
...
public void showPrizeMoney(){
```

```
        this.show_prize = true;
}

public void hidePrizeMoney(){
    this.show_prize = false;
}
```

When the request is complete, JSF will re-render the panel grid component with the ID `rnprizeid`; this was indicated in the `render` attribute of the `f:ajax` tag. As you can see, the re-rendered component is a panel that contains a simple `h:outputText` tag that outputs the `prize` property depending on the Boolean value of the EL expression present in the `rendered` attribute, as shown in the following code:

```
private int prize = 60941937;
...
public int getPrize() {
    return prize;
}
```

Showing and hiding text can be useful, but not enough. Usually, we need to show or hide the HTML content. For example, you may need to show or hide a picture:

```
<img src="resources/images/babolat.jpg" width="290" height="174"/>
```

This task can be easily accomplished by nesting the HTML code inside the Facelets `ui:fragment` tag, which supports the `rendered` attribute, as shown in the following code:

```
<ui:fragment rendered="#{playersBean.show_racquet}">
  <img src="#{resource['images:babolat.jpg']}" width="290"
    height="174"/>
</ui:fragment>
```

As you can see, the EL expression of the `rendered` attribute indicates a `boolean` property of the `PlayersBean` managed bean, as shown in the following code:

```
private boolean show_racquet = false;
...
public boolean isShow_racquet() {
    return show_racquet;
}
```

Now, you can let the user decide when to show or hide the image. You can easily adapt the preceding example, with two buttons labeled **Show Image** and **Hide Image**, or more elegant, you can use a checkbox, as shown in the following code:

```
...
<h:form>
  <h:selectBooleanCheckbox label="Show Image"
    valueChangeListener="#{playersBean.showHideRacquetPicture}">
    <f:ajax render="racquetId"/>
  </h:selectBooleanCheckbox>
  <h:panelGroup id="racquetId">
    <ui:fragment rendered="#{playersBean.show_racquet}">
    <img src="resources/images/babolat.jpg" width="290"
      height="174"/>
    </ui:fragment>
  </h:panelGroup>
</h:form>
...
```

The showHideRacquetPicture method sets the value of the show_racquet property to true or false, depending on the checkbox status. After this method is executed, JSF will re-render the content of the ui:fragment tag — this is accomplished via the HTML content rendered by the <h:panelGroup> tag, because the <ui:fragment> tag doesn't render the HTML content; therefore, it cannot be referenced by the ID. The following is the code for the showHideRacquetPicture method:

```
public void showHideRacquetPicture(ValueChangeEvent e){
  if(e.getNewValue() == Boolean.TRUE){
    this.show_racquet=true;
  } else {
    this.show_racquet=false;
  }
}
```

So, we can conclude that the rendered attribute can be used to conditionally output the HTML/non-HTML content. The user interaction and internal conditions can be used to play with this attribute value.

The complete application is named ch1_1.

# Writing a custom EL resolver

EL flexibility can be tested by extending it with custom implicit variables, properties, and method calls. This is possible if we extend the `VariableResolver` or `PropertyResolver` class, or even better, the `ELResolver` class that give us flexibility to reuse the same implementation for different tasks. The following are three simple steps to add custom implicit variables:

1. Create your own class that extends the `ELResolver` class.

2. Implement the inherited abstract methods.

3. Add the `ELResolver` class in `faces-config.xml`.

Next, you will see how to add a custom implicit variable by extending EL based on these steps. In this example, you want to retrieve a collection that contains the ATP singles rankings using EL directly in your JSF page. The variable name used to access the collection will be `atp`.

First, you need to create a class that extends the `javax.el.ELResolver` class. This is very simple. The code for the `ATPVarResolver` class is as follows:

```
public class ATPVarResolver extends ELResolver {

  private static final Logger logger =
    Logger.getLogger(ATPVarResolver.class.getName());
  private static final String PLAYERS = "atp";
  private final Class<?> CONTENT = List.class;
...
}
```

Second, you need to implement six abstract methods:

- `getValue`: This method is defined in the following manner:

```
public abstract Object getValue(ELContext context,
  Object base, Object property)
```

  This is the most important method of an `ELResolver` class. In the implementation of the `getValue` method, you will return the ATP items if the property requested is named `atp`. Therefore, the implementation will be as follows:

```
@Override
public Object getValue(ELContext ctx, Object base,
  Object property) {

logger.log(Level.INFO, "Get Value property : {0}",
  property);

  if ((base == null) && property.equals(PLAYERS)) {
```

```
        logger.log(Level.INFO, "Found request {0}", base);
        ctx.setPropertyResolved(true);
        List<String> values =
          ATPSinglesRankings.getSinglesRankings();
        return values;
        }
      return null;
    }
```

- `getType`: This method is defined in the following manner:

```
public abstract Class<?> getType(ELContext context,
  Object base,Object property)
```

This method identifies the most general acceptable type for our property. The scope of this method is to determine if a call of the `setValue` method is safe without causing a `ClassCastException` to be thrown. Since we return a collection, we can say that the general acceptable type is `List`. The implementation of the `getType` method is as follows:

```
@Override
public Class<?> getType(ELContext ctx, Object base, Object
  property) {

  if (base != null) {
    return null;
  }

  if (property == null) {
    String message = MessageUtils.getExceptionMessageString
      (MessageUtils.NULL_PARAMETERS_ERROR_MESSAGE_ID,
      "property");
    throw new PropertyNotFoundException(message);
  }

  if ((base == null) && property.equals(PLAYERS)) {
    ctx.setPropertyResolved(true);
    return CONTENT;
  }
  return null;
}
```

- `setValue`: This method is defined in the following manner:

```
public abstract void setValue(ELContext context,
  Object base, Object property, Object value)
```

This method tries to set the value for a given property and base. For read-only variables, such as `atp`, you need to throw an exception of type `PropertyNotWritableException`. The implementation of the `setValue` method is as follows:

```
@Override
public void setValue(ELContext ctx, Object base,
  Object property, Object value) {

  if (base != null) {
    return;
  }

  ctx.setPropertyResolved(false);
  if (property == null) {
    String message =
      MessageUtils.getExceptionMessageString(MessageUtils.
      NULL_PARAMETERS_ERROR_MESSAGE_ID, "property");
    throw new PropertyNotFoundException(message);
  }

  if (PLAYERS.equals(property)) {
    throw new PropertyNotWritableException((String)
      property);
  }
}
```

- `isReadOnly`: This method is defined in the following manner:

```
public abstract boolean isReadOnly(ELContext context,
  Object base, Object property)
```

This method returns `true` if the variable is read-only and `false` otherwise. Since the `atp` variable is read-only, the implementation is obvious. This method is directly related to the `setValue` method, meaning that it signals whether it is safe or not to call the `setValue` method without getting `PropertyNotWritableException` as a response. The implementation of the `isReadOnly` method is as follows:

```
@Override
public boolean isReadOnly(ELContext ctx, Object base,
  Object property) {
  return true;
}
```

- getFeatureDescriptors: This method is defined in the following manner:

```
public abstract Iterator<FeatureDescriptor>
  getFeatureDescriptors(ELContext context, Object base
```

This method returns a set of information about the variables or properties that can be resolved (commonly it is used by a design time tool (for example, JDeveloper has such a tool) to allow code completion of expressions). In this case, you can return null. The implementation of the getFeatureDescriptors method is as follows:

```
@Override
public Iterator<FeatureDescriptor>
  getFeatureDescriptors(ELContext ctx, Object base) {
    return null;
}
```

- getCommonPropertyType: This method is defined in the following manner:

```
public abstract Class<?> getCommonPropertyType(ELContext
  context, Object base)
```

This method returns the most general type that this resolver accepts. The implementation of the getCommonPropertyType method is as follows:

```
@Override
public Class<?> getCommonPropertyType(ELContext ctx,
  Object base) {
  if (base != null) {
    return null;
  }
  return String.class;
}
```

> How do you know if the ELResolver class acts as a VariableResolver class (these two classes are deprecated in JSF 2.2) or as a PropertyResolver class? The answer lies in the first part of the expression (known as the base argument), which in our case is null (the base is before the first dot or the square bracket, while property is after this dot or the square bracket). When the base is null, the ELresolver class acts as a VariableResolver class; otherwise, it acts as a PropertyResolver class.

The getSinglesRankings method (that populates the collection) is called from the getValue method, and is defined in the following ATPSinglesRankings class:

```
public class ATPSinglesRankings {

  public static List<String> getSinglesRankings(){

    List<String> atp_ranking= new ArrayList<>();

    atp_ranking.add("1 Nadal, Rafael (ESP)");
    ...

    return atp_ranking;
  }
}
```

Third, you register the custom ELResolver class in faces-config.xml using the <el-resolver> tag and specifying the fully qualified name of the corresponding class. In other words, you add the ELResolver class in the chain of responsibility, which represents the pattern used by JSF to deal with ELResolvers:

```
<application>
  <el-resolver>book.beans.ATPVarResolver</el-resolver>
</application>
```

Each time an expression needs to be resolved, JSF will call the default expression language resolver implementation. Each value expression is evaluated behind the scenes by the getValue method. When the <el-resolver> tag is present, the custom resolver is added in the chain of responsibility. The EL implementation manages a chain of resolver instances for different types of expression elements. For each part of an expression, EL will traverse the chain until it finds a resolver capable to resolve that part. The resolver capable of dealing with that part will pass true to the setPropertyResolved method; this method acts as a flag at the ELContext level.

Furthermore, EL implementation checks, after each resolver call, the value of this flag via the getPropertyResolved method. When the flag is true, EL implementation will repeat the process for the next part of the expression.

Done! Next, you can simply output the collection items in a data table, as shown in the following code:

```
<h:dataTable id="atpTableId" value="#{atp}" var="t">
  <h:column>
    #{t}
  </h:column>
</h:dataTable>
```

Well, so far so good! Now, our custom EL resolver returns the plain list of ATP rankings. But, what can we do if we need the list items in the reverse order, or to have the items in uppercase, or to obtain a random list? The answer could consist in adapting the preceding EL resolver to this situation.

First, you need to modify the getValue method. At this moment, it returns List, but you need to obtain an instance of the ATPSinglesRankings class. Therefore, modify it as shown in the following code:

```
public Object getValue(ELContext ctx, Object base,
  Object property) {

  if ((base == null) && property.equals(PLAYERS)) {
    ctx.setPropertyResolved(true);
    return new ATPSinglesRankings();
  }
  return null;
}
```

Moreover, you need to redefine the CONTENT constant accordingly as shown in the following line of code:

```
private final Class<?> CONTENT = ATPSinglesRankings.class;
```

Next, the ATPSinglesRankings class can contain a method for each case, as shown in the following code:

```
public class ATPSinglesRankings {

  public List<String> getSinglesRankings(){

    List<String> atp_ranking= new ArrayList<>();

    atp_ranking.add("1 Nadal, Rafael (ESP)");
    ...

    return atp_ranking;
```

```
   }

   public List<String> getSinglesRankingsReversed(){

      List<String> atp_ranking= new ArrayList<>();

      atp_ranking.add("5 Del Potro, Juan Martin (ARG)");
      atp_ranking.add("4 Murray, Andy (GBR)");
      ...

      return atp_ranking;
   }

   public List<String> getSinglesRankingsUpperCase(){

      List<String> atp_ranking= new ArrayList<>();

      atp_ranking.add("5 Del Potro, Juan Martin
        (ARG)".toUpperCase());
      atp_ranking.add("4 Murray, Andy (GBR)".toUpperCase());
      ...

      return atp_ranking;
   }
   ...
}
```

Since the EL resolver returns an instance of the ATPSinglesRankings class in the getValue method, you can easily call the getSinglesRankings, getSinglesRankingsReversed, and getSinglesRankingsUpperCase methods directly from your EL expressions, as shown in the following code:

```
<b>Ordered:</b><br/>
<h:dataTable id="atpTableId1"
  value="#{atp.singlesRankings}"
  var="t">
  <h:column>#{t}</h:column>
</h:dataTable>
<br/><br/><b>Reversed:</b><br/>
<h:dataTable id="atpTableId2"
  value="#{atp.singlesRankingsReversed}"
  var="t">
  <h:column>#{t}</h:column>
</h:dataTable>
<br/><br/><b>UpperCase:</b><br/>
```

```
<h:dataTable id="atpTableId3"
    value="#{atp.singlesRankingsUpperCase}" var="t">
  <h:column>#{t}</h:column>
</h:dataTable>
```

The complete applications to demonstrate custom ELResolvers are available in the code bundle of this chapter and are named ch1_2 and ch1_3.

In order to develop the last example of writing a custom resolver, let's imagine the following scenario: we want to access the ELContext object as an implicit object, by writing #{elContext} instead of #{facesContext.ELContext}. For this, we can use the knowledge accumulated from the previous two examples to write the following custom resolver:

```
public class ELContextResolver extends ELResolver {

  private static final String EL_CONTEXT_NAME = "elContext";

  @Override
  public Class<?> getCommonPropertyType(ELContext ctx,
    Object base){
    if (base != null) {
      return null;
    }
    return String.class;
  }

  @Override
  public Iterator<FeatureDescriptor>
    getFeatureDescriptors(ELContext ctx, Object base) {
    if (base != null) {
      return null;
    }
    ArrayList<FeatureDescriptor> list = new ArrayList<>(1);
    list.add(Util.getFeatureDescriptor("elContext", "elContext",
      "elContext", false, false, true,
    ELContext.class, Boolean.TRUE));
    return list.iterator();
  }

  @Override
  public Class<?> getType(ELContext ctx, Object base,
    Object property) {
    if (base != null) {
      return null;
```

```
      }
      if (property == null) {
        String message =
          MessageUtils.getExceptionMessageString(MessageUtils.
          NULL_PARAMETERS_ERROR_MESSAGE_ID, "property");
        throw new PropertyNotFoundException(message);
      }
      if ((base == null) && property.equals(EL_CONTEXT_NAME)) {
        ctx.setPropertyResolved(true);
      }
      return null;
    }


    @Override
    public Object getValue(ELContext ctx, Object base,
      Object property) {

      if ((base == null) && property.equals(EL_CONTEXT_NAME)) {
        ctx.setPropertyResolved(true);
        FacesContext facesContext =
          FacesContext.getCurrentInstance();
          return facesContext.getELContext();
      }
      return null;
    }


    @Override
    public boolean isReadOnly(ELContext ctx, Object base,
      Object property) {
      if (base != null) {
        return false;
      }
      if (property == null) {
        String message =
          MessageUtils.getExceptionMessageString(MessageUtils.
          NULL_PARAMETERS_ERROR_MESSAGE_ID, "property");
        throw new PropertyNotFoundException(message);
      }
      if (EL_CONTEXT_NAME.equals(property)) {
        ctx.setPropertyResolved(true);
        return true;
      }
      return false;
```

```
    }

    @Override
    public void setValue(ELContext ctx, Object base,
      Object property, Object value) {
      if (base != null) {
        return;
      }
      ctx.setPropertyResolved(false);
      if (property == null) {
        String message =
          MessageUtils.getExceptionMessageString(MessageUtils.
          NULL_PARAMETERS_ERROR_MESSAGE_ID, "property");
        throw new PropertyNotFoundException(message);
      }
      if (EL_CONTEXT_NAME.equals(property)) {
        throw new PropertyNotWritableException((String) property);
      }
    }
  }
}
```

The complete application is named, ch1_6. The goal of these three examples was to get you familiar with the main steps of writing a custom resolver. In *Chapter 3, JSF Scopes – Lifespan and Use in Managed Beans Communication*, you will see how to write a custom resolver for a custom scope.

# EL 3.0 overview

EL 3.0 (JSR 341, part of Java EE 7) represents a major boost of EL 2.2. The main features of EL 3.0 are as follows:

- New operators +, =, and ;
- Lambda expressions
- Collection objects support
- An API for standalone environments

In the upcoming sections, you will see how to use EL 3.0 features in JSF pages.

# Working with the assignment operator

In an expression of type, x = y, the assignment operator (=), assign the value of y to x. In order to avoid an error of the kind PropertyNotWritableException, the x value must be an lvalue. The following examples show you how to use this operator in two simple expressions:

- #{x = 3} evaluates to 3

- #{y = x + 5} evaluates to 8

The assignment operator is right-associative (z = y = x is equivalent with z = (y = x)). For example, #{z = y = x + 4} evaluates to 7.

# Working with the string concatenation operator

In an expression of type, x += y, the string concatenation operator (+=) returns the concatenated string of x and y. For example:

- #{x += y} evaluates to 37

- #{0 += 0 +=0 += 1 += 1 += 0 += 0 += 0} evaluates to 00011000

In EL 2.2, you can do this using the following code:

```
#{'0'.concat(0).concat(0).concat(1).concat(1).
    concat(0).concat(0).concat(0)}
```

# Working with the semicolon operator

In an expression of type, x; y, x is first evaluated, and its value is discarded. Next, y is evaluated and its value is returned. For example, #{x = 5; y = 3; z = x + y} evaluates to 8.

# Exploring lambda expressions

A lambda expression can be disassembled in three main parts: parameters, the lambda operator (->), and the function body.

Basically, in Java language, a lambda expression represents a method in an anonymous implementation of a functional interface. In EL, a lambda expression is reduced to an anonymous function that can be passed as an argument to a method.

It is important to not confuse Java 8 lambda expressions with EL lambda expressions, but in order to understand the next examples, it is important to know the fundamentals of Java 8 lambda expressions (http://docs.oracle.com/javase/tutorial/java/javaOO/lambdaexpressions.html). They don't have the same syntax, but they are similar enough to not cause notable discomfort when we need to switch between them.

An EL lambda expression is a parameterized `ValueExpression` object. The body of an EL lambda expression is an EL expression. EL supports several kinds of lambda expressions. The simplest type of EL lambda expressions are immediately invoked, for example:

- `#{(x->x+1)(3)}` evaluates to 4
- `#{((x,y,z)->x-y*z)(1,7,3)}` evaluates to -20

Further, we have assigned lambda expressions. These are invoked indirectly. For example, `#{q = x->x+1; q(3)}` evaluates to 4.

Indirectly, invocation can be used to write functions. For example, we can write a function to calculate `n mod m` (without using the `%` operator). The following example is evaluated to 3:

```
#{modulus = (n,m) -> m eq 0 ? 0 : (n lt m ? n: (modulus(n-m, m)));
    modulus(13,5)}
```

We can call this function from other expressions. For example, if we want to calculate the greatest common divisor of two numbers, we can exploit the preceding function; the following example is evaluated to 5:

```
#{gcd = (n,m) -> modulus(n,m) == 0 ? m: (gcd(m, modulus(n,m)));
    gcd(10, 15)}
```

Lambda expressions can be passed as arguments to methods. For example, in the following example, you call a method named `firstLambdaAction`—the lambda expression is invoked from this method:

```
#{lambdaBean.firstLambdaAction(modulus = (n,m) -> m eq 0 ? 0 :
    (n lt m ? n: (modulus(n-m, m))))}
```

Now, the `firstLambdaAction` method is as follows:

```
public Object firstLambdaAction(LambdaExpression lambdaExpression) {

    //useful in case of a custom ELContext
    FacesContext facesContext = FacesContext.getCurrentInstance();
    ELContext elContext = facesContext.getELContext();
```

```
    return lambdaExpression.invoke(elContext, 8, 3);

    //or simply, default ELContext:
    //return lambdaExpression.invoke(8, 3);
}
```

Another powerful feature of lambda expressions consists of nested lambda expressions. For example (first, is evaluated the inner expression to 7, afterwards the outer expression to as, 10 - 7): #{ (x->x-((x,y)->(x+y))(4,3))(10) } evaluates to 3.

Do you think EL lambda expressions rocks? Well, get ready for more. The real power is unleashed only when we bring collection objects into equations.

# Working with collection objects

EL 3.0 provides powerful support to manipulate collection objects by applying operations in a pipeline. The methods supporting the collection operations are implemented as ELResolvers, and lambda expressions are indicated as arguments for these methods.

The main idea behind manipulating collection objects is based on **streams**. More precisely, the specific operations are accomplished as method calls to the stream of elements obtained from the collection. Many operations return streams, which can be used in other operations that return streams, and so on. In such a case, we can say that we have a chain of streams or a pipeline. The entry in the pipeline is known as the **source**, and the exit from the pipeline is known as the **terminal operation** (this operation doesn't return a stream). Between the source and terminal operation, we may have zero or more **intermediate operations** (all of them return streams).

The pipeline execution begins when the terminal operation starts. Because intermediate operations are lazy evaluated, they don't preserve intermediate results of the operations (an exception is the sorted operation, which needs all the elements to sort tasks).

Now, let's see some examples. We begin by declaring a set, a list, and a map—EL contains syntaxes to construct sets, lists, and maps dynamically as follows:

```
#{nr_set = {1,2,3,4,5,6,7,8,9,10}}
#{nr_list = [1,2,3,4,5,6,7,8,9,10]}
#{nr_map = {"one":1,"two":2,"three":3,"four":4,"five":5,"six":6,
  "seven":7,"eight":8,"nine":9,"ten":10}}
```

Now, let's go a step further and sort the list in ascending/descending order. For this, we use the `stream`, `sorted` (this is like the ORDER BY statement of SQL), and `toList` methods (the latter returns a `List` that contains the elements of the source stream), as shown in the following code:

```
#{nr_list.stream().sorted((i,j)->i-j).toList()}
#{ nr_list.stream().sorted((i,j)->j-i).toList()}
```

Further, let's say that we have the following list in a managed bean named `LambdaBean`:

```
List<Integer> costBeforeVAT = Arrays.asList(34, 2200, 1350, 430,
    57, 10000, 23, 15222, 1);
```

Next, we can apply 24 percent of VAT and compute the total for costs higher than 1,000 using the `filter` (this is like SQL's WHERE and GROUP BY statements), `map` (this is like SQL's SELECT statement), and `reduce` (this is like the aggregate functions) methods. These methods are used as follows:

```
#{(lambdaBean.costBeforeVAT.stream().filter((cost)-> cost gt
    1000).map((cost) -> cost + .24*cost)).reduce((sum, cost) ->
    sum + cost).get()}
```

These were just a few examples of using collection objects in EL 3.0. A complete application named `ch1_4` is available for download in the code bundle of this chapter. Since, in this application you can see more than 70 examples, I recommend you to take a look at it. Moreover, a nice example can be found on Michael Müller's blog at `http://blog.mueller-bruehl.de/web-development/using-lambda-expressions-with-jsf-2-2/`.

But, what if we want to take advantage of lambda expressions, but we don't like to write such expressions? Well, a solution can be to write parameterized functions based on lambda expressions, and call them in the JSTL style. For example, the following function is capable of extracting a sublist of a `List`:

```
#{get_sublist = (list, left, right)->list.stream().substream(left,
    right).toList()}
```

Now, we can call it as shown in the following code:

```
<ui:repeat value="#{get_sublist(myList, from, to)}" var="t">
  #{t}
</ui:repeat>
```

In the complete application, named `ch1_5`, you can see a bunch of 21 parameterized functions that can be used with `List`s.

# Summary

In this chapter, we saw that EL 2.2 expressions can be used to dynamically access data (read and write) stored in JavaBeans components, to call arbitrary static and public methods, and to perform arithmetic and logic operations. Finally, we saw that EL allows us to extend its capabilities with custom resolvers. Starting with EL 3.0, we can take advantage of new operators, lambda expressions, and support when working with collection objects.

While reading this book, you will see many examples of EL expressions in real cases. For example, in the next chapter, you will use EL expressions to explore JSF communication capabilities.

See you in the next chapter, where we will discuss JSF communications.

# 2
# Communication in JSF

Communication is the core of a JSF application, and is one of the main aspects that dictate the architecture of such an application. Thinking of the big picture, you need to identify—right from the start—the main parts and how they will communicate with one another and with the end user. After selecting design patterns, drawing the UML diagrams, and sketching the architecture and the application flow, it's time to get to work and start implementing the communication pipes using forms, parameters, arguments, values, pages, beans, and so on.

Fortunately, JSF provides many solutions for ensuring a powerful and flexible communication layer between JSF components and also between JSF and XHTML pages, the JavaScript code, and other third-party components. In this chapter, we will cover the following topics:

- Using context parameters
- Passing request parameters with the `<f:param>` tag
- Working with view parameters
- Calling actions on GET requests
- Passing attributes with the `<f:attribute>` tag
- Setting property values via action listeners
- Passing parameters using the Flash scope
- Replacing the `<f:param>` tag with the JSTL `<c:set>` tag
- Sending data through cookies
- Working with hidden fields
- Sending passwords
- Accessing UI component attributes programmatically
- Passing parameters via method expressions
- Communicating via the `binding` attribute

# Passing and getting parameters

As you will see in the next sections, JSF provides several approaches to pass/get parameters to/from Facelets, managed beans, UI components, and so on.

## Using context parameters

Context parameters are defined in the `web.xml` file using the `<context-param>` tag. This tag allows two important children: `<param-name>`, which indicates the parameter name, and `<param-value>`, which indicates the parameter value. For example, a user-defined context parameter looks like the following code:

```
<context-param>
  <param-name>number.one.in.ATP</param-name>
  <param-value>Rafael Nadal</param-value>
</context-param>
```

Now, in a JSF page, you can access this parameter as shown in the following code:

```
<h:outputText value="#{initParam['number.one.in.ATP']}"/>
<h:outputText value="#{facesContext.externalContext.
  initParameterMap['number.one.in.ATP']}"/>
```

In a managed bean, the same context parameter can be accessed via the `getInitParameter` method:

```
facesContext.getExternalContext().getInitParameter
  ("number.one.in.ATP");
```

The complete application is named `ch2_27`.

## Passing request parameters with the `<f:param>` tag

Sometimes, you need to pass parameters from a Facelet to a managed bean or to another Facelet. In this case, you may need the `<f:param>` tag, which can be used to add query string name-value pairs to a request, or put simply, to send request parameters. Commonly, the `<f:param>` tag is used inside the `<h:commandButton>` and `<h:commandLink>` tags for sending request parameters to a managed bean. For example, the following snippet of code adds two parameters to the request when the form is submitted. These parameters are accessed in the `PlayersBean` bean; the first parameter is named `playerNameParam` and the second one is named `playerSurnameParam`.

```
<h:form>
  Click to send name, 'Rafael' surname, 'Nadal', with f:param:
```

```
    <h:commandButton value="Send Rafael Nadal"
      action="#{playersBean.parametersAction()}">
    <f:param id="playerName" name="playerNameParam" value="Rafael"/>
    <f:param id="playerSurname" name="playerSurnameParam"
      value="Nadal"/>
    </h:commandButton>
  </h:form>
```

As you can see, when the button is clicked, the request parameters are sent and the `parametersAction` method is called (via `action` or `actionListener`). When the application flow reaches this method, the two request parameters are already available for use. You can easily extract them inside this method by accessing the request parameters map through the current `FacesContext` instance as shown in the following code:

```
private String playerName;
private String playerSurname;
...
//getter and setter
...

public String parametersAction() {

  FacesContext fc = FacesContext.getCurrentInstance();
  Map<String, String> params =
    fc.getExternalContext().getRequestParameterMap();
  playerName = params.get("playerNameParam");
  playerSurname = params.get("playerSurnameParam");

  return "some_page";
}
```

The values of both the parameters are stored in the `playerName` and `playerSurname` managed beans' properties (these can be modified further without affecting the original parameters), but you can easily display the parameters' values using the `param` EL reserved word in *some_page* (remember the *EL implicit objects* section of *Chapter 1, Dynamic Access to JSF Application Data through Expression Language (EL 3.0)*, which explains that `param` is a predefined variable referring to the request parameter map):

```
Name: #{param.playerNameParam}
Surname: #{param.playerSurnameParam}
```

The `<f:param>` tag can also be used inside the `<h:outputFormat>` tag to substitute message parameters; `<f:param>` is used to pass parameters to a UI component as shown in the following code:

```
<h:outputFormat value="Name: {0} Surname: {1}">
  <f:param value="#{playersBean.playerName}" />
  <f:param value="#{playersBean.playerSurname}" />
</h:outputFormat>
```

The preceding code's output is as follows:

**Name: Rafael Surname: Nadal**

 If you want to execute some initialization tasks (or something else) after setting the managed bean properties but before an action method is called (if it exists), then you can define a public void method annotated with `@PostConstruct`. In this example, the init method will be called before the `parametersAction` method, and the passed request parameters are available through the request map.

The `init` method is shown in the following code:

```
@PostConstruct
public void init(){
  //do something with playerNameParam and playerSurnameParam
}
```

This example is wrapped into the application named `ch2_1`.

If you think that it is not a very convenient approach to access the request map in the managed bean, then you can use `@ManagedProperty`, which sets the parameter as a managed bean property and links its value to the request parameter:

```
@ManagedProperty(value = "#{param.playerNameParam}")
private String playerName;
@ManagedProperty(value = "#{param.playerSurnameParam}")
private String playerSurname;
```

The values are set immediately after the bean's construction and are available during `@PostConstruct`, but keep in mind that `@ManagedProperty` is usable only with beans managed by JSF (`@ManagedBean`), not with beans managed by CDI (`@Named`).

This example is wrapped into the application named `ch2_2` which is available in the code bundle of this chapter. You may also be interested in the application `ch2_3`, which is another example of using `<f:param>`, `@ManagedProperty`, and `@PostConstruct`. In this example, the `<h:commandButton>` action indicates another JSF page instead of a managed bean method.

The `<f:param>` tag can be used to pass request parameters directly between Facelets, without involving a managed bean. Usually, this happens in the `<h:link>` tag, as shown in the following code:

```
<h:link value="Send Rafael Nadal" outcome="result">
  <f:param id="playerName" name="playerNameParam" value="Rafael"/>
  <f:param id="playerSurname" name="playerSurnameParam"
    value="Nadal"/>
</h:link>
```

When the **Send Rafael Nadal** link is clicked, JSF will use the prepared URL containing the `result.xhtml` file's resource name and the request parameters, `playerNameParam` and `playerSurnameParam`. Both the parameters are displayed in the `result.xhtml` file as follows:

```
Name: #{param.playerNameParam}
Surname: #{param.playerSurnameParam}
```

If you check the URL generated by the `<h:link>` tag in the browser address bar, then you will see something like the following URL:

```
http://hostname/ch2_4/faces/result.xhtml?playerNameParam=Rafael&playerS
urnameParam=Nadal
```

This example is wrapped into the application named `ch2_4`. In that application, you can also see an example using the `<h:commandButton>` tag. Notice that, in this case, we need to wrap the `<h:commandButton>` tag in a `<h:form>` tag, which is submitted using the POST request; therefore, the request parameters are not visible in the URL anymore.

The `<f:param>` tag cannot be fortified with declarative/imperative validations and/or conversions. You need to accomplish this task by yourself.

Do not try to place the `<f:param>` tag inside the `<h:inputText>` tag or any other input component. That will simply not work.

# Working with view parameters

Starting with JSF 2.0, we can use a new category of parameters, known as **view parameters**. These kinds of parameters are implemented by the `UIViewParameter` class (that extends the `UIInput` class) and are defined in Facelets using the `<f:viewParam>` tag. Through this tag, we can declaratively register the `UIViewParameter` class as metadata for the parent view; this is why the `<f:viewParam>` tag is nested in the `<f:metadata>` tag.

Starting with JSF 2.0, the metadata concept was materialized in a section of a view, which provides the following two main advantages (the section is demarcated by the `<f:metadata>` tag):

- The content of this section is readable without having the entire view available

- At the initial request, components from this section can accomplish different things before the view is rendered

 Starting with JSF 2.2, the metadata section (and subsequent components) is detected via a public static method, named the `hasMetadata` (`UIViewRoot`) method. This method was added in `javax.faces.view.ViewMetadata` and returns `true` if there is a metadata section and `false` otherwise. Among other benefits, the main advantage of using the `<f:viewParam>` tag is the URL bookmarking support.

For better understanding, let's look at a simple example of using the `<f:viewParam>` tag. The following pieces of code are from the same page, `index.xhtml`:

```
<f:metadata>
  <f:viewParam name="playernameparam"
    value="#{playersBean.playerName}"/>
  <f:viewParam name="playersurnameparam"
    value="#{playersBean.playerSurname}"/>
</f:metadata>
...
<h:body>
  You requested name: <h:outputText
    value="#{playersBean.playerName}"/><br/>
  You requested surname: <h:outputText
    value="#{playersBean.playerSurname}"/>
</h:body>
```

Now, let's see what is happening at the initial request. First, let's focus on the first block of code: here, JSF gets the request parameter's values by their names (`playernameparam` and `playersurnameparam`) from the page URL and applies the specified converter/validators (these are optional). After conversion/validation succeeds, before the view is rendered, JSF binds the values of the `playernameparam` and `playersurnameparam` request parameters to the managed bean properties, `playerName` and `playerSurname`, by calling the `setPlayerName` and `setPlayerSurname` methods (called only if we provide request parameters in the URL). If the `value` attribute is missing, then JSF sets request parameters as request attributes on names, `playernameparam` and `playersurnameparam`, available via #{playernameparam} and #{playersurnameparam}.

The page's initial URL should be something like the following one:

```
http://hostname/ch2_5/?playernameparam=Rafael&playersurnameparam=Nadal
```

In the second block of code, the values of the managed bean properties, `playerName` and `playerSurname`, are displayed (the `getPlayerName` and `getPlayerSurname` methods are called); they should reflect the values of the request parameters.

 Since the `UIViewParameter` class extends the `UIInput` class, the managed bean properties are set during the **Update Model** phase only.

This example is wrapped into the application named `ch2_5`.

View parameters can be included in links (the GET query string) by using the `includeViewParams="true"` attribute in the `<h:link>` tag, or the `includeViewParams=true` request parameter in any URL. Both these cases can be seen in the upcoming examples.

In the `index.xhtml` file, you can have something like the following code, in which view parameters are included through the request parameter:

```
<f:metadata>
  <f:viewParam name="playernameparam"
    value="#{playersBean.playerName}"/>
  <f:viewParam name="playersurnameparam"
    value="#{playersBean.playerSurname}"/>
</f:metadata>
...
<h:body>
  <h:form>
    Enter name:<h:inputText value="#{playersBean.playerName}"/>
    Enter name:<h:inputText value="#{playersBean.playerSurname}"/>
```

```
    <h:commandButton value="Submit"
      action="results?faces-
      redirect=true&amp;includeViewParams=true"/>
    </h:form>
  </h:body>
```

The initial URL can be:

`http://hostname/ch2_6/?playernameparam=Rafael&playersurnameparam=Nadal`

The view parameters, `playernameparam` and `playersurnameparam`, will be extracted from this URL and bound to the managed bean properties, `playerName` and `playerSurname`. Optionally, both properties can be further altered by the user through two `<h:inputText>` tags, or other UI components. (If the initial URL does not contain the view parameters, then the `<h:inputText>` generated fields will be empty.) The button rendered through the `<h:commandButton>` tag will redirect the flow to the `results.xhtml` page and will include the view parameters in the new URL. The values of the view parameters will reflect the values of the corresponding managed bean properties, since the form is submitted before the following URL is composed:

`http://hostname/ch2_6/faces/results.xhtml?playernameparam=Rafael&player surnameparam=Nadal`

The `results.xhtml` file (or any other page that the `index.xhtml` file directs) will use the `<f:viewParam>` tag to take parameters from the GET request into bound properties, as shown in the following code:

```
<f:metadata>
  <f:viewParam name="playernameparam"
    value="#{playersBean.playerName}"/>
  <f:viewParam name="playersurnameparam"
    value="#{playersBean.playerSurname}"/>
</f:metadata>
...
<h:body>
  You requested name: <h:outputText
    value="#{playersBean.playerName}"/><br/>
  You requested surname: <h:outputText
    value="#{playersBean.playerSurname}"/>
</h:body>
```

If you prefer to use a `<h:link>` tag in conjunction with the `includeViewParams` attribute set to `true`, then the `index.xhtml` file will be as follows (in this case, there is no form submission and no POST request):

```
<f:metadata>
  <f:viewParam name="playernameparam"
    value="#{playersBean.playerName}"/>
 <f:viewParam name="playersurnameparam"
    value="#{playersBean.playerSurname}"/>
</f:metadata>
...
<h:body>
  <h:link value="Send"
    outcome="results?faces-redirect=true"
    includeViewParams="true"/>
</h:body>
```

These examples are wrapped into the application named `ch2_6`.

You can use the `includeViewParams` request parameter in any URL, which means that you can use it in managed beans to include view parameters in the navigation links as follows:

```
<f:metadata>
  <f:viewParam name="playernameparam"
  value="#{playersBean.playerName}"/>
  <f:viewParam name="playersurnameparam"
    value="#{playersBean.playerSurname}"/>
</f:metadata>
...
<h:body>
  <h:form>
    Enter name:<h:inputText value="#{playersBean.playerName}"/>
    Enter name:<h:inputText value="#{playersBean.playerSurname}"/>
    <h:commandButton value="Submit"
      action="#{playersBean.toUpperCase()}"/>
  </h:form>
</h:body>
```

And the action method is as follows:

```
public String toUpperCase(){
  playerName=playerName.toUpperCase();
  playerSurname=playerSurname.toUpperCase();

  return "results?faces-redirect=true&includeViewParams=true";
}
```

The complete application is named `ch2_7` and is available in the code bundle of this chapter on the Packt Publishing website.

As you know from the previous code, the `UIViewParameter` class extends the `UIInput` class, which means that it inherits all attributes, such as `required` and `requiredMessage`. When the URL must contain view parameters, you can use these two attributes to ensure that the application flow is controlled and the user is correctly informed. The following is the example code:

```
<f:metadata>
  <f:viewParam name="playernameparam" required="true"
    requiredMessage="Player name required!"
    value="#{playersBean.playerName}"/>
  <f:viewParam name="playersurnameparam" required="true"
    requiredMessage="Player surname required!"
    value="#{playersBean.playerSurname}"/>
</f:metadata>
```

If the initial URL does not contain the view parameters (one or both), then you will receive a message that report this fact. This example is wrapped into the application named `ch2_9`.

Moreover, view parameters support fine-grained conversion and validation. You can use `<f:validator>` and `<f:converter>`, or the `validator` and `converter` attributes inherited from the `UIInput` class. Supposing that you have a custom validator, named `PlayerValidator` (its implementation is not really relevant), the following is its code:

```
@FacesValidator("playerValidator")
public class PlayerValidator implements Validator {

  @Override
  public void validate(FacesContext context,
    UIComponent component,
  Object value) throws ValidatorException {
    //validation conditions
    ...
```

Then, you can attach it to a view parameter as shown in the following code:

```
<f:metadata>
  <f:viewParam id="nameId" name="playernameparam"
    validator="playerValidator"
    value="#{playersBean.playerName}"/>
  <f:viewParam id="surnameId" name="playersurnameparam"
    validator="playerValidator"
    value="#{playersBean.playerSurname}"/>
</f:metadata>
```

The preceding snippet of code accomplishes the following tasks:

- Gets the request parameters' values by their names, `playernameparam` and `playersurnameparam`
- Converts and validates (in this case, validates) parameters
- If conversions and validations end successfully, then the parameters are set in managed bean properties
- Any validation failure will result in a message being displayed

> For the customize messages style, you can attach a `<h:message>` tag to the `<f:viewParam>` tag.

This example is wrapped into the application named `ch2_10`.

> If you want to preserve the view parameters over validation failures, then you need to use a broader scope than `@RequestScoped`, such as `@ViewScoped`, or to manually preserve the request parameters for the subsequent requests through the `<f:param>` tag in the command components.

Sometimes, you may need a converter for a view parameter. For example, if you try to pass a `java.util.Date` parameter as a view parameter from a managed bean, you will probably will code it as follows:

```
private Date date = new Date();
...
public String sendDate() {
  String dateAsString = new SimpleDateFormat
    ("dd-MM-yyyy").format(date);
  return "date.xhtml?faces-redirect=true&date=" + dateAsString;
}
```

Now, in the `date.xhtml` file, you need to convert the view parameter from string to date, and for this, you may use the `<f:convertDateTime>` converter, as shown in the following code:

```
<f:viewParam name="date" value="#{dateBean.date}">
  <f:convertDateTime pattern="dd-MM-yyyy" />
</f:viewParam>
```

Of course, a custom converter can also be used. The complete application is named `ch2_29`.

Among so many advantages of using the `<f:viewParam>` tag, we have a gap. When view parameters are set in managed bean properties, the set values are not available in `@PostConstruct`; therefore, you cannot perform initialization or preload tasks directly. You can quickly fix this by attaching the `preRenderView` event listener, as shown in the following code:

```
<f:metadata>
  <f:viewParam name="playernameparam"
    value="#{playersBean.playerName}"/>
  <f:viewParam name="playersurnameparam"
    value="#{playersBean.playerSurname}"/>
  <f:event type="preRenderView"
    listener="#{playersBean.init()}"/>
</f:metadata>
```

The `init` method is shown as follows:

```
public void init() {
  // do something with playerName and playerSurname
}
```

> The set values are not available in `@PostConstruct` when using the `<f:viewParam>` tag. You can fix this by attaching the `preRenderView` event listener, or, as you will see next, the `<f:viewAction>` tag.

This example is wrapped into the application named `ch2_8`.

Well, there is one more aspect that I'd like to discuss here. The `UIViewParameter` class (`<f:viewParam>`) is a stateful component that stores its value in state. This is very nice as the value is available over postbacks, even if it doesn't come from the page URL anymore or the managed bean is request scoped. So, you need to indicate view parameters only once, and not for every request. But, there are a few drawbacks of this behavior—the most significant being calling the setter method at each postback (you don't want this in view beans). Another one is calling, for each postback, the method indicated through the `preRenderView` event handler; this can be fixed using a test as shown in the following code. The complete application is named `ch2_28`.

```
public void init() {
  if (!FacesContext.getCurrentInstance().isPostback()) {
    // do something with playerName and playerSurname
  }
}
```

Maybe the most painful drawback is converting and validating view parameters at each postback. Obviously, this is not the behavior you are expecting to see. In order to call a converter/validator only when the page URL contains the request parameters, you need to alter the `UIViewParameter` class implementation by writing a custom implementation. You can try to write a stateless `UIViewParameter` class or to control the conversion/validation calls. Of course, you have to keep in mind that altering the default implementation may lead to more or less unpredictable drawbacks. As an alternative, you can use the `<o:viewParam>` tag from OmniFaces, which fixes these issues. A relevant example can be seen at `http://showcase.omnifaces.org/components/viewParam`.

So, as a final conclusion of this section, the `<f:viewParam>` tag is used to capture the request parameters. Moreover, it can be used with the `<h:link>` and `<h:button>` tags to send outgoing request parameters, or in non-JSF forms, to send data to JSF pages that use the `<f:viewParam>` tag, or to make JSF results pages bookmarkable in a POST-redirect-GET flow. On the other hand, the `<f:viewParam>` tag doesn't sustain the `<h:form>` tag to use GET or provide access to random JSF pages via the GET request.

# Calling actions on GET requests

Starting with JSF 2.2, we can deal with calling actions on GET requests by using the new generic **view action** feature (well-known in Seam 2 and 3). This new feature is materialized in the `<f:viewAction>` tag, which is declared as a child of the metadata facet, `<f:metadata>`. This allows the view action to be part of the JSF life cycle for faces/non-faces requests.

In the preceding section, we saw how to attach a custom validator to a `<f:viewParam>` tag for validating view parameters. The same thing can be accomplished using the `<f:viewAction>` tag, when the validation method is declared in the managed bean instead of being a separate implementation of the `Validator` interface. For example, in the `index.xhtml` file, you may have the following code:

```
<f:metadata>
  <f:viewParam id="nameId" name="playernameparam"
    value="#{playersBean.playerName}"/>
  <f:viewParam id="surnameId" name="playersurnameparam"
    value="#{playersBean.playerSurname}"/>
  <f:viewAction action="#{playersBean.validateData()}"/>
</f:metadata>
```

As you can see, the following `validateData` method is just a common method declared in `PlayersBean`:

```
public String validateData() {
  //validation conditions
  return "index"; //or other page
}
```

This example is wrapped into the application named `ch2_11`.

 The `<f:viewAction>` tag and the `preRenderView` event listener are not the same!

The preceding note underlines our next discussion. You may think that they are the same because in the preceding example, you can replace `<f:viewAction>` with `preRenderView` and obtain the same effect (result). Well, it is true that they are partially the same, but a few existing differences are important, as you can see in the following four bullets:

- By default, the `preRenderView` event listener is executed on postback requests, while the view action is not. In the case of the `preRenderView` event listener, you need to overcome this by testing the request type as follows:

```
if (!FacesContext.getCurrentInstance().isPostback()) {
  // code that should not be executed in postback phase
}
```

For example, the following code will try to apply some modifications over the set values using the `preRenderView` event listener:

```
<f:metadata>
  <f:viewParam name="playernameparam"
    value="#{playersBean.playerName}"/>
  <f:viewParam name="playersurnameparam"
    value="#{playersBean.playerSurname}"/>
  <f:event type="preRenderView"
    listener="#{playersBean.init()}"/>
</f:metadata>
```

The `init` method is declared in `PlayersBean` and it just turns the set values to uppercase, as shown in the following code:

```
public void init() {
  if (playerName != null) {
    playerName = playerName.toUpperCase();
  }
  if (playerSurname != null) {
    playerSurname = playerSurname.toUpperCase();
  }
}
```

Next, when the JSF page is rendered, the set values are used in uppercase, and further requests can be accomplished (for example, you may want to call the method `#{playersBean.userAction()}` when a certain button is clicked). But, each further request will call the `init` method again (after the `userAction` method), because the `preRenderView` event listener is executed at postback time. Except for the case when this is the desired functionality, you need to programmatically test the postbacks to prevent the following `init` method code from being executed:

```
public void init() {
  if (!FacesContext.getCurrentInstance().isPostback()) {
    if (playerName != null) {
      playerName = playerName.toUpperCase();
    }
    if (playerSurname != null) {
      playerSurname = playerSurname.toUpperCase();
    }
  }
}
```

Well, this is not the same in the case of the `<f:viewAction>` tag. Replace the `preRenderView` event listener with the `<f:viewAction>` tag, as shown in the following code:

```
<f:metadata>
  <f:viewParam name="playernameparam"
    value="#{playersBean.playerName}"/>
  <f:viewParam name="playersurnameparam"
    value="#{playersBean.playerSurname}"/>
  <f:viewAction action="#{playersBean.init()}"/>
</f:metadata>
```

The `<f:viewAction>` tag supports an attribute named `onPostback` which is set to `false` by default, meaning that the `init` method will not be called on postback requests. Of course, if you set it to `true`, then it will function contrary; but, notice that in the case of the `preRenderView` event listener, the `init` method is called after the `userAction` method, while in the case of the `<f:viewAction>` tag, the `init` method is called before the `userAction` method, as shown in the following line of code:

```
<f:viewAction action="#{playersBean.init()}"
  onPostback="true"/>
```

The example based on the `preRenderView` event listener is wrapped in the application named `ch_12_1`, while for the `<f:viewAction>` tag it is named `ch_12_2`.

- The view action has navigation capabilities, while the `preRenderView` event listener doesn't. While the view action can naturally accomplish navigation tasks, the `preRenderView` event listener requires explicit navigation based on the JSF API.

  For example, if you modify the preceding `init` method to return the `start.xhtml` view, then you will probably change it as shown in the following code:

```
public String init() {
  if (playerName != null) {
    playerName = playerName.toUpperCase();
  }
  if (playerSurname != null) {
    playerSurname = playerSurname.toUpperCase();
  }
  return "start";
}
```

But, this will not work with the `preRenderView` event listener! You will need to add explicit navigation by returning void and replacing the return `"start"` code line with the following code:

```
ConfigurableNavigationHandler handler =
  (ConfigurableNavigationHandler)
  FacesContext.getCurrentInstance().
  getApplication().getNavigationHandler();
handler.performNavigation("start");
```

If you drop the `preRenderView` event listener and use the `<f:viewAction>` tag instead, then the preceding `init` method will correctly navigate to `start.xhtml` without involving an explicit call of the navigation handler.

The example based on the `preRenderView` event listener is wrapped in the application named `ch_13_1`, while for the `<f:viewAction>` tag it is named `ch_13_2`.

Moreover, the `<f:viewAction>` tag supports declarative navigation. So, you can write a navigation rule in the `faces-config.xml` file that is consulted before the page is rendered. For example:

```
<navigation-rule>
  <from-view-id>index.xhtml</from-view-id>
  <navigation-case>
    <from-action>#{playersBean.init()}</from-action>
    <from-outcome>start</from-outcome>
    <to-view-id>rafa.xhtml</to-view-id>
    <redirect/>
  </navigation-case>
</navigation-rule>
```

Now, the `rafa.xhtml` page will be rendered instead of the `start.xhtml` page. This example is wrapped into the application named `ch2_13_3`.

- By default, the view action is executed in the **Invoke Application** phase. But, it can be executed in the **Apply Request Values** phase by setting the `immediate` attribute to `true`, as shown in the following code:

```
<f:viewAction action="#{playersBean.init()}"
  immediate="true"/>
```

- Moreover, you can specify in which phase to execute the action using the `phase` attribute whose value represents the phase name as a predefined constant. For example:

```
<f:viewAction action="#{playersBean.init()}"
  phase="UPDATE_MODEL_VALUES"/>
```

The supported values are `APPLY_REQUEST_VALUES`, `INVOKE_APPLICATION`, `PROCESS_VALIDATIONS`, and `UPDATE_MODEL_VALUES`.

 The view action can be placed into a view metadata facet that doesn't contain other view parameters.

# Passing attributes with the <f:attribute> tag

When the `<f:param>` tag does not satisfy your needs, maybe the `<f:attribute>` tag will. This tag allows you to pass the value of an attribute of a component or to pass a parameter to a component.

For example, you can assign the value of the attribute named `value` of a `<h:commandButton>` tag as shown in the following code:

```
<h:commandButton actionListener="#{playersBean.parametersAction}">
  <f:attribute name="value" value="Send Rafael Nadal" />
</h:commandButton>
```

This will render a button labeled **Send Rafael Nadal**. Its code is given as follows:

```
<h:commandButton value="Send Rafael Nadal"
  actionListener="#{playersBean.parametersAction}">
```

Moreover, the `<f:attribute>` tag can be used to pass a parameter to a component, as shown in the following code:

```
<h:commandButton actionListener="#{playersBean.parametersAction}">
  <f:attribute id="playerName" name="playerNameAttr"
    value="Rafael"/>
  <f:attribute id="playerSurname" name="playerSurnameAttr"
    value="Nadal"/>
</h:commandButton>
```

In the action listener method, you can extract the attributes' values as shown in the following code:

```
private final static Logger logger =
  Logger.getLogger(PlayersBean.class.getName());
private String playerName;
private String playerSurname;
...
//getters and setters
...
public void parametersAction(ActionEvent evt) {

  playerName = (String) evt.getComponent().
    getAttributes().get("playerNameAttr");
  playerSurname = (String) evt.getComponent().
    getAttributes().get("playerSurnameAttr");

  logger.log(Level.INFO, "Name: {0} Surname: {1}",
    new Object[]{playerName, playerSurname});
}
```

This example is wrapped into the application named ch2_14.

If you are a fan of PrimeFaces (http://primefaces.org/), then you will probably find the next example useful. One of the greatest built-in components of PrimeFaces is the <p:fileUpload> tag, which can be used, obviously, to upload files. Sometimes, besides the files that will be uploaded, you need to pass some extra parameters, for example, the files' owner name and surname. Well, the <p:fileUpload> tag doesn't come with a solution for this, but the <f:attribute> tag can be helpful. The following is the code of a classic <p:fileUpload> tag with the <f:attribute> tag:

```
<h:form>
  <p:fileUpload
    fileUploadListener="#{fileUploadController.handleFileUpload}"
    mode="advanced" dragDropSupport="false"
    update="messages" sizeLimit="100000" fileLimit="3"
    allowTypes="/(\.|\/)(gif|jpe?g|png)$/">
  <f:attribute id="playerName" name="playerNameAttr"
    value="Rafael"/>
  <f:attribute id="playerSurname" name="playerSurnameAttr"
    value="Nadal"/>
  </p:fileUpload>
  <p:growl id="messages" showDetail="true"/>
</h:form>
```

The `handleFileUpload` method is responsible for the upload-specific steps (skipped in the following code), but it can also access the values passed by the `<f:attribute>` tag:

```
public void handleFileUpload(FileUploadEvent evt) {

  //upload specific tasks, see PrimeFaces documentation

  String playerName = (String) evt.getComponent().
    getAttributes().get("playerNameAttr");
  String playerSurname = (String) evt.getComponent().
    getAttributes().get("playerSurnameAttr");

  FacesMessage msg = new FacesMessage("Successful",
    evt.getFile().getFileName() + " is uploaded for "
    + playerName + " " + playerSurname);

  FacesContext.getCurrentInstance().addMessage(null, msg);
}
```

If you are not a fan of PrimeFaces, then you might probably think that this example is useless, but maybe you are a fan of some other third-party library, such as RichFaces, ICEFaces, and MyFaces. You can apply this technique for other component libraries as well.

This example is wrapped into the application named `ch2_15`.

Another case when the `<f:attribute>` tag can be useful is when dynamically passing parameters in conjunction with UI components bound to the managed bean using the `binding` attribute. This is very useful, especially because there is no solution provided by JSF for passing parameters to the getters/setters methods of the bound UI components, as shown in the following code:

```
<h:form>
  <h:inputText binding="#{playersBean.htmlInputText}"
    value="#{playersBean.playerNameSurname}">
    <f:attribute name="playerNameAttr" value="Rafael Nadal"/>
  </h:inputText>
</h:form>
```

Now, the value of the `<h:inputText>` tag should contain the value set via the `<f:attribute>` tag. Be careful to use only unique names for the attributes and to not interfere (try to overwrite) with the default attributes of the UI component.

Also, the `PlayersBean` managed bean's code is as follows:

```
@Named
@RequestScoped
public class PlayersBean {

  private UIInput htmlInputText= null;

  public PlayersBean() {
  }

  public UIInput getHtmlInputText() {
    return htmlInputText;
  }

  public void setHtmlInputText(UIInput htmlInputText) {
    this.htmlInputText = htmlInputText;
  }

  public String getPlayerNameSurname() {
    return (String)
      htmlInputText.getAttributes().get("playerNameAttr");
  }
}
```

As you can see, all the parameters passed this way are accessible via the `getAttributes` method of the parent UI component.

This example is wrapped into the application named `ch2_23`.

# Setting property values via action listeners

The `<f:setPropertyActionListener>` tag uses an action listener (created by the framework) to directly set a value into a managed bean property; it is placed within a component derived from the `ActionSource` class. The `target` attribute indicates the managed bean property, while the `value` attribute indicates the value of the property, as shown in the following code:

```
<h:commandButton value="Send Rafael Nadal 1">
  <f:setPropertyActionListener id="playerName"
    target="#{playersBean.playerName}" value="Rafael"/>
  <f:setPropertyActionListener  id="playerSurname"
    target="#{playersBean.playerSurname}" value="Nadal"/>
</h:commandButton>
```

Now, in the `PlayersBean` managed bean, the setter methods are called and the values are set; `logger` is useful to see the application flow and to understand how listeners are fired, as shown in the following code:

```
private final static Logger logger =
  Logger.getLogger(PlayersBean.class.getName());
private String playerName;
private String playerSurname;

public void setPlayerName(String playerName) {
  this.playerName = playerName;
  logger.log(Level.INFO, "Player name
    (from setPlayerName() method: {0}", playerName);
}

public void setPlayerSurname(String playerSurname) {
  this.playerSurname = playerSurname;
  logger.log(Level.INFO, "Player surname
    (from setPlayerSurname() method: {0}", playerSurname);
}
```

When the button labeled **Send Rafael Nadal 1** is clicked, the application output will be as follows:

```
INFO:    Player name (from setPlayerName() method: Rafael
INFO:    Player surname (from setPlayerSurname() method: Nadal
```

 Keep in mind that action listeners are executed in the order they are defined, which means that the presence of the `<f:setPropertyActionListener>` tag can affect the order in which the listeners are fired.

This note is important! For a clear understanding, take a look at the following snippet of code:

```
<h:commandButton value="Send Rafael Nadal 2"
  actionListener="#{playersBean.parametersAction}">
  <f:setPropertyActionListener id="playerName"
    target="#{playersBean.playerName}" value="Rafael"/>
  <f:setPropertyActionListener  id="playerSurname"
    target="#{playersBean.playerSurname}" value="Nadal"/>
</h:commandButton>
```

The following code is of the `parametersAction` method:

```
public void parametersAction(ActionEvent e) {
  logger.log(Level.INFO, "Player name
    (from parametersAction(ActionEvent) method: {0}", playerName);
  logger.log(Level.INFO, "Player surname
    (from parametersAction(ActionEvent) method: {0}",
    playerSurname);
}
```

Well, this code does not work as expected! Probably, you think that the setters method is called first and the `parametersAction` method later; therefore, the set values are available in the action method. But, the following output will prove the opposite:

```
INFO:     Player name (from parametersAction() method: null
INFO:     Player surname (from parametersAction() method: null
INFO:     Player name (from setPlayerName() method: Rafael
INFO:     Player surname (from setPlayerSurname() method: Nadal
```

So, the properties are set after the command action listener is fired! To fix this issue, you can use the `action` attribute instead of `actionListener`:

```
<h:commandButton value="Send Rafael Nadal 3"
    action="#{playersBean.parametersAction()}">
  <f:setPropertyActionListener id="playerName"
    target="#{playersBean.playerName}" value="Rafael"/>
  <f:setPropertyActionListener  id="playerSurname"
    target="#{playersBean.playerSurname}" value="Nadal"/>
</h:commandButton>
```

Of course, you need to adjust the `parametersAction` method accordingly, as shown in the following code:

```
public void parametersAction() {
  logger.log(Level.INFO, "Player name
    (from parametersAction() method: {0}", playerName);
  logger.log(Level.INFO, "Player surname
    (from parametersAction() method: {0}", playerSurname);
}
```

Now, the output will reflect the following desired result:

```
INFO:     Player name (from setPlayerName() method: Rafael
INFO:     Player surname (from setPlayerSurname() method: Nadal
INFO:     Player name (from parametersAction() method: Rafael
INFO:     Player surname (from parametersAction() method: Nadal
```

This example is wrapped into the application named `ch2_16`.

# Passing parameters using the Flash scope

The new JSF Flash scope is a very handy tool when you need to pass parameters between user views without the need to store them in the session. The Flash scope is simple to understand if you keep in mind that variables stored in the Flash scope will be available over a redirection and they will be eliminated afterwards. This is really useful when implementing a POST-redirect-GET pattern.

For a better understanding, let's suppose the following scenario:

- A player (user) needs to register on the ATP website. Among other information, he will provide his name and surname and click on the **Register** button. This is accomplished in the `index.xhtml` page.

- The application flow redirects the player to the page `terms.xhtml`. On this page, the user can see a welcome message containing his name and surname and some terms and conditions that must be accepted (using the **Accept** button) or rejected (using the **Reject** button).

- If the **Reject** button is clicked, then the user is redirected to the `index.xhtml` home page, and the form registration fields will reveal the information provided by him earlier. Moreover, he will see a generated message stating **Terms rejected! Player not registered!**. This is outputted by the `<h:message>` tag.

- If the **Accept** button is clicked, then the user is redirected to a page named `done.xhtml`. On this page, the user will see a generated message stating **Terms accepted and player registered!** and another message stating *Name Surname* **successfully registered!**. The first message is outputted by the `<h:message>` tag, while the second one by the `<h:outputText>` tag.

The following is a screenshot of both the scenarios:

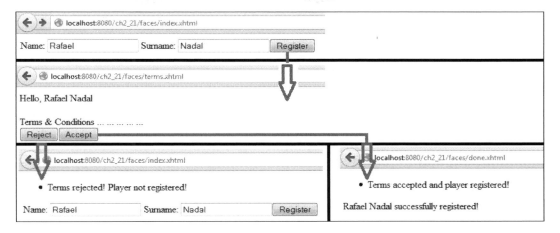

Obviously, you can implement this flow only if you store the submitted values somewhere, because they will not survive during the redirect process. This means that using a managed bean in the request scope cannot be a valid option. But, if we add in discussion the new Flash scope, then things become more favorable for the request scoped bean.

It will be much easier to follow this idea if you take a quick look at the following code of the request scoped bean, named `PlayersBean`:

```
@Named
@RequestScoped
public class PlayersBean {

  private final static Logger logger =
    Logger.getLogger(PlayersBean.class.getName());
  private String playerName;
  private String playerSurname;

...

  public String addValuesToFlashAction() {

    Flash flash = FacesContext.getCurrentInstance().
      getExternalContext().getFlash();
    flash.put("playerName", playerName);
```

```
        flash.put("playerSurname", playerSurname);

        return "terms?faces-redirect=true";
    }

    public void pullValuesFromFlashAction(ComponentSystemEvent e) {

        Flash flash = FacesContext.getCurrentInstance().
            getExternalContext().getFlash();
        playerName = (String) flash.get("playerName");
        playerSurname = (String) flash.get("playerSurname");
    }

    public String termsAcceptedAction() {

        Flash flash = FacesContext.getCurrentInstance().
            getExternalContext().getFlash();

        flash.setKeepMessages(true);
        pullValuesFromFlashAction(null);

        //do something with firstName, lastName
        logger.log(Level.INFO, "First name: {0}", playerName);
        logger.log(Level.INFO, "Last name: {0}", playerSurname);

        FacesContext.getCurrentInstance().addMessage(null, new
            FacesMessage("Terms accepted and player registered!"));
        return "done?faces-redirect=true";
    }

    public String termsRejectedAction() {

        Flash flash = FacesContext.getCurrentInstance().
            getExternalContext().getFlash();

        flash.setKeepMessages(true);
        pullValuesFromFlashAction(null);

        FacesContext.getCurrentInstance().addMessage(null, new
            FacesMessage("Terms rejected! Player not registered!"));
        return "index?faces-redirect=true";
    }
}
```

Also, take a look at the start page, `index.xhtml`. Its code is as follows:

```
<h:body>
  <f:metadata>
    <f:event type="preRenderView"
      listener="#{playersBean.pullValuesFromFlashAction}"/>
  </f:metadata>
  <h:messages />
  <h:form>
    Name: <h:inputText value="#{playersBean.playerName}"/>
    Surname: <h:inputText value="#{playersBean.playerSurname}"/>
   <h:commandButton value="Register"
      action="#{playersBean.addValuesToFlashAction()}"/>
  </h:form>
</h:body>
```

So, the submission process begins when the user clicks on the button labeled **Register**. JSF will call the `addValuesToFlashAction` method, which is responsible for putting the submitted values to the Flash scope; this will ensure that the values will survive during redirect to the `terms.xhtml` page.

If the user rejects the terms and conditions, then he is redirected to the `index.xhtml` page. Here, you need to repopulate the registration form fields with the user-inserted values. For this, you can use the `preRenderView` event, which will load the values from the Flash scope during the render response phase by calling the `pullValuesFromFlashAction` method.

Next, let's focus on the `terms.xhtml` page; its code is as follows:

```
<h:body>
  <h:messages />
    Hello, <h:outputText value="#{flash.keep.playerName}
      #{flash.keep.playerSurname}"/>
  <br/><br/>Terms &amp; Conditions ... ... ... ... ...
  <h:form>
  <h:commandButton value="Reject"
    action="#{playersBean.termsRejectedAction()}" />
  <h:commandButton value="Accept"
    action="#{playersBean.termsAcceptedAction()}" />
  </h:form>
</h:body>
```

First, this page displays the entered values wrapped into a welcome message. The values are obtained from the Flash scope using the following code:

```
#{flash.keep.playerName}
#{flash.keep.playerSurname}
```

Notice that this approach has two functions, which are listed as follows:

- It obtains the values from the Flash scope, which could also be accomplished with the following lines:

```
#{flash.playerName}
#{flash.playerSurname}
```

- It tells JSF to keep the values in the Flash scope for the next request. This is needed because values put to the Flash scope survive only one redirect and then are deleted. We have already fired a redirect when we have navigated from the `index.xhtml` page to the `terms.xhtml` page. But, another redirect will appear when the **Accept** or **Reject** button is clicked.

 Values stored in the Flash scope survive only one redirect and then are deleted.

Furthermore, the page displays both the buttons for navigating back to the `index.xhtml` page and forward to the `done.xhtml` page. The **Accept** button will call the `termsAcceptedAction` method, which will basically preserve messages across redirects (it calls the `setKeepMessages` method) and redirects the flow to the `done.xhtml` page. In the same manner, the **Reject** button calls the `termsRejectedAction` method, preserves messages in the Flash scope, and redirects the flow to the `index.xhtml` page.

The `done.xhtml` page is presented using the following code:

```
<h:body>
  <f:metadata>
   <f:event type="preRenderView"
     listener="#{playersBean.pullValuesFromFlashAction}"/>
  </f:metadata>
  <h:messages />
  <h:outputText value="#{playersBean.playerName}
    #{playersBean.playerSurname}"/> successfully registered!
</h:body>
```

The `preRenderView` event listener is used again for obtaining the values from the Flash scope.

This example is wrapped into the application named `ch2_21`.

# Replacing the <f:param> tag with the JSTL <c:set> tag

Sometimes, the JSTL `<c:set>` tag can solve issues that the JSF `<f:param>` tag can't. Probably, you know that we can pass parameters to the `<ui:include>` tag using the `<f:param>` tag, as shown in the following code:

```
<ui:include src="rafa.xhtml">
  <f:param name="rafa" value="Rafael Nadal Page"/>,
</ui:include>
```

Well, this approach triggers an issue! Now, the `Rafael Nadal Page` value will be available in the included page through EL, `#{rafa}`, but will not be available in the constructor of the managed bean of the included page!

It is time for the `<c:set>` tag to save the situation; therefore, the code will be changed to the following:

```
<ui:include src="rafa.xhtml">
  <c:set var="rafa" value="Rafael Nadal Page" scope="request"/>,
</ui:include>
```

Done! Now, in the constructor of the managed bean, the value can be extracted as shown in the following code:

```
public ConstructorMethod(){
  FacesContext facesContext = FacesContext.getCurrentInstance();
  HttpServletRequest httpServletRequest  = (HttpServletRequest)
    facesContext.getExternalContext().getRequest();
  String rafa = (String) request.getAttribute("rafa");
}
```

In the *Configuring system event listeners* section in *Chapter 4, JSF Configurations Using XML Files and Annotations – Part 1*, you will see how to work with system events dedicated to the Flash scope.

# Sending data through cookies

JSF provides a request cookie map that can be used to work with HTTP cookies. Setting cookies can be easily accomplished through JavaScript; the following are just some helper methods:

- The JavaScript method for setting a cookie is as follows:

```
function setCookie(cookie_name, value, expiration_days)
{
  var expiration_date = new Date();
  expiration_date.setDate(expiration_date.getDate() +
    expiration_days);
  var c_value = escape(value) + ((expiration_days == null)
    ? "" : ";
  expires=" + expiration_date.toUTCString());
  document.cookie = cookie_name + "=" + c_value;
}
```

The JavaScript method for deleting a cookie by the name is as follows:

```
function deleteCookie(cookie_name) {
  document.cookie = encodeURIComponent(cookie_name) +
    "=deleted; expires=" + new Date(0).toUTCString();
}
```

- The JavaScript method for extracting a cookie by the name is as follows:

```
function getCookie(cookie_name) {
  var i, part_1, part_2;
  var cookieslist = document.cookie.split(";");
  //<![CDATA[
  for (i = 0; i < cookieslist.length; i++)
  {
    part_1 = cookieslist[i].substr(0,
      cookieslist[i].indexOf("="));
    part_2 = cookieslist[i].substr
      (cookieslist[i].indexOf("=") + 1);
    part_1 = part_1.replace(/^\s+|\s+$/g, "");
    if (part_1 == cookie_name)
    {
      return unescape(part_2);
    }
  }
  //]]>
  return "nocookie";
}
```

Let's suppose that you have two cookies named `name` and `surname`, as shown in the following code:

```
setCookie('name', 'Rafael', 1);
setCookie('surname', 'Nadal', 1);
```

JSF can access these cookies through the following request cookie map:

```
Object name_cookie = FacesContext.getCurrentInstance().
  getExternalContext().getRequestCookieMap().get("name");
Object surname_cookie = FacesContext.getCurrentInstance().
  getExternalContext().getRequestCookieMap().get("surname");

//set playerName property
if (name_cookie != null) {
  playerName = (((Cookie) name_cookie).getValue());
}

//set playerSurname property
if (surname_cookie != null) {
  playerSurname = (((Cookie) surname_cookie).getValue());
}
```

JSF also provides several getters and setters methods for working with cookies. These methods are given in the following table:

| Getter methods | Setter methods |
| --- | --- |
| String getComment() | setComment(String arg) |
| String getDomain() | setDomain(String arg) |
| String getName() | setHttpOnly(boolean arg) |
| String getPath() | setPath(String arg) |
| String getValue() | setValue(String arg) |
| int getMaxAge() | setMaxAge(int arg) |
| boolean getSecure() | setSecure(boolean arg) |
| int getVersion() | setVersion(int arg) |
| boolean isHttpOnly() | |

This example is wrapped into the application named `ch2_18` and can be found in the code bundle of this chapter.

# Working with hidden fields

Hidden fields can sometimes be very useful! Passing data in a subtle manner can be the perfect choice for dealing with temporary data or information provided by the user that should be used again and again. JSF offers the `<h:inputHidden>` tag to pass hidden parameters. The following code passes two hidden parameters to a managed bean:

```
<h:form id="hiddenFormId">
  <h:commandButton value="Send Rafael Nadal"
    onclick="setHiddenValues();"
    action="#{playersBean.parametersAction()}"/>
  <h:inputHidden id="playerName"
    value="#{playersBean.playerName}"/>
 <h:inputHidden id="playerSurname"
    value="#{playersBean.playerSurname}"/>
</h:form>
```

Usually, setting hidden field values from JavaScript is a common practice. When the button **Send Rafael Nadal** is clicked, the JavaScript function named `setHiddenValues` is called; this happens before the form submission. The `setHiddenValues` function is given in the following code:

```
<script type="text/javascript">
  function setHiddenValues() {
    document.getElementById('hiddenFormId:playerName').
      value = "Rafael";
    document.getElementById('hiddenFormId:playerSurname').
      value = "Nadal";
  }
</script>
```

Next, the hidden parameters are set in the indicated managed bean properties and the `parametersAction` method is called—the set values are ready to use!

This example is wrapped into the application named `ch2_17` and can be found in the code bundle of this chapter.

# Sending passwords

JSF provides a dedicated tag named `<h:inputSecret>` for rendering the following well-known HTML code:

```
<input type="password">
```

For example, you can use it as shown in the following code:

```
<h:form>
  <h:inputSecret value="#{playersBean.playerPassword}"/>
  <h:commandButton value="Send Password"
    action="#{playersBean.passwordAction()}"/>
</h:form>
```

This example is wrapped into the application named `ch2_19`.

# Accessing UI component attributes programmatically

Accessing UI component attributes from managed beans using the JSF API is not a common approach, but sometimes you may find it useful. For example, let's suppose that we have the following form:

```
<h:form id="playerFormId">
  <h:inputText id="playerNameId"
    value="#{playersBean.playerName}"/>
  <h:inputText id="playerSurnameId"
    value="#{playersBean.playerSurname}"/>
  <h:commandButton value="Process"
    action="#{playersBean.processAction()}"/>
</h:form>
```

Now, you want to obtain the values of the components with IDs, `playerNameId` and `playerSurnameId`, in the `processAction` method. Moreover, you want to set the value of the component with the ID, `playerNameId`, as RAFAEL. Programmatically (using the JSF API), you can achieve this as follows:

```
public void processAction() {

  UIViewRoot view =
    FacesContext.getCurrentInstance().getViewRoot();
  UIComponent uinc =
    view.findComponent("playerFormId:playerNameId");
  Object prev = ((UIInput) uinc).getAttributes().put("value",
    "RAFAEL");


  UIComponent uisc =
    view.findComponent("playerFormId:playerSurnameId");
  Object current = ((UIInput) uisc).getAttributes().get("value");
}
```

First, you need to obtain access to `UIViewRoot`, which is the top level UI component—the root of the `UIComponent` tree. Then, you can search by the ID for the desired UI component through the UI components tree using the `findComponent` method. Each UI component provides the `getAttributes` method, which can be used to gain access to the UI component attributes by their names. At this point, you can extract an attribute value using the `get` method, or set a new attribute value using the `put` method.

This example is wrapped into the application named `ch2_20`.

# Passing parameters via method expressions

Passing parameters using method expressions is an elegant solution to send parameters as arguments to an action method of a managed bean. For example, let's focus on the following snippet of code:

```
<h:form>
  <h:commandButton value="Send Rafael Nadal"
     action="#{playersBean.parametersAction('Rafael','Nadal')}"/>
</h:form>
```

As you can see in the following code, the `action` attribute indicates a method that gets two arguments:

```
private String playerName;
private String playerSurname;

//getters and setters

public String parametersAction(String playerNameArg,
   String playerSurnameArg) {

   playerName = playerNameArg;
   playerSurname = playerSurnameArg;

   return "result";
}
```

In the same manner, you can pass numeric values or objects.

This example is wrapped into the application named `ch2_26`.

# Communicating via the binding attribute

JSF UI components support an attribute named `binding`, which is rarely used and, sometimes, poorly understood. The story behind its meaning can be stretched over several pages or summed up in some golden rules. We will start with the binding lifespan and a brief overview and will end with the important rules that should be taken into account when you decide to used it in production.

If we want to localize the moment in time when the `binding` attribute enters the fray, we can refer to the moment when the JSF view is built or restored; the result of building/restoring the view is present in the component tree. So, before the component tree is deliverable, JSF needs to inspect all `binding` attributes. For each of them, JSF will check the presence of a pre-existing (precreated) component. If a pre-existing component is found, then it is used; otherwise, JSF will automatically create a brand new one, and will pass it as an argument to the setter method that corresponds to that `binding` attribute. In addition, JSF adds a reference of the component in the view state. Furthermore, a postback request (a form submit) will tell JSF to restore the view, which will restore the components and bindings based on view state.

Now that you know what happens with the `binding` attribute, let's enumerate some important aspects of using it:

- After each request (initial or postback), JSF creates an instance of the component indicated by the `binding` attribute.

- At the restore view (at the postback), after the component instance is created, JSF populates it from the view state, based on the stored reference.

- When you bind a component to a bean property (of type `UIComponent`), you actually bind the whole component. This kind of binding is a very rare use case, and it may be useful when you want to work/expose a component's methods that are not available in the view or you need to alter the component's children in a programmatic fashion. Moreover, you can alter the component's attributes and instantiate the component rather than letting the page author do so.

- Since JSF instantiates the component at each request, the bean must be in the request scope; otherwise, the component may be shared between different views. The view scope may also be a solution.

- The `binding` attribute is also used to bind the component to the current view, without the need of a bean. This is useful to gain access to the state of a component from another component.

- Binding a component without a bean property will put the component in the EL scope. This happens when the component tree is built; therefore, EL is perfectly capable to reveal the bound component at the rendering stage, which takes place after the component tree was built.

For example, a `<h:dataTable>` tag has three useful properties: `first`, `rows`, and `rowCount`. If you bind a `<h:dataTable>` tag to the current view, then outside of this component, you can access these properties as shown in the following line of code:

```
<h:dataTable value="#{playersBean.dataArrayList}"
  binding="#{table}" var="t">
```

For example, you can set the `rows` property as follows:

```
#{table.rows = 3;''}
```

Also, display the `rowCount` and `first` properties as follows:

```
<h:outputText value="#{table.rowCount}"/>
<h:outputText value="#{table.first}"/>
```

The complete application is named `ch2_32`.

We can accomplish the same thing from a bean. First, we bind the `<h:dataTable>` tag to a bean property of type `HtmlDataTable` as follows:

```
<h:dataTable value="#{playersBean.dataArrayList}"
  binding="#{playersBean.table}" var="t">
```

Now, in `PlayersBean`, we add the following code:

```
private HtmlDataTable table;
...
//getter and setter
...
public void tableAction() {
  logger.log(Level.INFO, "First:{0}", table.getFirst());
  logger.log(Level.INFO, "Row count: {0}", table.getRowCount());
  table.setRows(3);
}
```

The complete application is named `ch2_31`.

# Managed bean communication

Until now, we have focused especially on the communication between Facelets and managed beans. In this section, we will cover another important aspect regarding JSF communication—managed beans communication. We will discuss the following topics:

- Injecting a managed bean into another bean
- Communication between managed beans using the application/session map
- Accessing other managed beans programmatically

# Injecting a managed bean into another bean

A managed bean can be injected into another managed bean using @ManagedProperty. For example, let's suppose that you have a managed bean in the session scope that stores a player name and surname, as shown in the following code:

```
@Named
@SessionScoped
public class PlayersBean implements Serializable{

  private String playerName;
  private String playerSurname;

  public PlayersBean() {
    playerName = "Rafael";
    playerSurname = "Nadal";
  }

//getters and setters
}
```

Now, let's suppose that you want to have access to this bean's properties from another view scoped bean, named ProfileBean. For this, you can use @ManagedProperty as shown in the following code:

```
@ManagedBean //cannot be @Named
@ViewScoped
public class ProfileBean implements Serializable{

  private final static Logger logger =
    Logger.getLogger(PlayersBean.class.getName());
  @ManagedProperty("#{playersBean}")
  private PlayersBean playersBean;
  private String greetings;

  public ProfileBean() {
  }

  public void setPlayersBean(PlayersBean playersBean) {
    this.playersBean = playersBean;
  }

  @PostConstruct
  public void init(){
```

```
    greetings = "Hello, " + playersBean.getPlayerName()
    + " " +playersBean.getPlayerSurname() + " !";
}

public void greetingsAction(){
  logger.info(greetings);
}

}
```

A Facelet that calls the `greetingsAction` method will draw something like the following line in the log:

```
INFO:   Hello, Rafael Nadal !
```

 The presence of the `@PostConstruct` method is optional, but it is good to know that this is the earliest place where an injected dependency is available.

This example is wrapped into the application named `ch2_22`.

If you want to use CDI beans, then you can accomplish the same thing as shown in the following code:

```
@Named
@ViewScoped
public class ProfileBean implements Serializable{

  @Inject
  private PlayersBean playersBean;
  private String greetings;
  ...
```

This example is wrapped into the application named `ch2_30`.

# Communication between managed beans using the application/session map

Communication between managed beans can be ensured through an application map or a session map, depending on what kind of communication is needed, during multiple browser sessions or during one browser session.

The advantage of using the application/session map is in the fact that multiple beans can communicate with each other independent of their scopes. First, you need to define a helper class that provides two static methods, one for adding a value into the application map and one for deleting a value from the application map, as shown in the following code:

```
public class ApplicationMapHelper {

    public static Object getValueFromApplicationMap(String key) {
        return FacesContext.getCurrentInstance().getExternalContext().
          getApplicationMap().get(key);
    }

    public static void setValueInApplicationMap(String key,
      Object value) {
        FacesContext.getCurrentInstance().getExternalContext().
          getApplicationMap().put(key, value);
    }
}
```

Now, you can improvise a simple scenario: in one managed bean (request scoped), put some values into the application map, and in another managed bean (session scoped), get those values. So, the first bean code is as follows:

```
@Named
@RequestScoped
public class PlayersBeanSet {

    public void playerSetAction() {
        ApplicationMapHelper.setValueInApplicationMap
          ("PlayersBeanSet.name", "Rafael");
        ApplicationMapHelper.setValueInApplicationMap
          ("PlayersBeanSet.surname", "Nadal");
    }
}
```

The managed beans that extract these values from the application map are given out as follows:

```
@Named
@SessionScoped
public class PlayersBeanGet implements Serializable{

    private final static Logger logger =
      Logger.getLogger(PlayersBeanGet.class.getName());

    public void playerGetAction() {
```

```
String name = String.valueOf(ApplicationMapHelper.
  getValueFromApplicationMap("PlayersBeanSet.name"));
String surname = String.valueOf(ApplicationMapHelper.
  getValueFromApplicationMap("PlayersBeanSet.surname"));

logger.log(Level.INFO, "Name: {0} Surname: {1}",
  new Object[]{name, surname});
  }
}
```

This example is wrapped into the application named `ch2_24`.

# Accessing other managed beans programmatically

Sometimes, you may need to access one managed bean from an event listener class or another managed bean. Suppose that we have a managed bean on session scope, named `PlayersBean`, and one on request scope, named `ProfileBean`, and you want to programmatically access `PlayersBean` inside `ProfileBean`. Supposing that `PlayersBean` has been created, you can accomplish this task in the following ways:

- Use the `evaluateExpressionGet` method inside `ProfileBean` as follows:

```
FacesContext context = FacesContext.getCurrentInstance();
PlayersBean playersBean = (PlayersBean)
  context.getApplication().evaluateExpressionGet(context,
  "#{playersBean}", PlayersBean.class);

if (playersBean != null) {
  //call the PlayersBean method
} else {
  logger.info("SESSION BEAN NOT FOUND!");
}
```

- Use the `createValueExpression` method inside `ProfileBean` as follows:

```
FacesContext context = FacesContext.getCurrentInstance();
ELContext elcontext = context.getELContext();

PlayersBean playersBean = (PlayersBean)
  context.getApplication().getExpressionFactory().
  createValueExpression(elcontext, "#{playersBean}",
  PlayersBean.class).getValue(elcontext);

if (playersBean != null) {
  //call the PlayersBean method
```

```
} else {
  logger.info("SESSION BEAN NOT FOUND!");
}
```

In order to make things simpler, when you need to programmatically create a value expression, you can use a simple helper method and pass only the expression and class, as follows:

```
private ValueExpression createValueExpression(String exp,
  Class<?> cls) {
  FacesContext facesContext =
    FacesContext.getCurrentInstance();
  ELContext elContext = facesContext.getELContext();
  return facesContext.getApplication().
    getExpressionFactory().createValueExpression(elContext,
    exp, cls);
}
```

- Use ELResolver inside ProfileBean as follows:

```
FacesContext context = FacesContext.getCurrentInstance();
ELContext elcontext = context.getELContext();

PlayersBean playersBean = (PlayersBean)
  elcontext.getELResolver().getValue(elcontext, null,
  "playersBean");

if (playersBean != null) {
  //call the PlayersBean method
} else {
  logger.info("SESSION BEAN NOT FOUND!");
}
```

> The evaluateExpressionGet method is the most common one.

This example is wrapped into the application named ch2_25.

# Summary

Communication in JSF is one of the most important aspects, since the entire application's flow spins around the capability of processing and sharing data between JSF components. As you have seen, there are many ways to pass/get parameters and to access managed beans from other managed beans, but choosing the right ones for obtaining a robust, harmonious, balanced application depends on experience. This chapter covers a wide range of solutions for building communication pipes between JSF components, but, as any developer knows, there is always a case that requires a new approach!

See you in the next chapter, where we will talk about JSF scopes.

# 3
# JSF Scopes – Lifespan and Use in Managed Beans Communication

If programming is an art, then working correctly with scopes is a part of it!

This affirmation is generally true, not just in JSF. Should I use the session scope now, or the request scope? Do I have too many session beans? Can I inject this scope into that scope? Is this session object too big? How many times have you asked yourself these kinds of questions? I know ... many times! Maybe in this chapter you will find answers to some of these questions and you will fortify your knowledge about working with JSF scopes.

We have a lot to accomplish; therefore, let's have a short overview of what you will see in this chapter:

- JSF scopes versus CDI scopes
- Request scope, session scope, view scope, application scope, conversation scope, flow scope, none scope, dependent scope, and custom scope
- Beans injection

## JSF scopes versus CDI scopes

Even a JSF beginner might have heard about JSF managed beans (regular JavaBeans classes managed by JSF) and CDI beans (regular JavaBeans classes managed by CDI), and knows that JSF supports JSF scopes and CDI scopes. Starting with Java EE 6, CDI is recognized as the managed bean framework, besides EJBs. This causes confusion among programmers, because EJBs, CDIs, and JSF managed beans raise a critical question: which one to use and when?

Focusing on JSF, the unanimous answer is that CDI beans are more powerful than JSF beans. But, when you know right from the start that CDI will not be a part of your application or you are running the application inside a servlet container (which does not have CDI support by default, like Apache Tomcat), then JSF beans is the right choice. In other words, when you need a simple way to define beans and a neat mechanism for a dependency injection, then JSF bean will do the job, but when you need heavy artillery, such as events, type safe injection, automatic injection, producer methods, and interceptors, then CDI will represent the complete solution.

Moreover, NetBeans IDE 8.0 warns us that the JSF bean's annotations will be deprecated in the next JSF version, while the CDI beans are recommended instead (as shown in the following screenshot). This warning and the new JSF 2.2 flow scope, introduced as a dependency on CDI, are powerful signals that JSF and CDI become closer and closer:

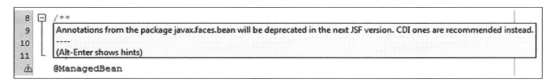

 CDI beans are much powerful than JSF beans; therefore, use CDI beans whenever possible.

So, strong arguments indicate CDI is often the right choice, but there are still instances where it is effective to use JSF beans, as you will soon discover.

JSF bean's main annotations (such as `@ManagedBean` and scopes annotations) are defined in the package `javax.faces.bean`, while CDI's main annotations are defined in the `javax.inject` (such as, `@Named`) and `javax.enterprise.context` (such as, scopes) packages.

A JSF managed bean is annotated with `@ManagedBean`, which allows us to inject it in to another bean (not CDI beans!) and to access the bean properties and methods from JSF pages using EL expressions. A CDI bean is annotated with `@Named`, which provides an EL name to be used in view technologies, such as JSP or Facelets.

Typically, a JSF bean is declared as shown in the following code:

```
package package_name;

import javax.faces.bean.ManagedBean;
```

```
import javax.faces.bean.jsfScoped;

@ManagedBean
@jsfScoped
public class JSFBeanName {
...
}
```

The JSF bean, `@ManagedBean`, supports an optional parameter, `name`. The provided name can be used to reference the bean from JSF pages in the following manner:

```
@ManagedBean(name="custom name")
```

A CDI bean has the same shape, with different annotations, as shown in the following code:

```
package package_name;

import javax.inject.Named;
import javax.enterprise.context.cdiScoped;

@Named
@cdiScoped
public class CDIBeanName {
...
}
```

The CDI bean, `@Named`, supports an optional parameter, `value`. The provided name can be used to reference the bean from JSF pages in the following manner:

```
@Named(value="custom name")
```

Notice that CDI annotations cannot be mixed with JSF annotations in the same bean, only in the same application. For example, you cannot define a bean using @ManagedBean and a CDI scope (or any other combination between them), but you can have, in the same application, a managed bean (or more) and a CDI bean (or more).

In the following figure, you can see a short overview of JSF 2.2 scopes:

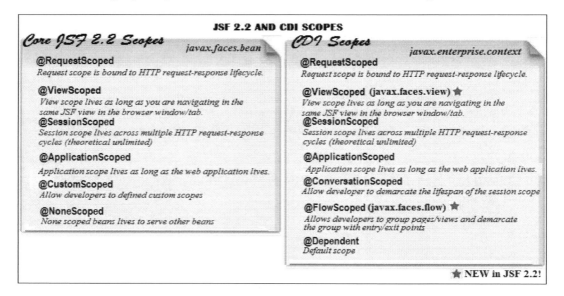

In the next section, you will see how each JSF/CDI scope works.

# The request scope

The **request scope** is bound to the HTTP request-response life cycle.

The request scope is very useful in any web application, and an object defined in the request scope usually has a short lifespan; beans live as long as the HTTP request-response lives. When the container accepts an HTTP request from the client, the specified object is attached to the request scope and it is released when the container has finished transmitting the response to that request. A new HTTP request always comes in a new request scope object. In short, a request scope represents a user's interaction with a web application in a single HTTP request. Commonly, a request scope is useful for simple GET requests that expose some data to the user without requiring to store the data.

 The request scope is present in JSF and CDI and functions in the same way. It can be used for nonrich AJAX and non-AJAX requests. For JSF managed beans (@ManagedBean), this is the default scope, when none is specified.

For example, let's suppose that we have a predefined list of tennis players, and we randomly extract them one-by-one from this list and store them in another list. The current generated player and the list of extracted players are managed bean's properties and their values are rendered in a JSF page.

 The request scope annotation is @RequestScoped and is defined in the javax.enterprise.context package for CDI, and in the javax.faces.bean package for JSF.

The code for the CDI bean can be written as follows:

```
@Named
@RequestScoped
public class PlayersBean {

    final String[] players_list = {"Nadal, Rafael (ESP)","Djokovic,
       Novak (SRB)", "Ferrer, David (ESP)", "Murray, Andy (GBR)",
       "Del Potro, Juan Martin (ARG)"};

    private ArrayList players = new ArrayList();
    private String player;

    //getters and setters

    public void newPlayer() {
       int nr = new Random().nextInt(4);
       player = players_list[nr];
       players.add(player);
    }
}
```

The relevant part of the JSF page is as follows:

```
<h:body>
   Just generated:
   <h:outputText value="#{playersBean.player}"/><br/>

   List of generated players:
   <h:dataTable var="t" value="#{playersBean.players}">
     <h:column>
        <h:outputText value="#{t}"/>
     </h:column>
   </h:dataTable>
   <h:form>
```

```
    <h:commandButton value="Get Players In Same View"
      actionListener="#{playersBean.newPlayer()}"/>
    <h:commandButton value="Get Players With Page Forward"
      actionListener="#{playersBean.newPlayer()}"
      action="index.xhtml"/>
    <h:commandButton value="Get Players With Page Redirect"
      actionListener="#{playersBean.newPlayer()}"
      action="index.xhtml?faces-redirect=true;"/>
  </h:form>
</h:body>
```

When you click on the button labeled **Get Players With Page Forward** or **Get Players In Same View**, you will see something as shown in the following screenshot:

Request Scope (CDI):
Just generated: Djokovic, Novak (SRB)
List of generated players:
Djokovic, Novak (SRB)

| Get Players In Same View | Get Players With Page Forward | Get Players With Page Redirect |

Since a request scope lives as long as the HTTP request-response lives and page forward implies a single HTTP request-response, you will see the player extracted at the current request and the list of extracted players, which will always only contain this player. The list is created for each request and filled with the current player, which makes the list useless.

> The request scope doesn't lose the object's state while forwarding, because the source page and the destination page (the forwarded page) are part of the same request-response cycle. This is not true in the case of redirect actions.

When you click on the button labeled **Get Players With Page Redirect**, you will see something as shown in the following screenshot:

Request Scope (CDI):
Just generated:
List of generated players:

| Get Players In Same View | Get Players With Page Forward | Get Players With Page Redirect |

The current extracted player and the list content is not available in this case, because a JSF redirect implies two requests, instead of one as in the forward case.

Programmatically, you can access the request map using the following code:

```
FacesContext context = FacesContext.getCurrentInstance();
Map<String, Object> requestMap =
  context.getExternalContext().getRequestMap();
```

Submitting a form defined in page 1 to page 2 via a bean, and then you have the following cases:

- If the same view or forward is used, then the data is available for display on page 2
- If redirect is used, then data will be lost and not available for display on page 2

The JSF version of the CDI beans is as follows:

```
import javax.faces.bean.ManagedBean;
import javax.faces.bean.RequestScoped;

@ManagedBean
@RequestScoped
public class PlayersBean {
   ...
}
```

And it works the same as the CDI bean!

> A method annotated with @PostConstruct will be called for each request, since each request requires a separate instance of the request scoped bean.

The case of the CDI bean is wrapped into the application named ch3_1_1, while the case of the JSF bean is wrapped into application named ch3_1_2.

# The session scope

The **session scope** lives across multiple HTTP request-response cycles (theoretical unlimited).

The request scope is very useful in any web application when you need a single interaction per HTTP request-response cycle. However, when you need objects visible for any HTTP request-response cycle that belongs to a user session, then you need a session scope; in this case, the bean lives as long as the HTTP session lives. The session scope allows you to create and bind objects to a session. It gets created upon the first HTTP request involving this bean in the session and gets destroyed when the HTTP session is invalidated.

> The session scope is present in JSF and CDI and it functions the same way in both. Commonly, it is used for AJAX and non-AJAX requests that process user-specific data (such as credentials, shopping carts, and so on).

Therefore, the first HTTP request initializes the session and stores the objects, while the subsequent requests have access to these objects for further tasks. A session invalidation occurs when the browser is closed, a timeout is fired, the logout is clicked, or a programmatic subroutine forces it. Normally, each time you need to preserve data across the whole session (multiple requests and pages), the session scope is the right choice.

For example, you can add the session scope to the previous applications of this chapter for storing the list of randomly extracted players across multiple requests.

> The session scope annotation is @SessionScoped and is defined in the javax.enterprise.context package for CDI, and in the javax.faces.bean package for JSF.

The CDI bean is modified as follows:

```
import java.io.Serializable;
import javax.enterprise.context.SessionScoped;
import javax.inject.Named;

@Named
@SessionScoped
public class PlayersBean implements Serializable{
    ...
}
```

Alternatively, the JSF version is as follows:

```
import java.io.Serializable;
import javax.faces.bean.ManagedBean;
import javax.faces.bean.SessionScoped;

@ManagedBean
@SessionScoped
public class PlayersBean implements Serializable{
    ...
}
```

 Notice that the session scope bean might get passivated by the container and should be capable of passivity, which means that the session beans should be serializable (implement the `java.io.Serializable` interface); refer to the capability to persist/restore session data to/from the hard disk.

The session objects lives across forward and redirect mechanisms. In the following screenshot, you can see the current extracted player and the list of extracted players after several requests belonging to the same session:

Session Scope (CDI):
Just generated: Nadal, Rafael (ESP)
List of generated players:
  Murray, Andy (GBR)
  Djokovic, Novak (SRB)
  Ferrer, David (ESP)
  Djokovic, Novak (SRB)
  Nadal, Rafael (ESP)

| Get Players In Same View | Get Players With Page Forward | Get Players With Page Redirect |

Now the list is not useless anymore! You can add methods for manipulating its content, such as order or delete.

Programmatically, you can access the session map as follows:

```
FacesContext context = FacesContext.getCurrentInstance();
Map<String, Object> sessionMap =
    context.getExternalContext().getSessionMap();
```

Also, you can invalidate a session as follows:

```
FacesContext.getCurrentInstance().
    getExternalContext().invalidateSession();
```

Obviously, data submitted through forms across the session scope will be available in subsequent requests.

> A method annotated with `@PostConstruct` will be called only once during a session, when the session bean is instantiated. Subsequent requests will use this instance, so it can be a good place to add initialization stuff.

The case of the CDI bean is wrapped into the application named `ch3_2_1`, while the case of the JSF bean is wrapped into the application named `ch3_2_2`.

# The view scope

The **view scope** lives as long as you are navigating in the same JSF view in the browser window/tab.

The view scope is useful when you need to preserve data over multiple requests without leaving the current JSF view by clicking on a link, returning a different action outcome, or any other interaction that dumps the current view. It gets created upon an HTTP request and gets destroyed when you postback to a different view; as long as you postback to the same view, the view scope is alive.

> Notice that the view scope bean might get passivated by the container and should be capable of passivity by implementing the `java.io.Serializable` interface.

Since the view scope is particularly useful when you are editing some objects while staying in the same view, it can be the perfect choice for rich AJAX requests. Moreover, since the view scope is bounded to the current view, it does not reflect the stored information in another window or tab of a browser; this is an issue specific to the session scope!

> In order to keep the view active, the bean methods (actions/listeners) must return `null` or `void`.

The view scope is not available in CDI, but JSF 2.2 has introduced it through the new annotation, @ViewScoped. This is defined in the javax.faces.view.ViewScoped package and it is compatible with CDI. Do not confuse this @ViewScoped with the one defined in the javax.faces.bean package, which is JSF compatible!

 The view scope annotation is @ViewScoped and is defined in the javax.faces.view package for CDI, and in the javax.faces.bean package for JSF.

You can see the view scope in action by modifying the PlayersBean scope as follows:

```
import java.io.Serializable;
import javax.faces.view.ViewScoped;
import javax.inject.Named;

@Named
@ViewScoped
public class PlayersBean implements Serializable{
    ...
}
```

Firing multiple HTTP requests by clicking on the button labeled **Get Players In Same View** will reveal something like the following screenshot. Notice the action method (newPlayer) returns void and the button doesn't contain the action attribute, which means that you are in the same JSF view during the execution of these requests.

View Scope (CDI):
Just generated: Nadal, Rafael (ESP)
List of generated players:
Murray, Andy (GBR)
Nadal, Rafael (ESP)
Nadal, Rafael (ESP)

| Get Players In Same View | Get Players With Page Forward | Get Players With Page Redirect |

The other two buttons contain the action attribute and indicate an explicit navigation, which means that the current view is changed at every request and the data is lost.

You can easily adapt PlayersBean (and any other bean) to use the JSF version of @ViewScoped as follows:

```
import java.io.Serializable;
import javax.faces.bean.ManagedBean;
```

```
import javax.faces.bean.ViewScoped;

@ManagedBean
@ViewScoped
public class PlayersBean implements Serializable{
   ...
}
```

Data submitted through forms across the view scope will be available in subsequent requests as long as you are in the same view.

A method annotated with @PostConstruct will be called only when the view scoped bean is instantiated. Subsequent requests, from this view, will use this instance. As long as you are in the same view, this method will not be called again; therefore, it can be a good place to add initialization stuff specific to the current view.

The case of the CDI bean is wrapped into the application named ch3_6_1, while the case of the JSF bean is wrapped into the application named ch3_6_2.

Starting with JSF 2.2, we can use the UIViewRoot.restoreViewSc opeState(FacesContext context, Object state) method for restoring the view scope when it is not available. This will be exemplified in *Chapter 12, Facelets Templating*.

# The application scope

The **application scope** lives as long as the web application lives.

An application scope extends the session scope with the shared state across all users' interactions with a web application; this scope lives as long as the web application lives. Since the beans in the application scope lives until the application shuts down (or they are programmatically removed), we can say that this scope lives most. More precisely, objects settled on the application scope can be accessed from any page that is part of the application (for example, JSF, JSP, and XHTML).

The application scope should be used only for data that is safe to be shared. Since an application scoped bean is shared by all users, you need to be sure that the bean has an immutable state or you need to synchronize access.

Usually, application scope objects are used as counters, but they can be used for many other tasks, such as initializations and navigations. For example, the application scope can be used to count how many users are online or to share that information with all users. Practically, it can be used to share data among all sessions, such as constants, common settings, and tracking variables.

 The application scope annotation is @ApplicationScoped and is defined in the javax.enterprise.context package for CDI, and in the javax.faces.bean package for JSF.

If you put the PlayersBean managed bean in the application scope, then the list of randomly extracted players will be available across all sessions. You can do it as shown in the following code:

```
import javax.enterprise.context.ApplicationScoped;
import javax.inject.Named;

@Named
@ApplicationScoped
public class PlayersBean {
    ...
}
```

The JSF version is shown in the following code:

```
import javax.faces.bean.ApplicationScoped;
import javax.faces.bean.ManagedBean;

@ManagedBean
@ApplicationScoped
public class PlayersBean {
    ...
}
```

For testing the application scope, you need to open multiple browsers or use multiple machines.

Be careful when you provide data from an application scoped bean to multiple sessions beans (for example, using injection), since the data shared by all sessions can be modified by each session separately. This can lead to inconsistent data across multiple users; therefore, be sure that the exposed application data isn't modified in sessions.

A method annotated with `@PostConstruct` will be called only when the application scoped bean is instantiated. Subsequent requests will use this instance. Usually, this happens when the application starts; therefore, place inside this method the initialization tasks specific to the application in the context of this bean.

Programmatically, you can access the application map using the following code:

```
FacesContext context = FacesContext.getCurrentInstance();
Map<String, Object> applicationMap =
    context.getExternalContext().getApplicationMap();
```

The case of the CDI bean is wrapped into the application named `ch3_3_1`, while the case of the JSF bean is wrapped into the application named `ch3_3_2`.

# The conversation scope

The **conversation scope** allows developers to demarcate the lifespan of the session scope.

The conversation scope is committed to the user's interaction with JSF applications and represents a unit of work from the point of view of the user; a bean in this scope is able to follow a conversation with a user. We may charge the conversation scope as a developer-controlled session scope across multiple invocations of the JSF life cycle; while session scoped lives across unlimited requests, the conversation scopes lives only across a limited number of requests.

The conversation scope bean might get passivated by the container and should be capable of passivity by implementing the `java.io.Serializable` interface.

The developer can explicitly set the conversation scope boundaries and can start, stop, or propagate the conversation scope based on the business logic flow. All long-running conversations are scoped to a particular HTTP servlet session and may not cross session boundaries. In addition, conversation scope keeps the state associated with a particular Web browser window/tab in a JSF application.

The conversation scope annotation is `@ConversationScoped` and is defined in the `javax.enterprise.context` package for CDI. This scope is not available in JSF!

Dealing with the conversation scope is slightly different from the rest of the scopes. First, you mark the bean with `@ConversationScope`, represented by the `javax.enterprise.context.ConversationScoped` class. Second, CDI provides a built-in bean (`javax.enterprise.context.Conversation`) for controlling the life cycle of conversations in a JSF application—its main responsibility is to manage the conversation context. This bean may be obtained by injection, as shown in the following code:

```
private @Inject Conversation conversation;
```

By default, the `Conversation` object is in transient state and it should be transformed into a long-running conversation by calling the `begin` method. You also need to prepare for the destruction of the conversation by calling the `end` method.

 If we try to call the `begin` method when the conversation is active, or the `end` method when the conversation is inactive, `IllegalStateException` will be thrown. We can avoid this by testing the transitivity state of the `Conversation` objects using the method named `isTransient`, which returns a Boolean value.

Now, add the `begin`, `end`, and `isTransient` methods together to the following conversations:

- For start conversation, the code is as follows:

```
if (conversation.isTransient()) {
  conversation.begin();
}
```

- For stop conversation, the code is as follows:

```
if (!conversation.isTransient()) {
  conversation.end();
}
```

For example, you can add the conversation scope in `PlayersBean` as follows:

```java
@Named
@ConversationScoped
public class PlayersBean implements Serializable {

    private @Inject
    Conversation conversation;

    final String[] players_list = {"Nadal, Rafael (ESP)","Djokovic,
        Novak (SRB)", "Ferrer, David (ESP)", "Murray, Andy (GBR)",
        "Del Potro, Juan Martin (ARG)"};
    private ArrayList players = new ArrayList();
    private String player;

    public PlayersBean() {
    }

    //getters and setters

    public void newPlayer() {
        int nr = new Random().nextInt(4);
        player = players_list[nr];
        players.add(player);
    }

    public void startPlayerRnd() {
        if (conversation.isTransient()) {
            conversation.begin();
        }
    }

    public void stopPlayerRnd() {
        if (!conversation.isTransient()) {
            conversation.end();
        }
    }
}
```

Besides injecting the built-in CDI bean, notice that you have defined a method (`startPlayerRnd`) for demarcating the conversation start point and another method (`stopPlayerRnd`) for demarcating the conversation stop point. In this example, both the methods are exposed to the user through two buttons, but you can control the conversation programmatically by calling them conditionally.

Running the example inside a conversation will reveal something as shown in the following screenshot:

Conversation scope (CDI):
Just generated: Ferrer, David (ESP)
List of generated numbers:
Nadal, Rafael (ESP)
Nadal, Rafael (ESP)
Ferrer, David (ESP)
Ferrer, David (ESP)

**Start Conversation** | Get Players In Same View | Get Players With Page Forward | Get Players With Page Redirect | **Stop Conversation**

The list of randomly extracted players will be empty or will contain only the current extracted player until the button labeled **Start Conversation** is clicked. At that moment the list will be stored in session, until the button labeled **Stop Conversation** is clicked.

> During the conversation, the user may execute AJAX/non-AJAX requests against the bean or perform navigations to other pages that still reference this same managed bean. The bean will keep its state across user interactions using a **conversation identifier** generated by the container, and this is why the conversation scope can be the right choice when you need to implement wizards. But it might be a good idea to take into account the new JSF 2.2 flow scope as well, which solves several gaps of the conversation scope. See the upcoming section!

In this example, the conversation context automatically propagates with any JSF faces request or redirection (this facilitates the implementation of the common POST-then-redirect pattern), but it does not automatically propagate with non-faces requests, such as links. In this case, you need to include the unique identifier of the conversation as a request parameter. The CDI specification reserves the request parameter `cid` for this use. The following code will propagate the conversation context over a link:

```
<h:link outcome="/link.xhtml" value="Conversation Propagation">
  <f:param name="cid" value="#{conversation.id}"/>
</h:link>
```

A method annotated with @PostConstruct will be called for each request as long as the bean is not involved in a conversation. When the conversation begins, the method is called for that instance and subsequent requests will use this instance until the conversation ends. Therefore, be careful how you manage this method content.

This example is wrapped into the application named ch3_4 and is available in the code bundle of this chapter.

# The flow scope

The **flow scope** allows developers to group pages/views and demarcate the group with entry/exit points.

Between the request scope and the session scope, we have the CDI flow scope. This scope exists for a while in Spring Web Flow or ADF flow, and now is available in JSF 2.2 as well. Basically, the flow scope allows us to demarcate a set of related pages/views (usually, logic related) with an entry point (known as **start node**) and an exit point (known as **return node**).

The flow scope is a good choice for applications that contain wizards, such as multiscreen subscriptions/registrations, bookings, and shopping carts. Generally speaking, any chunk of an application that has a logical start point and an end point can be encapsulated into the flow scope.

In the same application, we can define multiple flows, which can be seen as modules that are reusable and capable to communicate. They can be called sequentially, can be encapsulated as Matrioska dolls or can create any custom design. Moreover, it is very easy to move, delete, or add a flow into such an application just by plugging in/out the entry and exit point.

To understand the benefits of using the flow scope, you have to identify some disadvantages of the applications that don't use it. They are listed as follows:

- Each application is a big flow, but usually pages do not follow any intuitive logical design. Apparently, a disordered order governs even when pages are logically related, such as pages of a wizard or of a shopping cart.

 The flow scope allows us to define logical units of work.

- Reusing pages can be a difficult task to accomplish, since pages are so tied up to UI components and user interaction.

 The flow scope provides reusability.

- CDI provides conversation scope capable of stretching over several pages, but the flow scope fits better for JSF.

- As the conversation scope, the flow scope covers a set of pages/views, but it has several main advantages, such as it is much more flexible, doesn't need that clumsy begin/end operation, flow scoped beans are created and destroyed automatically when the user enters or exists into/from a flow, provides easy-to-use support for inbound/outbound parameters, and prehandlers and posthandlers. A normal flow cannot be opened in multiple windows/tabs because information travels between pages with the session scope.

 Data in a flow is scoped to that flow alone; therefore, flows can be opened in multiple windows/tabs.

- The **nodes** define the entry and exit points of a flow and there are five types of nodes, which are listed as follows:
    - **View**: This represents any JSF page in the application that participates in the flow. It is known as a **view node** of the flow.
    - **The method call**: This indicates an invocation of a method using EL. The called method may return an outcome that indicates which node should be navigated next.

- ○ **Switch**: The `switch` case statements are a substitute for long `if` statements. The cases are represented by EL expressions and are evaluated to Boolean values. Each case is accompanied by an outcome that will be used when the condition is evaluated to `true`. There is also a default outcome that will be used when all cases are evaluated to `false`.

- ○ **The flow call**: This is used to call another flow in the current flow — these are transition points between flows. The called flow (known as inner or nested flow) is nested in the flow that calls it (known as calling flow or outer flow). When the nested flow finishes its tasks, it will return a view node from the calling flow, which means that the calling flow will have control only after the nested flow's lifespan comes to an end.

- ○ **The flow return**: This can be used for returning an outcome to the calling flow.

Flows can pass parameters from one to the other. Parameters sent by a flow to another flow are known as **outbound parameters**, while parameters received by a flow from another flow are known as **inbound parameters**.

Well, at this point, you should have enough information about the flow scope to develop some examples. But, before doing this, you need to be aware of some tags, annotations, and conventions.

The flow definition is based on a set of conventions over configuration. A flow has a name, a folder in the web root of the application reflecting the flow name, and a view representing the start node that also reflects the flow name. This folder groups the pages/views that belong to the same flow.

In order to use a flow, you need to accomplish some configuration tasks. These can be done through a configuration file or programmatically. If you choose the first approach, then the configuration file can be limited to one flow, which means that it is stored in the flow folder and is named in the format *flowname*-`flow.xml`, or you can use the `faces-config.xml` file for having all flows in a single place.

Since our first example uses the configuration file, we need to use tags. The main tags used for configuring a flow are as follows:

- • `< flow-definition>`: This tag contains an `id` attribute that uniquely identifies the flow. The value of this ID is the flow name used to reference the flow from JSF pages or beans.

- `<view>`: It is nested in the `<flow-definition>` tag and indicates the JSF pages that represent the flow nodes; it associates an explicit ID to each page (Facelet) path (further, you can refer to each page by its ID). The page path is mapped in a `<vdl-document>` tag, nested in the `<view>` tag. The presence of this tag is optional, but as a convention, at least the `<view>` tag indicating the start node (start page) is present, especially if you want to set another start node besides the default one, which is represented by the page in the flow with the same name (ID) as the flow. Further, you can use the optional `<start-node>`*ID*`</start-node>` tag and indicate the ID of the `<view>` tag that maps the custom starting page. As an alternative, the start node of the flow can be indicated by setting the value of the `id` attribute of a `<view>` tag as the flow ID, and the content of the encapsulated `<vdl-document>` tag as the path of the custom starting page. When you refer to the flow ID, JSF will go to that page and automatically put you in the flow.

- `<flow-return>`: It is nested in the `<flow-definition>` tag and returns an outcome to the calling flow. You can refer to it through the value of the `id` attribute. There are at least three ways of getting out of a flow: using `<flow-return>`, using `<flow-call>` (presented later), or by abandoning the flow.

We just said that a flow is identified by an ID (by a name). But, when the same flow name is defined in multiple documents (like in big projects that use multiple packaged flows from different vendors), there is one more ID needed. This ID is known as the **document ID**. Thus, when you need to identify a flow whose name appears in different documents, we need the flow ID and the defining document ID. Most of the time the document ID is omitted; therefore, it is not demonstrated in this section. In this section, you will see just a few hints about it.

In order to define the simplest flow, you need to be aware of the following diagram:

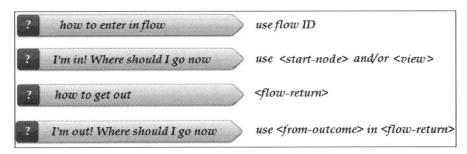

# The simple flow

With these three tags, `<start-node>` and/or `<view>`, `<flow-return>`, and `<from-outcome>`, you can configure a simple flow, like a peddling registration form. Let's suppose that a tennis player registers online to a tournament through a flow made up of two JSF pages (the flow name will be `registration`): a page containing a form used for collecting data and a confirmation page. Moreover, there will be two pages outside the flow, one for entering into the flow (like the first page of the website), and one that is called after confirmation.

In the following diagram, you can see an image of our flow:

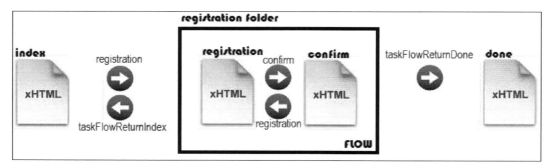

Let's have a look at the code for the first page that is outside the flow and outside the registration folder (`index.xhtml`) as follows:

```
<h:body>
  <h1><b>In flow ?
  #{null != facesContext.application.flowHandler.currentFlow}
  </b></h1><br/><br/>
  Flow Id: #{facesContext.application.flowHandler.currentFlow.id}
  REGISTER NEW PLAYER
  <h:form>
    <h:commandButton value="Start Registration"
      action="registration" immediate="true"/>
  </h:form>
</h:body>
```

Two important things can be observed here. First, the following lines:

```
#{null != facesContext.application.flowHandler.currentFlow}
#{facesContext.application.flowHandler.currentFlow.id}
```

The first line returns a Boolean value indicating whether the current page is or is not in a flow. Obviously, the `index.xhtml` page is not in a flow; therefore, `false` will be returned. You can use it for tests. The second line displays the ID of the current flow.

Further, you need to take a look at the value of the attribute `action` of the `<h:commandButton>` tag. This value is the name (ID) of our flow; after the window context is enabled, JSF will search the indicated flow and navigate to the start node of the flow. By default, the window context is disabled.

Therefore, when the button labeled **Start Registration** is clicked, the application steps in the registration flow and loads the start node page represented by the `registration.xhtml` page. The code for this page is as follows:

```
<h:body>
    <h1><b>First page in the 'registration' flow</b></h1>
    <h1><b>In flow ?
    #{null != facesContext.application.flowHandler.currentFlow}
    </b></h1><br/><br/>

    You are registered as:#{flowScope.value}
    <h:form prependId="false">
      Name &amp; Surname:
      <h:inputText id="nameSurnameId" value="#{flowScope.value}" />
      <h:commandButton value="Register To Tournament"
        action="confirm"/>
      <h:commandButton value="Back(exit flow)"
        action="taskFlowReturnIndex"/>
    </h:form>
</h:body>
```

Since we are in the flow, `currentFlow` will return `true`.

It is more important to focus on the implicit object, `flowScope`; however, as you know from *Chapter 1, Dynamic Access to JSF Application Data through Expression Language (EL 3.0)*, the `flowScope` implicit object (which indicates the current flow) is used for sharing data through the entire flow and maps to `facesContext.getApplication().getFlowHandler().getCurrentFlowScope()`. For example, the value of the `<h:inputText>` tag can be put into the `flowScope` object and can be read from the flow scope in the next page, as follows:

```
#{flowScope.value}
```

The button labeled **Register To Tournament** navigates to the second page in the flow, `confirm.xhtml`; this is a usual navigation case, there is nothing to say here. But the other button navigates outside the flow (to `index.xhtml`) by indicating the ID of a flow return. In the configuration file, this flow return is as shown in the following code:

```
<flow-return id="taskFlowReturnIndex">
  <from-outcome>/index</from-outcome>
</flow-return>
```

The code of the `confirm.xhtml` page is as follows:

```
<h:body>
  <h1><b>Second page in the 'registration' flow</b></h1>
  <h1><b>In flow ?
  #{null != facesContext.application.flowHandler.currentFlow}
  </b></h1><br/><br/>
  You are registered as:#{flowScope.value}
  <h:form prependId="false">
    <h:commandButton value="Back (still in flow)"
      action="registration"/>
    <h:commandButton value="Next (exit flow)"
      action="taskFlowReturnDone"/>
  </h:form>
</h:body>
```

This page displays the data that was entered and stored on the flow scope along with both the buttons. The first button navigates back to the `registration.xhtml` page, while the other one navigates to the `done.xhtml` page, which is outside the flow. The flow return is identified by the ID, as shown in the following code:

```
<flow-return id="taskFlowReturnDone">
  <from-outcome>done</from-outcome>
</flow-return>
```

The `done.xhtml` page just checks to see if the page is in flow and displays a simple message, as shown in the following code:

```
<h:body>
  <h1><b>In flow ?
  #{null != facesContext.application.flowHandler.currentFlow}
  </b></h1><br/><br/>
  REGISTER NEW PLAYER ENDED
</h:body>
```

The final step is to define the flow in a configuration file. Since you have a single flow, you can create a file `registration-flow.xml` in the `registration` folder. The following is the code of the `registration-flow.xml` file:

```
<faces-config version="2.2"
  xmlns="http://xmlns.jcp.org/xml/ns/javaee"
  xmlns:xsi="http://www.w3.org/2001/XMLSchema-instance"
```

```
xsi:schemaLocation="http://xmlns.jcp.org/xml/ns/javaee
http://xmlns.jcp.org/xml/ns/javaee/web-facesconfig_2_2.xsd">

<flow-definition id="registration">
  <view id="registration">
    <vdl-document>/registration/registration.xhtml</vdl-
      document>
  </view>
  <flow-return id="taskFlowReturnIndex">
    <from-outcome>/index</from-outcome>
  </flow-return>
  <flow-return id="taskFlowReturnDone">
    <from-outcome>/done</from-outcome>
  </flow-return>
</flow-definition>
</faces-config>
```

You can also place the following code inside the `faces-config.xml` file in the `<faces-flow-definition>` tag:

```
<faces-flow-definition>
  <flow-definition id="registration">
  ...
</faces-flow-definition>
```

This example is wrapped into the application named `ch3_7_1` that is available in the code bundle of this chapter.

# Flows with beans

Beside pages, a flow can contain beans. A bean defined in a flow is annotated with `@FlowScoped`; this is a CDI annotation that enables automatic activation (when the scope is entered) and passivation (when the scope is exited). The `@FlowScoped` bean requires an attribute named `value` that contains the flow ID. The data stored in such a bean is available in all pages that belong to that flow.

 The flow scope bean might get passivated by the container and should be capable of passivity by implementing the `java.io.Serializable` interface.

Adding a bean in the registration flow can modify the initial diagram, as shown in the following diagram:

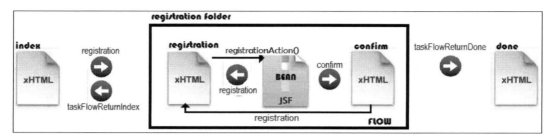

As you can see, the bean will store the data collected from the registration form in the flow scope (in the previous example, this data was passed using the `flowScope` implicit object). The button labeled **Register To Tournament** will call the `registrationAction` bean method, which will decide if the data is valid and return the flow back to the `registration.xhtml` page or next to the `confirm.xhtml` page.

The `registration.xhtml` page's code is modified as follows:

```
<h:body>
  <h1><b>First page in the 'registration' flow</b></h1>
  <h1><b>In flow ?
  #{null != facesContext.application.flowHandler.currentFlow}
  </b></h1><br/><br/>
  Your registration last credentials:
  #{registrationBean.playerName} #{registrationBean.playerSurname}
  <h:form prependId="false">
    Name: <h:inputText value="#{registrationBean.playerName}"/>
    Surname: <h:inputText
      value="#{registrationBean.playerSurname}"/>
    <h:commandButton value="Register To Tournament"
      action="#{registrationBean.registrationAction()}"/>
    <h:commandButton value="Back (exit flow)"
      action="taskFlowReturnIndex"/>
  </h:form>
</h:body>
```

The code of `RegistrationBean` is as follows:

```
@Named
@FlowScoped(value="registration")
public class RegistrationBean implements Serializable {

    private String playerName;
```

```
    private String playerSurname;

    ...
    //getters and setters
    ...

    public String getReturnValue() {
      return "/done";
    }

    public String registrationAction(){

      //simulate some registration conditions
      Random r= new Random();
      int nr = r.nextInt(10);

      if(nr < 5){
        playerName="";
        playerSurname="";
        FacesContext.getCurrentInstance().addMessage("password",
        new FacesMessage(FacesMessage.SEVERITY_ERROR,
        "Registration failed!",""));
        return "registration";
      } else {
        return "confirm";
      }
    }
}
```

The code is self explanatory, but what about the `getReturnValue` method? Well, this is just an example of how a flow scoped bean can indicate the outcome of a flow return. Instead of using the following code:

```
<flow-return id="taskFlowReturnDone">
  <from-outcome>/done</from-outcome>
</flow-return>
```

You can use the following code:

```
<flow-return id="taskFlowReturnDone">
  <from-outcome>#{registrationBean.returnValue}</from-outcome>
</flow-return>
```

This example is wrapped into the application named ch3_7_2 that is available in the code bundle of this chapter.

# Nested flows

Well, now let's complicate things by adding another flow under the existing one. Let's suppose that after the registration, the player has to indicate the day and the hour when he is available to play the first match. This can be accomplished in a new flow named `schedule`. The `registration` flow will call the `schedule` flow and will pass some parameters to it. The `schedule` flow will return in the `registration` flow, which will provide a simple button for navigation outside the `registration` flow.

 The nested flow returns only in the calling flow. You have to refer to a page of the calling flow in the `<flow-return>` tag of the nested flow, including the pages returned by the calling flow.

Passing parameters is a thing that requires more tags in the configuration tag. Therefore, you need to know the following tags:

- `<flow-call>`: This calls another flow in the current flow. This tag requires the `id` attribute. The value of this attribute will be used to refer to this flow call.

- `<flow-reference>`: This is nested in the `<flow-call>` tag and contains the ID of the flow that must be called.

- `<outbound-parameter>`: This is nested in the `<flow-call>` tag and defines parameters that must be passed to the called flow.

- `<inbound-parameter>`: This defines the parameters passed from another flow.

In order to see these tags at work, you need to take a look at the application flow. The diagram of the application will change as follows:

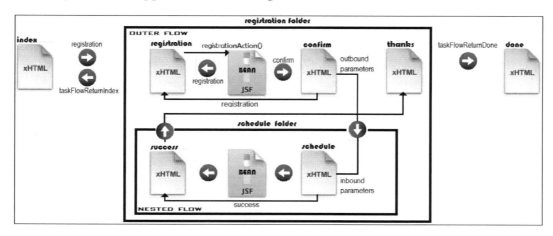

We resume our discussion from the `confirm.xhtml` page (defined in the `registration` flow). From this page, we want to navigate to the `schedule.xhtml` page, which is available in the `schedule` flow (the `schedule` folder). For this, we can add a new button, labeled **Schedule**, as shown in the following code:

```
<h:form prependId="false">
  <h:commandButton value="Back (still in flow)"
    action="registration"/>
  <h:commandButton id="Next" value="Schedule"
    action="callSchedule" />
  <h:commandButton value="Next (exit flow)"
    action="taskFlowReturnDone"/>
</h:form>
```

The button's `action` attribute value is the ID of the `<flow-call>` tag. When the button is clicked, JSF locates the corresponding `<flow-call>` tag and follows the flow with the ID indicated by the `<flow-id>` tag, as shown in the following code:

```
<flow-call id="callSchedule">
  <flow-reference>
    <flow-id>schedule</flow-id>
  </flow-reference>
...
</flow-call>
```

Moreover, we want to pass several parameters from the `registration` flow to the `schedule` flow: the player name and surname (stored in the flow scoped `RegistrationBean` bean) and a constant representing some registration code (it can also be generated based on certain rules). This can be accomplished by the `<outbound-parameter>` tag, as shown in the following code:

```
<flow-call id="callSchedule">
  <flow-reference>
    <flow-id>schedule</flow-id>
  </flow-reference>
  <outbound-parameter>
    <name>playernameparam</name>
    <value>#{registrationBean.playerName}</value>
  </outbound-parameter>
  <outbound-parameter>
    <name>playersurnameparam</name>
    <value>#{registrationBean.playerSurname}</value>
  </outbound-parameter>
  <outbound-parameter>
```

```
      <name>playerregistrationcode</name>
      <value>349CF0YO122</value>
    </outbound-parameter>
  </flow-call>
```

The `schedule.xhtml` page displays a hello message based on the received parameters and a form that allows to the player to enter the day and hour when he is available for playing the first match, as shown in the following code:

```
<h:body>
  <h1><b>First page in the 'schedule' flow</b></h1>
  <h1><b>In flow ?
  #{null != facesContext.application.flowHandler.currentFlow}
  </b></h1><br/><br/>
  Hello, #{flowScope.name} #{flowScope.surname}
    (#{scheduleBean.regcode})
  <h:form prependId="false">
    Day: <h:inputText value="#{scheduleBean.day}"/>
    Starting At Hour: <h:inputText
      value="#{scheduleBean.hourstart}"/>
    <h:commandButton value="Save" action="success"/>
  </h:form>
</h:body>
```

Notice that the name and surname are obtained from the flow scope using the `flowScope` object, while the registration code is obtained from the flow scoped `ScheduleBean`; this bean stores the day, hour (received from the player), and registration code (received from the `registration` flow). Each piece of information received from the registration bean was guided to the place of storage using the `<inbound-parameter>` tag in the `schedule-flow.xml` file, as shown in the following code:

```
<flow-definition id="schedule">
  <view id="schedule">
    <vdl-document>/schedule/schedule.xhtml</vdl-document>
  </view>

  <inbound-parameter>
    <name>playernameparam</name>
    <value>#{flowScope.name}</value>
  </inbound-parameter>
  <inbound-parameter>
    <name>playersurnameparam</name>
    <value>#{flowScope.surname}</value>
  </inbound-parameter>
```

```
    <inbound-parameter>
      <name>playerregistrationcode</name>
      <value>#{scheduleBean.regcode}</value>
    </inbound-parameter>
</flow-definition>
```

After the day and hour are inserted, the button labeled **Save** should save the data and navigate to the `success.xhtml` page, which is a simple page that displays all data provided by the player. From this page, we can return to the calling flow, `registration`, via a simple button labeled **Exit Registration**, as shown in the following code:

```
<h:body>
  <h1><b>Second page in the 'schedule' flow</b></h1>
  <h1><b>In flow ?
  #{null != facesContext.application.flowHandler.currentFlow}
  </b></h1><br/><br/>
  You are registered as
  #{flowScope.name} #{flowScope.surname} (#{scheduleBean.regcode})
  You will play first match
  #{scheduleBean.day} after #{scheduleBean.hourstart}
  <h:button value="Exit Registration"
    outcome="taskFlowReturnThanks"/>
</h:body>
```

The outcome, `taskFlowReturnThanks`, is defined in the `schedule-flow.xml` file as follows:

```
<flow-return id="taskFlowReturnThanks">
  <from-outcome>/registration/thanks.xhtml</from-outcome>
</flow-return>
```

The `thanks.xhtml` page is just a final step before the user exists from the `registration` flow, as shown in the following code:

```
<h:body>
  <h1><b>Third page in the 'registration' flow</b></h1>
  <h1><b>In flow ? #{null !=
    facesContext.application.flowHandler.currentFlow}</b></h1>
    <br/><br/>
  Thanks for your patience, Mr :#{registrationBean.playerName}
  #{registrationBean.playerSurname}<br/>
  <b>We wish you beautiful games!</b><br/><br/>
  <h:button value="Bye Bye, #{registrationBean.playerSurname}"
    outcome="taskFlowReturnDone"/>
</h:body>
```

If you want to jump over the `thanks.xhtml` page, directly outside of both flows, then you can define the flow return, `taskFlowReturnThanks`, to point out the `done.xhtml` page, which is returned by the calling flow via the `taskFlowReturnDone` flow return. Therefore, we can use the following code:

```
<flow-return id="taskFlowReturnThanks">
  <from-outcome>taskFlowReturnDone</from-outcome>
</flow-return>
```

This example is wrapped into the application named `ch3_7_3` that is available in the code bundle of this chapter.

 Flows can be configured declaratively or programmatically using the JSF 2.2 `FlowBuilder` API.

# Configuring flows programmatically

In all the previous examples, you saw how to configure a flow using the declarative approach. But, flows can be configured programmatically also. The steps for configuring a flow programmatically are as follows:

1. Create a class and name it as the flow. This is more like a convention, not a requirement!

2. In this class, write a method as shown in the following code; the `@FlowDefinition` annotation is a class-level annotation that allows the flow definition to be defined using the `FlowBuilder` API. The name of this method can be any valid name, but `defineFlow` is like a convention. So, the name `defineFlow` is not mandatory, and you can even define more flows in the same class as long as you have annotated them correctly.

   ```
   @Produces
   @FlowDefinition
   public Flow defineFlow(@FlowBuilderParameter FlowBuilder
     flowBuilder) {
     ...
   }
   ```

3. Use the `FlowBuilder` API to configure the flow.

Using the `FlowBuilder` API is pretty straightforward and intuitive. For example, you can write the `registration-flow.xml` file programmatically, as follows:

```
public class Registration implements Serializable {

  @Produces
```

```
@FlowDefinition
public Flow defineFlow(@FlowBuilderParameter FlowBuilder
  flowBuilder) {

  String flowId = "registration";
  flowBuilder.id("", flowId);
  flowBuilder.viewNode(flowId, "/" + flowId + "/"
    + flowId + ".xhtml").markAsStartNode();
  flowBuilder.viewNode("confirm-id", "/" + flowId +
    "/confirm.xhtml");
  flowBuilder.viewNode("thanks-id", "/" + flowId +
    "/thanks.xhtml");
  flowBuilder.returnNode("taskFlowReturnIndex").
    fromOutcome("/index");
  flowBuilder.returnNode("taskFlowReturnDone").
    fromOutcome("#{registrationBean.returnValue}");

  flowBuilder.flowCallNode("callSchedule").
    flowReference("", "schedule").
    outboundParameter("playernameparam",
    "#{registrationBean.playerName}").
    outboundParameter("playersurnameparam",
    "#{registrationBean.playerSurname}").
    outboundParameter("playerregistrationcode", "349CF0YO122");

  return flowBuilder.getFlow();
  }
}
```

As you can see, for each tag used in the declarative approach, there is a corresponding method in the `FlowBuilder` API. For example, the `flowBuilder.id` method accepts two arguments: the first one represents the document ID (usually, an empty space), and the second one represents the flow ID.

The `schedule-flow.xml` file can be programmatically translated as shown in the following code:

```
public class Schedule implements Serializable {

  @Produces
  @FlowDefinition
  public Flow defineFlow(@FlowBuilderParameter FlowBuilder
    flowBuilder) {

  String flowId = "schedule";
  flowBuilder.id("", flowId);
```

```
flowBuilder.viewNode(flowId, "/" + flowId + "/"
 + flowId + ".xhtml").markAsStartNode();
flowBuilder.viewNode("success-id", "/" + flowId +
"/success.xhtml");
flowBuilder.returnNode("taskFlowReturnThanks").
  fromOutcome("/registration/thanks.xhtml");

flowBuilder.inboundParameter("playernameparam",
  "#{flowScope.name}");
flowBuilder.inboundParameter("playersurnameparam",
  "#{flowScope.surname}");
flowBuilder.inboundParameter("playerregistrationcode",
  "#{scheduleBean.regcode}");

return flowBuilder.getFlow();
 }
}
```

A method annotated with @PostConstruct will be called when the application enters into the current flow and the flow scoped bean is instantiated, while subsequent requests will use this instance until the flow is dumped. This is repeated if the application enters in this flow again. So, initializations specific to the current flow can be placed here.

This example is wrapped into the application named ch3_7_5 that is available in the code bundle of this chapter.

Declarative and programmatic configurations can be mixed in the same application. For example, check the application named ch3_7_4, which uses programmatic configuration for the registration flow and declarative configuration for the schedule flow.

# Flows and navigation cases

Navigation cases can be used for navigating inside flows. At this moment, when you click on the button labeled **Register To Tournament**, the flow goes in the confirm. xhtml page based on implicit navigation. But we can easily exemplify an explicit navigation in the flow by replacing the value of the action attribute as follows:

```
<h:commandButton value="Register To Tournament"
  action="confirm_outcome"/>
```

Now, `confirm_outcome` cannot be automatically fetched to the `confirm.xhtml` page; therefore, in the `registration-flow.xml` file, we can add an explicit navigation case, as shown in the following code:

```
<navigation-rule>
  <from-view-id>/registration/registration.xhtml</from-view-id>
  <navigation-case>
    <from-outcome>confirm_outcome</from-outcome>
    <to-view-id>/registration/confirm.xhtml</to-view-id>
    <redirect/>
  </navigation-case>
</navigation-rule>
```

When you need to use a navigation case to enter in a flow, you will have to specify the `<to-flow-document-id>`*document_ID*`</to-flow-document-id>` statement nested in the `<navigation-case>` tag. If there is no document ID, that uses `<to-flow-document-id/>`. Moreover a `<h:button>` (or `<h:link>`) can be used to enter in such a flow, as follows:

```
<h:button id="..." value="enter flow" outcome="flow">
  <f:attribute name="to-flow-document-id"
    value="unique"/>
</h:button>
```

If you choose to write a programmatic navigation case, then JSF 2.2 comes with a method named, `getToFlowDocumentId`, which should be overridden for indicating the document ID.

At this point, everything comes to normal. Therefore, we can use explicit navigation cases for navigation between the flow's pages. The complete application is named `ch3_11_1`.

In order to accomplish the same thing in a programmatic fashion, you need to use the `NavigationCaseBuilder` API, as shown in the following code; this is the same navigation case, so we have used only the needed methods:

```
flowBuilder.navigationCase().
  fromViewId("/registration/registration.xhtml").
  fromOutcome("confirm_outcome").
  toViewId("/registration/confirm.xhtml").
  redirect();
```

This example is wrapped in the complete application named `ch3_11_2`.

Moreover, you can even use a custom navigation handler. The new
`NavigationHandlerWrapper` class (added in JSF 2.2) provides a simple
implementation of the `NavigationHandler` class. Therefore, we can easily
extend it to prove a navigation case using a custom navigation handler,
as shown in the following code:

```
public class CustomNavigationHandler extends
  NavigationHandlerWrapper {

  private NavigationHandler configurableNavigationHandler;

  public CustomNavigationHandler() {}

  public CustomNavigationHandler(NavigationHandler
    configurableNavigationHandler){
    this.configurableNavigationHandler =
      configurableNavigationHandler;
  }

  @Override
  public void handleNavigation(FacesContext context,
    String fromAction, String outcome) {

    if (outcome.equals("confirm_outcome")) {
      outcome = "confirm";
    }

    getWrapped().handleNavigation(context, fromAction, outcome);
  }

  @Override
  public NavigationHandler getWrapped() {
    return configurableNavigationHandler;
  }
}
```

Finally, a quick configuration in the `faces-config.xml` file is as follows:

```
<application>
  <navigation-handler>
    book.beans.CustomNavigationHandler
  </navigation-handler>
</application>
```

When the flow has a document ID, you need to override the handleNavigation(FacesContext context, String fromAction, String outcome, String toFlowDocumentId) method.

The complete application is named ch3_11_3.

# Inspecting flow navigation cases

Whatever approach you choose for using navigation cases inside flows, you can always inspect them via the ConfigurableNavigationHandler.inspectFlow method. This method is invoked by the flow system to cause the flow to be inspected for navigation rules. You can easily override it to obtain information about navigation cases, by writing a custom configurable navigation handler. The easiest way to accomplish this is to extend the new ConfigurableNavigationHandlerWrapper class (introduced in JSF 2.2), which represents a simple implementation of ConfigurableNavigationHandler. For example, the following snippet of code sends in log information about each found navigation case:

```
public class CustomConfigurableNavigationHandler extends
  ConfigurableNavigationHandlerWrapper {

  private final static Logger logger =
    Logger.getLogger(CustomConfigurableNavigationHandler.
    class.getName());
  private ConfigurableNavigationHandler
    configurableNavigationHandler;

  public CustomConfigurableNavigationHandler() {}

  public CustomConfigurableNavigationHandler
    (ConfigurableNavigationHandler configurableNavigationHandler){
    this.configurableNavigationHandler =
    configurableNavigationHandler;
  }

  @Override
  public void inspectFlow(FacesContext context, Flow flow) {
    getWrapped().inspectFlow(context, flow);
    if (flow.getNavigationCases().size() > 0) {
      Map<String, Set<NavigationCase>> navigationCases =
        flow.getNavigationCases();
```

```
        for (Map.Entry<String, Set<NavigationCase>> entry :
          navigationCases.entrySet()) {
          logger.log(Level.INFO, "Navigation case: {0}",
            entry.getKey());
          for (NavigationCase nc : entry.getValue()) {
            logger.log(Level.INFO, "From view id: {0}",
              nc.getFromViewId());
            logger.log(Level.INFO, "From outcome: {0}",
              nc.getFromOutcome());
            logger.log(Level.INFO, "To view id: {0}",
              nc.getToViewId(context));
            logger.log(Level.INFO, "Redirect: {0}",
              nc.isRedirect());
          }
        }
      }
    }

    @Override
    public ConfigurableNavigationHandler getWrapped() {
      return configurableNavigationHandler;
    }
}
```

If you attach this custom configurable navigation handler to one of the preceding three examples, then you will get information about the presented navigation case. The complete example is named ch3_15.

# Using the initializer and finalizer

By using the FlowBuilder API, we can attach callback methods that will be automatically called when a flow is created and right before it is destroyed. The FlowBuilder.initializer method has the following signatures, which are called when the flow is created:

```
public abstract FlowBuilder initializer(String methodExpression)
public abstract FlowBuilder initializer(javax.el.MethodExpression
  methodExpression)
```

The FlowBuilder.finalizer signature is called before the flow is destroyed, as follows:

```
public abstract FlowBuilder finalizer(String methodExpression)
public abstract FlowBuilder finalizer(javax.el.MethodExpression
  methodExpression)
```

For example, the `initializer` method can be used to pass external parameters into a flow. Let's suppose that in the `index.xhtml` page (outside the flow), when we click on the button labeled **Start Registration**, we want to pass the tournament name and place into the flow, as follows:

```
<h:form prependId="false">
  <h:inputHidden id="tournamentNameId" value="Roland Garros"/>
  <h:inputHidden id="tournamentPlaceId" value="France"/>
  <h:commandButton value="Start Registration"
    action="registration"/>
</h:form>
```

These two parameters must be available when the flow starts, because the wrapped information is displayed in the `registration.xhtml` page (the start node of the flow) via two properties from `RegistrationBean`, namely `tournamentName` and `tournamentPlace`. For this, we need to call a method from `RegistrationBean` capable of extracting this information and store it in these two properties, as shown in the following code:

```
//initializer method
public void tournamentInitialize() {
   tournamentName = FacesContext.getCurrentInstance().
     getExternalContext().getRequestParameterMap().
     get("tournamentNameId");
   tournamentPlace = FacesContext.getCurrentInstance().
     getExternalContext().getRequestParameterMap().
     get("tournamentPlaceId");
}
```

Now is the interesting part, because we can use the `initializer` method to indicate the `tournamentInitialize` method as the callback method that should be invoked when the flow is created. This can be done in the `registration-flow.xml` file as follows:

```
<initializer>
   #{registrationBean.tournamentInitialize()}
</initializer>
```

So, at this moment, we can use the tournament name and place right from the beginning of the flow and during the flow's lifespan.

Going further, another simple scenario can be the justification for using a `finalizer` method. Let's suppose that we count the registered players via an application scoped bean named `PlayersCounterBean`, as shown in the following code:

```
@Named
@ApplicationScoped
```

```
public class PlayersCounterBean {

  private int count = 0;

  public int getCount() {
    return count;
  }

  public void addPlayer() {
    count++;
  }
}
```

The `count` variable should be increased when the player exits the flow, and the registration is successfully done; therefore, we can place a `finalizer` method in the `registration-flow.xml` file as follows:

```
<finalizer>
  #{registrationBean.tournamentFinalize()}
</finalizer>
```

The `tournamentFinalize` method is implemented in `RegistrationBean`, as shown in the following code:

```
@Named
@FlowScoped(value = "registration")
public class RegistrationBean {

  @Inject
  private PlayersCounterBean playersCounterBean;
  ...
  //finalizer method
  public void tournamentFinalize() {
    playersCounterBean.addPlayer();
  }
}
```

Since the `PlayersCounterBean` is an application bean, we can use its goodies outside the flow. The complete application is named `ch3_12_1`.

The same output can be programmatically achieved using the following code:

```
flowBuilder.initializer("#{registrationBean.
  tournamentInitialize(param['tournamentNameId'],
  param['tournamentPlaceId'])}");
flowBuilder.finalizer("#{registrationBean.tournamentFinalize()}");
```

For the sake of variation, in this case we didn't extract the parameter values using the request parameter `Map`. We preferred to use the implicit object `param` and to pass the values as arguments of the `tournamentInitialize` method as follows:

```
//initializer method
public void tournamentInitialize(String tn, String tp) {
    tournamentName = tn;
    tournamentPlace = tp;
}
```

The complete application is named `ch3_12_2`.

# Using the flow switch

The `switch` case statements are a substitute for long `if` statements and are useful to do conditional outcome mapping. In order to see it at work, we can suppose that for each tournament we have a separate `confirm.xhtml` page. Let's have the four grand slams in tennis and the associated XHTML confirmation pages, as follows:

- Roland Garros and `confirm_rg.xhtml`
- Wimbledon and `confirm_wb.xhtml`
- US Open and `confirm_us.xhtml`
- Australian Open and `confirm_ao.xhtml`

The name and place of the tournament are passed in the flow via a simple form (one form per tournament), as follows (you already know from the preceding section how this information may be obtained inside the flow):

```
<h:form prependId="false">
  <h:inputHidden id="tournamentNameId" value="Australian Open"/>
  <h:inputHidden id="tournamentPlaceId" value="Australia"/>
  <h:commandButton value="Start Registration (Australian Open)"
    action="registration"/>
</h:form>
```

Now, after clicking on the button labeled **Register To...**, we need to choose the right confirmation page. For this, we can use a programmatic switch, as shown in the following code:

```
public class Registration implements Serializable {

    @Produces
    @FlowDefinition
```

```
public Flow defineFlow(@FlowBuilderParameter FlowBuilder
  flowBuilder) {

  String flowId = "registration";
  flowBuilder.id("", flowId);
  flowBuilder.viewNode(flowId, "/" + flowId + "/" + flowId +
    ".xhtml").markAsStartNode();
  flowBuilder.viewNode("no-tournament-id", "/" + flowId +
    "/notournament.xhtml");
  flowBuilder.viewNode("confirm-rg-id", "/" + flowId +
    "/confirm_rg.xhtml");
  flowBuilder.viewNode("confirm-wb-id", "/" + flowId +
    "/confirm_wb.xhtml");
  flowBuilder.viewNode("confirm-us-id", "/" + flowId +
    "/confirm_us.xhtml");
  flowBuilder.viewNode("confirm-ao-id", "/" + flowId +
    "/confirm_ao.xhtml");
  flowBuilder.returnNode("taskFlowReturnDone").
    fromOutcome("#{registrationBean.returnValue}");

  flowBuilder.switchNode("confirm-switch-id").
    defaultOutcome("no-tournament-id").
    switchCase().condition("#{registrationBean.tournamentName eq
    'Roland Garros'}").fromOutcome("confirm-rg-id").
    condition("#{registrationBean.tournamentName eq
    'Wimbledon'}").fromOutcome("confirm-wb-id").
    condition("#{registrationBean.tournamentName eq 'US
    Open'}").fromOutcome("confirm-us-id").
    condition("#{registrationBean.tournamentName eq 'Australian
    Open'}").fromOutcome("confirm-ao-id");
  flowBuilder.initializer("#{registrationBean.
    tournamentInitialize(param['tournamentNameId'],
    param['tournamentPlaceId'])}");
  flowBuilder.finalizer("#{registrationBean.
    tournamentFinalize()}");

  return flowBuilder.getFlow();
  }
}
```

Notice that when no condition is evaluated to `true`, the selected node will be the `notournament.xhtml` page, which represents the default outcome. This is just a simple XHMTL page containing some specific text.

The complete application is named `ch3_13`. Declaratively, this can be achieved in the `registration-flow.xml` file as shown in the following code. You can use `<view>` tags to hide the outcome's path behind some IDs (map outcomes to pages), as we saw in the programmatic example:

```
<switch id="confirm-switch-id">
  <default-outcome>
    /registration/notournament.xhtml
  </default-outcome>
  <case>
    <if>#{registrationBean.tournamentName eq 'Roland Garros'}</if>
    <from-outcome>/registration/confirm_rg.xhtml</from-outcome>
  </case>
  <case>
    <if>#{registrationBean.tournamentName eq 'Wimbledon'}</if>
    <from-outcome>/registration/confirm_wb.xhtml</from-outcome>
  </case>
  <case>
    <if>#{registrationBean.tournamentName eq 'US Open'}</if>
    <from-outcome>/registration/confirm_us.xhtml</from-outcome>
  </case>
  <case>
    <if>#{registrationBean.tournamentName eq 'Australian
      Open'}</if>
    <from-outcome>/registration/confirm_ao.xhtml</from-outcome>
  </case>
</switch>
```

So, switch can be useful when you don't want to map each outcome to a single page.

This example wasn't wrapped in a complete application.

# Packaging flows

Flows act as logical units of work; therefore, they are portable across multiple applications. The portability is obtained by packaging the flow artifacts in a JAR file. Further, the JAR file can be added in any application CLASSPATH and the flow is ready to be used. To package a flow, you need to follow some conventions, which are listed as follows:

1. Explicitly define the flows in the `faces-config.xml` file.
2. In the JAR root, create a `META-INF` folder.
3. Add the `faces-config.xml` file in this folder.

4. Add the `beans.xml` file in this folder.

5. In the same folder, `META-INF`, create a subfolder named `flows`.

6. In the `flows` folder, add all nodes (pages) of the flow.

7. In the JAR root, outside the `META-INF` folder, add all the Java code (classes) needed by the flow.

Based on the preceding steps, the flow described in the *Flows with beans* section can be packaged in a JAR file named `registration.jar`, as shown in the following screenshot:

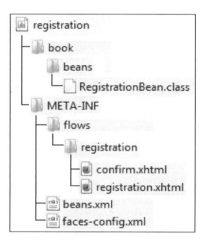

The complete application that uses this JAR file is named `ch3_14`.

# Programmatic flow scope

Programmatically speaking, the flow scope can be accessed via the `javax.faces.flow.FlowHandler` class. After obtaining a `FlowHandler` class's object, you can easily access the current flow, add a new flow, and manipulate the flow map represented by `#{flowScope}`, as follows:

```
FacesContext context = FacesContext.getCurrentInstance();
Application application = context.getApplication();
FlowHandler flowHandler = application.getFlowHandler();

//get current flow
Flow flow = flowHandler.getCurrentFlow();
Flow flowContext = flowHandler.getCurrentFlow(context);

//add flow
```

```
flowHandler.addFlow(context, flow);

//get access to the Map that backs #{flowScope}
Map<Object,Object> flowMap = flowHandler.getCurrentFlowScope();
```

Obviously, the `FlowHandler` class is the most important class involved in the interaction between runtime and the faces flow feature. This is an abstract class that can be extended to provide a custom flow handler implementation. In order to do that, you can start by creating a new `FlowHandlerFactory` class, which is used by the `Application` class to create the singleton instance of the `FlowHandler` class. This class has a simple implementation named `FlowHandlerFactoryWrapper`, which can be easily extended to return a custom flow handler, as shown in the following code:

```
public class CustomFlowHandlerFactory extends
  FlowHandlerFactoryWrapper {

  private FlowHandlerFactory flowHandlerFactory;

  public CustomFlowHandlerFactory(){}

  public CustomFlowHandlerFactory(FlowHandlerFactory
    flowHandlerFactory){
    this.flowHandlerFactory = flowHandlerFactory;
  }

  @Override
  public FlowHandler createFlowHandler(FacesContext context){
    FlowHandler customFlowHandler = new
      CustomFlowHandler(getWrapped().createFlowHandler(context));
    return customFlowHandler;
  }

  @Override
  public FlowHandlerFactory getWrapped() {
    return this.flowHandlerFactory;
  }
}
```

This factory should be configured in the `faces-config.xml` file, as shown in the following code:

```
<factory>
  <flow-handler-factory>
    book.beans.CustomFlowHandlerFactory
  </flow-handler-factory>
</factory>
```

Further, the `CustomFlowHandler` class represents an extension of the `FlowHandler` class. Since the `FlowHandler` class is an abstract class, you need to provide an implementation for each of its methods, as shown in the following code:

```
public class CustomFlowHandler extends FlowHandler {

    private FlowHandler flowHandler;

    public CustomFlowHandler() {}

    public CustomFlowHandler(FlowHandler flowHandler) {
        this.flowHandler = flowHandler;
    }

    ...
    //Overrided methods
    ...

}
```

For example, you know from the previous sections that the `registration` flow passed several outbound parameters to the nested `schedule` flow. You saw how to accomplish that declaratively, in the `registration-flow.xml` file, and programmatically, via the `FlowBuilder` API, in the `Registration` class. You can do the same thing from a custom flow handler in the method named, `transition`, which is capable to perform a transition between a source flow (for example, `registration`) and a target flow (for example, `schedule`). When the `registration` flow calls the `schedule` flow, you can write the following code:

```
@Override
public void transition(FacesContext context, Flow sourceFlow,
    Flow targetFlow, FlowCallNode outboundCallNode, String toViewId)
{
    if ((sourceFlow != null) && (targetFlow != null)) {
        if ((sourceFlow.getStartNodeId().equals("registration")) &&
            (targetFlow.getStartNodeId().equals("schedule"))) {

            FlowCallNode flowCallNode =
                sourceFlow.getFlowCalls().get("callSchedule");
            Map<String, Parameter> outboundParameters =
                flowCallNode.getOutboundParameters();

            CustomParameter playernameparamO = new
                CustomParameter("playernameparam",
                "#{registrationBean.playerName}");
```

```
    CustomParameter playersurnameparamO = new
      CustomParameter("playersurnameparam",
      "#{registrationBean.playerSurname}");
    CustomParameter playerregistrationcodeO = new
      CustomParameter("playerregistrationcode",
      "349CF0YO122");

    outboundParameters.put("playernameparam",
      playernameparamO);
    outboundParameters.put("playersurnameparam",
      playersurnameparamO);
    outboundParameters.put("playerregistrationcode",
      playerregistrationcodeO);
    }
  }
  flowHandler.transition(context, sourceFlow, targetFlow,
    outboundCallNode, toViewId);
}
```

The target inbound parameters can be accessed as follows (the Map parameter cannot be altered):

```
Map<String, Parameter> inboundParameters =
  targetFlow.getInboundParameters();
```

Flow parameters are represented by the javax.faces.flow.Parameter abstract class. The CustomParameter class provides an implementation as follows:

```
public class CustomParameter extends Parameter {

  private String name;
  private String value;

  public CustomParameter(String name, String value) {
    this.name = name;
    this.value = value;
  }

  @Override
  public String getName() {
    return name;
  }

  @Override
  public ValueExpression getValue() {
    return createValueExpression(value, String.class);
```

```
    }

    private ValueExpression createValueExpression(String exp,
      Class<?> cls) {
      FacesContext facesContext = FacesContext.getCurrentInstance();
      ELContext elContext = facesContext.getELContext();
      return facesContext.getApplication().getExpressionFactory().
      createValueExpression(elContext, exp, cls);
    }
}
```

# Dependent pseudo-scope

This is the default scope of a CDI bean (@Named) when nothing is specified. In this case, an object exists to serve exactly one bean and has the same life cycle as that bean; an instance of a dependent scoped bean is not shared between different users or different points of injection. It can also be explicitly specified by annotating the bean with the @Dependent annotation and importing javax.enterprise.context. Dependent. This scope is available only in CDI and is the only **non-contextual** scope.

 All CDI scopes, except this one, are known as **normal** scopes. More details about normal scopes versus pseudo-scopes can be found in the *Normal scopes and pseudo-scopes* section at http://docs.jboss. org/cdi/spec/1.0/html/contexts.html.

If you put the PlayersBean in the dependent scope, then the current extracted player and the list of randomly extracted players (which will be empty or will contain this player) is available only inside the bean, as shown in the following code:

```
import javax.enterprise.context.Dependent;
import javax.inject.Named;

@Named
@Dependent
public class PlayersBean {
  ...
}
```

A method annotated with @PostConstruct will be called for each request. Actually, it might be called multiple times during the same request, if the bean is used in several EL expressions. Initially, there is one instance of the bean, and this instance is reused if the bean EL name appears multiple times in the EL expression, but is not reused in the case of another EL expression or in the case of a re-evaluation of the same EL expression.

This example is wrapped into the application named ch3_5 that is available in the code bundle of this chapter.

# The none scope

The **none scoped** beans lives to serve other beans.

The none scope seems to be the black sheep of JSF scopes. Even its name doesn't inspire something useful. Practically, a managed bean in this scope lives as long as a single EL expression evaluation and is not visible in any JSF page. If the application scope lives the longest, this scope lives the shortest. But, if you inject the none scoped managed beans in other managed beans, then they will live as long as their hosts. Actually, this is their job, to serve other beans.

The none scoped objects used in the configuration file indicate managed beans that are used by other managed beans in the application.

So, whenever you need a humble managed bean that is ready to be a part of a cool scope, such as a request or a session, you can annotate it with @NoneScoped, available in the javax.faces.bean package. Moreover, objects with the none scope can use other objects with the none scope.

# The custom scope

When none of the previous scopes meet your application needs, you have to pay attention to the JSF 2 custom scope. Most likely, you will never want to write a custom scope, but if it is necessary, then, in this section, you can see how to accomplish this task.

The custom scope annotation is `@CustomScoped` and is defined in the `javax.faces.bean` package. It is not available in CDI!

In order to implement a custom scope, let's suppose that you want to control the life cycle of several beans that live in the application scope. Normally they live as long as the application lives, but you want to be able to add/remove them from the application scope at certain moments of the application flow. Of course, there are many approaches to do that, but remember that we look for a reason to implement a custom scope; therefore, we will try to write a custom scope nested in the application scope that will allow us to add/remove a batch of beans. Creating and destroying the scope itself will be reflected in creating and destroying the beans, which means that you don't need to refer to each bean.

Actually, since this is just a demo, we will use only two beans: one will stay in the classical application scope (it can be useful for comparison of the application and custom scope lifespan), while the other one will be added/destroyed through the custom scope. The application purpose is not relevant; you should focus on the technique used to write a custom scope and paper over the assumptions and gaps. Think more on the lines that you can use this knowledge when you really need to implement a custom scope.

# Writing the custom scope class

The custom scope is represented by a class that extends the `ConcurrentHashMap<String, Object>` class. We need to allow concurrent access to an usual map because the exposed data may be accessed concurrently from multiple browsers. The code of the `CustomScope` class is as follows:

```
public class CustomScope extends ConcurrentHashMap<String, Object> {

  public static final String SCOPE = "CUSTOM_SCOPE";

  public CustomScope(){
    super();
  }

  public void scopeCreated(final FacesContext ctx) {

    ScopeContext context = new ScopeContext(SCOPE, this);
    ctx.getApplication().publishEvent(ctx,
      PostConstructCustomScopeEvent.class, context);
```

```
    }

    public void scopeDestroyed(final FacesContext ctx) {

      ScopeContext context = new ScopeContext(SCOPE,this);
      ctx.getApplication().publishEvent(ctx,
        PreDestroyCustomScopeEvent.class, context);
    }
  }
```

When our scope is created/destroyed, other components will be informed through events. In the `scopeCreated` method, you register `PostConstructCustomScopeEvent`, while in the `scopeDestroyed` method, you register `PreDestroyCustomScopeEvent`.

Now we have a custom scope, it is time to see how to declare a bean in this scope. Well, this is not hard and can be done with the `@CustomScoped` annotations and an EL expression, as follows:

```
import javax.faces.bean.CustomScoped;
import javax.faces.bean.ManagedBean;

@ManagedBean
@CustomScoped("#{CUSTOM_SCOPE}")
public class SponsoredLinksBean {

  ...
}
```

# Resolving a custom scope EL expression

At this point, JSF will iterate over the chain of existing resolvers in order to resolve the custom scope EL expression. Obviously, this attempt will end with an error, since no existing resolver will be able to satisfy this EL expression. So, you need to write a custom resolver as you saw in *Chapter 1, Dynamic Access to JSF Application Data through Expression Language (EL 3.0)*. Based on that, you should obtain something as shown in the following code:

```
public class CustomScopeResolver extends ELResolver {

  private static final Logger logger =
    Logger.getLogger(CustomScopeResolver.class.getName());

  @Override
```

```java
public Object getValue(ELContext context,
  Object base, Object property) {

  logger.log(Level.INFO, "Get Value property : {0}", property);

  if (property == null) {
    String message = MessageUtils.getExceptionMessageString
      (MessageUtils.NULL_PARAMETERS_ERROR_MESSAGE_ID,
      "property");
    throw new PropertyNotFoundException(message);
  }

  FacesContext facesContext = (FacesContext)
    context.getContext(FacesContext.class);

  if (base == null) {
    Map<String, Object> applicationMap =
      facesContext.getExternalContext().getApplicationMap();
    CustomScope scope = (CustomScope)
      applicationMap.get(CustomScope.SCOPE);

    if (CustomScope.SCOPE.equals(property)) {
      logger.log(Level.INFO, "Found request | base={0}
        property={1}", new Object[]{base, property});
      context.setPropertyResolved(true);
      return scope;
    } else {
      logger.log(Level.INFO, "Search request | base={0}
        property={1}", new Object[]{base, property});
      if (scope != null) {
        Object value = scope.get(property.toString());
        if (value != null) {
          logger.log(Level.INFO, "Found request | base={0}
            property={1}", new Object[]{base, property});
          context.setPropertyResolved(true);
        }else {
          logger.log(Level.INFO, "Not found request | base={0}
            property={1}", new Object[]{base, property});
          context.setPropertyResolved(false);
        }
        return value;
      } else {
        return null;
      }
    }
  }
```

```
    }

    if (base instanceof CustomScope) {

      CustomScope baseCustomScope = (CustomScope) base;
        Object value = baseCustomScope.get(property.toString());
      logger.log(Level.INFO, "Search request | base={0}
        property={1}", new Object[]{base, property});

      if (value != null) {
        logger.log(Level.INFO, "Found request | base={0}
          property={1}", new Object[]{base, property});
        context.setPropertyResolved(true);
      } else {
        logger.log(Level.INFO, "Not found request | base={0}
          property={1}", new Object[]{base, property});
        context.setPropertyResolved(false);
      }

    return value;
  }

  return null;
}

@Override
public Class<?> getType(ELContext context, Object base,
  Object property) {
  return Object.class;
}

@Override
public void setValue(ELContext context, Object base,
  Object property, Object value) {

  if (base != null) {
    return;
  }

  context.setPropertyResolved(false);

  if (property == null) {
    String message = MessageUtils.getExceptionMessageString
      (MessageUtils.NULL_PARAMETERS_ERROR_MESSAGE_ID,
      "property");
```

```
        throw new PropertyNotFoundException(message);
    }

    if (CustomScope.SCOPE.equals(property)) {
      throw new PropertyNotWritableException((String) property);
    }
  }

  @Override
  public boolean isReadOnly(ELContext context,
    Object base, Object property) {
    return true;
  }

  @Override
  public Iterator<FeatureDescriptor> getFeatureDescriptors
    (ELContext context, Object base) {
    return null;
  }

  @Override
  public Class<?> getCommonPropertyType(ELContext context,
    Object base) {
    if (base != null) {
      return null;
    }
    return String.class;
  }
}
```

Do not forget to put the following resolver into the chain by adding it in the
`faces-config.xml` file:

```
<el-resolver>book.beans.CustomScopeResolver</el-resolver>
```

Done! So far, you have created a custom scope, you put a bean into this scope,
and learned that the brand new resolver provides access to this bean.

The custom scope must be stored somewhere, so nested in the application scope can
be a choice (of course, other scopes can also be a choice, depending on your needs).
When the scope is created, it has to be placed in the application map, and when it is
destroyed, it has to be removed from the application map. The question is when to
create it and when to destroy it? And the answer is, *it depends*. Most likely, this is a
decision strongly tied to the application flow.

# Controlling the custom scope lifespan with action listeners

Using action listeners can be a good practice even if it involves control from view declaration. Let's suppose that the button labeled **START** will add the custom scope in the application map, as shown in the following code:

```
<h:commandButton value="START">
  <f:actionListener type="book.beans.CreateCustomScope" />
</h:commandButton>
```

The following `CreateCustomScope` class is a straightforward action listener as it implements the `ActionListener` interface:

```
public class CreateCustomScope implements ActionListener {

  private static final Logger logger =
    Logger.getLogger(CreateCustomScope.class.getName());

  @Override
  public void processAction(ActionEvent event)
    throws AbortProcessingException {

    logger.log(Level.INFO, "Creating custom scope ...");

    FacesContext context = FacesContext.getCurrentInstance();
    Map<String, Object> applicationMap =
      context.getExternalContext().getApplicationMap();
    CustomScope customScope = (CustomScope)
      applicationMap.get(CustomScope.SCOPE);

    if (customScope == null) {
      customScope = new CustomScope();
      applicationMap.put(CustomScope.SCOPE, customScope);

      customScope.scopeCreated(context);
    } else {
      logger.log(Level.INFO, "Custom scope exists ...");
    }
  }
}
```

Following the same approach, the button labeled **STOP** will remove the custom scope from the application map as follows:

```
<h:commandButton value="STOP">
  <f:actionListener type="book.beans.DestroyCustomScope" />
</h:commandButton>
```

The following `DestroyCustomScope` class is the action listener as it implements the `ActionListener` interface:

```
public class DestroyCustomScope implements ActionListener {

    private static final Logger logger =
      Logger.getLogger(DestroyCustomScope.class.getName());

    @Override
    public void processAction(ActionEvent event) throws
      AbortProcessingException {

      logger.log(Level.INFO, "Destroying custom scope ...");

      FacesContext context = FacesContext.getCurrentInstance();
      Map<String, Object> applicationMap =
        context.getExternalContext().getApplicationMap();
      CustomScope customScope = (CustomScope)
        applicationMap.get(CustomScope.SCOPE);

      if (customScope != null) {
        customScope.scopeDestroyed(context);
        applicationMap.remove(CustomScope.SCOPE);
      } else {
        logger.log(Level.INFO, "Custom scope does not exists ...");
      }
    }
}
```

This example is wrapped into the application named `ch3_8` that is available in the code bundle of this chapter. Just a run and a quick look over the code will clarify that the spaghetti-code is missing here.

# Controlling the custom scope lifespan with the navigation handler

Another approach is to control the custom scope lifespan based on the page's navigation. This solution is more flexible and is hidden from the user. You can write a custom navigation handler by extending NavigationHandler. The next implementation puts the custom scope in the application map when the navigation reaches the page named sponsored.xhtml, and will remove it from the application map in any other navigation case. The code of the CustomScopeNavigationHandler class is as follows:

```
public class CustomScopeNavigationHandler extends
  NavigationHandler {

  private static final Logger logger =
    Logger.getLogger(CustomScopeNavigationHandler.
    class.getName());
  private final NavigationHandler navigationHandler;

  public CustomScopeNavigationHandler(NavigationHandler
    navigationHandler) {
    this.navigationHandler = navigationHandler;
  }

  @Override
  public void handleNavigation(FacesContext context,
    String fromAction, String outcome) {

    if (outcome != null) {
      if (outcome.equals("sponsored")) {
        logger.log(Level.INFO, "Creating custom scope ...");

        Map<String, Object> applicationMap =
          context.getExternalContext().getApplicationMap();
        CustomScope customScope = (CustomScope)
          applicationMap.get(CustomScope.SCOPE);

        if (customScope == null) {
          customScope = new CustomScope();
          applicationMap.put(CustomScope.SCOPE, customScope);

          customScope.scopeCreated(context);
        } else {
          logger.log(Level.INFO, "Custom scope exists ...");
        }
```

```
      } else {
        logger.log(Level.INFO, "Destroying custom scope ...");

        Map<String, Object> applicationMap =
          context.getExternalContext().getApplicationMap();
        CustomScope customScope = (CustomScope)
          applicationMap.get(CustomScope.SCOPE);

        if (customScope != null) {
          customScope.scopeDestroyed(context);
          applicationMap.remove(CustomScope.SCOPE);
        } else {
          logger.log(Level.INFO,
            "Custom scope does not exist");
        }
      }
    }
  }

  navigationHandler.handleNavigation(context, fromAction,
    outcome);
  }
}
```

Do not forget to register the following navigation handler in the `faces-config.xml` file:

```
<navigation-handler>
  book.beans.CustomScopeNavigationHandler
</navigation-handler>
```

This example is wrapped into the application named `ch3_9` that is available in the code bundle of this chapter. A quick look over the code will clarify that the spaghetti-code is missing here.

As I said earlier, JSF 2.2 comes with a wrapper class for `NavigationHandler`. This is a simple implementation that can be easily extended by developers. An instance of the class being wrapped is returned in the `getWrapped` method. For example, you can rewrite the `CustomScopeNavigationHandler` class, as shown in the following code:

```
public class CustomScopeNavigationHandler
  extends NavigationHandlerWrapper {

  private static final Logger logger =
    Logger.getLogger(CustomScopeNavigationHandler.
    class.getName());
```

```java
    private final NavigationHandler navigationHandler;

  public CustomScopeNavigationHandler(NavigationHandler
    navigationHandler){
    this.navigationHandler = navigationHandler;
  }

@Override
  public void handleNavigation(FacesContext context,
    String fromAction, String outcome) {

    if (outcome != null) {
      if (outcome.equals("sponsored")) {
        logger.log(Level.INFO, "Creating custom scope ...");

        Map<String, Object> applicationMap =
          context.getExternalContext().getApplicationMap();
        CustomScope customScope = (CustomScope)
          applicationMap.get(CustomScope.SCOPE);

        if (customScope == null) {
          customScope = new CustomScope();
          applicationMap.put(CustomScope.SCOPE, customScope);

          customScope.scopeCreated(context);
        } else {
          logger.log(Level.INFO, "Custom scope exists ...");
        }
      } else {
        logger.log(Level.INFO, "Destroying custom scope ...");

        Map<String, Object> applicationMap =
          context.getExternalContext().getApplicationMap();
        CustomScope customScope = (CustomScope)
          applicationMap.get(CustomScope.SCOPE);

        if (customScope != null) {
          customScope.scopeDestroyed(context);
          applicationMap.remove(CustomScope.SCOPE);
        } else {
          logger.log(Level.INFO, "Custom scope does not exist");
        }
      }
    }
```

```
    }

    getWrapped().handleNavigation(context, fromAction, outcome);
  }

  @Override
  public NavigationHandler getWrapped() {
    return navigationHandler;
  }
}
```

This example is wrapped into the application named `ch3_10` that is available in the code bundle of this chapter.

# Managed bean instantiation

By default, a managed bean is instantiated at first reference to it (a request, for example) — this is known as **lazy instantiation**. You can alter the default behavior by adding the `eager` attribute and set its value to `true`. This will instantiate the managed bean when the application starts, before any request is made. But, it is important to know that this works only for application scoped beans and the eager instantiated bean is placed in the application scope, as shown in the following lines of code:

```
@ManagedBean(eager=true)
@ApplicationScoped
```

# Beans injection

Normally, solutions depend on the concrete functional requirements, but finding the right solutions is what makes the difference between developers. Sometimes, developers get stuck or make mistakes when they work with objects in a scope that uses objects from another scope. From the following figure, you can seek some guidance for dealing with some of the most popular cases:

| Working with scoped objects | | | |
| --- | --- | --- | --- |
| **Request Objects** | **Session Objects** | **Application Objects** | **None Objects** |
| Request Objects ✓ | Request Objects ✗ | Request Objects ✗ | Request Objects ✗ |
| Session Objects ✓ | Session Objects ✓ | Session Objects ✗ | Session Objects ✗ |
| Application Objects ✓ | Application Objects ✓ | Application Objects ✓ | Application Objects ✗ |
| None Objects ✓ | None Objects ✓ | None Objects ✓ | None Objects ✓ |

As you can see, there are some restrictions. As a general rule in JSF, don't use objects that have shorter lifespan than the objects you are calling it from. In other words, use objects whose lifespan is the same as, or longer than, the object being injected into. Breaking this rule will end up in a JSF exception.

The logic behind this rule can be explained through the two most common mistakes, which are as follows:

- **Use request objects in session objects**: This is a bad thing, because we will have lots of requests (lots of instances) and only one session (one instance). Usually, requests belong to all users, while a session is one per user; therefore, it is unclear request object is injected? To be more clear, lots of requests means lots of associated beans, while a session means one bean. Now, it is illogical to inject one particular instance and skip all others. Moreover, how and when will you fetch the correct instance, since the request objects are transient, and usually, have a short lifespan! Even if you find a plausible use case, JSF will not allow you to do this via JSF managed beans.

- **Use session objects in application objects**: The same logic can be applied further when we want to use session objects in application objects. Sessions are many as users, but the application is only one; therefore, you cannot inject all sessions in the application ... it is useless! Of course, you may want to fetch a certain session to the application, but you have to be sure that the pointed session exists; this is not a problem if you are interested in the session of the current user, but it may be an issue if you are interested in sessions of other users. Moreover, if there are many sessions, you have to correctly identify the desired session. Even if you find a plausible use case, JSF will not allow you to do this via JSF managed beans.

Nevertheless, for CDI, these cases are not such a big issue. When you are using an object that has a shorter lifespan than the object you are calling it from (for example, injecting a request scoped bean into a session scoped bean), CDI classifies the use case as a mismatched injection and fixes the issue via CDI proxies. For each request, the CDI proxy re-establishes the connection to a live instance of the request scoped bean.

Even when we follow the written rules, we are still vulnerable to the unwritten rules. One of the unwritten rules that can cause undesirable results is named **overuse** or **abuse**. The following are some cases to avoid:

- Overusing a view scoped bean for request scoped data may affect memory.

- Overusing a request scoped bean for view scoped data may cause forms with unexpected behavior.

- Overusing an application scoped bean for request/view/session scoped data may cause an undesirably wide visibility of data across users and will affect memory.

- Overusing a session scoped bean for request/view data may cause an undesirably wide visibility of data across multiple browser windows/tabs in that session. As you know, view data are specific to a single browser window/tab, which allows us to open multiple tabs and keeps the data integrity while switching between tabs. On the other hand, if this data was exposed via the session scope, then the modifications in one window/tab will be reflected in the browser session; therefore, switching between tabs will lead to an apparently strange behavior, known as inconsistency of data. In case of using the session scope for request/view data, will also affect memory, since request/view scopes are meant to have a shorter lifespan than session scope.

Starting with JSF 2.0, managed beans can be injected (dependency injection) into the property of another managed bean using the @ManagedProperty annotation. You already know that from the previous chapter, where an example is provided.

Another way to inject beans is to use the @Inject annotation, which is part of the CDI powerful injection mechanism.

So when do we use @ManagedProperty and when do we use @Inject ? Well, we know that both of them do the same thing in different ways and different containers, so maybe it is a good idea to use @ManagedProperty when you are working in a servlet container or just don't need CDI. Another good argument for @ManagedProperty is that you can use EL with it. But, if you are in a proper CDI environment where you can exploit CDI benefits, such as proxy scope leak prevention or better deploy-time dependency, then use CDI.

The pacifist approach will combine these two in the same application. In this case, you have two options: to avoid any interaction between the managed beans and CDI beans or, obviously, to encourage the interaction between them for better performance. If you choose the second option, then it is important to keep in mind some simple rules of injection as shown in the following figure:

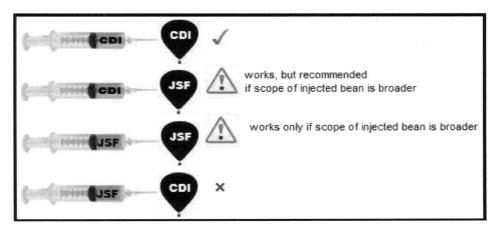

# Summary

In this chapter, we have browsed through an overview of JSF/CDI scopes. It begins with an open discussion about JSF scopes versus CDI scopes, meant to provide a few advantages/disadvantages of choosing either one (or both). After a short overview of JSF/CDI scopes, each scope was detailed by covering fundamental knowledge, such as definition, usability, functionality, restrictions, and examples.

The chapter ends with a bunch of thoughts regarding beans injections. You can find several rules, tips, and bad practices commonly used in JSF applications mentioned out here.

See you in the next two chapters, where we will cover many kinds of JSF artifacts and configuration stuff.

# 4
# JSF Configurations Using XML Files and Annotations – Part 1

Starting with JSF 2.0, there is no need to create the configuration file, `faces-config.xml`. Well, this affirmation is partially true, because JSF annotations still don't cover several configurations, such as resource bundles, factories, phase listeners, and so on. Usually, JSF annotations provide sufficient support for our applications; however, as you will see in this chapter, there are still many cases when `faces-config.xml` is mandatory, or additional configurations must be added in the `web.xml` file.

Nevertheless, JSF 2.2 provides a programmatic approach that can be used to reproduce `faces-config.xml`, without writing it in the classical approach. Later in this chapter, you will see how to take advantage of this new feature. For now, you will see a mix of creating and configuring different kinds of JSF artifacts. They will be arbitrarily presented—some of them are well known, from JSF 1.x and 2.0, while others are new, starting with JSF 2.2. Since these configurations are straightforward, they can be listed as barren documentation, but gluing each configuration into an example is more useful and provides a good point to start when you need to use them.

Therefore, in this chapter you will learn about JSF artifacts' configurations, but you will also see some examples of working with these artifacts. The following is a short overview of what we will cover:

- JSF 2.2 new namespaces
- JSF 2.2 programmatic configuration
- Configuring managed beans in XML

- Working with multiple configuration files
- Configuring locales and resource bundles
- Configuring validators and converters
- Configuring navigation
- Configuring action listeners
- Configuring system event listeners
- Configuring phase listeners
- Working with `@ListenerFor` and `@ListenersFor`

Obviously, we have a lot of work to do and a lot of JSF 2.2 features to cover (for example, JSF 2.2 injection in more artifacts then before), so let's begin!

# JSF 2.2 new namespaces

JSF 2.2 modified the existing JSF namespaces, as you can see in the following table:

| Namespace | Before JSF 2.2 | JSF 2.2 |
| --- | --- | --- |
| Faces Core | `http://java.sun.com/jsf/core` | `http://xmlns.jcp.org/jsf/core` |
| HTML_BASIC | `http://java.sun.com/jsf/html` | `http://xmlns.jcp.org/jsf/html` |
| Facelets Templating | `http://java.sun.com/jsf/facelets` | `http://xmlns.jcp.org/jsf/facelets` |
| Composite Components | `http://java.sun.com/jsf/composite` | `http://xmlns.jcp.org/jsf/composite` |
| JSTL Core | `http://java.sun.com/jsp/jstl/core` | `http://xmlns.jcp.org/jsp/jstl/core` |
| JSTL Functions | `http://java.sun.com/jsp/jstl/functions` | `http://xmlns.jcp.org/jsp/jstl/functions` |
| Pass Through Attributes | `http://java.sun.com/jsf/passthrough` | `http://xmlns.jcp.org/jsf/passthrough` |
| Pass Through Elements | `http://java.sun.com/jsf` | `http://xmlns.jcp.org/jsf` |
| `@FacesComponent` default namespace | | `http://xmlns.jcp.org/jsf/component` |

# JSF 2.2 programmatic configuration

Starting with JSF 2.2, we can programmatically reproduce the content and tasks of `faces-config.xml`. The starting point consists of a callback method, named `populateApplicationConfiguration`, which gets a single argument of type `org.w3c.dom.Document` — this class belongs to DOM API. Basically, a `Document` (tree node) is a representation in memory of an XML document, and we can manipulate it by adding, removing, importing, or adopting nodes, elements, and text. For each of these operations, there are dedicated methods. For some JSF developers, this API can be something new that should be learned; therefore, this can be a drawback of programmatic configuration.

For now, let's resume the dissertation from the callback method. The `populateApplicationConfiguration` method is provided by a class that extends and implements the abstract class `ApplicationConfigurationPopulator` found in the `javax.faces.application` package. In order to tell JSF about this class, you need to:

1. Create a JAR package (for example, `faces-config.jar` or by using any other name).

2. In this JAR package, create a folder named `META-INF`.

3. In the `META-INF` folder, create a folder named `services`.

4. In the `services` folder, create an empty file named `javax.faces.application.ApplicationConfigurationPopulator`.

5. In this file, write the fully qualified name of the class that extends and implements the abstract class `ApplicationConfigurationPopulator`.

6. In the JAR root, place the class that extends and implements the abstract class `ApplicationConfigurationPopulator`.

Done! Now when you add this JAR package in your project `CLASSPATH`, JSF will process it and apply the found configurations.

Supposing that the class that extends and implements the abstract class `ApplicationConfigurationPopulator` is named `faces.config.Initializer` (you can use any other name), then the JAR content will look like in the following screenshot:

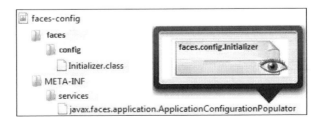

In this chapter, you will see some programmatic examples as an alternative to classical `faces-config.xml`. When we are working directly on a DOM tree node, we tend to make stupid mistakes, like forgetting to add the text of an element, or placing an element in an improper place, and so on. In order to eliminate these errors without headaches, you can write a simple method to serialize the DOM in an XML file, which can be easily debugged visually or using a specialized tool. The following method accomplishes this task, and you will find it in all the examples in this chapter:

```
private void serializeFacesConfig(Document document,String path) {

    FileOutputStream fileOutputStream = null;
    OutputFormat outputFormat = new OutputFormat();
    outputFormat.setIndent(5);
    outputFormat.setLineWidth(150);


    ...
    fileOutputStream = new FileOutputStream(path);

    XMLSerializer xmlSerializer = new XMLSerializer();
    xmlSerializer.setOutputFormat(outputFormat);
    xmlSerializer.setOutputByteStream((OutputStream)
                                        fileOutputStream);

    xmlSerializer.serialize(document);
    ...
}
```

# Configuring managed beans in XML

JSF managed bean configuration was essentially improved starting with JSF 2.0. Most commonly, a managed bean is annotated with @ManagedBean and another annotation indicating a JSF scope (for example, @RequestScoped). But managed beans can be configured in `faces-config.xml` as well, and this approach is not deprecated or obsolete. The simplest configuration contains the managed bean's name, class, and scope:

```
<managed-bean>
    <managed-bean-name>playersBean</managed-bean-name>
    <managed-bean-class>book.beans.PlayersBean</managed-bean-class>
    <managed-bean-scope>request</managed-bean-scope>
    ...
</managed-bean>
```

In case that you need a managed bean that should be eagerly initialized, you can use the `eager` attribute of the `<managed-bean>` tag:

```
<managed-bean eager="true">
```

Managed beans' properties can be initialized from `faces-config.xml` using the `<managed-property>` tag as follows:

```
<managed-property>
  <property-name>name</property-name>
  <value>Nadal</value>
</managed-property>
<managed-property>
  <property-name>surname</property-name>
  <value>Rafael</value>
</managed-property>
```

Inside the `<value>` tag, we can use EL expressions as well. For example, we can initialize a property of managed bean A with the value of a property belonging to managed bean B. But, it is important to know that JSF doesn't support cyclic dependency for managed bean reference—you cannot refer managed bean A from managed bean B, and vice versa.

An interesting case involves setting a property with the value of a context initialization parameter. Such parameters are configured in the deployment descriptor (`web.xml`):

```
<context-param>
  <param-name>rafakey</param-name>
  <param-value>Vamos Rafa!</param-value>
</context-param>
```

Programmatically, these kinds of parameters can be extracted through the initialization map or by their name, as follows:

```
FacesContext.getCurrentInstance().getExternalContext().
  getInitParameterMap();
FacesContext.getCurrentInstance().getExternalContext().
  getInitParameter(param_name);
```

These parameters can be accessed from `faces-config.xml` using the EL implicit object, `initParam`. JSF provides the ability to reference EL implicit objects from a managed bean property, as follows:

```
<managed-property>
  <property-name>rafakey</property-name>
  <value>#{initParam.rafakey}</value>
</managed-property>
```

From `faces-config.xml`, we can initialize more complex properties such as enumerations and collections. Consider the following enumeration:

```
public enum Plays {
    Left, Right
    };

private Plays play;

//getters and setters
...
```

The preceding property can be initialized as follows:

```
<managed-property>
  <property-name>play</property-name>
  <value>Left</value>
</managed-property>
```

In case of collections, we can easily initialize maps and lists. A map (`java.util.Map`) can be initialized as follows:

```
<managed-property>
  <property-name>matchfacts</property-name>
  <map-entries>
    <map-entry>
      <key>Aces</key>
      <value>12</value>
    </map-entry>
    <map-entry>
      <key>Double Faults</key>
      <value>2</value>
    </map-entry>
    <map-entry>
      <key>1st Serve</key>
      <value>70%</value>
```

```
        </map-entry>
      </map-entries>
  </managed-property>
```

While a list `java.util.List` (or array) can be initialized as follows:

```
<managed-property>
    <property-name>titles_2013</property-name>
    <list-entries>
        <value-class>java.lang.String</value-class>
        <value>Sao Paulo</value>
        <value>Acapulco</value>
        <value>Barcelona</value>
        <value>...</value>
    </list-entries>
</managed-property>
```

 A property can be initialized with a `null` value by using the `<null-value/>` tag.

If you prefer to configure managed beans in the XML descriptor (instead of using annotations), then it is a good practice is to place them into another descriptor and not in `faces-config.xml`. Keep this descriptor for application-level configurations. For example, you can name it `faces-beans.xml`. JSF will know how to use this file when it inspects the application descriptor, `web.xml`, for the following predefined context parameter:

```
<context-param>
    <param-name>javax.faces.CONFIG_FILES</param-name>
    <param-value>/WEB-INF/faces-beans.xml</param-value>
</context-param>
```

Now you can keep `faces-config.xml` for other configurations.

Obviously, it is much easier to use annotations instead of tags, but sometimes this approach can be really useful. For example, you can have some annotated managed beans whose behavior you want to change, but for different reasons you cannot edit the source code. In such a scenario, you can write the modifications in an XML file, because at runtime, configurations from the XML file will take precedence against annotations.

A complete example, named `ch4_12`, is available in the code bundle of this chapter.

The JSF 2.2 programmatic approach can reproduce the configuration file of the ch4_12 application as follows:

```
public class Initializer extends
  ApplicationConfigurationPopulator {

  @Override
  public void populateApplicationConfiguration
    (Document toPopulate) {

    String ns = toPopulate.getDocumentElement().getNamespaceURI();

    Element managedbeanEl = toPopulate.
      createElementNS(ns, "managed-bean");

    Element managedbeannameEl =
      toPopulate.createElementNS(ns, "managed-bean-name");
    managedbeannameEl.appendChild(toPopulate.createTextNode
      ("playersBean"));
    managedbeanEl.appendChild(managedbeannameEl);

    Element managedbeanclassEl = toPopulate.createElementNS
      (ns, "managed-bean-class");
    managedbeanclassEl.appendChild(toPopulate.
        createTextNode("book.beans.PlayersBean"));
    managedbeanEl.appendChild(managedbeanclassEl);

    Element managedbeanscopeEl = toPopulate.
        createElementNS(ns, "managed-bean-scope");
    managedbeanscopeEl.appendChild(toPopulate.
        createTextNode("request"));
    managedbeanEl.appendChild(managedbeanscopeEl);

    Element managedproperty0El = toPopulate.
        createElementNS(ns, "managed-property");
    Element propertyNameEl = toPopulate.
        createElementNS(ns, "property-name");
    propertyNameEl.appendChild(toPopulate.createTextNode("name"));
    Element valueNameEl = toPopulate.createElementNS(ns, "value");
    valueNameEl.appendChild(toPopulate.createTextNode("Nadal"));
    managedproperty0El.appendChild(propertyNameEl);
    managedproperty0El.appendChild(valueNameEl);
    managedbeanEl.appendChild(managedproperty0El);
    ...
    Element managedproperty5El = toPopulate.
```

```
      createElementNS(ns, "managed-property");
Element propertyMatchfactsEl = toPopulate.
      createElementNS(ns, "property-name");
propertyMatchfactsEl.appendChild(toPopulate.
      createTextNode("matchfacts"));
Element mapEntriesEl = toPopulate.
      createElementNS(ns, "map-entries");
Element mapEntry0El = toPopulate.
      createElementNS(ns, "map-entry");
Element key0El = toPopulate.createElementNS(ns, "key");
key0El.appendChild(toPopulate.createTextNode("Aces"));
Element value0El = toPopulate.createElementNS(ns, "value");
value0El.appendChild(toPopulate.createTextNode("12"));
mapEntry0El.appendChild(key0El);
mapEntry0El.appendChild(value0El);
...
mapEntriesEl.appendChild(mapEntry0El);
mapEntriesEl.appendChild(mapEntry1El);
mapEntriesEl.appendChild(mapEntry2El);
managedproperty5El.appendChild(propertyMatchfactsEl);
managedproperty5El.appendChild(mapEntriesEl);
managedbeanEl.appendChild(managedproperty5El);

Element managedproperty6El = toPopulate.
      createElementNS(ns, "managed-property");
Element propertyTitles_2013El = toPopulate.
      createElementNS(ns, "property-name");
propertyTitles_2013El.appendChild(toPopulate.
      createTextNode("titles_2013"));
Element listEntriesEl = toPopulate.
      createElementNS(ns, "list-entries");
Element valueClassEl = toPopulate.
      createElementNS(ns, "value-class");
valueClassEl.appendChild(toPopulate.
      createTextNode("java.lang.String"));
Element value01El = toPopulate.createElementNS(ns, "value");
value01El.appendChild(toPopulate.createTextNode("Sao Paulo"));
...
listEntriesEl.appendChild(valueClassEl);
listEntriesEl.appendChild(value01El);
listEntriesEl.appendChild(value11El);
listEntriesEl.appendChild(value21El);
listEntriesEl.appendChild(value31El);
listEntriesEl.appendChild(nullValue1El);
```

```
managedproperty6El.appendChild(propertyTitles_2013El);
managedproperty6El.appendChild(listEntriesEl);
managedbeanEl.appendChild(managedproperty6El);

toPopulate.getDocumentElement().appendChild(managedbeanEl);

//serializeFacesConfig(toPopulate, "D://faces-config.xml");
}
...
}
```

The complete application is named `ch4_14_1`.

# Working with multiple configuration files

JSF 2.0 provides support for ordering the configuration resources. We can use **partial ordering** (represented by the `<ordering>` tag) and **absolute ordering** (represented by the `<absolute-ordering>` tag).

 Each document that is involved in the ordering plan is identified by the top-level tag, `<name>`.

Partial ordering is specific to a single configuration document. We can use the `<before>` and `<after>` tags to indicate that a certain document should be processed before or after another document. Nested inside the `<before>` and `<after>` tags, we may have the `<others/>` tag, which indicates that a certain document should be processed before (respectively after) all the other documents that are sorted.

Listed here is an example where we have documents A, B, C, and `faces-config.xml` alias D:

1.  Document C needs to be executed before others; hence, it will be executed first:

    ```
    <name>C</name>
    <ordering>
      <before>
        <others/>
      </before>
    </ordering>
    ```

2.  Document B has no specified order; hence, it will be executed second:

    ```
    <name>B</name>
    ```

3. Document A needs to be executed after document B; hence, it will be executed third:

```
<name>A</name>
<ordering>
  <after>
    <name>B</name>
  </after>
</ordering>
```

4. Document D (`faces-config.xml`) is executed last and doesn't need any ordering specifications.

The order will be implementation-specific configuration resource, that is, C, B, A, and `faces-config.xml` (D).

> The ordering process (partial or absolute) has no effect over two documents: the respective implementation's (Mojarra or MyFaces) default configuration resource is always processed first, and `faces-config.xml` (if exists) is always processed last.

A simple test can be performed using several phase listeners and firing some customized messages. Each phase listener is configured in a separate document and some partial ordering schema is applied. A complete example can be found in the code bundle of this chapter and is named `ch4_13_1`. The console output will reveal the effect of partial ordering.

> If a document has ordering requirements, but no name, then the ordering requirements will be ignored.

The absolute ordering is accomplished by the `<absolute-ordering>` tag. This tag can appear only in `faces-config.xml` and provides us control over the order that configuration documents will be processed. For example, we have added the absolute ordering in the `faces-config.xml` document (alias document D) as follows:

```
<absolute-ordering>
  <others/>
  <name>C</name>
  <name>B</name>
  <name>A</name>
</absolute-ordering>
```

And, the processing order is: implementation specific configuration resource , C, B, A, and `faces-config.xml` (D).

The complete example for absolute ordering is named, `ch4_13_2`.

# Configuring locales and resource bundles

A properties file that contains messages can be named `PlayerMessages.properties`. When we have messages in several languages, we can create a properties file for each language and name it accordingly. For example, for English it will be `PlayerMessages_en.properties`, and for French it will be `PlayerMessages_fr.properties`. A convenient place to store them is in the application source folder directly or in subfolders (or, in NetBeans, under `Other Sources` folder in a Maven web application project). A resource bundle is capable of loading and displaying messages from these files.

A resource bundle can be configured locally or globally. A local resource bundle loads the properties file for the specified page only. For this, use the `<f:loadBundle>` tag as follows:

```
<f:loadBundle basename="players.msgs.PlayerMessages" var="msg"/>
```

A global resource bundle loads the properties file for all the JSF pages. In this case, we need a declarative loading in `faces-config.xml`:

```
<application>
  <resource-bundle>
    <base-name>players.msgs.PlayerMessages</base-name>
    <var>msg</var>
  </resource-bundle>
</application>
```

When we have files for multiple languages, we also have to indicate the locale. Locally, this is accomplished in the `<f:view>` tag by adding the locale attribute, as follows (here we indicate the French language):

```
<f:view locale="fr">
```

Globally, in `faces-config.xml`, we indicate the default locale via `<default-locale>` and the list of supported locales using the `<supported-locale>` tag:

```
<application>
  <locale-config>
    <default-locale>en</default-locale>
```

```
    <supported-locale>fr</supported-locale>
    <supported-locale>en</supported-locale>
  </locale-config>
  <resource-bundle>
    <base-name>players.msgs.PlayerMessages</base-name>
    <var>msg</var>
  </resource-bundle>
</application>
```

Programmatically, we may depict the locale as follows:

```
UIViewRoot viewRoot =
  FacesContext.getCurrentInstance().getViewRoot();
viewRoot.setLocale(new Locale("fr"));
```

A simple entry in the properties file will be as follows:

```
HELLO = Hello from Rafael Nadal!
```

The messages will be displayed using the `msg` variable (declared by the `var` attribute or the `<var>` tag):

```
#{msg['HELLO']}
```

But, messages can be more complex than static text. For example, they can be parameterized, as follows:

```
HELLOPARAM = Hello from {0} {1}!
```

And parameters can be replaced using the `<h:outputFormat>` tag:

```
<h:outputFormat value="#{msg['HELLOPARAM']}">
 <f:param value="Roger" />
 <f:param value="Federer" />
</h:outputFormat>
```

But, how about a message of the following type:

```
REGISTERED = You have {0} players registered!
```

When you have one player, the message will be as follows:

```
You have 1 players registered!
```

This is grammatically incorrect; therefore, you need to use a pattern similar to the following:

```
REGISTERED = You have {0} {0, choice, 0#players|1#player|2#players}
registered!
```

This will fix the problem. The arguments used here are explained as follows:

- `0, choice`: Take the first parameter and base the output on a choice of available formats
- `0#players`: If the first parameter contains 0 (or below), then it should print "players"
- `1#player`: If the first parameter contains 1, then it should print "player"
- `2#players`: If the first parameter contains 2 (or above), then it should print "players"

You can find the complete example under the name `ch4_4`, in the code bundle of this chapter.

 Do not confuse the `<resource-bundle>` tag with `<message-bundle>`. The former is used for registering custom localized static text, while the latter is used for registering custom error/info/warn messages, which are displayed by `<h:message>` and `<h:messages>`.

The `<message-bundle>` option is ideally used as follows:

```
<message-bundle>
    players.msgs.ErrorsMessages
</message-bundle>
```

The message file can be loaded with the `<f:loadBundle>` tag.

# Configuring validators and converters

Data validation is an important part of a JSF application (which has existed since JSF 1.2), because it allows us to separate the business logic from the tedious checks that help us to obtain only valid information from the user. Data is validated in the *Process Validations* phase (if the `immediate` attribute is set to `true`, this processing will occur at the end of the *Apply Request Values* phase instead) and should be valid and ready to be used before the *Update Model Values* phase.

Besides the built-in validators, we can write our own customized validators. A public class that implements the `Validator` interface and overrides the `validate` method is recognized by JSF as a **validator**. There are two ways to configure a validator in JSF: using the `@FacesValidator` annotation or the `<validator>` tag in `faces-config.xml`.

Suppose that we have the following e-mail validator configured using
`@FacesValidator`:

```
@FacesValidator(value = "emailValidator")
public class EmailValidator implements Validator {

  @Override
  public void validate(FacesContext context, UIComponent
    component, Object value) throws ValidatorException {

    ...
  }
}
}
```

 In JSF 2.2, the name can now be omitted from components, converters, and validators, so the preceding code will become `@FacesValidator`. Here, we need to note that when the name is omitted, JSF will use the class name, without the package name, with the first letter de-capitalized.

If you prefer to use `faces-config.xml`, then `EmailValidator` can be configured as follows:

```
<validator>
  <validator-id>emailValidator</validator-id>
  <validator-class>book.beans.EmailValidator</validator-class>
</validator>
```

Now, you can easily link `validator` to an input component:

```
<h:inputText value="#{bean property}">
  <f:validator validatorId="emailValidator"/>
</h:inputText>
```

An alternate way to do this is as follows:

```
<h:inputText value="#{bean property}" validator="emailValidator"/>
```

The complete example of `EmailValidator` is available in the code bundle of this chapter and is named `ch4_3_1`. Besides this application, consider, as a bonus, two applications that are useful when validators are involved. The first one is named `ch4_2`, and requires passing extra parameters to a validator using `<f:attribute>`, and the other one is named `ch4_11`, which is an example of validating multiple fields using a custom validator and the `<f:attribute>` tag. The latter one is also developed using the `PostValidateEvent` system event—check the *Configuring system event listeners* section later in this chapter.

Well, there are many articles about JSF validators, but just a few discuss injection in JSF validators. By default, JSF 2.0 does not support injection in validators, since only managed beans are injection targets, but there are several tricks that can bring dependency injection in discussion.

In order to obtain a validator eligible for injection, you need to apply the following modifications, which basically transform the validator into a bean:

1. Replace the @FacesValidator annotation with @Named or @ManagedBean (or even with a Spring annotation, @Component).

2. Put the bean in a request scope (use the proper @RequestScoped annotation)

```
@Named(value="emailValidator")
@RequestScoped
public class EmailValidator implements Validator {

    @Override
    public void validate(FacesContext context,
      UIComponent component, Object value)
      throws ValidatorException {
      ...
    }
}
```

3. Refer to it using the proper EL expression:

```
<h:inputText value="#{bean property}"
               validator="#{emailValidator.validate}" />
```

Done! Now, you can use @Inject in this validator.

The complete example is available in the code bundle of this chapter and is named ch4_3_2.

A more complicated task is to use @EJB for injecting **Enterprise JavaBeans (EJB)** session beans. In this case, we need to manually lookup the EJB session bean from **Java Naming and Directory Interface (JNDI)**. When the EJBs are deployed in **Web application ARchive (WAR)** the lookup generally is of the following type:

```
java:app/app-name/bean-name[! fully-qualified-interface-name]
```

When the EJBs are in an **Enterprise ARchive (EAR)**, the common lookup type is as follows:

```
java:global/app-name/module-name/bean-name[! fully-qualified-interface-name]
```

When EJBs are deployed in WAR, use the following approach:

```
@FacesValidator
public class EmailValidator implements Validator {

  private LoginEJBBean loginEJBBean;

  @Override
  public void validate(FacesContext context, UIComponent
    component, Object value) throws ValidatorException {

    try {
      loginEJBBean = (LoginEJBBean) new InitialContext().
              lookup("java:app/ch4_3_5/LoginEJBBean");
      } catch (NamingException e) {
        throw new ExceptionInInitializerError(e);
  }
}
...
```

When EJBs are deployed in the EAR, use the following approach:

```
@FacesValidator public class EmailValidator implements Validator {

  private LoginEJBBean loginEJBBean;

  @Override
  public void validate(FacesContext context,
        UIComponent component, Object value) throws ValidatorException
{

  try {
      loginEJBBean = (LoginEJBBean) new InitialContext().
      lookup("java:global/ch4_3_6/ch4_3_6-ejb/LoginEJBBean");
      } catch (NamingException e) {
        throw new ExceptionInInitializerError(e);
  }
}
...
```

You can find the complete examples in the code bundle of this chapter. The example for EJBs deployed in the WAR is named ch4_3_5, and the EJBs deployed in EAR case is named ch4_3_6.

These approaches are just some engrafts for bringing dependency injection in validators and this seems to be the only workaround in JSF 2.0. Starting with JSF 2.2, injection is possible in many more artifacts, but as the specification says, converters and validators are still not injection targets. It seems that this will be available from JSF 2.3.

Contrary to this affirmation, I tried to write a validator and use the injection as it should natively work. I used `@Inject` as follows where `LoginBean` is a CDI application scoped bean:

```
@FacesValidator
public class EmailValidator implements Validator {

 @Inject
 LoginBean loginBean;

 @Override
 public void validate(FacesContext context,
        UIComponent component, Object value) throws ValidatorException
{
. . .
```

Moreover, I also tried to inject an EJB using `@EJB` and `@Inject` where `LoginEJBBean` is a stateless session bean, as shown in the following code:

```
@FacesValidator
public class EmailValidator implements Validator {

 @EJB
 LoginEJBBean loginEJBBean;
 //@Inject
 //LoginEJBBean loginEJBBean;

 @Override
 public void validate(FacesContext context,
        UIComponent component, Object value) throws ValidatorException
{
. . .
```

I have to admit that I was expecting to see a `null` value for the injected resource, but surprisingly, everything worked as expected in all cases. There are rumors that, initially, the injection mechanism for validators and convertors was added in JSF 2.2, but it was removed at the last moment because some tests failed. Even if the preceding examples worked fine, it doesn't mean that is a good practice to use this approach in production. You'd better wait until it is guaranteed by the JSF team.

If you are a fan of OmniFaces, then you can use @Inject and @EJB with @FacesValidator. This great facility was added starting with Version 1.6 (http://showcase.omnifaces.org/cdi/FacesValidator). Moreover, MyFaces CODI (http://myfaces.apache.org/ extensions/cdi/) can also be a workaround, but it requires an additional @Advanced annotation.

The complete examples are available in the code bundle of this chapter and they are named ch4_3_3 (web application) and ch4_3_4 (enterprise application), respectively.

When discussing **converters**, let's remember that the conversion between two UIInput instances happens in the *Process Validations* phase (default), which can be moved to *Apply Request Values* phase using the immediate attribute set to true. For UIOutput, the conversion happens in the *Render Response* phase.

Beside the built-in converters, we can write our custom converters. A public class that implements the Converter interface and overrides the getAsObject and getAsString methods is recognized by JSF as a **converter**. There are two ways to configure a converter in JSF: using the @FacesConverter annotation or the <converter> tag in faces-config.xml.

Concerning we have the following converter configured using @FacesConverter (remember that JSF 2.2 doesn't need the value attribute):

```
@FacesConverter(value="playerConverter")
public class PlayerConverter implements Converter{

  @Override
  public Object getAsObject(FacesContext context,
              UIComponent component, String value) {
    PlayerName playerName = new
          PlayerName(value.toLowerCase(), value.toUpperCase());

    return playerName;
  }

  @Override
  public String getAsString(FacesContext context,
        UIComponent component, Object value) {

    PlayerName playerName = (PlayerName)value;

    return "Mr. " + playerName.getUppercase();
  }
}
```

If you prefer to use `faces-config.xml`, then `PlayerConverter` can be configured as follows:

```
<converter>
 <converter-id>playerConverter</converter-id>
 <converter-class>book.beans.PlayerConverter</converter-class>
</converter>
```

Now, you can easily link the converter to an input component as follows:

```
<h:inputText value="#{bean property}">
 <f:converter converterId="playerConverter"/>
</h:inputText>
```

An alternate way to do this is as follows:

```
<h:inputText value="#{bean property}" converter="playerConverter"/>
```

Moreover, you can write this as follows:

```
<h:inputText value="#{bean property}"/>
```

If you configure the converter using the `forClass` attribute, skip the `value` attribute as follows:

```
@FacesConverter(forClass=PlayerName.class)
```

The complete example of `PlayerConverter` is available in the code bundle of this chapter and it is named `ch4_6_1`.

Speaking about dependency injection, having converters as targets is pretty similar with the situation of validators:

1. Replace the `@FacesConverter` annotation with `@Named` and `@ManagedBean` (for Spring, you can use `@Component` also)

2. Put the bean in the request scope (use the proper `@RequestScoped` annotation) as follows:

```
@Named(value="playerConverter")
@RequestScoped
public class PlayerConverter implements Converter{

 @Override
 public Object getAsObject(FacesContext context,
         UIComponent component, String value) {
```

```
...
}

@Override
public String getAsString(FacesContext context,
        UIComponent component, Object value) {
...
}
}
```

3. Refer to it using the proper EL expression as follows:

```
<h:inputText value="#{bean property}" converter="#{playerConverter}"/>
```

The complete example can be found in the code bundle of this chapter and it is named ch4_6_2. EJBs can be injected in converters by looking up the EJB session bean from JNDI. Refer to the examples ch4_6_5 (EJBs in EAR) and ch4_6_6 (EJBs in WAR).

- The following block of code in the ch4_6_5 application; RandomEJBBean is a stateless session bean:

```
@FacesConverter(value = "playerConverter")
public class PlayerConverter implements Converter {

  private static RandomEJBBean randomEJBBean;

  static {
      try {
        randomEJBBean = (RandomEJBBean) new InitialContext().
         lookup("java:global/ch4_6_5/ch4_6_5-ejb/RandomEJBBean");
      } catch (NamingException e) {
        throw new ExceptionInInitializerError(e);
      }
}
...
```

- The following block of code in the ch4_6_6 application; RandomEJBBean is a stateless session bean:

```
@FacesConverter(value = "playerConverter")
public class PlayerConverter implements Converter {

    private static RandomEJBBean randomEJBBean;

    static {
```

```
        try {
            randomEJBBean = (RandomEJBBean) new InitialContext().
            lookup("java:app/ch4_6_6/RandomEJBBean");
        } catch (NamingException e) {
            throw new ExceptionInInitializerError(e);
        }
    }
    ...
```

Moreover, under GlassFish 4.0 and Mojarra 2.2.x, I was able to successfully run two applications that use injection in converters without any fancy workaround. See examples ch4_6_3 and ch4_6_4. Do remember that this approach is not officially adopted, however.

# Configuring navigation

Starting with JSF 2, navigation became much easier. Navigation can be accomplished using:

- Implicit navigation
- Conditional navigation
- Preemptive navigation
- Programmatic navigation

We can talk for hours and hours about JSF navigation, but there are a few golden rules that save us from falling for the most common mistakes when we need to choose between GET and POST. It might be useful to know that:

- It is recommended to use the GET request for page-to-page navigation, search forms, URLs that you want to be visible and bookmarkable, and, in general, for any idempotent request. By specification, GET, HEAD, PUT, DELETE, OPTIONS, and TRACE are idempotent.
- For requests that shouldn't be bookmarkable, use the same view repeatedly (use forward, not redirect).
- For requests that shouldn't be bookmarkable, but have bookmarkable targets, use POST and redirect.

# Implicit navigation

**Implicit navigation** interprets navigation outcomes as target view IDs. The simplest implicit navigation case is accomplished by JSF itself whenever you perform an action and no navigation is indicated. In this case, JSF will post a form (via HTTP POST) back to the current view (render the current view again).

Without declarative navigation in `faces-config.xml`, we can easily write navigation cases, such as the following where JSF 2 knows how to treat `outcome` (or the `action` value) as the targeted page name:

```
<h:outputLink value="success.xhtml">Success</h:outputLink>
<h:link value="Success" outcome="success"/>
<h:button value="Success" outcome="success"/>
<h:commandButton value="Success" action="success"/>
<h:commandLink value="Success" action="success"/>
```

> If the `success.xhtml` page exists, then all the given examples will navigate to this page. The `<h:outputLink>` element will navigate independently of JSF (that means it doesn't interact with JSF). The `<h:link>` and `<h:button>` elements will navigate via a bookmarkable GET request and aren't capable of form submissions (as you will see, this is actually preemptive navigation). The `<h:commandButton>` and `<h:commandLink>` elements are the main components for navigating within a JSF application. They fire POST requests and are capable of form submissions. Whenever you want to add the application context path in a URL (for example, the URL generated via `<h:outputLink>`, you can use the `ExternalContext.getApplicationContextPath` method of JSF 2.2. For example, take a look at the following code:
>
> ```
> <h:outputLink value="#{facesContext.externalContext.
> applicationContextPath}/next.xhtml">Next</h:outputLink>
> ```

The declarative version of this is as follows—thanks to implicit navigation, this code is not needed:

```
<navigation-rule>
 <from-view-id>*</from-view-id>
 <navigation-case>
  <from-outcome>success</from-outcome>
  <to-view-id>/success.xhtml</to-view-id>
 </navigation-case>
</navigation-rule>
```

The outcome of `<h:link>` and `<h:button>` are evaluated during the *Render Response* phase; therefore, the URLs are available right from the start of the corresponding view. On the other hand, when the button (`<h:commandButton>`) or link (`<h:commandLink>`) is clicked, JSF will merge the `action` value `success` with the XHTML extension and find the view name `success.xhtml` in the current page directory.

[ Wildcard ("*") is supported to specify a navigation rule that applies to all pages. It can be useful for a logout page. ]

The navigation case can also pass through a bean method, as follows:

```
<h:commandButton value="Success" action="#{playerBean.playerDone()}"/>
```

Also, the `PlayerBean` method is defined as follows:

```
public String playerDone() {
  logger.log(Level.INFO, "playerDone method called ...");
  return "success";
}
```

In these examples, the `outcome/action` values and the target view ID matches. However, the `outcome/action` values and target view ID are not always that simple. The `outcome/action` values are used to determine the target view ID even if they don't have the same root. For example, refer to the following code:

```
<h:commandButton value="Success" action="done"/>
```

The preceding code indicates the `done.xhtml` page, but this page doesn't exist; therefore, no navigation happens. We need to add a declarative navigation rule in `faces-config.xml` in order to link the `action` value (or the `outcome` value that is fetched via preemptive navigation, which we will see soon), `done`, with target view ID, `success.xhtml`. This navigation rule can be seen in the following code:

```
<navigation-rule>
 <from-view-id>/index.xhtml</from-view-id>
 <navigation-case>
   <from-outcome>done</from-outcome>
   <to-view-id>/success.xhtml</to-view-id>
 </navigation-case>
</navigation-rule>
```

If the bean method returns the outcome `done`, then the navigation rules are modified as follows:

```
<navigation-rule>
 <from-view-id>/index.xhtml</from-view-id>
 <navigation-case>
  <from-action>#{playerBean.playerDone()}</from-action>
  <from-outcome>done</from-outcome>
  <to-view-id>/success.xhtml</to-view-id>
 </navigation-case>
</navigation-rule>
```

By default, between **forward** and **redirect**, JSF will navigate from one page to another using the forward mechanism (HTTP POST). When JSF receives the user action, it will forward the user to the determined target page, which means that the URL displayed by the browser will not be updated to reflect the current target. Keeping the browser URL updated implies the page redirection mechanism; in this case, JSF, delegates the browser to send a separate GET request to the target page.

You can use the page redirection mechanism by attaching the `faces-redirect=true` parameter to the outcome query string as follows:

```
<h:commandButton value="Success" action="success?faces-
redirect=true;"/>
```

Alternatively, you can use the `<redirect/>` tag inside the navigation rule as follows:

```
<navigation-rule>
 <from-view-id>/index.xhtml</from-view-id>
 <navigation-case>
  <from-outcome>done</from-outcome>
  <to-view-id>/success.xhtml</to-view-id>
  <redirect/>
 </navigation-case>
</navigation-rule>
```

> In the forward case, the browser URL is not updated (is with a step behind navigation URL), but there is a single request. In the redirect case, the browser URL is up to date, but there are two requests. Since forward needs a single request, it is faster than page redirection. The speed is lower, but page redirection solves the duplicated form submission problem found in the Post-Redirect-Get design pattern. Of course, this is not the case for `<h:link>`, `<h:button>`, and `<h:outputLink>`.

These examples are grouped in the `ch4_5_1` application in the code bundle of this chapter.

# Conditional navigation

**Conditional navigation** allows us to specify preconditions for choosing the desired navigation case; a precondition must be met in order for the navigation case to be accepted. For this, we use the `<if>` tag as a child of the `<navigation-case>` tag and use an EL expression that can be evaluated to a Boolean value; here the `true` value matches the navigation case.

Let's have a simple button that logs the user into the application. This is done using the following code:

```
<h:commandButton value="Login" action="#{playerBean.playerLogin()}"/>
```

When the **Login** button is clicked, JSF will call the `playerLogin` method. This method will not return an outcome, actually it returns `void`. In this example, we simulate a login process through a random number and set a Boolean value, `login`, accordingly, as shown in the following code:

```
private boolean login  = false;
...
public boolean isLogin() {
  return login;
}

public void setLogin(boolean login) {
  this.login = login;
}

public void playerLogin() {

  Random random = new Random();
  int r = random.nextInt(10);
  if (r <= 5) {
   login = false;
   } else {
     login = true;
   }
 }
```

Next, we can use the `<if>` tag to decide if we navigate to the `success.xhtml` page (equivalent to `login` equals `true`) or to the `failed.xhtml` page (equivalent to `login` equals `false`):

```
<navigation-rule>
 <from-view-id>/index.xhtml</from-view-id>
 <navigation-case>
```

```
  <from-action>#{playerBean.playerLogin()}</from-action>
  <if>#{playerBean.login}</if>
  <to-view-id>/success.xhtml</to-view-id>
  <redirect/>
 </navigation-case>
 <navigation-case>
  <from-action>#{playerBean.playerLogin()}</from-action>
  <if>#{!playerBean.login}</if>
  <to-view-id>/failed.xhtml</to-view-id>
  <redirect/>
 </navigation-case>
</navigation-rule>
```

> In conditional navigation, the navigation cases are evaluated even when the outcome is null or void. Notice that there is no `<else>` tag or multiple conditional checking; therefore, in such cases, you have to emulate a switch statement. If you want to simply match the null outcome in any case, then you can use a condition of type: `<if>#{true}</if>`.
>
> Moreover, the sequence of the navigation rule affects the navigation flow; therefore, it is a good practice to prioritize conditions.

You can find the complete example in the code bundle of this chapter, under the name ch4_5_2.

We can write conditional navigation cases without the `<if>` tag by delegating the decision of choosing the navigation case to a bean method. For this, we have to replace the static value of the `<to-view-id>` tag with an EL expression, as follows:

```
<navigation-rule>
 <from-view-id>/index.xhtml</from-view-id>
 <navigation-case>
  <from-action>#{playerBean.playerLogin()}</from-action>
  <to-view-id>#{playerBean.navigateHelper()}</to-view-id>
  <redirect/>
 </navigation-case>
</navigation-rule>
```

Notice that this is not a real conditional navigation (since `<if>` is missing); therefore, we need to return an outcome from the `playerLogin` method:

```
public String playerLogin() {

  Random random = new Random();
  int r = random.nextInt(10);
  login = r > 5;
  return "done";
}
```

When the `login` property is set and the outcome `done` is returned, JSF will follow the preceding navigation case and reach for the `navigateHelper` method:

```
public String navigateHelper() {
  if (!login) {
   return "failed.xhtml";
  } else {
   return "success.xhtml";
  }
}
```

In a real application, the method that returns the outcome and the method that chooses the navigation case will probably be in different beans. If you take into account that you can pass arguments to the decisional method, then many navigation cases can be solved.

You can find the complete example in the code bundle of this chapter, under the name `ch4_5_3`.

# Preemptive navigation

**Preemptive navigation** is available starting with JSF 2.0. The navigation rules are more permissive and they are evaluated during the *Render Response* phase instead of the *Invoke Application* phase.

> This is known as predetermined navigation or preemptive navigation. The current view ID and specified outcome are used to determine the target view ID. Afterwards, the target view ID is translated into a bookmarkable URL and used as the hyperlink's target. Practically, the URL is prepared without user interaction.

The main usage of preemptive navigation appears in bookmarkable component tags, `<h:link>` and `<h:button>`. For example, the following are two classical examples of preemptive navigation:

```
<h:link value="Success" outcome="success"/>
<h:button value="Success" outcome="success"/>
```

When the application starts, you can check the source code of the page to see how the corresponding URLs were mapped in the HTML tag `<a>` in case of `<h:link>`, and the HTML tag `<input type="button">` in case of `<h:button>`. Even if you never use those URLs, they are ready to serve.

Well, before JSF 2.0, navigation rules were explicitly the domain of POST requests (`NavigationHandler.handleNavigation` was doing the dirty job behind the scene), but the new support for GET-based navigation and bookmarkability takes navigation to another level of flexibility and transparency (for example, the `ConfigurableNavigationHandler` API).

The interesting part here is how the query string of a URL is assembled. The simplest case consists of the implicit query string parameter as shown in the following code:

```
<h:link value="Done" outcome="done?id=done"/>
```

In *Chapter 2, Communication in JSF*, you saw how to build the query string using `<f:param>` and `<f:viewParam>`.

Another way consists in using the `<view-param>` tag nested in a `<redirect>` tag in a navigation case. For example, we can add query string parameters to a redirect URL in the navigation rules. Let's create the following button:

```
<h:commandButton value="Success" action="#{playerBean.playerDone()}"/>
```

Also, a silly method named `playerDone` is as follows:

```
private String player;

 public String getPlayer() {
  return player;
 }

 public void setPlayer(String player) {
  this.player = player;
 }

 public String playerDone() {
  player = "Rafael Nadal";
  return "done";
 }
```

Now, we can add the `player` property value (of course, you can add any other value) as a parameter in the query string of the redirection navigation URL:

```
<navigation-rule>
 <from-view-id>/index.xhtml</from-view-id>
 <navigation-case>
  <from-action>#{playerBean.playerDone()}</from-action>
  <from-outcome>done</from-outcome>
  <to-view-id>/success.xhtml</to-view-id>
  <redirect>
   <view-param>
    <name>playerparam</name>
    <value>#{playerBean.player}</value>
   </view-param>
  </redirect>
 </navigation-case>
</navigation-rule>
```

A URL like this will be of the format (notice how the request parameter was attached based on the navigation rule) http://*host*:*port*/*app-name*/faces/success. xhtml?playerparam=Rafael+Nadal.

The `playerparam` value will be available through the `param` implicit object:

```
#{param['playerparam']}
```

You can find the complete example in the code bundle of this chapter, under the name ch4_5_4.

# Programmatic Navigation

Sometimes, you need to control navigation directly from the application. JSF provides the `NavigationHandler` and `ConfigurableNavigationHandler` APIs that can be used for tasks such as accessing navigation cases, customizing navigation handlers, conditional navigations, and so on. It is good to know that, programmatically speaking, we can do the following:

1.  Obtain access to navigation handler (`NavigationHandler`) using the following code:

    ```
    FacesContext context = FacesContext.getCurrentInstance();
    Application application = context.getApplication();
    NavigationHandler nh = application.getNavigationHandler();
    ```

2. Invoke navigation case using `NavigationHandler` as follows:

```
nh.handleNavigation(context,fromAction,outcome);
nh.handleNavigation(context,fromAction,outcome,toFlowDocumentId);
```

3. Access the `ConfigurableNavigationHandler` API using the following code:

```
ConfigurableNavigationHandler cnh =
  (ConfigurableNavigationHandler) FacesContext.
  getCurrentInstance().getApplication().
  getNavigationHandler();
```

4. Invoke navigation case using `ConfigurableNavigationHandler` as follows:

```
cnh.handleNavigation(context,fromAction,outcome);
cnh.handleNavigation(context,fromAction,outcome,
 toFlowDocumentId);
```

5. Retrieve one `NavigationCase` object by the action expression signature and outcome as shown in the following code:

```
NavigationCase case = cnh.getNavigationCase(context,
 fromAction,outcome);
NavigationCase case = cnh.getNavigationCase(context,
 fromAction,outcome, toFlowDocumentId);
```

6. Access all navigation rules into `Map<String, Set<NavigationCase>>`, where the keys are the `<from-view-id>` values as follows:

```
Map<String, Set<NavigationCase>> cases =
  cnh.getNavigationCases();
```

> Starting with JSF 2.2, we have **wrappers** for many classes that provide basic implementations and help developers to extend those classes and override only the necessary methods. Among them, we have a wrapper class for `NavigationHandler`, named `NavigationHandlerWrapper`, one for `ConfigurableNavigationHandler`, named `ConfigurableNavigationHandlerWrapper`, and one for `NavigationCase`, named `NavigationCaseWrapper`.

In *Chapter 3, JSF Scopes – Lifespan and Use in Managed Beans Communication*, you saw a custom implementation of `ConfigurableNavigationHandler` in *The flow scope* section, and you saw a custom implementation of `NavigationHandler` in the *Controlling the custom scope lifespan with the navigation handler* section.

# Configuring action listeners

Action listeners are a great facility provided by JSF for dealing with action events. Commonly, action listeners are attached to command buttons (`<h:commandButton>`) or command links (`<h:commandLink>`) using the `actionListener` attribute.

When a button/link is clicked, JSF calls the action listener during the *Invoke Application* phase. Notice that if you are using `immediate="true"`, then the action listener is called during the *Apply Request Values* phase. The method, indicated as a listener, should be public, should return `void`, and should accept an `ActionEvent` object (this object can be used to access the component that invoked the action), which can perform specific tasks. When its execution has finished, JSF will call the method bound by the `action` attribute (if it exists!). This method is responsible to indicate the navigation case. The action listener method can alter the response returned by the action method.

As a practice, `actionListener` is used to have some "fun" before the real business and navigation task, which is the responsibility of `action`. So, do not abuse `actionListener` for solving business logic tasks!

Let's use an example of a simple command button that uses an action listener, as shown in the following code:

```
<h:commandButton value="Player Listener 1"
                 actionListener="#{playerBean.playerListener}"
                 action="#{playerBean.playerDone()}"/>
```

The `PlayerBean` contains the following code:

```
public void playerListener(ActionEvent e) {
  logger.log(Level.INFO, "playerListener method called ...");
}

public String playerDone() {
  logger.log(Level.INFO, "playerDone method called ...");
  return "done";
}
```

Well, the log messages reveal the order of calls as follows:

```
INFO:    playerListener method called ...
INFO:    playerDone method called ...
```

This kind of listener doesn't need any special configuration.

Another type of listener can be written by implementing the `ActionListener` interface and overriding the `processAction` method. In this case, we need to use the `<f:actionListener>` tag for attaching the action listener to a command button/link:

```
<h:commandButton value="Player Listener 2"
                 action="#{playerBean.playerDone()}">
  <f:actionListener type="book.beans.PlayerListener"/>
</h:commandButton>
```

Well, the `PlayerListener` is defined as follows:

```
public class PlayerListener implements ActionListener {

  private static final Logger logger =
        Logger.getLogger(PlayerListener.class.getName());

 @Override
 public void processAction(ActionEvent event)
                           throws AbortProcessingException {

  logger.log(Level.INFO, "Player listener class called ...");
 }
}
```

And, the output of the log messages will be as follows:

```
INFO:    Player listener class called ...
INFO:    playerDone method called ...
```

Again, these kinds of listeners do not need any special configurations.

> Starting with JSF 2.2 the `ActionListener` interface was wrapped in a simple implementation named, `ActionListenerWrapper`. You need to extend this class and override `getWrapped` to return the wrapped instance.

For example, the `PlayerListener` may be called via the following wrapper:

```
public class PlayerListenerW extends ActionListenerWrapper {

    PlayerListener playerListener = new PlayerListener();

    @Override
    public ActionListener getWrapped() {
        return playerListener;
    }
}
```

You can even combine these two listeners into a single command button, as follows:

```
<h:commandButton value="Player Listener 3"
                actionListener="#{playerBean.playerListener}"
                action="#{playerBean.playerDone()}">
  <f:actionListener type="book.beans.PlayerListener"/>
</h:commandButton>
```

In this case, the log messages are as follows:

```
INFO:    playerListener method called ...
INFO:    Player listener class called ...
INFO:    playerDone method called ...
```

 Well, this example gives us an important rule: the action listeners are invoked before `action` and in the same order as they are declared inside the component.

# Application action listeners

So far so good! The last category of action listeners are known as application action listeners. They are set on the application level and are called by JSF even for command buttons/links that do not specify any action listener explicitly. Such an action listener may look like the following code:

```
public class ApplicationPlayerListener implements ActionListener {

  private static final Logger logger =
          Logger.getLogger(PlayerListener.class.getName());
  private ActionListener actionListener;

  public ApplicationPlayerListener() {
  }

  public ApplicationPlayerListener(ActionListener actionListener) {
    this.actionListener = actionListener;
  }

  @Override
  public void processAction(ActionEvent event)
                    throws AbortProcessingException {

    logger.log(Level.INFO, "Application player listener class called
...");
```

```
        actionListener.processAction(event);
    }
}
```

This action listener will be called for a command button/link even if it doesn't specify it, as shown in the following code:

```
<h:commandButton value="Player Listener 4"
                 action="#{playerBean.playerDone()}" />
```

The output will be as follows:

```
INFO:    Application player listener class called ...
INFO:    playerDone method called ...
```

In JSF 2.2, we can write this implementation by extending ActionListenerWrapper as follows:

```
public class ApplicationPlayerListenerW extends ActionListenerWrapper
{

  private ActionListener actionListener;
  private static final Logger logger =
         Logger.getLogger(ApplicationPlayerListenerW.class.getName());

  public ApplicationPlayerListenerW(){}

  public ApplicationPlayerListenerW(ActionListener actionListener){
    this.actionListener = actionListener;
  }

  @Override
  public void processAction(ActionEvent event)
         throws AbortProcessingException {
  logger.log(Level.INFO, "Application player listener
                                   (wrapper) class called ...");
  getWrapped().processAction(event);
  }

  @Override
  public ActionListener getWrapped() {
   return this.actionListener;
  }
}
```

Application action listeners are called after the action listeners that are explicitly set via the `actionListener` attribute or the `<f:actionListener>` tag.

In order to be called, such listeners must be configured in `faces-config.xml`. For example, the preceding listener can be configured as follows:

```
<application>
 <action-listener>book.beans.ApplicationPlayerListener</action-
listener>
</application>
```

When you are using application action listeners, it is important to keep in mind a few things:

- Application action listeners cannot invoke other listeners.
- Application action listeners are responsible for processing the `action` attribute.
- Application action listeners cannot catch events from other listeners.

You have probably noticed that an action listener throws an `AbortProcessingException` exception. When this exception appears, JSF will directly jump to render the response and ignore further action listeners. The error is *swallowed* by default, so don't expect to see it! You can make it visible by altering the default mechanism of treating exceptions.

You might think that action listeners rock! Wait till you see this starting with JSF 2.2. We can use the injection mechanism for injecting CDI managed beans and EJBs in action listener classes. For example, the simple bean shown in the following code:

```
@Named
@RequestScoped
public class DemoBean {

    private String demo = "TEST INJECTION VALUE ...";

    public String getDemo() {
        return demo;
    }

    public void setDemo(String demo) {
        this.demo = demo;
    }
}
```

This bean can be injected in our application action listener as follows:

```
public class ApplicationPlayerListener implements ActionListener {

    @Inject
    private DemoBean demoBean;
...
```

Obviously, this facility opens new perspectives in implementing applications. And, as you will see next, injection mechanism is available for many other JSF artifacts that do not support it in JSF 2.0.

A complete example named ch4_1, is available in the code bundle of this chapter.

# Configuring system event listeners

JSF 2.0 allows us to use **system events**. These are events that can be fired by arbitrary objects at arbitrary points during the request processing lifecycle. Since the number of these events is quite big, you will not see them entirely covered here, but the next five examples should clarify the basic aspects of system events. You can find all of them in the javax.faces.event package.

# Using <f:event>

The easiest way to use system event listeners consists in passing the name of the managed bean method in the listener attribute of the <f:event> tag. For example, PostValidateEvent is a system event that gets fired after all components are validated. This can be useful to validate multiple components. Suppose, that a user submits a form that contains his name, surname, bank account, and the confirmation of that bank account (like a password that should be typed twice for confirmation). In order to check if the same bank account was typed in both fields, we can use PostValidateEvent, as follows:

```
<h:body>
 <h:form id="registerForm">
  <f:event listener="#{playersBean.validateAccount}"
          type="postValidate" />
  ...
  <h:inputText id="bankAccountId" value="#{playersBean.bank}"
              required="true" />
  <h:message for="bankAccountId" style="color: red;" />
  <h:inputText id="confirmBankAccountId"
```

```
            value="#{playersBean.cbank}" required="true" />
    <h:message for="confirmBankAccountId" style="color: red;" />
    <h:commandButton action="done" value="Send" />
  </h:form>
</h:body>
```

Now, in `PlayersBean`, we need to implement the `validateAccount` method as follows:

```
public void validateAccount(ComponentSystemEvent event) {

  UIComponent uis = event.getComponent();

  //obtain bank account
  String bankAccount = null;
  UIInput uiBankAccount = (UIInput)
        uis.findComponent("bankAccountId");
  Object bankAccountObj = uiBankAccount.getLocalValue();
  if (bankAccountObj != null) {
      bankAccount = String.valueOf(bankAccountObj).trim();
  }

  //obtain bank account confirmation
  String bankAccountC = null;
  UIInput uiBankAccountC = (UIInput)
        uis.findComponent("confirmBankAccountId");
  Object bankAccountCObj = uiBankAccountC.getLocalValue();
  if (bankAccountCObj != null) {
      bankAccountC = String.valueOf(bankAccountCObj).trim();
  }

  if ((bankAccount != null) && (bankAccountC != null)) {
      if (!bankAccount.equals(bankAccountC)) {
          FacesContext facesContext =
              FacesContext.getCurrentInstance();
          FacesMessage facesMessage = new FacesMessage("Bank
              account must match bank account confirmation !");

          facesMessage.setSeverity(FacesMessage.SEVERITY_ERROR);

          facesContext.addMessage(uiBankAccount.getClientId(),
              facesMessage);
          facesContext.renderResponse();
      }
  }
}
```

Done! If you don't provide the same bank account, then you will see the corresponding message. The complete application is named `ch4_7`.

# Implementing SystemEventListener

Another approach of handling system events is based on the following steps:

1. Implementing the `SystemEventListener` interface.
2. Overriding the `processEvent` and `isListenerForSource` methods.
3. Configuring the listener in `faces-config.xml`.

The registered system event can be fired by many kinds of sources (components). We can sort and accept certain sources in the `isListenerForSource` method. It returns `true` when the listener should receive events from the source passed to it as an argument (usually a simple test using the `instanceof` operator should do the work). When a source is accepted, the `processEvent` method is called and we can add a custom behavior.

For example, let's suppose that we want to remove certain resources included by JSF, such as CSS style sheets or JS scripts (it could be even resources added by third-party libraries). Speaking about CSS resources, they are always rendered in the HEAD section of an HTML page. Knowing that, we can configure our listener to be executed if the event source is a `UIViewRoot` instance. Further, we exploit JSF API to loop through the CSS resources and remove some of them (or, all of them). The code of our listener is pretty simple, as you can see in the following code:

```
public class ResourcesListener implements SystemEventListener {

  @Override
  public void processEvent(SystemEvent event)
            throws AbortProcessingException {

    FacesContext context = FacesContext.getCurrentInstance();

    int i = context.getViewRoot().
          getComponentResources(context, "HEAD").size() - 1;

    while (i >= 0) {
      UIComponent resource = context.getViewRoot().
              getComponentResources(context, "HEAD").get(i);

      String resourceLibrary = (String)
              resource.getAttributes().get("library");
```

```
    String resourceName = (String) resource.getAttributes().
get("name");

    if ((resourceLibrary.equals("default")) &&
            (resourceName.equals("css/roger.css"))) {
     context.getViewRoot().removeComponentResource
                            (context, resource, "HEAD");
    }
   i--;
   }
  }

  @Override
  public boolean isListenerForSource(Object source) {
   return (source instanceof UIViewRoot);
  }
 }
```

The listener should be configured in `faces-config.xml`, as follows:

```
<system-event-listener>
 <system-event-listener-class>
  book.beans.ResourcesListener
 </system-event-listener-class>
 <system-event-class>
  javax.faces.event.PreRenderViewEvent
 </system-event-class>
 <source-class>
  javax.faces.component.UIViewRoot
 </source-class>
</system-event-listener>
```

So, even if initially we write the following code:

```
<h:head>
 <h:outputStylesheet library="default" name="css/rafa.css"/>
 <h:outputStylesheet library="default" name="css/roger.css"/>
</h:head>
```

JSF will render the following code:

```
<head>
 <title></title>
 <link type="text/css" rel="stylesheet"
      href="/ch4_9_1/faces/javax.faces.resource/css/rafa.
css?ln=default">
</head>
```

The `<source-class>` tag is actually overriding the condition from the `isListenerForSource` method. So, you can always return `true` from the `isListenerForSource` method and use this tag, or vice versa.

You can find the complete example under the name `ch4_9_1`, in the code bundle of this chapter.

Now, let's see another example. A common approach, when some form input fields are invalid, is to color the background in red. In JSF 2.0, we can do that using the following code:

```
.ui-invalid {
    background-color:red
}
...
<h:inputText value="#{...}" required="true" styleClass="#{not
component.valid ? 'ui-invalid' : ''}" />
```

Well, that is really cool! But, if the form has several input fields, then we have to repeat the condition again and again, which isn't cool anymore! But, with a little magic, we can generalize this behavior. We can write a listener that will be executed only from the `UIInput` objects and modify their `styleClass` attribute based on the result returned by the `isValid` method:

```
public class InputValidationListener implements SystemEventListener {

  @Override
  public void processEvent(SystemEvent event)
            throws AbortProcessingException {

    UIInput inputSource = (UIInput) event.getSource();

    if(!inputSource.isValid()) {
      inputSource.getAttributes().put("styleClass", "ui-invalid");
    }
  }

  @Override
  public boolean isListenerForSource(Object source) {
   return (source instanceof UIInput);
  }
}
```

Of course, this is simple and there is nothing to explain. Actually, the key lies in the configuration file, because we have to choose the right system event from the plethora of available events. Since we need to color the background of invalid input fields in red, the right choice should be `PostValidateEvent`, as shown in the following code:

```
<system-event-listener>
 <system-event-listener-class>
  book.beans.InputValidationListener
 </system-event-listener-class>
 <system-event-class>
  javax.faces.event.PostValidateEvent
 </system-event-class>
 <source-class>
  javax.faces.component.html.HtmlInputText
 </source-class>
</system-event-listener>
```

Done! A functional example is available in the code bundle of this chapter and is named ch4_9_3. The JSF 2.2 programmatic reflection of this configuration is listed as follows:

```
public class Initializer extends
        ApplicationConfigurationPopulator {

  @Override
  public void populateApplicationConfiguration
        (Document toPopulate) {

   String ns = toPopulate.getDocumentElement().getNamespaceURI();

   Element applicationEl = toPopulate.
           createElementNS(ns, "application");
   Element systemeventlistenerEl = toPopulate.
           createElementNS(ns, "system-event-listener");
   Element systemeventlistenerclassEl =
           toPopulate.createElementNS(ns,
           "system-event-listener-class");
   systemeventlistenerclassEl.appendChild
           (toPopulate.createTextNode
           ("book.beans.InputValidationListener"));
```

```
Element systemeventclassEl = toPopulate.
        createElementNS(ns, "system-event-class");
systemeventclassEl.appendChild(toPopulate.
        createTextNode("javax.faces.event.PostValidateEvent"));
Element sourceclassEl = toPopulate.
        createElementNS(ns, "source-class");
sourceclassEl.appendChild(toPopulate.createTextNode
        ("javax.faces.component.html.HtmlInputText"));

systemeventlistenerEl.appendChild(systemeventlistenerclassEl);
systemeventlistenerEl.appendChild(systemeventclassEl);
systemeventlistenerEl.appendChild(sourceclassEl);
applicationEl.appendChild(systemeventlistenerEl);
toPopulate.getDocumentElement().appendChild(applicationEl);

//serializeFacesConfig(toPopulate, "D://faces-config.xml");
}
...
}
```

The complete application is named ch4_14_2.

 Starting with JSF 2.2, we can use dependency injection in system event listeners(@Inject and @EJB). For example, instead of hardcoding the CSS resources that we need to remove from HEAD, we can pass them through injection of a CDI bean or an EJB session bean. You can see a complete example in the code bundle of this chapter. This one is named ch4_9_2.

After you map the CSS classes names in a CDI bean (for example StyleResourcesBean) or EJB bean (for example StyleResourcesEJBBean), you can use any of the following injections:

```
@Inject
StyleResourcesBean styleResourcesBean;
@Inject
StyleResourcesEJBBean styleResourcesEJBBean;
@EJB
StyleResourcesEJBBean styleResourcesEJBBean;
```

Besides the injection facility, JSF 2.2 comes with a set of four brand new system events dedicated to Flash scope. These are:

- `PostKeepFlashValueEvent`: This event is fired when a value is kept in the Flash
- `PostPutFlashValueEvent`: This event is fired when a value is stored in the Flash
- `PreClearFlashEvent`: This event is fired before the Flash is cleared
- `PreRemoveFlashValueEvent`: This event is fired when a value is removed from the Flash

Remember that in *Chapter 2, Communication in JSF*, you saw an application based on the Flash scope. In this chapter, we will write a system event listener to monitor two of these events, `PostKeepFlashValueEvent` and `PreClearFlashEvent`. The code for this is as follows:

```java
public class FlashListener implements SystemEventListener {

private final static Logger LOGGER =
        Logger.getLogger(FlashListener.class.getName());

@Override
public void processEvent(SystemEvent event)
        throws AbortProcessingException {

if (event.getSource() instanceof String) {
  LOGGER.log(Level.INFO, "The following parameter was added
                     in flash scope: {0}", event.getSource());
} else if (event.getSource() instanceof Map) {
    LOGGER.info("Preparing to clear flash scope ...");
    LOGGER.info("Current content:");
    Iterator iterator = ((Map) event.getSource()).entrySet().
iterator();
    while (iterator.hasNext()) {
        Map.Entry mapEntry = (Map.Entry) iterator.next();
        LOGGER.log(Level.INFO, "{0}={1}", new
                Object[]{mapEntry.getKey(), mapEntry.getValue()});
    }
  }
}

@Override
public boolean isListenerForSource(Object source) {
  return ((source instanceof String) || (source instanceof Map));
}
}
```

Do not forget to configure the listener in `faces-config.xml` as follows:

```
<system-event-listener>
 <system-event-listener-class>
  book.beans.FlashListener
 </system-event-listener-class>
 <system-event-class>
  javax.faces.event.PostKeepFlashValueEvent
 </system-event-class>
</system-event-listener>
<system-event-listener>
 <system-event-listener-class>
  book.beans.FlashListener
 </system-event-listener-class>
 <system-event-class>
  javax.faces.event.PreClearFlashEvent
 </system-event-class>
</system-event-listener>
```

A functional example is available in the code bundle of this chapter, and is named `ch4_9_4`.

Generally speaking, from JSF 2.2 onwards, the `PostRestoreStateEvent` system event is published using `Application.publishEvent` without making `UIComponents` default listeners, but still doing the traditional tree traversal. This event was an exception for the rule in the previous JSF versions!

# Configuring phase listeners

As the name suggests, a **phase listener** is capable to listen to the start and end of each of the six JSF life-cycle phases (a detailed diagram of how JSF phases interact with each other is available in *Appendix, The JSF Life Cycle*):

- Restore the View phase
- Apply the Request Values phase
- Process the Validations phase
- Update the Model Values phase
- Invoke the Application phase
- Render the Response phase

You can easily capture the events of each phase by following these three steps:

1. Implementing the `PhaseListener` interface.
2. Overriding the `afterPhase`, `beforePhase`, and `getPhaseId` methods.
3. Configuring the phase listener in `faces-config.xml`.

A good point to start is a simple but useful `PhaseListener` that can be used to debug the phases. If you ever had the curiosity to see what is happening in JSF request lifecycle, then you can use this phase listener, which is defined as follows:

```java
public class DebugPhaseListener implements PhaseListener {

    public DebugPhaseListener() {
    }

    @Override
    public void afterPhase(PhaseEvent event) {
        System.out.println("After Phase: " + event.getPhaseId());
    }

    @Override
    public void beforePhase(PhaseEvent event) {
        System.out.println("Before Phase:" + event.getPhaseId());
    }

    @Override
    public PhaseId getPhaseId() {
        return PhaseId.ANY_PHASE;
    }
}
```

Finally, configure the custom phase listener in `faces-config.xml` as follows:

```xml
<lifecycle>
  <phase-listener>book.beans.DebugPhaseListener</phase-listener>
</lifecycle>
```

Now, you can play different scenarios with different pages and components to see the output. A simple scenario consists in an implicit navigation case, as you can see in application ch4_8_3, available in the code bundle of this chapter.

The programmatic reflection of this configuration in JSF 2.2 is as follows:

```java
public class Initializer extends
        ApplicationConfigurationPopulator {

  @Override
  public void populateApplicationConfiguration
        (Document toPopulate) {

  String ns = toPopulate.getDocumentElement().getNamespaceURI();

  Element lifecycleEl = toPopulate.createElementNS(ns, "lifecycle");
  Element phaselistenerEl = toPopulate.
        createElementNS(ns, "phase-listener");
  phaselistenerEl.appendChild(toPopulate.
        createTextNode("book.beans.DebugPhaseListener"));
  lifecycleEl.appendChild(phaselistenerEl);
  toPopulate.getDocumentElement().appendChild(lifecycleEl);

  serializeFacesConfig(toPopulate, "D://faces-config.xml");
  }
  ...
}
```

The complete application is named ch4_14_3.

 The get PhaseId method is used to determine the phases that pass through the listener. For capturing all the phase events, the method needs to return PhaseId.ANY_PHASE.

Phase listeners can also be used to alter components. For example, you can color the background of UIInput, based on the submitted value, by intercepting the *Render Response* phase as follows:

```java
public class PlayerPhaseListener implements PhaseListener {

  @Override
  public void afterPhase(PhaseEvent event) {
  }

  @Override
  public void beforePhase(PhaseEvent event) {
```

```
    processComponents(event.getFacesContext().getViewRoot());
  }

  @Override
  public PhaseId getPhaseId() {
   return PhaseId.RENDER_RESPONSE;
  }

  private void processComponents(UIComponent root) {
    for (UIComponent child : root.getChildren()) {
        if (child.getId().equals("playerId")) {
           HtmlInputText inputText = (HtmlInputText) child;
           String value = (String) inputText.getValue();

           if (value != null) {
              if (value.equalsIgnoreCase("rafa")) {
                  inputText.setStyleClass("rafa-style");
              } else if (value.equalsIgnoreCase("roger")) {
                       inputText.setStyleClass("roger-style");
              }
           }
        }
     processComponents(child);
    }
  }
}
```

The complete example is available in the code bundle of this chapter, and is named ch4_8_1.

> Starting with JSF 2.2, we can use dependency injection in phase listeners (@Inject and @EJB). For example, instead of hardcoding the CSS classes or the text against which we choose the CSS class, we can pass them through the injection of a CDI bean or an EJB session bean. You can see a complete example in the code bundle of this chapter under the name ch4_8_2.

After you map the CSS class' names in a CDI bean (for example, StyleResourcesBean) or an EJB bean (for example, StyleResourcesEJBBean), you can use any of the following injections in the phase listener as follows:

```
@Inject
StyleResourcesBean styleResourcesBean;
@Inject
```

```
StyleResourcesEJBBean styleResourcesEJBBean;
@EJB
StyleResourcesEJBBean styleResourcesEJBBean;
```

A phase listener can alter many kinds of JSF artifacts, not just UI components. For example, the following phase listener collects all FacesMessages and modifies the global ones. Obviously, you can choose to do anything else such as filter them by ID or save them in a special place.

```
public class MsgPhaseListener implements PhaseListener {

  private static final Logger logger =
   Logger.getLogger(MsgPhaseListener.class.getName());

  @Override
  public void afterPhase(PhaseEvent event) {}

  @Override
  public void beforePhase(PhaseEvent event) {
   FacesContext facesContext = event.getFacesContext();
   Iterator<String> ids = facesContext.getClientIdsWithMessages();

   while (ids.hasNext()) {
     String id = ids.next();
     Iterator<FacesMessage> messages = facesContext.getMessages(id);
     while (messages.hasNext()) {
           FacesMessage message = messages.next();
           logger.log(Level.INFO, "User ID:{0} Message: {1}"
                   , new Object[]{id, message.getSummary()});
           if(id == null){
              message.setSummary(message.getSummary() +
                         "alerted by a phase listener!");
           }
     }
   }
  }

  @Override
  public PhaseId getPhaseId() {
   return PhaseId.RENDER_RESPONSE;
  }
}
```

The complete application is named ch4_15.

# Working with @ListenerFor and @ListenersFor

The @ListenerFor annotation is an interesting annotation available from JSF 2.0. This annotation allows a component to subscribe to particular events with the component itself being the listener. For this, we need to follow the ensuing steps:

1. Implement the ComponentSystemEventListener interface (the name indicates that the event will always be associated with a UIComponent instance).

2. Override the processEvent method (here we can *play* with the component).

3. Use the @ListenerFor to indicate the event that the UI component will subscribe for, and the source class of the UI component.

For example, the UIInput component can subscribe to the PostAddToViewEvent event for adding attributes to the component, for example, following is a case, where we add some CSS to each UIInput component:

```
@ListenerFor(systemEventClass = PostAddToViewEvent.class, sourceClass
= javax.faces.component.UIInput.class)
public class PlayerRenderer extends TextRenderer
            implements ComponentSystemEventListener {

  @Override
  public void processEvent(ComponentSystemEvent event)
            throws AbortProcessingException {

   UIInput inputSource = (UIInput) event.getComponent();
   inputSource.getAttributes().put("styleClass", "rafa-style");
  }
}
```

The complete application is available in the code bundle of this chapter and is named ch4_10_1.

The @ListenersFor annotation allows a component to subscribe to more than one event. In the previous example, we have added some CSS to each UIInput component. Next, we want to extend this functionality by adding a separate CSS to the invalid UIInput components. For this, the UIInput components must subscribe to PostValidateEvent. This approach will help us to distinguish between the valid UIInput instances and invalid UIInput instances. The code for the same is as follows:

```
@ListenersFor({
  @ListenerFor(systemEventClass=PostAddToViewEvent.class,
            sourceClass = javax.faces.component.UIInput.class),
```

```
@ListenerFor(systemEventClass=PostValidateEvent.class,
                sourceClass = javax.faces.component.UIInput.class)
})
public class PlayerRenderer extends TextRenderer
        implements ComponentSystemEventListener {

@Override
 public void processEvent(ComponentSystemEvent event)
                            throws AbortProcessingException {

  UIInput inputSource = (UIInput) event.getComponent();
  inputSource.getAttributes().put("styleClass", "rafa-style");

  if(!inputSource.isValid()){
     inputSource.getAttributes().put("styleClass", "ui-invalid");
    }
  }
}
```

The complete application is available in the code bundle of this chapter and is named ch4_10_2.

 Starting with JSF 2.2, we can use dependency injection with `@ListenerFor`/`@ListenersFor` (`@Inject` and `@EJB`). For example, instead of hardcoding the CSS classes from the previous examples, we can pass them through injection of a CDI bean or an EJB session bean. You can see a complete example in the code bundle of this chapter, under the name ch4_10_3.

# Summary

Well, this was a pretty heavy chapter, but many of the important aspects in JSF were touched upon here. You learned how to create, extend, and configure several of the main JSF 2.x artifacts and how they have been improvised upon by JSF 2.2, especially with the dependency injection mechanism.

There are still a lot of things that were not discussed here; however, in the next chapter, we will continue this journey and cover other things, such as renders, handlers, and factories.

**5**

# JSF Configurations Using XML Files and Annotations – Part 2

In this chapter, we will continue to explore more situations where the `faces-config.xml` file will help us to accomplish different configuration tasks (of course, for some of them we have the alternative of annotations, while for others, we need to switch to the XML configuration level). Besides the examples presented in the previous chapter, this chapter will go deeper and cover the further list of tasks, which are as follows:

- Configuring resource handlers
- Configuring the View handler
- Overriding JSF renders
- Working with client behavior functionality
- Configuring the Global Exception handler
- Configuring render kit factory
- Configuring partial view context
- Configuring visit context
- Configuring external context
- Configuring Flash
- JSF 2.2 Window ID API

- Configuring lifecycle
- Configuring application
- Configuring VDL
- Combining multiple factory's powers

# Configuring resource handlers

Starting with JSF 2.0, all the web resources, such as CSS, JavaScript, and images are loaded from a folder named `resources`, present under the root of your web application or from `/META-INF/resources` in JAR files. A folder under the `resources` folder is known as a `library` or `theme`, which is like a collection of client artifacts. We can also create a special folder matching the regex `\d+(_\d+)*` under the `library` folder for providing versioning. In this case, the default JSF resource handler will always retrieve the newest version to display. The various approaches that can be followed for structuring the `resources` folder are as shown in the following figure:

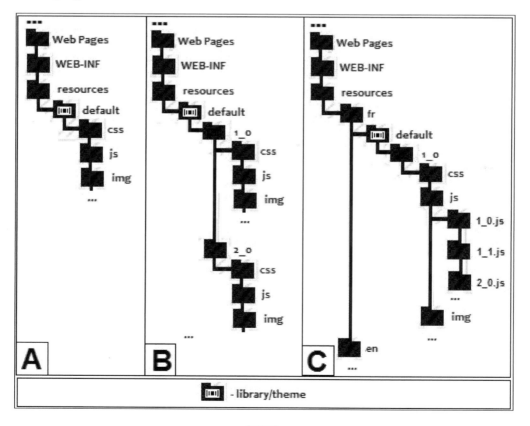

In the preceding figure, part **A** depicts a common structure of the `resources` folder without versioning, and in part **B**, you have the versioning approach. The folders `css`, `js`, `img`, and others usually denote the content type of files inside them; however, this is not mandatory.

 Note that the library name shouldn't denote the content type.

Part **C**, represents the complete structure of the subfolders supported under the `resources` folder. In this case, we entirely exploit the automatic localization and version management, which works if we respect the following structure under the `resources` folder and is known as *resourceIdentifier* (the `[]` demarcate optional parts):

```
[localePrefix/] [libraryName/] [libraryVersion/] resourceName [/
resourceVersion]
```

 In the case of face flows packaged within JAR files, resources packaged in `CLASSPATH` must reside under the JAR entry name `META-INF/flows/resourceIdentifier`.

We will also discuss the case referred to in part **A**, since this is the most used case. But for the sake of completeness, you can check the complete application named `ch5_12`, which represents an implementation case from part **C** (that includes part **B** as well).

So, having the structure from the preceding figure, we can easily load a CSS file (`rafa.css`) using the following code:

```
<h:outputStylesheet library="default" name="css/rafa.css"/>
```

Alternatively, you can load a JavaScript file (`rafa.js`) using the following code:

```
<h:outputScript library="default" name="js/rafa.js"/>
```

Alternatively, you can load an image file (`rafa.png`) using the following code:

```
<h:graphicImage library="default" name="img/rafa.png"/>
```

So, this is how the JSF default resource handler deals with resources. But what can we do if we don't respect this inflexible structure of folders? For example, if we have the CSS files under the application web root in `/players/css/`, or we want to place resources in a protected folder, such as `WEB-INF` (probably the biggest disadvantage of the `resources` folder is that everything in it is accessible from outside by default). In this case, there is no directly accessible `resources` folder and we have no idea what a library is. If we write something like the following code, it will not work:

```
<h:outputStylesheet name="rafa.css"  />
```

Among the possible solutions, we have the facility to write a custom resource handler. It is much simpler than it sounds, because JSF provides several wrappers (implements `FacesWrapper`) that help us to write custom handlers and factories by overriding only the methods that we want to affect. In case of a custom resource handler, we need to perform the following steps:

1.  Extend the `ResourceHandlerWrapper` class.
2.  Write a delegating constructor. JSF will call this constructor for passing the standard resource handler, which we will wrap in a `ResourceHandler` instance. We can also obtain this instance by overriding the `getWrapped` method.
3.  Override the `createResource` method. Here, we can sort the resources and decide which of them go to the default resource handler and which of them go to our custom resource handler.

The following implementation is based on the preceding three steps:

```
public class CustomResourceHandler extends
               javax.faces.application.ResourceHandlerWrapper {

  private ResourceHandler wrapped;

  public CustomResourceHandler(ResourceHandler wrapped) {
   this.wrapped = wrapped;
  }

  @Override
  public ResourceHandler getWrapped() {
   return this.wrapped;
  }

  @Override
```

```
public Resource createResource(String resourceName, String
libraryName){

    if ((!resourceName.equals("rafa.css")) &&
        (!resourceName.equals("roger.css"))) {
        //in JSF 2.0 and JSF 2.2
        //return super.createResource(resourceName, libraryName);
        //only in JSF 2.2
        return super.createResourceFromId
          (libraryName+"/"+resourceName);
    } else {
        return new PlayerResource(resourceName);
    }


  }
}
```

The PlayerResource class is our custom resource. The main aim of PlayerResource is to indicate the correct path /players/css/, which is not recognized by default. For this, we extend another wrapper named ResourceWrapper and override the method getRequestPath, as follows, where we delegate all calls to ResourceWrapper except one call, getRequestPath:

```
public class PlayerResource extends
        javax.faces.application.ResourceWrapper {

  private String resourceName;

  public PlayerResource(String resourceName) {
   this.resourceName = resourceName;
  }

  @Override
  public Resource getWrapped() {
   return this;
  }

  @Override
  public String getRequestPath() {
   return "players/css/" + this.resourceName;
  }
}
```

Next, you have to configure the custom resource handler in `faces-config.xml` as follows:

```
<application>
 <resource-handler>book.beans.CustomResourceHandler</resource-handler>
</application>
```

Now, if you try to load the `rafa.css` (or `roger.css`) file, you can add the following lines of code:

```
<h:outputStylesheet name="rafa.css"/>
<h:outputStylesheet name="roger.css"/>
```

The complete application is named `ch5_1_1` and is available in the code bundle of this chapter.

However, remember that I said "Among the possible solutions ..."? Well, starting with JSF 2.2, we can indicate the folder of resources through a context parameter in the `web.xml` descriptor, as follows (mapped by the `ResourceHandler.WEBAPP_RESOURCES_DIRECTORY_PARAM_NAME` field):

```
<context-param>
 <param-name>javax.faces.WEBAPP_RESOURCES_DIRECTORY</param-name>
 <param-value>/players/css</param-value>
</context-param>
```

Or, we can place the `resources` folder under `WEB-INF`, which can be accessed by JSF from inside `WEB-INF` but never from outside:

```
<context-param>
 <param-name>javax.faces.WEBAPP_RESOURCES_DIRECTORY</param-name>
 <param-value>/WEB-INF/resources</param-value>
</context-param>
```

A complete example named `ch5_1_2` is available in the code bundle of this chapter.

A custom resource handler can be useful to pass extra parameters to the linking file (for example CSS, JS, images, and so on). We can use this approach to reset the browser cache. Browsers cache static resources such as CSS, JS, and images; therefore they are not requested from the server each time the web page loads. We can force this by adding a parameter to the linking file in the query string, representing a version number or something that makes the browser to understand that it should load the resource from the server, not from the cache.

In this case, we assume that the `rafa.css` file is under the `/resources/default/css/` folder and it is loaded using the following code:

```
<h:outputStylesheet library="default" name="css/rafa.css"/>
```

At this moment, the generated HTML is as follows:

```
<link type="text/css" rel="stylesheet"
  href="/ch5_1_3/faces/javax.faces.resource/css/rafa.css?ln=
  default" />
```

Also, we want to obtain something like the following code:

```
<link type="text/css" rel="stylesheet" href="/ch5_1_3/faces/javax.
faces.resource/css/rafa.css?ln=default&amp;v=v4.2.1">
```

For this, we need to override the `createResource` method as follows:

```
@Override
public Resource createResource(String resourceName, String
libraryName) {
    Resource resource = super.createResource(resourceName, libraryName);
    return new PlayerResource(resource);
}
```

Also, `PlayerResource` is responsible to add the version parameter in the `getRequestPath` method:

```
@Override
public String getRequestPath() {
  String requestPath = resource.getRequestPath();

  logger.log (Level.INFO, "Initial request path is: {0}", requestPath);

  String new_version = "v4.2.1";

  if(requestPath.contains("?"))
     requestPath = requestPath + "&v=" + new_version;
  else
     requestPath = requestPath + "?v=" + new_version;

  logger.log (Level.INFO, "New request path is: {0}", requestPath);

  return requestPath;
}
```

The complete application is available in the code bundle named ch5_1_3.

Of course, in real cases, unlike in the preceding code, the version number is not hardcoded. Knowing that JSF 2.2 allows us to use dependency injection in custom resource handlers, we can inject the parameter values from a bean that can play the role of a version tracking system using the following code:

```
public class CustomResourceHandler extends
        javax.faces.application.ResourceHandlerWrapper {

@Inject
private VersionBean versionBean;

. . .
@Override
public Resource createResource(String resourceName, String
libraryName) {

  Resource resource = super.createResource(resourceName, libraryName);
  return new PlayerResource(resource, versionBean.getVersion());
}
. . .
```

The complete example is named ch5_1_4.

> You can also use the versioning system of JSF for invalidate browser cache, but you need to create the right folder under the library folder. - JSF will automatically load the last version. Passing parameters as we have seen earlier can be useful for many other things, such as generating customized JS and CSS response. Servers can access such parameters and JS as well.

Browser caching can also be controlled with two context parameters in the web.xml descriptor (specific to Mojarra) as follows:

- com.sun.faces.defaultResourceMaxAge: This parameter can be used to set the expiry time in milliseconds.

- com.sun.faces.resourceUpdateCheckPeriod: This parameter gives frequency in minutes to check for changes in web application artifacts that contain resources.

JSF resource handling provides solid advantages such as caching and loading resources within a JAR or writing custom UI components that contain CSS or JS, but it also has some disadvantages. For example, web designers use the static approach to add images in CSS, as follows:

```
background-image: url(link_to_image)
```

However, when importing CSS style sheets using `<h:outputStyleSheet>`, the style sheet is imported and processed by FacesServlet through the `/javax.faces. resource/*` folder, which makes the picture relative path unavailable (in this case, the CSS file becomes a JSF resource). One of the solutions is to force the image URL to become a JSF resource, using the resource mapper in EL, `#{resource}`, as `#{re source['library:location']}`. For example, in `rafa.css` (loaded in the page via `<h:outputStylesheet>`), we can load the `rafa.png` image using the following code:

```
body {
    background-image: url('#{resource["default:img/rafa.png"]}')
}
```

Based on this, `<h:graphicImage>` can load `rafa.png` as follows:

```
<h:graphicImage value="#{resource['default:img/rafa.png']}"/>
```

You can check these examples in the application named `ch5_13`.

As an alternative, you can use OmniFaces library's `UnmappedResourceHandler`, which spares us from modifying the CSS files (`http://showcase.omnifaces.org/ resourcehandlers/UnmappedResourceHandler`). Moreover, another approach consists in writing a custom `ResourceHandler` that can fix this issue.

 From JSF 2.2 onwards, `ResourceResolver` has been merged into `ResourceHandler`, and `ResourceResolver` itself has been deprecated. These two are detailed in *Chapter 12, Facelets Templating*.

# Adding CSS and JS resources programmatically

Sometimes, you may need to load the CSS and JS resources by specifying them in a managed bean method. For example, the following method loads `rafa.css` and `rafa.js` in a programmatic fashion:

```
public void addResourcesAction() {
  FacesContext facesContext = FacesContext.getCurrentInstance();
  UIOutput rafa_css = new UIOutput();
```

```
UIOutput rafa_js = new UIOutput();

rafa_css.setRendererType("javax.faces.resource.Stylesheet");
rafa_css.getAttributes().put("library", "default");
rafa_css.getAttributes().put("name", "css/rafa.css");
rafa_js.setRendererType("javax.faces.resource.Script");
rafa_js.getAttributes().put("library", "default");
rafa_js.getAttributes().put("name", "js/rafa.js");
facesContext.getViewRoot().addComponentResource
        (facesContext, rafa_css, "head");
facesContext.getViewRoot().addComponentResource
        (facesContext, rafa_js, "head");
}
```

The complete application is named ch5_14.

# Configuring the view handler

JSF provides a view handler that can be used for working with views. It can be a very handy tool when you want to interact with a view or create/restore/extend/modify a view. It is also good practice to deal with URLs here, which is exactly what you will see next.

 A view handler is not a good choice when you need to work with components! Even if this is possible, view handlers were not created for such tasks.

Sometimes you may need to convert absolute URLs into relative URLs. For example, if you run an application behind a reverse proxy, you may need to provide relative URLs. By default, the browser appends each absolute URL to the host, which is obviously a big issue.

In order to convert absolute URLs into relative URLs, we need to perform the following steps:

- Create a new view handler by extending the ViewHandlerWrapper class. Extending this wrapper allows us to override only the required methods.
- Override the getActionURL and getResourceURL methods.
- Configure the view handler in faces-config.xml.

Although it may sound pompous, the following code is self-explanatory:

```java
public class URLHandler extends ViewHandlerWrapper {

 private ViewHandler baseViewHandler;

 public URLHandler(ViewHandler baseViewHandler) {
  this.baseViewHandler = baseViewHandler;
 }

 @Override
  public String getActionURL(FacesContext context, String viewId) {
   return convertToRelativeURL(context,
         baseViewHandler.getActionURL(context, viewId));
 }

 @Override
 public String getResourceURL(FacesContext context, String path) {
  return convertToRelativeURL(context,
        baseViewHandler.getResourceURL(context, path));
 }

 @Override
 public ViewHandler getWrapped() {
  return baseViewHandler;
 }

 private String convertToRelativeURL(FacesContext context,
                                            String theURL){

 final HttpServletRequest request = ((HttpServletRequest)
                         context.getExternalContext().getRequest());
 final URI uri;
 String prefix = "";

 String string_uri = request.getRequestURI();

 try {
     uri = new URI(string_uri);
 } catch (URISyntaxException ex) {
     Logger.getLogger(URLHandler.class.getName()).
                            log(Level.SEVERE, null, ex);
```

```
        return "";
    }


    String path = uri.getPath();
    String new_path = path.replace("//", "/");

    if (theURL.startsWith("/")) {
        int count = new_path.length() - new_path.replace("/", "").
length();
        for (int i = 0; i < (count - 1); i++) {
            prefix = prefix + "/..";
        }
        if (prefix.length() > 0) {
            prefix = prefix.substring(1);
        }
    }


    return (prefix + theURL);
    }
}
```

The required configuration in `faces-config.xml` is as follows:

```
...
<application>
 <view-handler>book.beans.URLHandler</view-handler>
</application>
...
```

The complete application is available in the code bundle named `ch5_2_1`.

If you check the source code of the `index.xhtml` page, you will notice that instead of an absolute URL for the CSS resource, there is a relative one, of the following type:

```
<link type="text/css" rel="stylesheet" href="../ch5_2_1/faces/javax.
faces.resource/css/rafa.css?ln=default">
```

Done! Now you can run the application behind a reverse proxy.

Another useful view handler is the one that "swallows" the `ViewExpiredException` exception. This exception is thrown when a user session expires. Through a view handler, we can treat this exception by recreating the user view. Redirect the flow to a special page (let's name it `expired.xhtml`).

When the user session expires, `UIViewRoot` of the application is set to `null`. We can use this check in the `restoreView` method, as follows:

```java
public class ExceptionHandler extends ViewHandlerWrapper {

  private static final Logger logger =
          Logger.getLogger(ExceptionHandler.class.getName());
  private ViewHandler baseViewHandler;

  public ExceptionHandler(ViewHandler baseViewHandler) {
          this.baseViewHandler = baseViewHandler;
  }

  @Override
  public UIViewRoot restoreView(FacesContext context, String viewId) {

    UIViewRoot root;

    root = baseViewHandler.restoreView(context, viewId);
    if (root == null) {
        logger.info("The session has expired ...
                    I will not allow ViewExpiredException ...");
        root = createView(context, viewId);

        //root = createView(context, "/expired.xhtml");
        //context.renderResponse();
    }
    return root;
  }

  @Override
  public ViewHandler getWrapped() {
    return baseViewHandler;
  }
}
```

The configuration in `faces-config.xml` is as follows:

```xml
...
<application>
 <view-handler>book.beans.ExceptionHandler</view-handler>
</application>
...
```

The complete application is available in the code bundle and is named `ch5_2_2`.

 Starting with JSF 2.2, we can use dependency injection with the view handler (`@Inject` and `@EJB`).

# Overriding JSF renders

The main responsibilities of a `Renderer` consists of generating the appropriate client-side markup, such as HTML, WML, and XUL, and converting information coming from the client to the proper type for the component.

JSF provides a set of built-in renders and has the capability to extend them with custom behavior. If you consider a proper workaround to override a built-in render, then perform the following steps:

1. Extend the desired built-in renderer (for example, `Renderer`, `TextRenderer`, `LabelRenderer`, `MessagesRenderer`, and so on).

2. Override the built-in renderer methods.

3. Configure the new renderer in `faces-config.xml` or using the `@FacesRenderer` annotation.

Well, let's see some examples of writing a custom render. For example, let's suppose that we have three attributes (`player-nickname`, `player-mother-name`, and `player-father-name`) that we want to use inside the `<h:inputText>` tag. If you try to write the following code:

```
<h:inputText value="Rafael Nadal" player-nickname="Rafa"
   player-mother-name="Ana Maria Parera" player-father-name=
   "Sebastián Nadal" player-coach-name=" Toni Nadal"/>
```

Then, the built-in renderer will give the following output:

```
<input id="..." name="..."
        value="Rafael Nadal" type="text">
```

Obviously, our three attributes were ignored. We can fix this by extending `TextRenderer` as follows:

```
public class PlayerInputTextRenderer extends TextRenderer {

public PlayerInputTextRenderer(){}

@Override
 protected void getEndTextToRender(FacesContext context,
```

```
                    UIComponent component, String currentValue)
                    throws java.io.IOException {

    String[] attributes = {"player-nickname",
            "player-mother-name", "player-father-name"};
    ResponseWriter writer = context.getResponseWriter();
    for (String attribute : attributes) {
        String value = (String) component.getAttributes().
get(attribute);
        if (value != null) {
            writer.writeAttribute(attribute, value, attribute);
        }
    }
    super.getEndTextToRender(context, component, currentValue);
    }
}
```

Done! Configure the new renderer in `faces-config.xml` as follows:

```
<application>
 <render-kit>
  <renderer>
   <component-family>javax.faces.Input</component-family>
   <renderer-type>javax.faces.Text</renderer-type>
   <renderer-class>book.beans.PlayerInputTextRenderer</renderer-class>
  </renderer>
 </render-kit>
</application>
```

Now, the renderer input field will be as follows:

```
<input id="..." name="..." player-nickname="Rafa" player-mother-
name="Ana Maria Parera" player-father-name="Sebastián Nadal"
value="Rafael Nadal" type="text">
```

Instead of configuring the custom renderer in `faces-config.xml`,
we could use the `@FacesRenderer` annotation, as follows:

```
@FacesRenderer(componentFamily="javax.faces.
Input",rendererType="javax.faces.Text")
```

But, unfortunately this isn't working. There seems to be a bug here!

The complete example is named `ch5_4_1`.

Let's look at another example in order to fortify the knowledge about writing custom renderers. The next example will modify the built-in `LabelRenderer` class by adding an image in front of each `<h:outputText>` tag, as shown in the following code:

```
public class RafaLabelRenderer extends LabelRenderer{

  public RafaLabelRenderer(){}

  @Override
  public void encodeEnd(FacesContext context,
              UIComponent component)throws IOException{

   ResponseWriter responseWriter = context.getResponseWriter();
   responseWriter.write("<img src='resources/default/img/logo.png'/>");
  }
 }
```

Don't forget to configure the renderer in `faces-config.xml` as follows:

```
<component-family>javax.faces.Output</component-family>
<renderer-type>javax.faces.Text</renderer-type>
<renderer-class>book.beans.RafaLabelRenderer</renderer-class>
```

 Starting with JSF 2.2, we can use dependency injection in renderers (`@Inject` and `@EJB`). The complete example of the preceding renderer is named ch5_4_2 (the image name was provided by another bean through injection dependency).

The upcoming example in this section is a little bit tricky.

If you have used PrimeFaces, especially the `<p:messages>` tag, then you know that this tag accepts an attribute named `escape`. The attribute's value can be `true` or `false`, and it defines whether HTML would be escaped or not (defaults to `true`).

Unfortunately, JSF 2.2 still doesn't provide such attributes for the `<h:messages>` tag, but there is at least a workaround to solve this. You can implement a custom renderer that is capable of understanding the `escape` attribute.

JSF provides a class named `ResponseWriter`, which is useful in this case because it provides methods capable of producing elements and attributes for markup languages such as HTML and XML. Moreover, JSF provides a wrapper for this class named `ResponseWriterWrapper`. We can easily extend this class, and override the method `writeText`, which is useful for writing escaped strings obtained from objects by conversions. Un-escaped strings are written by the `write` method.

So, based on this information, we can easily write our response writer, as follows:

```java
public class EscapeResponseWriter extends ResponseWriterWrapper {

  private ResponseWriter responseWriter;

  public EscapeResponseWriter(ResponseWriter responseWriter) {
    this.responseWriter = responseWriter;
  }

  @Override
  public ResponseWriter getWrapped() {
    return responseWriter;
  }

  @Override
  public void writeText(Object text, UIComponent component,
                        String property) throws IOException {

    String escape = (String) component.getAttributes().get("escape");
    if (escape != null) {
        if ("false".equals(escape)) {
            super.write(String.valueOf(text));
        } else {
            super.writeText(String.valueOf(text), component, property);
        }
    }
  }
}
```

So far, so good! Now we need to write the custom renderer, as shown in the following code, by extending the `MessagesRenderer` class, which is the default renderer for JSF messages. The only method we need to affect is the `encodeEnd` method, by placing our response writer instead of the default one. In the end, we restore it to default.

```java
public class EscapeMessagesRenderer extends MessagesRenderer {

  public EscapeMessagesRenderer(){}

  @Override
  public void encodeEnd(FacesContext context,
          UIComponent component) throws IOException {

    ResponseWriter responseWriter = context.getResponseWriter();
```

```
context.setResponseWriter(new EscapeResponseWriter(responseWriter));
super.encodeEnd(context, component);
context.setResponseWriter(responseWriter);
  }
}
```

Finally, configure the new renderer in `faces-config.xml` as follows:

```
<renderer>
  <component-family>javax.faces.Messages</component-family>
  <renderer-type>javax.faces.Messages</renderer-type>
  <renderer-class>book.beans.EscapeMessagesRenderer</renderer-class>
</renderer>
```

Now, you can add HTML content in your messages by setting the `escape` attribute as follows:

```
<h:messages escape="false" />
```

The complete example is named `ch5_4_3`.

In the preceding examples, we saw a few use cases of extending an existing renderer. The last example of this section will go a little bit further, and will represent a use case for writing a custom `RenderKit` and a custom renderer by extending the abstract class `Renderer`.

While the `Renderer` class converts the internal representation of UI components into the output stream, `RenderKit` represents a collection of `Renderer` instances capable to render JSF UI component's instances for a specific client (for example, a specific device). Each time JSF needs to render a UI component, it will call the `RenderKit.getRenderer` method which is capable of returning an instance of the corresponding renderer based on two arguments that uniquely identifies it: the **component family** and the **renderer type**.

Let's suppose that we want to alter the default behavior of the renderer used for all UI components grouped under the `javax.faces.Input` family, by adding a custom style using some CSS. This can be easily accomplished by writing a custom `RenderKit` and overriding the `getRenderer` method. Starting with JSF 2.2, we can do this pretty fast, because we can extend the new wrapper class that represents a simple implementation of the abstract class, `RenderKit`. This is named `RenderKitWrapper` and allows us to override only the desired methods.

For example, we override the `getRenderer` method as follows:

```
public class CustomRenderKit extends RenderKitWrapper {

 private RenderKit renderKit;

 public CustomRenderKit() {}

 public CustomRenderKit(RenderKit renderKit) {
  this.renderKit = renderKit;
 }

 @Override
 public Renderer getRenderer(String family, String rendererType) {
  if (family.equals("javax.faces.Input")) {
      Renderer inputRenderer = getWrapped().
               getRenderer(family, rendererType);
      return new RafaRenderer(inputRenderer);
  }
  return getWrapped().getRenderer(family, rendererType);
 }

 @Override
 public RenderKit getWrapped() {
  return renderKit;
 }
}
```

So, when JSF needs to render a UI component that belongs to `javax.faces.Input` family, we take the original renderer used for this task and wrap it into a custom renderer named `RafaRenderer`. This custom renderer will extend the JSF 2.2 `RendererWrapper` (a simple implementation of `Renderer`) and will override the `encodeBegin` method, as follows:

```
@ResourceDependencies({
@ResourceDependency(name = "css/rafastyles.css",
                    library = "default", target = "head")
})
@FacesRenderer(componentFamily = "javax.faces.Rafa",
               rendererType = RafaRenderer.RENDERER_TYPE)
public class RafaRenderer extends RendererWrapper {

 private Renderer renderer;
 public static final String RENDERER_TYPE =
```

```
                    "book.beans.RafaRenderer";

    public RafaRenderer() {}

    public RafaRenderer(Renderer renderer) {
     this.renderer = renderer;
    }

    @Override
    public void encodeBegin(FacesContext context,
                UIComponent uicomponent) throws IOException {
     ResponseWriter responseWriter = context.getResponseWriter();
     responseWriter.writeAttribute("class", "rafastyle", "class");
     getWrapped().encodeBegin(context, uicomponent);
    }

    @Override
    public Renderer getWrapped() {
     return renderer;
    }
}
```

 It is good to know that we can specify external resources (such as CSS and JS) for a JSF renderer using the @ResourceDependency and @ResourceDependecies annotations.

Finally, you need to configure the custom RenderKit in faces-config.xml, as follows:

```
<render-kit>
 <render-kit-class>
   book.beans.CustomRenderKit
 </render-kit-class>
</render-kit>
```

The complete application is named ch5_15.

# Working with client behavior functionality

JSF 2 comes with the ability to define specific client-side behavior to a component in a reusable approach. The client-side behavior is actually a piece of JavaScript code that can be executed in a browser.

For example, when the user has access to buttons that perform irreversible changes; for example, deletion, copy, and move is a good practice to inform the user about consequences and ask for a confirmation before the action is performed.

For implementing a client behavior functionality, we perform the following steps:

1. Extend the `ClientBehaviorBase` class.

2. Override the `getScript` method.

3. Annotate the created class with the `@FacesBehavior` (value=*"developer_id"*) annotation where *developer_id* is used to refer to our custom client behavior. This is needed when we define a tag for the behavior.

4. Define a custom tag for the behavior — a tag is needed for specifying in the JSF pages, which components receive our client behavior (the JS code).

5. Register the custom tag in the descriptor of the `web.xml` file.

The following code shows you how to write a client behavior for displaying a JavaScript confirmation dialog when the user clicks on a button that emulates a deletion action, which covers the first three steps mentioned earlier:

```
@FacesBehavior(value = "confirm")
public class ConfirmDeleteBehavior extends ClientBehaviorBase {

@Override
 public String getScript(ClientBehaviorContext behaviorContext) {
   return "return confirm('Are you sure ?');";
  }
}
```

The fourth step consists of writing a custom tag for the behavior. Create a file named `delete.taglib.xml` under the `WEB-INF` folder as follows:

```
<?xml version="1.0" encoding="UTF-8"?>
<facelet-taglib version="2.2"
  xmlns="http://xmlns.jcp.org/xml/ns/javaee"
  xmlns:xsi="http://www.w3.org/2001/XMLSchema-instance"
  xsi:schemaLocation="http://xmlns.jcp.org/xml/ns/javaee
    http://xmlns.jcp.org/xml/ns/javaee/web-
                             facelettaglibrary_2_2.xsd">
 <namespace>http://www.custom.tags/jsf/delete</namespace>
 <tag>
  <tag-name>confirmDelete</tag-name>
  <behavior>
   <behavior-id>confirm</behavior-id>
  </behavior>
 </tag>
</facelet-taglib>
```

The `<behavior-id>` tag value must match the `value` member of the `FacesBehavior` annotation (*developer_id*). The tag name can be freely chosen.

The final step consists of registering the tag in `web.xml`:

```xml
<context-param>
 <param-name> javax.faces.FACELETS_LIBRARIES</param-name>
 <param-value>/WEB-INF/delete.taglib.xml</param-value>
</context-param>
```

We can attach a client behavior to every component that implements the `ClientBehaviourHolder` interface. Fortunately, almost all components implement this interface, such as buttons, links, input fields, and so on.

Done! Now, we can pick up the fruits in a JSF page as follows:

```xml
<?xml version='1.0' encoding='UTF-8' ?>
<!DOCTYPE html PUBLIC "-//W3C//DTD XHTML 1.0 Transitional//EN"
"http://www.w3.org/TR/xhtml1/DTD/xhtml1-transitional.dtd">
<html xmlns="http://www.w3.org/1999/xhtml"
      xmlns:h="http://xmlns.jcp.org/jsf/html"
      xmlns:b="http://www.custom.tags/jsf/delete">
 <h:head>
  <title></title>
 </h:head>
 <h:body>
  <h:form>
   <h:commandButton value="Delete" action="done">
    <b:confirmDelete/>
   </h:commandButton>
  </h:form>
 </h:body>
</html>
```

If the user doesn't confirm deletion, the action is aborted.

Starting with JSF 2.2, we can use dependency injection with client behavior (`@Inject` and `@EJB`). For example, instead of hardcoding the confirmation question, "Are you sure?", we can pass it through injection of a CDI bean or an EJB session bean. A complete example can be found in the code bundle of this chapter. It is named ch5_5_1.

Notice that the example works fine even if we do not specify any event that starts the client behavior JS code. This is happening because the JS code is attached to the `onclick` event of the button, which is the default event for `<h:commandButton>`. Now, we will write another example that will attach the client behavior to two other events simultaneously.

We can attach the client behavior code to some other event by specifying the event name with the `event` attribute of the tag.

In the next example, we assume the following scenario: an input field that is colored in green when it gains focus (`onfocus` JS event) and turns back to blank when it loses focus (`onblur` JS event). Now, we have to subscribe to two events.

In the previous example, we explicitly link the client behavior functionality to the `<confirmDelete>` tag. Even if this is still possible for this scenario, we choose to come with another approach. Instead of a direct link, we will use a tag handler (`TagHandler`).

A custom tag handler allows us to manipulate the created DOM tree (add/remove nodes from the tree).

When we write a custom tag handler, we need to focus on the apply method, especially on the second argument of this method that is named parent and represents the parent of the tag, which in our case will be `<h:inputText>`. We can add both the events to `<h:inputText>`, as follows:

```
public class FocusBlurHandler extends TagHandler {

  private FocusBlurBehavior onfocus = new FocusBlurBehavior();
  private FocusBlurBehavior onblur = new FocusBlurBehavior();

  public FocusBlurHandler(TagConfig tagConfig) {
    super(tagConfig);
  }

  @Override
  public void apply(FaceletContext ctx, UIComponent parent)
        throws IOException {

    if (parent instanceof ClientBehaviorHolder) {
        ClientBehaviorHolder clientBehaviorHolder =
```

```
                            (ClientBehaviorHolder) parent;

        clientBehaviorHolder.addClientBehavior("focus", onfocus);
        clientBehaviorHolder.addClientBehavior("blur", onblur);
      }
    }
  }
```

Remember that in the preceding section, we saw how to override a few JSF renderers. Well, here is one more! Instead of overriding the `getScript` method of the `ClientBehaviorBase`, as in the previous example, we will write a custom renderer, which is easy to achieve because JSF provides a dedicated renderer for client behavior, named `ClientBehaviorRenderer`. This renderer contains its own `getScript` method as shown in the following code:

```
@FacesBehaviorRenderer(rendererType = "focusblurrenderer")
@ResourceDependency(name="player.css", target="head")
public class FocusBlurRenderer extends ClientBehaviorRenderer {

  private static final String FOCUS_EVENT = "focus";
  private static final String BLUR_EVENT = "blur";

  @Override
  public String getScript(ClientBehaviorContext behaviorContext,
        ClientBehavior behavior) {

    if (FOCUS_EVENT.equals(behaviorContext.getEventName())) {
        return "this.setAttribute('class','focus-css');";
    }

    if (BLUR_EVENT.equals(behaviorContext.getEventName())) {
        return "this.setAttribute('class','blur-css');";
    }

  return null;
  }
}
```

 The `@ResourceDependency` annotation can be used for loading resources such as CSS and JS in custom `UIComponent` and `Renderer` components. In several versions of JSF, `@ResourceDependency` is not working as expected for `Renderers` (seems to be a bug). In case you have such issues, you have to hardcode the CSS for testing.

Finally, the client behavior will point out the above renderer as follows:

```
@FacesBehavior(value = "focusblur")
public class FocusBlurBehavior extends ClientBehaviorBase {

 @Override
 public String getRendererType() {
  return "focusblurrenderer";
 }
}
```

The complete example containing the CSS source, the tag definition, and specific configurations is available in the code bundle and is named ch5_5_2.

# JSF factories

The following note is a good point to start for the last part of this chapter, which is dedicated to JSF factories. In JSF, the factories are initialized by `FactoryFinder`, which recognizes if a custom factory has a delegating constructor—a one argument constructor for the type of the factory.

> This is useful when we want to wrap standard factory from JSF, because `FactoryFinder` will pass in the previously known factory, usually the built-in one. Factory instances are obtained as follows:
>
> ```
> XXXFactory factory = (XXXFactory)     FactoryFinder.
> getFactory(FactoryFinder.XXX_FACTORY);
> ```
>
> For example, `RenderKitFactory` can be found using the following code:
>
> ```
> RenderKitFactory factory = (RenderKitFactory)
>    FactoryFinder.getFactory(FactoryFinder.
>    RENDER_KIT_FACTORY);
> ```
>
> Next to `FaceletFactory`, another new factory obtainable via `FactoryFinder` in JSF 2.2 is the new `FlashFactory`. We will discuss about `FaceletFactory` in the last chapter of this book, *Chapter 12, Facelets Templating*.

# Configuring the global exception handler

During the JSF lifecycle, we need to treat different kinds of exceptions in different points of the application. Starting with JSF 2, we have a generic API that allows us to write a global exception handler. This can be very handy, especially when we need to avoid "silent" exceptions that are not caught by the application.

In order to write a global exception handler, we need to do the following:

- Extend ExceptionHandlerFactory, which is a factory object that is capable of creating and returning a new ExceptionHandler instance — the central point for handling unexpected Exceptions that are thrown during the JSF lifecycle.

- Extend ExceptionHandlerWrapper, which is a simple implementation of ExceptionHandler.

- Configure the custom exception handler in faces-config.xml.

Therefore, we can write a custom exception handler factory as follows:

```
public class CustomExceptionHandlerFactory
                    extends ExceptionHandlerFactory {

  private ExceptionHandlerFactory exceptionHandlerFactory;

  public CustomExceptionHandlerFactory(){}

  public CustomExceptionHandlerFactory(ExceptionHandlerFactory
                                        exceptionHandlerFactory) {
    this.exceptionHandlerFactory = exceptionHandlerFactory;
  }

  @Override
  public ExceptionHandler getExceptionHandler() {
    ExceptionHandler handler = new CustomExceptionHandler
                (exceptionHandlerFactory.getExceptionHandler());

    return handler;
  }
}
```

Our implementation for dealing with the exception is to send each error to a log and navigate to an error page, as shown in the following code (notice that `ViewExpiredException` can be caught here as well):

```
public class CustomExceptionHandler extends ExceptionHandlerWrapper {

  private static final Logger logger =
          Logger.getLogger(CustomExceptionHandler.class.getName());
  private ExceptionHandler exceptionHandler;

  CustomExceptionHandler(ExceptionHandler exceptionHandler) {
    this.exceptionHandler = exceptionHandler;
  }

  @Override
  public ExceptionHandler getWrapped() {
    return exceptionHandler;
  }

  @Override
  public void handle() throws FacesException {

    final Iterator<ExceptionQueuedEvent> queue =
          getUnhandledExceptionQueuedEvents().iterator();

    while (queue.hasNext()) {

      //take exceptions one by one
      ExceptionQueuedEvent item = queue.next();
      ExceptionQueuedEventContext exceptionQueuedEventContext =
                      (ExceptionQueuedEventContext) item.getSource();

      try {
          //log error
          Throwable throwable = exceptionQueuedEventContext.
getException();
          logger.log(Level.SEVERE, "EXCEPTION: ", throwable.
getMessage());

          //redirect error page
          FacesContext facesContext = FacesContext.getCurrentInstance();
          Map<String, Object> requestMap =
                      facesContext.getExternalContext().getRequestMap();
          NavigationHandler nav =
```

```
                           facesContext.getApplication().
       getNavigationHandler();

              requestMap.put("errmsg", throwable.getMessage());
              nav.handleNavigation(facesContext, null, "/error");
              facesContext.renderResponse();
              } finally {
                //remove it from queue
                queue.remove();
                }
        }


        getWrapped().handle();
      }
}
```

Finally, we need to configure the exception handler in `faces-config.xml` as follows:

```
<factory>
 <exception-handler-factory>
  book.beans.CustomExceptionHandlerFactory
 </exception-handler-factory>
</factory>
```

The complete example is named `ch5_3`.

 Starting with JSF 2.2, we can use dependency injection with exception handler (`@Inject` and `@EJB`).

Notice that a special case exists in treating AJAX exceptions. By default, most of them are invisible to the client. AJAX errors are returned to the client, but unfortunately JSF AJAX clients aren't prepared to deal with arbitrary error messages, so they simply ignore them. But a custom exception handler is specially created for this task by OmniFaces (it works for AJAX and non-AJAX exceptions). The handler is named `FullAjaxExceptionHandler`, and the factory is named `FullAjaxExceptionHandlerFactory`.

Once you install OmniFaces, you can exploit the AJAX exception handler with a simple configuration in `faces-config.xml`:

```
<factory>
 <exception-handler-factory>
  org.omnifaces.exceptionhandler.FullAjaxExceptionHandlerFactory
 </exception-handler-factory>
</factory>
```

The behavior of the OmniFaces exception handler is configured in `web.xml`:

```
<error-page>
  <exception-type>
    java.lang.NullPointerException
  </exception-type>
  <location>/null.jsf</location>
</error-page>
<error-page>
  <exception-type>
    java.lang.Throwable
  </exception-type>
  <location>/ throwable.jsf</location>
</error-page>
```

> Error pages for OmniFaces exception handler should be JSF
> 2.0 (or more) pages. A comprehensive demo can be found in
> OmniFaces showcase at `http://showcase.omnifaces.org/`
> `exceptionhandlers/FullAjaxExceptionHandler`.

# Configuring RenderKit factory

Earlier in this chapter, we have written a custom `RenderKit`, which was loaded by JSF because we have configured it in `faces-config.xml` using the `<render-kit>` tag. But, behind the scene, JSF uses `RenderKitFactory`, which is capable of registering and returning `RenderKit` instances. Therefore, we can write custom `RenderKitFactory` for returning our custom `RenderKit`. For writing such a factory, you need to do the following:

1. Extend the `RenderKitFactory` class that is responsible for registering and returning `RenderKit` instances.

2. Override the `addRenderKit` method that registers the specified `RenderKit` instance using the specified ID.

3. Override the `getRenderKit` method that returns `RenderKit` with the specified ID.

4. Override the `getRenderKitIds` method and return an `Iterator` over the set of render kit identifiers registered with this factory.

Based on these steps, we can register our custom `RenderKit` as follows:

```java
public class CustomRenderKitFactory extends RenderKitFactory {

  private RenderKitFactory renderKitFactory;

  public CustomRenderKitFactory() {}

  public CustomRenderKitFactory(RenderKitFactory renderKitFactory){
    this.renderKitFactory = renderKitFactory;
  }

  @Override
  public void addRenderKit(String renderKitId,
                                RenderKit renderKit){
    renderKitFactory.addRenderKit(renderKitId, renderKit);
  }

  @Override
  public RenderKit getRenderKit(FacesContext context,
                                String renderKitId) {
    RenderKit renderKit = renderKitFactory.
            getRenderKit(context, renderKitId);
    return (HTML_BASIC_RENDER_KIT.equals(renderKitId)) ?
            new CustomRenderKit(renderKit)  : renderKit;
  }

  @Override
  public Iterator<String> getRenderKitIds() {
    return renderKitFactory.getRenderKitIds();
  }
}
```

Now, instead of configuring the custom `RenderKit` using the `<render-kit>` tag, we can configure the custom `RenderKitFactory`, as follows:

```xml
<factory>
 <render-kit-factory>
  book.beans.CustomRenderKitFactory
 </render-kit-factory>
</factory>
```

The complete application is named `ch5_16`.

# Configuring PartialViewContext

The `PartialViewContext` class is responsible for processing partial requests and rendering partial responses on a view. In other words, JSF processes execution, rendering, and so on, of AJAX requests and responses using `PartialViewContext`. We refer to it as follows:

```
FacesContext.getCurrentInstance().getPartialViewContext();
```

Writing a custom `PartialViewContext` implementation implies the following steps:

1. Extending `PartialViewContextFactory`, will result in a factory object capable of creating and returning a new `PartialViewContext` instance, the central point for handling partial request-responses.

2. Extending `PartialViewContextWrapper`, which is a simple implementation of `PartialViewContext`.

3. Configuring the custom `PartialViewContext` implementation in `faces-config.xml`.

Now, let's suppose that we have multiple forms that are submitted through AJAX. Each `<f:ajax>` tag will contain the `execute` attribute and the one that we are especially interested in, the `render` attribute. This attribute should contain client IDs for the components to re-render. When multiple partial requests re-render the same component, the ID of that component is present in each partial request (in each `render` attribute).

A common case is the global `<h:messages>` tag. The ID of this tag should be added to each partial request that needs to re-render it. Instead of re-typing the client IDs in the `render` attribute, we can write a custom `PartialViewContext` implementation to do that. First, we create the factory instance as follows:

```
public class CustomPartialViewContextFactory
            extends PartialViewContextFactory {

  private PartialViewContextFactory partialViewContextFactory;

  public CustomPartialViewContextFactory(){}

  public CustomPartialViewContextFactory
        (PartialViewContextFactory partialViewContextFactory) {
    this.partialViewContextFactory = partialViewContextFactory;
  }

  @Override
```

```
public PartialViewContext getPartialViewContext(FacesContext context)
{

  PartialViewContext handler = new CustomPartialViewContext
     (partialViewContextFactory.getPartialViewContext(context));

  return handler;
  }
}
```

Next, we write our custom `PartialViewContext` and override the `getRenderIds` method. Basically, we locate the ID of the `<h:messages>` tag, check if this ID is already in the render IDs list, and add it to the list if it has not yet been added, as follows:

```
public class CustomPartialViewContext extends
PartialViewContextWrapper {

  private PartialViewContext partialViewContext;

  public CustomPartialViewContext(PartialViewContext
partialViewContext) {
    this.partialViewContext = partialViewContext;
  }

  @Override
  public PartialViewContext getWrapped() {
    return partialViewContext;
  }

  @Override
  public Collection<String> getRenderIds() {

    FacesContext facesContext = FacesContext.getCurrentInstance();
    if (PhaseId.RENDER_RESPONSE == facesContext.getCurrentPhaseId()) {
        UIComponent component = findComponent("msgsId",
                             facesContext.getViewRoot());
        if (component != null && component.isRendered()) {
            String componentClientId = component.
getClientId(facesContext);
            Collection<String> renderIds = getWrapped().getRenderIds();
            if (!renderIds.contains(componentClientId)) {
                renderIds.add(componentClientId);
            }
        }
```

```
    }
    return getWrapped().getRenderIds();
  }

  private UIComponent findComponent(String id, UIComponent root) {
    if (root == null) {
        return null;
    } else if (root.getId().equals(id)) {
            return root;
    } else {
      List<UIComponent> childrenList = root.getChildren();
      if (childrenList == null || childrenList.isEmpty()) {
          return null;
      }
      for (UIComponent child : childrenList) {
          UIComponent result = findComponent(id, child);
          if (result != null) {
              return result;
          }
      }
    }
    return null;
  }
}
```

Finally, we need to configure `PartialViewContext` in `faces-config.xml` as follows:

```
<factory>
  <partial-view-context-factory>
    book.beans.CustomPartialViewContextFactory
  </partial-view-context-factory>
</factory>
```

The complete example is named `ch5_6_1`.

 Starting with JSF 2.2, we can use dependency injection with partial view context (`@Inject` and `@EJB`). A complete example can be found in the code bundle of this chapter, under the name `ch5_6_2`.

# Configuring visitContext

According to the documentation, VisitContext is an object used to hold the state relating to performing a component tree visit.

Why do we need such an object? Well, imagine that you want to programmatically find a certain component. You will probably think of findComponent or invokeOnComponent built-in methods. When you need to find several components, you can apply the process recursively (as you saw in a few examples earlier). The recursive process performs a clean traversal of the component's tree (or subtree) by visiting each node in a hierarchical approach.

However, JSF 2 also provides an out-of-the-box method to accomplish a component's tree traversal named UIComponent.visitTree, declared as follows:

```
public boolean visitTree(VisitContext context,
                VisitCallback callback)
```

The first argument is an instance of VisitContext, and the second one is an instance of the VisitCallback interface that provides a method, named visit, which is called for each node that is visited. If the tree was successfully traversed, then visitTree returns true.

Based on this knowledge, we can write a custom VisitContext implementation for resetting the editable components of a form. Such a component implements the EditableValueHolder interface and provides a method resetValue.

The steps for writing a custom VisitContext implementation are as follows:

1. Extending VisitContextFactory, which is a factory object capable of creating and returning a new VisitContext instance.
2. Extending VisitContextWrapper, which is a simple implementation of VisitContext.
3. Configuring the custom VisitContext implementation in faces-config.xml.

So, first we need to extend the built-in factory as follows:

```
public class CustomVisitContextFactory extends VisitContextFactory {

    private VisitContextFactory visitContextFactory;

    public CustomVisitContextFactory() {}

    public CustomVisitContextFactory(VisitContextFactory
                                        visitContextFactory){
        this.visitContextFactory = visitContextFactory;
```

```
}

@Override
public VisitContext getVisitContext(FacesContext context,
                      Collection<String> ids, Set<VisitHint> hints)
{
  VisitContext handler = new CustomVisitContext(visitContextFactory.
                       getVisitContext(context, ids, hints));

  return handler;
  }
}
```

 Note that we can also specify a collection of client IDs to be visited. We can also specify some visit hints. When all components should be visited with the default visit hints, these arguments can be null.

The custom visit context is represented programmatically as follows—the method invokeVisitCallback is called by visitTree to visit a single component:

```
public class CustomVisitContext extends VisitContextWrapper {

private static final Logger logger =
        Logger.getLogger(CustomVisitContext.class.getName());
private VisitContext visitContext;

public CustomVisitContext(VisitContext visitContext) {
  this.visitContext = visitContext;
}

@Override
public VisitContext getWrapped() {
  return visitContext;
}

@Override
public VisitResult invokeVisitCallback(UIComponent component,
                                 VisitCallback callback) {
  logger.info("Custom visit context is used!");
  return getWrapped().invokeVisitCallback(component, callback);
}
}
```

So, our custom `VisitContext` implementation doesn't do much; it just fires some log messages and delegates the control to the original `VisitContext` class. Our aim is to write a custom `VisitCallback` implementation for resetting editable values of a form using the following code:

```
public class CustomVisitCallback implements VisitCallback{

@Override
public VisitResult visit(VisitContext context, UIComponent target) {

  if (!target.isRendered()) {
      return VisitResult.REJECT;
  }

  if (target instanceof EditableValueHolder) {
      ((EditableValueHolder)target).resetValue();
  }

  return VisitResult.ACCEPT;
  }
}
```

Well, we are almost done! Just configure the custom `VisitContext` implementation in `faces-config.xml` form using the following code:

```
<factory>
 <visit-context-factory>
  book.beans.CustomVisitContextFactory
 </visit-context-factory>
</factory>
```

Let's start the process of visiting nodes using the following code:

```
FacesContext context = FacesContext.getCurrentInstance();
UIComponent component = context.getViewRoot();
CustomVisitCallback customVisitCallback = new CustomVisitCallback();
component.visitTree(VisitContext.createVisitContext
            (FacesContext.getCurrentInstance()), customVisitCallback);
```

Note that the starting point in the traversal process is the view root. This is not mandatory; you can pass any other subtree.

An obvious question arises here! Since this custom `VisitContext` doesn't do something important (only fires some log messages), why don't we skip it?

Yes, it is true that we can skip this custom `VisitContext`, since all we need is the custom `VisitCallback` implementation, but it was a good opportunity to see how it can be done. Maybe you can modify `invokeVisitCallback` to implement some kind of client ID filtration before getting the action into the `VisitCallback.visit` method.

A complete example can be found in the code bundle of this chapter, which is named ch5_7.

 Starting with JSF 2.2, we can use dependency injection with visit context (@Inject and @EJB).

# Configuring ExternalContext

The `FacesContext` and `ExternalContext` objects are two of the most important objects in JSF. Each of them provides powerful capabilities and each of them covers an important area of artifacts provided by JSF (in case of `FacesContext`) and Servlet/Portlet (in case of `ExternalContext`).

Furthermore, both of them can be extended or modified by the developers. For example, in this section we will write a custom `ExternalContext` implementation for downloading a file. Sometimes, you may need to download a file by programmatically sending its content to the user. The default `ExternalContext` can do that, as shown in the following code — of course, you can easily adapt this code for other files:

```
public void readFileAction() throws IOException, URISyntaxException {

    FacesContext facesContext = FacesContext.getCurrentInstance();
    ExternalContext externalContext = facesContext.getExternalContext();
    Path path = Paths.get(((ServletContext)externalContext.getContext())
            .getRealPath("/resources/rafa.txt"));

    BasicFileAttributes attrs = Files.readAttributes(path,
                                BasicFileAttributes.class);

    externalContext.responseReset();
    externalContext.setResponseContentType("text/plain");
    externalContext.setResponseContentLength((int) attrs.size());
    externalContext.setResponseHeader("Content-Disposition",
                "attachment; filename=\"" + "rafa.txt" + "\"");

    int nRead;
    byte[] data = new byte[128];
```

```
    InputStream inStream = externalContext.
        getResourceAsStream("/resources/rafa.txt");

    try (OutputStream output = externalContext.getResponseOutputStream())
    {
        while ((nRead = inStream.read(data, 0, data.length)) != -1) {
                output.write(data, 0, nRead);
        }
        output.flush();
    }

    facesContext.responseComplete();
}
```

Normally, this approach uses the default response output stream. But let's suppose that we have written our "dummy" response output stream which, obviously, does a dummy action: for each chunk of bytes, replace the 'a' character with the 'A' character as shown in the following code:

```
public class CustomResponseStream extends OutputStream {

    private OutputStream responseStream;

    public CustomResponseStream(OutputStream responseStream) {
      this.responseStream = responseStream;
    }

    @Override
    public void write(byte[] b, int off, int len) throws IOException {
      String s = new String(b, off, len);
      s = s.replace('a', 'A');

      byte[] bb = s.getBytes();
      responseStream.write(bb, off, len);
    }

    @Override
    public void write(int b) throws IOException {
    }
}
```

Now, we want to use this response output stream instead of the default one, but there is no externalContext.setResponseOutputStream(OutputStream os) method. Instead, we can write a custom ExternalContext, by performing the following steps:

1. Extending ExternalContextFactory, which is a factory object capable of creating and returning a new ExternalContext.

2. Extending ExternalContextWrapper, which is a simple implementation of ExternalContext.

3. Configuring the custom ExternalContext implementation in faces-config.xml.

The custom external context factory code is as follows:

```
public class CustomExternalContextFactory extends
ExternalContextFactory{

  private ExternalContextFactory externalContextFactory;

  public CustomExternalContextFactory(){}

  public CustomExternalContextFactory(ExternalContextFactory
          externalContextFactory){
    this.externalContextFactory = externalContextFactory;
  }

  @Override
  public ExternalContext getExternalContext(Object context,
          Object request, Object response) throws FacesException {

    ExternalContext handler = new
          CustomExternalContext(externalContextFactory
              .getExternalContext(context, request, response));

      return handler;
  }
}
```

The custom external context is given as follows. Here, we override the `getResponseOutputStream` method to return our custom response output stream.

```
public class CustomExternalContext extends ExternalContextWrapper {

  private ExternalContext externalContext;

  public CustomExternalContext(ExternalContext externalContext) {
   this.externalContext = externalContext;
  }

  @Override
  public ExternalContext getWrapped() {
   return externalContext;
  }

  @Override
  public OutputStream getResponseOutputStream() throws IOException {
   HttpServletResponse response =
               (HttpServletResponse)externalContext.getResponse();
   OutputStream responseStream = response.getOutputStream();
   return new CustomResponseStream(responseStream);
  }
}
```

Finally, do not forget to configure the custom external context in `faces-config.xml`:

```
<factory>
 <external-context-factory>
   book.beans.CustomExternalContextFactory
 </external-context-factory>
</factory>
```

The complete example can be downloaded from the code bundle of this chapter named ch5_8.

 Starting with JSF 2.2, we can use dependency injection with external context and faces context (@Inject and @EJB).

JSF also provides factory (FacesContextFactory) and wrapper (FacesContextWrapper) classes for extending the default FacesContext class. This can be extended when you need to adapt JSF to Portlet environment, or use JSF to run inside another environment.

# Configuring Flash

Starting with JSF 2.2, we have a hook for overriding and/or wrapping the default implementation of Flash. Usually, we refer a Flash instance using the following code:

```
FacesContext.getCurrentInstance().getExternalContext().getFlash();
```

When advanced topics require a custom implementation, you can perform the following steps:

1. Extend `FlashFactory`, which is a factory object capable of creating and returning a new `Flash` instance.
2. Extend `FlashWrapper`, which is a simple implementation of `Flash` that allows us to selectively override methods.
3. Configure the custom `Flash` implementation in `faces-config.xml`.

For example, a custom Flash factory can be written using the following code:

```
public class CustomFlashFactory extends FlashFactory {

  private FlashFactory flashFactory;

  public CustomFlashFactory() {}

  public CustomFlashFactory(FlashFactory flashFactory) {
    this.flashFactory = flashFactory;
  }

  @Override
  public Flash getFlash(boolean create) {
    Flash handler = new CustomFlash(flashFactory.getFlash(create));

    return handler;
  }
}
```

The `CustomFlash` instance returned by the `getFlash` method is as follows:

```
public class CustomFlash extends FlashWrapper {

  private Flash flash;

  public CustomFlash(Flash flash){
```

```
    this.flash = flash;
  }

//... override here Flash methods

 @Override
 public Flash getWrapped() {
  return this.flash;
  }
}
```

In the `CustomFlash` class, you can override the methods of `javax.faces.context.Flash` that need to have a custom behavior. For example, you can override the `setKeepMessages` method to output some logs using the following code:

```
@Override
public  void setKeepMessages(boolean newValue){
  logger.log(Level.INFO, "setKeepMessages()
                        was called with value: {0}", newValue);
  getWrapped().setKeepMessages(newValue);
}
```

A custom flash factory is configured in `faces-config.xml` using the following code:

```
<factory>
 <flash-factory>book.beans.CustomFlashFactory</flash-factory>
</factory>
```

The complete example is named `ch5_9`.

 Starting with JSF 2.2, we can use dependency injection with Flash (`@Inject` and `@EJB`).

# JSF 2.2 Window ID API

The origin of the Window ID mechanism relies on an HTML gap—this protocol is stateless, which means that it doesn't associate clients with requests. JSF solves this issue using a cookie for tracking user sessions, but sometimes this is not enough, and a fine-grained tracking mechanism is needed. For example, if a user opens several tabs/windows, then the same session is used in all of them, meaning that the same cookie is sent to the server and the same login account is used (when login exists). This can be a real issue if the user operates modifications in these tabs/windows.

In order to provide a workaround for this problem, JSF 2.2 has introduced the Window ID API, which allows developers to identify separate tabs/windows of the same session.

 Under certain circumstances, you can track users' window IDs using view scope and flash scope. But Window ID is easier to use and is dedicated to this purpose.

Developers can choose the method used for tracking window IDs by setting the context parameter `javax.faces.CLIENT_WINDOW_MODE` in `web.xml` as follows—in JSF 2.2, the supported values are `url` (tracking activated) and `none` (tracking deactivated):

```
<context-param>
  <param-name>javax.faces.CLIENT_WINDOW_MODE</param-name>
  <param-value>url</param-value>
</context-param>
```

When `url` is specified, the user's window IDs are tracked using a hidden field or a request parameter named `jfwid`. In the following screenshot, you can see both of them, the request parameter and hidden field:

**Request parameter (jfwid):**

 localhost:8080/ch4_22_2/faces/index.xhtml?jfwid=9cf5d0ff8cad2615a2f561816efb:0

**Hidden field:**
```
<input name="javax.faces.ClientWindow" id="j_id1:javax.faces.ClientWindow:0"
       value="9cf5d0ff8cad2615a2f561816efb:0" autocomplete="off" type="hidden">
```

 When the hidden field (available after a postback) and request parameter are available, the hidden field has a bigger precedence.

You can easily get the Window ID using the following code:

```
public void pullWindowIdAction() {
  FacesContext facesContext = FacesContext.getCurrentInstance();
  ExternalContext externalContext=facesContext.getExternalContext();

  ClientWindow clientWindow = externalContext.getClientWindow();
  if (clientWindow != null) {
      logger.log(Level.INFO, "The current client window id is:{0}",
        clientWindow.getId());
```

```
    } else {
        logger.log(Level.INFO, "Client Window cannot be determined!");
    }
}
```

 The `ClientWindow` instance can be obtained using `ExternalContext.getClientWindow` and can be provided as `ExternalContext.setClientWindow`.

You can enable/disable user window tracking in at least two ways which are as follows:

- In `<h:button>` and `<h:link>`, you can use the `disableClientWindow` attribute whose value can be `true` or `false`, as shown in the following code:

```
Enable/Disable client window using h:button:<br/>
<h:button value="Enable Client Window" outcome="index"
                            disableClientWindow="false"/><br/>
<h:button value="Disable Client Window" outcome="index"
                            disableClientWindow="true"/><br/>
<hr/>
Enable/Disable client window using h:link:<br/>
<h:link value="Enable Client Window" outcome="index"
                            disableClientWindow="false"/><br/>
<h:link value="Disable Client Window" outcome="index"
                            disableClientWindow="true"/>
```

- Alternatively, we can use the `disableClientWindowRenderMode` and `enableClientWindowRenderMode` methods as shown in the following code:

```
private FacesContext facesContext;
private ExternalContext externalContext;
...
ClientWindow clientWindow = externalContext.getClientWindow();
//disable
clientWindow.disableClientWindowRenderMode(facesContext);
//enable
clientWindow.enableClientWindowRenderMode(facesContext);
```

A complete application is available in the code bundle of this chapter which is named `ch5_10_1`.

Developers can write custom `ClientWindow` implementations by extending the `ClientWindowWrapper` class, which is a simple and convenient implementation that allows us to override only the necessary methods. One way to tell JSF to use your custom `ClientWindow` is based on the following steps:

1. Extend `ClientWindowFactory`, which is a factory that is capable of creating `ClientWindow` instances based on the incoming request.

2. Override `ClientWindowFactory.getClientWindow` to create an instance of the custom `ClientWindow` implementation for the current request.

3. Check the value of the context parameter `ClientWindow.CLIENT_WINDOW_MODE_PARAM_NAME`, before creating an instance of the custom `ClientWindow` implementation. The value of the context parameter should be equal to `url`.

Based on these three steps, we can write a custom `ClientWindowFactory` implementation using the following code:

```
public class CustomClientWindowFactory
            extends ClientWindowFactory {

 private ClientWindowFactory clientWindowFactory;
 public CustomClientWindowFactory() {}

 public CustomClientWindowFactory(ClientWindowFactory
            clientWindowFactory) {
  this.clientWindowFactory = clientWindowFactory;
 }

 @Override
 public ClientWindow getClientWindow(FacesContext context) {
  if (context.getExternalContext().getInitParameter
     (ClientWindow.CLIENT_WINDOW_MODE_PARAM_NAME).equals("url")) {
     ClientWindow defaultClientWindow =
            clientWindowFactory.getClientWindow(context);
     ClientWindow customClientWindow = new
            CustomClientWindow(defaultClientWindow);
     return customClientWindow;
  }
  return null;
 }

 @Override
 public ClientWindowFactory getWrapped() {
  return clientWindowFactory;
 }
}
```

The CustomClientWindow implementation is an extension of ClientWindowWrapper, which allows us to override only the needed methods. In our case, we are interested in two methods. The first one is named getId, which returns a String value that uniquely identifies ClientWindow within the scope of the current session. The other one is named decode, which is responsible for providing the value returned by getId. In order to provide this value, the decode method should follow the given checks:

1.  Request a parameter under the name given by the value of ResponseStateManager.CLIENT_WINDOW_PARAM.

2.  If this check doesn't return a favorable ID, look for a request parameter under the name given by the value of ResponseStateManager.CLIENT_WINDOW_URL_PARAM.

3.  If an ID value is not found, then fabricate an ID that uniquely identifies this ClientWindow within the scope of the current session.

Furthermore, we can write a custom ClientWindow implementation that will generate a custom ID, of type CUSTOM—current date in milliseconds. The code is listed as follows–pay attention to see how the decode method is implemented:

```java
public class CustomClientWindow extends ClientWindowWrapper {

  private ClientWindow clientWindow;
  String id;

  public CustomClientWindow() {}

  public CustomClientWindow(ClientWindow clientWindow) {
  this.clientWindow = clientWindow;
  }

  @Override
  public void decode(FacesContext context) {

   Map<String, String> requestParamMap =
    context.getExternalContext().getRequestParameterMap();
   if (isClientWindowRenderModeEnabled(context)) {
       id = requestParamMap.
           get(ResponseStateManager.CLIENT_WINDOW_URL_PARAM);
   }
   if (requestParamMap.containsKey
       (ResponseStateManager.CLIENT_WINDOW_PARAM)) {
   id = requestParamMap.get
       (ResponseStateManager.CLIENT_WINDOW_PARAM);
   }
   if (id == null) {
```

```
        long time = new Date().getTime();
        id = "CUSTOM-" + time;
    }
}

@Override
public String getId() {
  return id;
}

@Override
public ClientWindow getWrapped() {
  return this.clientWindow;
}
}
```

Finally, configure the custom `ClientWindowFactory` implementation in `faces-config.xml` using the following code:

```
<factory>
 <client-window-factory>
  book.beans.CustomClientWindowFactory
 </client-window-factory>
</factory>
```

Done! The complete application is named ch5_10_3.

If you want to create an ID of type `UUID-uuid::counter` then, you can write the decode method, as follows:

```
@Override
public void decode(FacesContext context) {
 Map<String, String> requestParamMap =
  context.getExternalContext().getRequestParameterMap();
 if (isClientWindowRenderModeEnabled(context)) {
    id = requestParamMap.get
        (ResponseStateManager.CLIENT_WINDOW_URL_PARAM);
 }
 if (requestParamMap.
    containsKey(ResponseStateManager.CLIENT_WINDOW_PARAM)) {
      id = requestParamMap.get
          (ResponseStateManager.CLIENT_WINDOW_PARAM);
 }
 if (id == null) {
    synchronized (context.getExternalContext().getSession(true)) {
      final String clientWindowKey = "my.custom.id";
```

```
      ExternalContext externalContext =
                    context.getExternalContext();
      Map<String, Object> sessionAttrs =
       externalContext.getSessionMap();
      Integer counter = (Integer) sessionAttrs.get(clientWindowKey);
      if (counter == null) {
          counter = 0;
      }
      String uuid = UUID.randomUUID().toString();
      id = "UUID-" + uuid + "::" + counter;
      sessionAttrs.put(clientWindowKey, ++counter);
    }
  }
}
```

In this case, the complete application is named `ch5_10_4`.

Using a counter may be very useful when you decide to use an ID of type `SESSION_ID::counter`. Since the session ID will be the same over multiple windows/tabs, you need the counter to differentiate between the IDs. This kind of ID can be easily obtained thanks to the `ExternalContext.getSessionId` method of JSF 2.2, which is as follows:

```
      String sessionId = externalContext.getSessionId(false);
      id = sessionId + "::" + counter;
```

# Configuring lifecycle

As you know, JSF lifecycle contains six phases. In order to be processed, each JSF request will go through all these phases, or only through a part of them. The abstraction of lifecycle model is represented by the `javax.faces.lifecycle.Lifecycle` class, which is responsible for executing JSF phases in two methods:

- The `execute` method will execute all the phases except the sixth phase, that is, the *Render Response* phase.

- The `render` method will execute the sixth phase.

The custom `Lifecycle` can be written by implementing the following steps:

1. Extend `LifecycleFactory`, which is a factory object capable of creating and returning a new `Lifecycle` instance.

2. Extend `LifecycleWrapper`, which is a simple implementation of `LifecycleLifecycle` that allows us to selectively override methods.

3. Configure the custom `Lifecycle` implementation in `faces-config.xml`.

4. Configure the custom `Lifecycle` implementation in `web.xml`.

Let's begin with a generic custom `Lifecycle`, by extending `LifecycleFactory` as follows—notice how we register a custom `Lifecycle` implementation using a unique identifier:

```
public class CustomLifecycleFactory extends LifecycleFactory {

  public static final String CUSTOM_LIFECYCLE_ID = "CustomLifecycle";
  private LifecycleFactory lifecycleFactory;

  public CustomLifecycleFactory(){}

  public CustomLifecycleFactory(LifecycleFactory lifecycleFactory) {
   this.lifecycleFactory = lifecycleFactory;
   Lifecycle defaultLifecycle = this.lifecycleFactory.
          getLifecycle(LifecycleFactory.DEFAULT_LIFECYCLE);
   addLifecycle(CUSTOM_LIFECYCLE_ID, new
          CustomLifecycle(defaultLifecycle));
  }

  @Override
  public final void addLifecycle(String lifecycleId,Lifecycle
  lifecycle) {
   lifecycleFactory.addLifecycle(lifecycleId, lifecycle);
  }

  @Override
  public Lifecycle getLifecycle(String lifecycleId) {
   return lifecycleFactory.getLifecycle(lifecycleId);
  }

  @Override
  public Iterator<String> getLifecycleIds() {
   return lifecycleFactory.getLifecycleIds();
  }
}
```

Furthermore, `CustomLifecycle` extends `LifecycleWrapper` and overrides
the required methods. In order to have access to the instance of the class being
wrapped, we need to override the `getWrapped` method as follows:

```
public class CustomLifecycle extends LifecycleWrapper {

  private Lifecycle lifecycle;

  public CustomLifecycle(Lifecycle lifecycle) {
   this.lifecycle = lifecycle;
  }

  ...
 @Override
  public Lifecycle getWrapped() {
   return lifecycle;
  }
}
```

Next, we need to configure our custom lifecycle factory in `faces-config.xml`
as follows:

```
<factory>
 <lifecycle-factory>book.beans.CustomLifecycleFactory</lifecycle-
factory>
</factory>
```

Finally, we need to register the custom lifecycle in `web.xml` using its identifier (see
the highlighted code):

```
<servlet>
 <servlet-name>Faces Servlet</servlet-name>
 <servlet-class>javax.faces.webapp.FacesServlet</servlet-class>
 <init-param>
  <param-name>javax.faces.LIFECYCLE_ID</param-name>
  <param-value>CustomLifecycle</param-value>
 </init-param>
 <load-on-startup>1</load-on-startup>
</servlet>
```

At this moment, we have a functional dummy custom lifecycle. Next, we will add some real functionality, and for this we focus on the `Lifecycle.attachWindow` method. This method was introduced in JSF 2.2 and is used for attaching a `ClientWindow` instance to the current request. The `ClientWindow` instance is associated with the incoming request during the `Lifecycle.attachWindow` method. This method will cause a new instance of `ClientWindow` to be created, to be assigned an ID, and then to be passed to `ExternalContext.setClientWindow(ClientWindow)`.

In the *JSF 2.2 Window ID API* section, you saw how to explore the default mechanism for identifying different windows/tabs of users. Based on this knowledge, we have written a custom `ClientWindow` implementation to provide a custom ID for the `jfwid` request parameter of type `CUSTOM`—`current date in milliseconds`—and of type `UUID::counter`. The custom client window was set via a custom `ClientWindowFactory` implementation. Further, we set the same custom client window by overriding the `attachWindow` method as shown in the following code:

```
public class CustomLifecycle extends LifecycleWrapper {

  private static final Logger logger =
   Logger.getLogger(CustomLifecycle.class.getName());
  private Lifecycle lifecycle;

  public CustomLifecycle(Lifecycle lifecycle) {
   this.lifecycle = lifecycle;
  }

  @Override
  public void attachWindow(FacesContext context) {

   if (context.getExternalContext().getInitParameter
      (ClientWindow.CLIENT_WINDOW_MODE_PARAM_NAME).equals("url")) {
      ExternalContext externalContext =
       context.getExternalContext();
      ClientWindow clientWindow = externalContext.getClientWindow();
      if (clientWindow == null) {
         clientWindow = createClientWindow(context);
         if (clientWindow != null) {
            CustomClientWindow customClientWindow = new
             CustomClientWindow(clientWindow);
            customClientWindow.decode(context);

            externalContext.setClientWindow(customClientWindow);
      }
```

```
        }
      }
    }

    private ClientWindow createClientWindow(FacesContext context) {
      ClientWindowFactory clientWindowFactory = (ClientWindowFactory)
      FactoryFinder.getFactory(FactoryFinder.CLIENT_WINDOW_FACTORY);
      return clientWindowFactory.getClientWindow(context);
    }
    ...
  }
```

Done! The complete application is named ch5_10_2.

# Configuring the application

The application represents a per-web-application singleton object, which is the heart of the JSF runtime. Through this object we can accomplish many tasks, such as adding components, converters, validators, subscribing to events, setting listeners, locales, and messaging bundles. It represents the entry point for many JSF artifacts. We refer to it using the following code:

```
FacesContext.getCurrentInstance().getApplication();
```

The application can be extended and customized by following these steps:

1. Extend ApplicationFactory, which is a factory object capable of creating and returning a new Application instance.
2. Extend ApplicationWrapper, which is a simple implementation of Application that allows us to selectively override methods.
3. Configure the custom Application implementation in faces-config.xml.

For example, we can use a custom Application implementation for adding a list of validators to an application. We start by writing a custom application factory as follows:

```
public class CustomApplicationFactory extends ApplicationFactory {

  private ApplicationFactory applicationFactory;

  public CustomApplicationFactory(){}

  public CustomApplicationFactory(ApplicationFactory
  applicationFactory) {
    this.applicationFactory = applicationFactory;
```

```
}

@Override
public void setApplication(Application application) {
 applicationFactory.setApplication(application);
}

@Override
public Application getApplication() {
 Application handler = new CustomApplication(
                      applicationFactory.getApplication());
 return handler;
}
}
```

Now, the job is accomplished by CustomApplication as follows:

```
public class CustomApplication extends ApplicationWrapper {

 private Application application;

 public CustomApplication(Application application) {
  this.application = application;
 }

 @Override
 public Application getWrapped() {
  return application;
 }

 @Override
 public void addValidator(java.lang.String validatorId,
                     java.lang.String validatorClass) {
boolean
  flag = false;
  Iterator i = getWrapped().getValidatorIds();
  while (i.hasNext()) {
       if (i.next().equals("emailValidator")) {
           flag = true;
           break;
       }
  }

  if (flag == false) {
      getWrapped().addValidator("emailValidator",
```

```
                              "book.beans.EmailValidator");
     }

   getWrapped().addValidator(validatorId, validatorClass);
   }
 }
```

Finally, configure the new custom application in `faces-config.xml` as follows:

```xml
<factory>
 <application-factory>
  book.beans.CustomApplicationFactory
 </application-factory>
</factory>
```

 Starting with JSF 2.2, we can use dependency injection with application objects (@`Inject` and @`EJB`). The preceding example, with the list of validators provided by a CDI bean as a `Map`, is available in the code bundle of this chapter under the name `ch5_11`.

# Configuring VDL

The abbreviation VDL stands for **View Declaration Language**, which represents the contract that a view declaration language must implement in order to interact with the JSF runtime. The `ViewDeclarationLanguageFactory` class is used to create and return instances of the `ViewDeclarationLanguage` class.

In order to alter how the runtime transforms an input file into a tree of components, you need to write a custom `ViewDeclarationLanguageFactory` implementation, which can be accomplished by extending the original class and overriding the `getViewDeclarationLanguage` method, as shown in the following code:

```java
public class CustomViewDeclarationLanguageFactory
        extends ViewDeclarationLanguageFactory{

 private ViewDeclarationLanguageFactory
        viewDeclarationLanguageFactory;

 public CustomViewDeclarationLanguageFactory
  (ViewDeclarationLanguageFactory viewDeclarationLanguageFactory){
  this.viewDeclarationLanguageFactory =
```

```
                    viewDeclarationLanguageFactory;
   }

   @Override
   public ViewDeclarationLanguage
           getViewDeclarationLanguage(String viewId) {
     return new
       CustomViewDeclarationLanguage(viewDeclarationLanguageFactory.
        getViewDeclarationLanguage(viewId));
   }
}
```

The `CustomViewDeclarationLanguage` implementation can be written by extending `ViewDeclarationLanguage` and overriding all methods, or extending the new JSF 2.2 `ViewDeclarationLanguageWrapper` class and overriding only the needed method. Our `CustomViewDeclarationLanguage` implementation represents a simple skeleton based on the wrapper class as shown in the following code:

```
public class CustomViewDeclarationLanguage extends
                     ViewDeclarationLanguageWrapper {

  private ViewDeclarationLanguage viewDeclarationLanguage;

  public CustomViewDeclarationLanguage
          (ViewDeclarationLanguage viewDeclarationLanguage) {
    this.viewDeclarationLanguage = viewDeclarationLanguage;
  }

  //override here the needed methods

  @Override
  public ViewDeclarationLanguage getWrapped() {
    return viewDeclarationLanguage;
  }
}
```

This factory can be configured in `faces-config.xml` as follows:

```
<factory>
 <view-declaration-language-factory>
  book.beans.CustomViewDeclarationLanguageFactory
 </view-declaration-language-factory>
</factory>
```

Done! The complete application is named `ch5_17`.

At https://code.google.com/p/javavdl/, you can see an implementation of a JSF VDL that allows pages or complete JSF applications to be authored in pure Java, without the need for any XML or other declarative markup (for example, Facelets).

# Combined power of multiple factories

In the last several sections, you saw how to customize and configure the most used JSF factories. In the final section of this chapter, you will see how to exploit a few factories in the same application. For example, a convenient scenario will assume that we want to fire a non-JSF request and get as response a JSF view. An approach of this scenario consists in writing a Java Servlet capable of converting a non-JSF request into a JSF view.

In order to write such a Servlet, we need to obtain access to FacesContext. For this, we can combine the power of the default LifecycleFactory class with the power of the default FacesContextFactory class. Further, we can access Application via FacesContext, which means that we can obtain the ViewHandler that is responsible for creating JSF views via the createView method. Once the view is created, all we need to do is to set UIViewRoot and tell Lifecycle to render the response (execute the *Render Response* phase). In lines of code, the Servlet looks like the following:

```
@WebServlet(name = "JSFServlet", urlPatterns = {"/jsfServlet"})
public class JSFServlet extends HttpServlet {
...
protected void processRequest(HttpServletRequest request,
 HttpServletResponse response)
 throws ServletException, IOException {

String page = request.getParameter("page");

LifecycleFactory lifecycleFactory = (LifecycleFactory)
  FactoryFinder.getFactory(FactoryFinder.LIFECYCLE_FACTORY);
Lifecycle lifecycle = lifecycleFactory.getLifecycle
(LifecycleFactory.DEFAULT_LIFECYCLE);

FacesContextFactory facesContextFactory = (FacesContextFactory)
  FactoryFinder.getFactory(FactoryFinder.FACES_CONTEXT_FACTORY);
FacesContext facesContext = facesContextFactory.getFacesContext
  (request.getServletContext(), request, response, lifecycle);

Application application = facesContext.getApplication();
ViewHandler viewHandler = application.getViewHandler();
UIViewRoot uiViewRoot = viewHandler.
  createView(facesContext, "/" + page);
```

```
    facesContext.setViewRoot(uiViewRoot);
    lifecycle.render(facesContext);
}
...
```

Now, you can test very easily using the `<h:outputLink>` tag as follows:

```
Navigate page-to-page via h:outputLink - WON'T WORK!
<h:outputLink value="done.xhtml">done.xhtml</h:outputLink>
Navigate page-to-page via h:outputLink, but add context path for the
application to a context-relative path - WORK!
<h:outputLink value="#{facesContext.externalContext.
 applicationContextPath}/faces/done.xhtml">
 done.xhtml</h:outputLink>
Navigate to a JSF view via a non-JSF request using servlet - WORK!
<h:outputLink value="jsfServlet?page=done.xhtml">
 done.xhml</h:outputLink>
```

The complete application is named `ch5_18`.

# Summary

Well, this was a pretty heavy chapter, but JSF's important aspects were touched upon here. You learned how to create, extend, and configure several of the main JSF 2.x artifacts, and how they have been improved by JSF 2.2, especially with the dependency injection mechanism. There are still a lot of things that were not discussed in this chapter, such as state management, facelet factory, and so on, but keep on reading.

See you in the next chapter, where we will discuss about working with tabular data in JSF.

# 6
# Working with Tabular Data

Data that makes sense when displayed in a spreadsheet (or a tabular structure) is known as **tabular data**. In web applications, tabular data is commonly obtained from databases, where the data is natively represented in relational tables. The main JSF component for displaying tabular data is represented by the `<h:dataTable>` tag, which is capable of producing HTML classical tables. This chapter is a tribute to this tag, since tabular data is very commonly used and can be manipulated in many ways. Therefore, in this chapter, you will learn about the following topics:

- Creating a simple JSF table
- The `CollectionDataModel` class of JSF 2.2
- Sorting tables
- Deleting a table row
- Editing/updating a table row
- Adding a new row
- Displaying a row number
- Selecting a single row
- Selecting multiple rows
- Nesting tables
- Paginating tables
- Generating tables with the JSF API
- Filtering tables
- Styling tables

This chapter focuses more on the tables that are populated with data that comes from collections (databases). But, you can include in and manipulate the content in the table with almost any JSF UI component.

# Creating a simple JSF table

Most commonly, everything starts from a POJO class (or a EJB entity class), as shown in the following code—note that tables with hardcoded information were skipped:

```java
public class Players {

    private String player;
    private byte age;
    private String birthplace;
    private String residence;
    private short height;
    private byte weight;
    private String coach;
    private Date born;
    private int ranking;

    public Players() {}

    public Players(int ranking, String player, byte age, String
        birthplace, String residence, short height, byte weight,
        String coach, Date born) {

        this.ranking = ranking;
        this.player = player;
        this.age = age;
        this.birthplace = birthplace;
        this.residence = residence;
        this.height = height;
        this.weight = weight;
        this.coach = coach;
        this.born = born;
    }
    ...
    //getters and setters

}
```

Each instance of this POJO class is actually a row in the table displayed to the user (it's not mandatory, but usually this is how things work). Next, a JSF bean (or CDI bean) will provide a collection of POJO's instances. (The `List`, `Map`, and `Set` instances are the ones that are most commonly used.) In the following code, the `List` instance is shown:

```
@Named
@ViewScoped
public class PlayersBean implements Serializable{

  List<Players> data = new ArrayList<>();
  final SimpleDateFormat sdf = new SimpleDateFormat("dd.MM.yyyy");

  public PlayersBean() {
    try {
      data.add(new Players(2, "NOVAK DJOKOVIC", (byte) 26,
        "Belgrade, Serbia", "Monte Carlo, Monaco", (short) 188,
        (byte) 80, "Boris Becker, Marian Vajda",
        sdf.parse("22.05.1987")));
      data.add(new Players(1, "RAFAEL NADAL", (byte) 27, "Manacor,
        Mallorca, Spain", "Manacor, Mallorca, Spain", (short) 185,
        (byte) 85, "Toni Nadal", sdf.parse("03.06.1986")));
      data.add(new Players(7, "TOMAS BERDYCH", (byte) 28,
        "Valasske Mezirici, Czech", "Monte Carlo, Monaco",
        (short) 196, (byte) 91, "Tomas Krupa",
        sdf.parse("17.09.1985")));

      ...

    } catch (ParseException ex) {
      Logger.getLogger(PlayersBean.class.getName()).
        log(Level.SEVERE, null, ex);
    }
  }

  public List<Players> getData() {
    return data;
  }

  public void setData(List<Players> data) {
    this.data = data;
  }
}
```

Note that, usually, data is queried from a database, but this is not quite relevant here.

This common scenario ends with a piece of code that displays the data on the screen. The code is shown as follows:

```
...
<h:dataTable value="#{playersBean.data}" var="t">
  <h:column>
    <f:facet name="header">Ranking</f:facet>
    #{t.ranking}
  </h:column>
  <h:column>
    <f:facet name="header">Name</f:facet>
    #{t.player}
  </h:column>
  <h:column>
    <f:facet name="header">Age</f:facet>
    #{t.age}
  </h:column>
  <h:column>
    <f:facet name="header">Birthplace</f:facet>
    #{t.birthplace}
  </h:column>
  <h:column>
    <f:facet name="header">Residence</f:facet>
    #{t.residence}
  </h:column>
  <h:column>
    <f:facet name="header">Height (cm)</f:facet>
    #{t.height}
  </h:column>
  <h:column>
    <f:facet name="header">Weight (kg)</f:facet>
    #{t.weight}
  </h:column>
  <h:column>
    <f:facet name="header">Coach</f:facet>
    #{t.coach}
  </h:column>
  <h:column>
    <f:facet name="header">Born</f:facet>
    <h:outputText value="#{t.born}">
      <f:convertDateTime pattern="dd.MM.yyyy" />
    </h:outputText>
  </h:column>
</h:dataTable>
...
```

The output is shown in the following screenshot:

| Ranking | Name | Age | Birthplace | Residence |
|---|---|---|---|---|
| 2 | NOVAK DJOKOVIC | 26 | Belgrade, Serbia | Monte Carlo, Monaco |
| 1 | RAFAEL NADAL | 27 | Manacor, Mallorca, Spain | Manacor, Mallorca, S |
| 7 | TOMAS BERDYCH | 28 | Valasske Mezirici, Czech | Monte Carlo, Monaco |
| 8 | STANISLAS WAWRINKA | 28 | Lausanne, Switzerland | St. Barthelemy, Switze |
| 4 | ANDY MURRAY | 26 | Dunblane, Scotland | London, England |
| 5 | JUAN MARTIN DEL POTRO | 25 | Tandil, Argentina | Tandil, Argentina |
| 10 | JO-WILFRIED TSONGA | 28 | Le Mans, France | Gingins, Switzerland |
| 6 | ROGER FEDERER | 32 | Basel, Switzerland | Bottmingen, Switzerla |
| 9 | RICHARD GASQUET | 27 | Beziers, France | Neuchatel, Switzerlan |
| 3 | DAVID FERRER | 31 | Javea, Spain | Valencia, Spain |

The complete example is available in the code bundle of this chapter, and is named `ch6_1`.

# The CollectionDataModel class of JSF 2.2

Until JSF 2.2, the supported types for the `<h:dataTable>` tag contains `java.util.List`, **arrays**, `java.sql.ResultSet`, `javax.servlet.jsp.jstl.sql.Result`, `javax.faces.model.DataModel`, null (or empty list), and types used as scalar values.

 Starting with JSF 2.2, we can also use `java.util.Collection`. This is especially useful to Hibernate/JPA users, who are usually using the `Set` collections for entity relationships. Therefore, nothing can stop us from using a `HashSet`, `TreeSet`, or `LinkedHashSet` set for feeding our JSF tables.

The next example is like a test case for the most-used Java collections. First, let's declare some collections of `Players` as follows:

- `java.util.ArrayList`: This library implements `java.util.Collection`. The `java.util.ArrayList` collection is declared as follows:

  ```
  ArrayList<Players> dataArrayList = new ArrayList<>();
  ```

- `java.util.LinkedList`: This library implements `java.util.Collection`. The `java.util.LinkedList` collection is declared as follows:

  ```
  LinkedList<Players> dataLinkedList = new LinkedList<>();
  ```

- `java.util.HashSet`: This library implements `java.util.Collection`. The `java.util.HashSet` collection is declared as follows:

  ```
  HashSet<Players> dataHashSet = new HashSet<>();
  ```

- `java.util.TreeSet`: This library implements `java.util.Collection`. The `java.util.TreeSet` collection is declared as follows:

  ```
  TreeSet<Players> dataTreeSet = new TreeSet<>();
  ```

> For the `TreeSet` collection, you have to use `Comparable` elements, or provide `Comparator`. Otherwise, the `TreeSet` collection can't do its job since it wouldn't know how to order the elements. This means that the `Players` class should implement `Comparable<Players>`.

- `java.util.LinkedHashSet`: This library implements `java.util.Collection`. The `java.util.LinkedHashSet` collection is declared as follows:

  ```
  LinkedHashSet<Players> dataLinkedHashSet = new
    LinkedHashSet<>();
  ```

- `java.util.HashMap`: This library doesn't implement `java.util.Collection`. The `java.util.HashMap` collection is declared as follows:

  ```
  HashMap<String, Players> dataHashMap = new HashMap<>();
  ```

- `java.util.TreeMap`: This library doesn't implement `java.util.Collection`. The `java.util.TreeMap` collection is declared as follows:

  ```
  TreeMap<String, Players> dataTreeMap = new TreeMap<>();
  ```

- `java.util.LinkedHashMap`: This library doesn't implement `java.util.Collection`. The `java.util.LinkedHashMap` collection is declared as follows:

  ```
  LinkedHashMap<String, Players> dataLinkedHashMap = new
    LinkedHashMap<>();
  ```

Supposing that these collections are populated and the getters are available; they are used to display their content in a table in the following ways:

- `java.util.ArrayList`: This library implements `java.util.Collection`.. The following is the code of the `java.util.ArrayList` collection:

  ```
  <h:dataTable value="#{playersBean.dataArrayList}" var="t">
    <h:column>
      <f:facet name="header">Ranking</f:facet>
      #{t.ranking}
  ```

```
    </h:column>
  . . .
  </h:dataTable>
```

 In the same manner, we can display in a table the LinkedList, HashSet, TreeSet, and LinkedHashSet collection classes.

- `java.util.LinkedList`: This library implements `java.util.Collection`. The following is the code of the `java.util.LinkedList` collection:

```
<h:dataTable value="#{playersBean.dataLinkedList}" var="t">
  <h:column>
    <f:facet name="header">Ranking</f:facet>
    #{t.ranking}
  </h:column>
  . . .
</h:dataTable>
```

- `java.util.HashSet`: This library implements `java.util.Collection`. The following is the code of the `java.util.HashSet` collection:

```
<h:dataTable value="#{playersBean.dataHashSet}" var="t">
  <h:column>
    <f:facet name="header">Ranking</f:facet>
    #{t.ranking}
  </h:column>
  . . .
</h:dataTable>
```

- `java.util.TreeSet`: This library implements `java.util.Collection`. The following is the code of the `java.util.TreeSet` collection:

```
<h:dataTable value="#{playersBean.dataTreeSet}" var="t">
  <h:column>
    <f:facet name="header">Ranking</f:facet>
    #{t.ranking}
  </h:column>
  . . .
</h:dataTable>
```

- `java.util.LinkedHashSet`: This library implements `java.util.Collection`. The following is the code of the `java.util.LinkedHashSet` collection:

```
<h:dataTable value="#{playersBean.dataLinkedHashSet}"
  var="t">
  <h:column>
    <f:facet name="header">Ranking</f:facet>
    #{t.ranking}
  </h:column>
  ...
</h:dataTable>
```

 Use the following examples to display a `Map` collection in a table. (`HashMap`, `TreeMap`, and `LinkedHashMap` are displayed in the same way.)

- `java.util.HashMap`: This library doesn't implement `java.util.Collection`. The following is the code of the `java.util.HashMap` collection:

```
<h:dataTable value="#{playersBean.dataHashMap.entrySet()}"
  var="t">
  <h:column>
    <f:facet name="header">Ranking</f:facet>
    #{t.key}
  </h:column>
  <h:column>
    <f:facet name="header">Name</f:facet>
    #{t.value.player}
  </h:column>
  ...
</h:dataTable>
```

- `java.util.TreeMap`: This library doesn't implement `java.util.Collection`. The following is the code of the `java.util.TreeMap` collection:

```
<h:dataTable value="#{playersBean.dataTreeMap.entrySet()}"
  var="t">
  <h:column>
    <f:facet name="header">Ranking</f:facet>
    #{t.key}
  </h:column>
  <h:column>
```

```
        <f:facet name="header">Name</f:facet>
        #{t.value.player}
      </h:column>
    ...
    </h:dataTable>
```

- `java.util.LinkedHashMap`: This library doesn't implement `java.util.Collection`. The following is the code of the `java.util.LinkedHashMap` collection:

```
<h:dataTable value="#{playersBean.dataLinkedHashMap.
  entrySet()}" var="t">
  <h:column>
    <f:facet name="header">Ranking</f:facet>
    #{t.key}
  </h:column>
  <h:column>
    <f:facet name="header">Name</f:facet>
    #{t.value.player}
  </h:column>
  ...
</h:dataTable>
```

For a `Map` collection, you can have a getter method, as follows:

```
HashMap<String, Players> dataHashMap = new HashMap<>();

public Collection<Players> getDataHashMap() {
  return dataHashMap.values();
}
```

In this case, the code of the table will be as follows:

```
<h:dataTable value="#{playersBean.dataHashMap}" var="t">
  <h:column>
    <f:facet name="header">Ranking</f:facet>
    #{t.ranking}
  </h:column>
  ...
</h:dataTable>
```

The `CollectionDataModel` class is an extension of the `DataModel` class that wraps a `Collection` class of Java objects. Furthermore, in this chapter, you will see some examples that will alter this new class.

The complete example is available in the code bundle of this chapter, and is named ch6_2.

# Sorting tables

In the previous examples, the data is arbitrarily displayed. Sorting the data provides more clarity and accuracy in reading and using the information; for example, see the screenshot of the *Creating a simple JSF table* section. You can try to visually localize the number 1 in the ATP ranking, and number 2 and number 3, and so on, but it is much more useful to have the option of sorting the table by the **Ranking** column. This is a pretty simple task to implement, especially if you are familiar with Java's `List`, `Comparator`, and `Comparable` features. It is beyond the scope of this book to present these features, but you can accomplish most of the sorting tasks by overriding the `compare` method, which has a straightforward flow: it compares both of its arguments for order and returns a negative integer, zero, or a positive integer, as the first argument is less than, equal to, or greater than the second. For example, let's see some common sortings:

- Sort the list of strings, such as player's names. To do this sorting, the code of the `compare` method is as follows:

```
...
String dir="asc"; //or "dsc" for descending sort

Collections.sort(data, new Comparator<Players>() {
  @Override
  public int compare(Players key_1, Players key_2) {
    if (dir.equals("asc")) {
      return key_1.getPlayer().
        compareTo(key_2.getPlayer());
    } else {
      return key_2.getPlayer().
        compareTo(key_1.getPlayer());
    }
  }
});
...
```

- Sort the list of numbers, such as the player's rankings. To do this sorting, the code of the `compare` method is as follows:

```
...
int dir = 1; //1 for ascending, -1 for descending

Collections.sort(data, new Comparator<Players>() {
  @Override
  public int compare(Players key_1, Players key_2) {
    return dir * (key_1.getRanking() - key_2.getRanking());
  }
});
...
```

- Sort the list of dates, such as player's birthdays (this works as in the case of strings). To do this sorting, the code of the `compare` method is as follows:

```
...
String dir="asc"; //or "dsc" for descending sort

Collections.sort(data, new Comparator<Players>() {
  @Override
  public int compare(Players key_1, Players key_2) {
    if (dir.equals("asc")) {
      return key_1.getBorn().compareTo(key_2.getBorn());
    } else {
      return key_2.getBorn().compareTo(key_1.getBorn());
    }
  }
});
...
```

> The `data` argument stands for a `List` collection type because not all types of collections can take the place of this one. For example, `List` will work perfectly, while `HashSet` won't. There are different workarounds to sort collections that are not `List` collections. You have to ensure that you choose the right collection for your case.

If you know how to write comparators for the selected collection, then everything else is simple. You can encapsulate the comparators in managed beans methods and attach buttons, links, or anything else that calls those methods. For example, you can add these comparators to the `PlayersBean` backing bean, as shown in the following code:

```
@Named
@ViewScoped
public class PlayersBean implements Serializable{

  List<Players> data = new ArrayList<>();
  final SimpleDateFormat sdf = new SimpleDateFormat("dd.MM.yyyy");

  public PlayersBean() {
    try {
      data.add(new Players(2, "NOVAK DJOKOVIC", (byte) 26,
        "Belgrade, Serbia", "Monte Carlo, Monaco", (short) 188,
        (byte) 80, "Boris Becker, Marian Vajda",
        sdf.parse("22.05.1987")));
...
    } catch (ParseException ex) {
      Logger.getLogger(PlayersBean.class.getName()).
        log(Level.SEVERE, null, ex);
    }
  }

  public List<Players> getData() {
    return data;
  }

  public void setData(List<Players> data) {
    this.data = data;
  }

  public String sortDataByRanking(final int dir) {

    Collections.sort(data, new Comparator<Players>() {
      @Override
      public int compare(Players key_1, Players key_2) {
        return dir * (key_1.getRanking() - key_2.getRanking());
      }
    });
```

```
      return null;
   }

   public String sortDataByName(final String dir) {

      Collections.sort(data, new Comparator<Players>() {
         @Override
         public int compare(Players key_1, Players key_2) {
            if (dir.equals("asc")) {
               return key_1.getPlayer().compareTo(key_2.getPlayer());
            } else {
               return key_2.getPlayer().compareTo(key_1.getPlayer());
            }
         }
      });
      return null;
   }

   public String sortDataByDate(final String dir) {

      Collections.sort(data, new Comparator<Players>() {
         @Override
         public int compare(Players key_1, Players key_2) {
            if (dir.equals("asc")) {
               return key_1.getBorn().compareTo(key_2.getBorn());
            } else {
               return key_2.getBorn().compareTo(key_1.getBorn());
            }
         }
      });
      return null;
   }
   . . .
```

Next, you can easily modify the code of the index.xhtml page to provide access to the sorting feature as follows:

```
   . . .
   <h:dataTable value="#{playersBean.data}" var="t" border="1">
      <h:column>
         <f:facet name="header">
            <h:commandLink action="#{playersBean.sortDataByRanking(1)}">
               Ranking ASC
            </h:commandLink>
```

```
        <h:commandLink action="#{playersBean.
          sortDataByRanking(-1)}">
          Ranking DSC
        </h:commandLink>
      </f:facet>
      #{t.ranking}
    </h:column>
    <h:column>
      <f:facet name="header">
        <h:commandLink
          action="#{playersBean.sortDataByName('asc')}">
          Name ASC
        </h:commandLink>
        |
        <h:commandLink
          action="#{playersBean.sortDataByName('dsc')}">
          Name DSC
        </h:commandLink>
      </f:facet>
      #{t.player}
    </h:column>
    ...
    <h:column>
      <f:facet name="header">
        <h:commandLink
          action="#{playersBean.sortDataByDate('asc')}">
          Born ASC
        </h:commandLink>
        |
        <h:commandLink
          action="#{playersBean.sortDataByDate('dcs')}">
          Born DSC
        </h:commandLink>
      </f:facet>
      <h:outputText value="#{t.born}">
        <f:convertDateTime pattern="dd.MM.yyyy" />
      </h:outputText>
    </h:column>
  </h:dataTable>
  ...
```

The output is shown in the following screenshot:

| Ranking ASC \| Ranking DSC | Name ASC \| Name DSC | Age | | Coach | Born ASC \| Born DSC |
|---|---|---|---|---|---|
| 2 | NOVAK DJOKOVIC | 26 | Belgra | ːer, Marian Vajda | 21.05.1987 |
| 1 | RAFAEL NADAL | 27 | Manac | l | 02.06.1986 |
| 7 | TOMAS BERDYCH | 28 | Valass | ːpa | 16.09.1985 |
| 8 | STANISLAS WAWRINKA | 28 | Lausaː | orman | 27.03.1985 |
| 4 | ANDY MURRAY | 26 | Dunblː | | 14.05.1987 |
| 5 | JUAN MARTIN DEL POTRO | 25 | Tandil | vin | 22.09.1988 |
| 10 | JO-WILFRIED TSONGA | 28 | Le Mː | cude & Thierry Ascione | 16.04.1985 |
| 6 | ROGER FEDERER | 32 | Basel, | ːerg, Severin Luthi | 07.08.1981 |
| 9 | RICHARD GASQUET | 27 | Bezier | uera and Sebastien | 17.06.1986 |
| 3 | DAVID FERRER | 31 | Javea, | isco Altur | 01.04.1982 |

The complete example is available in the code bundle of this chapter, and is named ch6_3_1.

As you can see, each sorting provides two links: one for ascending and one for descending. We can easily glue these links in a switch-link, by using an extra property in our view scoped bean. For example, we can declare a property named sortType, as follows:

```
...
private String sortType = "asc";
...
```

Add a simple condition to make it act as a switch between ascending and descending sort as shown in the following code:

```
...
public String sortDataByRanking() {

  Collections.sort(data, new Comparator<Players>() {
    @Override
    public int compare(Players key_1, Players key_2) {
      if(sortType.equals("asc")){
        return key_1.getRanking() - key_2.getRanking();
      } else {
        return (-1) * (key_1.getRanking() - key_2.getRanking());
      }
    }
  });

  sortType = (sortType.equals("asc")) ? "dsc" : "asc";
  return null;
}
...
```

Now, the `index.xhtml` page contains a single link per sort, as shown in the following code:

```
...
<h:dataTable value="#{playersBean.data}" var="t" border="1">
  <h:column>
    <f:facet name="header">
      <h:commandLink action="#{playersBean.sortDataByRanking()}">
        Ranking
      </h:commandLink>
    </f:facet>
    #{t.ranking}
  </h:column>
...
```

The output of this trick can be seen in the following screenshot:

The complete example is available in the code bundle of this chapter, and is named `ch6_3_2`.

# Sorting and DataModel – CollectionDataModel

A more complex sorting example involves a decorator class that extends the `javax.faces.model.DataModel` class. JSF uses a `DataModel` class even if we are not aware of it, because each collection (`List`, array, `HashMap` and so on) is wrapped by JSF in a `DataModel` class (or, in a subclass, as `ArrayDataModel`, `CollectionDataModel`, `ListDataModel`, `ResultDataModel`, `ResultSetDataModel`, or `ScalarDataModel`). JSF will call the table `DataModel` class's methods when it renders/decodes table data. In the following screenshot, you can see all directly known subclasses of the `DataModel` class:

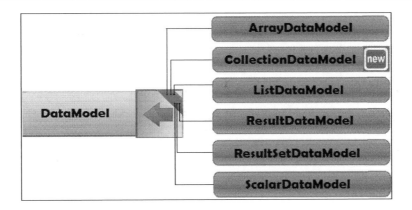

As you will see in this chapter, sometimes you need to be aware of the `DataModel` class because you need to alter its default behavior. (It is recommended that you take a quick look at the official documentation of this class's section at `https://javaserverfaces.java.net/nonav/docs/2.2/javadocs/` to obtain a better understanding.) The most common cases involve the rendering row numbers, sorting, and altering the row count of a table. When you do this, you will expose the `DataModel` class instead of the underlying collection.

For example, let's suppose that we need to use a collection, such as `HashSet`. This collection doesn't guarantee that the iteration order will remain constant over time, which can be a problem if we want to sort it. Of course, there are a few workarounds, such as converting it to `List` or using `TreeSet` instead, but we can alter the `DataModel` class that wraps the `HashSet` collection, which is the new JSF 2.2 class, `CollectionDataModel`.

We can accomplish this in a few steps, which are listed as follows:

1.  Extend the `CollectionDataModel` class for overriding the default behavior of its methods, as shown in the following code:

    ```
    public class SortDataModel<T> extends
      CollectionDataModel<T> {
    . . .
    ```

2.  Provide a constructor and use it for passing the original model (in this case, `CollectionDataModel`). Besides the original model, we need an array of integers representing the indexes of rows (For example, `rows[0]=0`, `rows[1]=1`, ... `rows[n] = model.getRowCount()`). Sorting the row indexes will actually sort the `HashSet` collection, as shown in the following code:

    ```
    . . .
    CollectionDataModel<T> model;
    ```

```
    private Integer[] rows;

    public SortDataModel(CollectionDataModel<T> model) {
      this.model = model;
      initRows();
    }

    private void initRows() {
      int rowCount = model.getRowCount();
      if (rowCount != -1) {
        this.rows = new Integer[rowCount];
        for (int i = 0; i < rowCount; ++i) {
          rows[i] = i;
        }
      }
    }
    ...
```

3.  Next, we need to override the setRowIndex method to replace the default row index, as shown in the following code:

```
@Override
public void setRowIndex(int rowIndex) {

    if ((0 <= rowIndex) && (rowIndex < rows.length)) {
      model.setRowIndex(rows[rowIndex]);
    } else {
      model.setRowIndex(rowIndex);
    }
}
```

4.  Finally, provide a comparator as follows:

```
public void sortThis(final Comparator<T> comparator) {
    Comparator<Integer> rowc = new Comparator<Integer>() {
      @Override
      public int compare(Integer key_1, Integer key_2) {
        T key_1_data = getData(key_1);
        T key_2_data = getData(key_2);
        return comparator.compare(key_1_data, key_2_data);
      }
    };
    Arrays.sort(rows, rowc);
}

private T getData(int row) {
```

```
    int baseRowIndex = model.getRowIndex();
    model.setRowIndex(row);
    T newRowData = model.getRowData();
    model.setRowIndex(baseRowIndex);

    return newRowData;
}
```

5. Now, our custom `CollectionDataModel` class with sorting capabilities is ready. We can test it by declaring and populating `HashSet`, wrapping it in the original `CollectionDataModel` class, and passing it to the custom `SortDataModel` class, as shown in the following code:

```
private HashSet<Players> dataHashSet = new HashSet<>();
private SortDataModel<Players> sortDataModel;
...
public PlayersBean() {
  dataHashSet.add(new Players(2, "NOVAK DJOKOVIC",
    (byte) 26, "Belgrade, Serbia", "Monte Carlo, Monaco",
    (short) 188, (byte) 80, "Boris Becker, Marian Vajda",
    sdf.parse("22.05.1987")));
...

  sortDataModel = new SortDataModel<>(new
    CollectionDataModel<>(dataHashSet));
}
...
```

6. Since we are the caller, we need to provide a comparator. The complete example is available in the code bundle of this chapter, and is named `ch6_3_3`.

# Deleting a table row

Deleting a table row can be easily implemented by performing the following steps:

1. Define a method in the managed bean that receives information about the row that should be deleted, and remove it from the collection that feeds the table.

   For example, for a `Set` collection, the code will be as follows (`HashSet<Players>`):

```
public void deleteRowHashSet(Players player) {
  dataHashSet.remove(player);
}
```

For `Map<String, Players>`, the code will be as follows:

```
public void deleteRowHashMap(Object key) {
  dataHashMap.remove(String.valueOf(key));
}
```

2. Besides columns containing data, add a new column in the table named **Delete**. Each row can be a link to the delete*XXX* method.

For example, we can delete a value from `Set` (`HashSet<Players>`), as shown in the following code:

```
<h:dataTable value="#{playersBean.dataHashSet}" var="t">
...
  <h:column>
    <f:facet name="header">Delete</f:facet>
    <h:commandLink value="Delete"
      action="#{playersBean.deleteRowHashSet(t)}" />
  </h:column>
...
</h:dataTable>
```

And from `Map<String, Players>`, as follows:

```
<h:dataTable value="#{playersBean.dataHashMap.entrySet()}"
  var="t">
...
  <h:column>
    <f:facet name="header">Delete</f:facet>
    <h:commandLink value="Delete"
      action="#{playersBean.deleteRowHashMap(t.key)}" />
  </h:column>
...
</h:dataTable>
```

In the following screenshot, you can see a possible output:

| Weight (kg) | Coach | Born | Delete |
|---|---|---|---|
| 80 | Boris Becker, Marian Vajda | 21.05.1987 | Delete |
| 85 | Toni Nadal | 02.06.1986 | Delete |
| 81 | Magnus Norman | 27.03.1985 | Delete |
| 97 | Franco Davin | 22.09.1988 | Delete |
| 91 | Nicolas Escude & Thierry Ascione | 16.04.1985 | Delete |
| 73 | Jose Francisco Altur | 01.04.1982 | Delete |
| 91 | Tomas Krupa | 16.09.1985 | Delete |
| 84 | Ivan Lendl | 14.05.1987 | Delete |
| 75 | Sergi Bruguera and Sebastien | 17.06.1986 | Delete |
| 85 | Stefan Edberg, Severin Luthi | 07.08.1981 | Delete |

**after deleting three rows**

| ight (kg) | Coach | Born | Delete |
|---|---|---|---|
| | Boris Becker, Marian Vajda | 21.05.1987 | Delete |
| | Toni Nadal | 02.06.1986 | Delete |
| | Franco Davin | 22.09.1988 | Delete |
| | Nicolas Escude & Thierry Ascione | 16.04.1985 | Delete |
| | Tomas Krupa | 16.09.1985 | Delete |
| | Sergi Bruguera and Sebastien | 17.06.1986 | Delete |
| | Stefan Edberg, Severin Luthi | 07.08.1981 | Delete |

The complete example is available in the code bundle of this chapter, and is
named ch6_4.

# Editing/updating a table row

One of the most convenient approaches for editing/updating a table row consists
of using a special property to track the row edit status. This property can be named
edited and it should be of the type boolean (default false). Define it in the POJO
class, as shown in the following code:

```
public class Players {
  ...
  private boolean edited;
  ...
  public boolean isEdited() {
    return edited;
  }

  public void setEdited(boolean edited) {
    this.edited = edited;
  }
}
```

> If your POJO class is an entity class, then define this new property as
> transient, using the @Transient annotation or transient modifier.
> This annotation will tell JPA that this property doesn't participate in
> persistence and that its values are never stored in the database.

Next, assign an **Edit** link to each row. Using the rendered attribute, you can
easily show/hide the link using a simple EL condition; initially, the link is
visible for each row. For example, take a look at the following use cases:

- For a Set collection, the code is as follows:

```
...
<h:column>
  <f:facet name="header">Edit</f:facet>
  <h:commandLink value="Edit"
    action="#{playersBean.editRowHashSet(t)}"
    rendered="#{not t.edited}" />
</h:column>
...
```

- For a `Map` collection, the code is as follows:

```
...
<h:column>
  <f:facet name="header">Edit</f:facet>
  <h:commandLink value="Edit"
    action="#{playersBean.editRowHashMap(t.value)}"
    rendered="#{not t.value.edited}"/>
</h:column>
...
```

When the link is clicked, the `edited` property will be switched from `false` to `true` and the table will be re-rendered as follows:

- For a `Set` collection, the code of the `editRowHashSet` method is as follows:

```
public void editRowHashSet(Players player) {
  player.setEdited(true);
}
```

- For a `Map` collection, the code of the `editRowHashSet` method is as follows:

```
public void editRowHashMap(Players player) {
  player.setEdited(true);
}
```

This means that the link is not rendered anymore and the user should be able to edit that table row. You need to switch between the `<h:outputText>` tag, used to display data (visible when the `edited` property is `false`), and the `<h:inputText>` tag, which is used to collect data (visible when the `edited` property is `true`). Using the `rendered` attribute again will do the trick, as follows:

- For a `Set` collection, the code is modified as follows:

```
...
<h:column>
  <f:facet name="header">Name</f:facet>
  <h:inputText value="#{t.player}"
    rendered="#{t.edited}" />
  <h:outputText value="#{t.player}"
    rendered="#{not t.edited}" />
</h:column>
...
```

- For a `Map` collection, the code is modified as follows:

```
...
<h:column>
  <f:facet name="header">Name</f:facet>
```

```
<h:inputText value="#{t.value.player}"
  rendered="#{t.value.edited}" />
<h:outputText value="#{t.value.player}"
  rendered="#{not t.value.edited}" />
</h:column>
...
```

Finally, you need a button to save changes; this button will set the `edited` property back to `false`, preparing the table for more edits, as follows:

- For a `Set` collection, the code for the button is as follows:

```
<h:commandButton value="Save Hash Set Changes"
  action="#{playersBean.saveHashSet()}" />
```

- For a `Map` collection, the code for the button is as follows:

```
<h:commandButton value="Save Hash Map Changes"
  action="#{playersBean.saveHashMap()}" />
```

This is a straightforward action, as you can see in the following points—values inserted in the input textbox are automatically saved in the collection:

- For a `Set` collection, the code is as follows:

```
public void saveHashSet() {
  for (Players player : dataHashSet) {
    player.setEdited(false);
  }
}
```

- For a `Map` collection, the code is as follows:

```
public void saveHashMap() {
  for (Map.Entry pairs : dataHashMap.entrySet()) {
    ((Players) pairs.getValue()).setEdited(false);
  }
}
```

Done! In the following screenshot, you can see a possible output:

| No | Ranking | Name | Age | Birthplace | Weight (kg) | Coach | Born | Delete | Edit |
|----|---------|------|-----|------------|-------------|-------|------|--------|------|
| 1. | 4 | ANDY MURRAY | 26 | Dunblane, Scotland | 4 | Ivan Lendl | 14.05.1987 | Delete | Edit |
| 2. | 9 | RICHARD GASQUET | 27 | Beziers, France | 5 | Sergi Bruguera and Sebastien | 17.06.1986 | Delete | Edit |
| 3. | 5 | JUAN MARTI | 25 | Tandil, Argent | 7 | Franco Davin | 22.09.1988 | Delete | |
| 4. | 8 | STANISLAS WAWRINKA | 28 | Lausanne, Switzerland | 1 | Magnus Norman | 27.03.1985 | Delete | Edit |
| 5. | 2 | NOVAK DJOK | 26 | Belgrade, Ser | 0 | Boris Becker, | 21.05.1987 | Delete | |
| 6. | 3 | DAVID FERRER | 31 | Javea, Spain | 3 | Jose Francisco Altur | 01.04.1982 | Delete | Edit |

The complete example is available in the code bundle of this chapter, and is named `ch6_5`.

# Adding a new row

Adding a new row is also a simple task. First, you need to provide a form that reflects a table row content, as shown in the following screenshot:

This form can be easily implemented using the following code:

```
...
<h:inputText value="#{playersBean.player}"/>
<h:inputText value="#{playersBean.age}"/>
<h:inputText value="#{playersBean.birthplace}"/>
<h:inputText value="#{playersBean.residence}"/>
<h:inputText value="#{playersBean.height}"/>
<h:inputText value="#{playersBean.weight}"/>
<h:inputText value="#{playersBean.coach}"/>
<h:inputText value="#{playersBean.born}">
  <f:convertDateTime pattern="dd.MM.yyyy" />
</h:inputText>
<h:inputText value="#{playersBean.ranking}"/>
<h:commandButton value="Add Player"
  action="#{playersBean.addNewPlayer()}"/>
...
```

The button labeled **Add Player** will call a managed bean method that creates a new Players instance and adds it in the collection that feeds the table, as shown in the following code:

```
public void addNewPlayer() {
    Players new_player = new Players(ranking, player, age,
      birthplace, residence, height, weight, coach, born);
    //adding in a Set
```

```
    dataHashSet.add(new_player);
    //adding in a Map
    dataHashMap.put(String.valueOf(ranking), new_player);
}
```

In the following screenshot, you can see the newly added row from the data shown in the preceding screenshot:

| 8 | STANISLAS WAWRINKA | 28 | Lausanne, Switzerland | St. Barthelemy, Switzerland | 183 | 81 | Magnus Norman | 27.03.1985 | Delete |
| 11 | MILOS RAONIC | 23 | Podgorica, Montenegro | Thornhill, Canada | 196 | 88 | Ivan Ljubicic | 27.12.1990 | Delete |

The complete example is available in the code bundle of this chapter, and is named ch6_6_1.

A more elegant approach is to add a row directly in the table and eliminate this user form. This can be easily accomplished by following these simple steps:

1. Use linked collections (for example, use LinkedHashSet instead of HashSet or LinkedHashMap instead of HashMap). A table is populated by iterating the corresponding collection, but some collections, such as HashSet or HashMap, do not provide an iteration order, which means that the iteration order is unpredictable. This is important because we want to add a row at the end of the table, but this is hard to achieve with an unpredictable iteration order. But a linked collection would fix this issue, which is shown in the following code:

   ```
   LinkedHashSet<Players> dataHashSet = new LinkedHashSet<>();
   LinkedHashMap<String, Players> dataHashMap = new
     LinkedHashMap<>();
   ```

2. Add a new row by creating a new item in the corresponding collection and activate the editable mode using the Set and Map collections as follows:

   ° The following is the code for a linked Set collection:

   ```
   . . .
   <h:commandButton value="Add New Row"
     action="#{playersBean.addNewRowInSet()}" />
   . . .
   public void addNewRowInSet() {
     Players new_player = new Players();
     new_player.setEdited(true);
     dataHashSet.add(new_player);
   }
   ```

- ° The following is the code for a linked `Map` collection:

```
...
<h:commandButton value="Add New Row"
  action="#{playersBean.addNewRowInMap()}" />
...

public void addNewRowInMap() {
  Players new_player = new Players();
  new_player.setEdited(true);
  dataHashMap.put(String.valueOf(dataHashMap.size() + 1),
    new_player);
}
```

Check out the following screenshot for a possible output:

| 3 | DAVID FERRER | 31 | | 73 | Jose Francisco Altur | 01.04.1982 | Delete | Edit |
| 11 | | 0 | | 0 | | | Delete | |
| Save Hash Map Changes | Add New Row | | | | | | | |

The complete example is available in the code bundle of this chapter, and is named `ch6_6_2`.

# Displaying row numbers

By default, JSF doesn't provide a method for displaying row numbers. But as you can see in the screenshot depicting the output in the *Editing/updating a table row* section, there is a column named **No** that displays row numbers. You can obtain this column in at least two ways. The simplest workaround consists of binding the table to the current view, as shown in the following code:

```
<h:dataTable value="..." binding="#{table}" var="t">
  <h:column>
    <f:facet name="header">No</f:facet>
    #{table.rowIndex+1}.
  </h:column>
  ...
```

Another approach is to obtain it using the `DataModel` class, which has the `getRowIndex` method to return the currently selected row number. In order to do that, you need to wrap the collection in a `DataModel` class.

The example named `ch6_7` contains the first approach of this task.

# Selecting a single row

The easiest implementation of such a task is to provide a button for each row in the table. When a button is clicked, it can pass the selected row, as shown in the following code:

```
<h:dataTable value="#{playersBean.dataHashSet}" var="t"
  border="1">
  <h:column>
    <f:facet name="header">Select</f:facet>
    <h:commandButton value="#"
      action="#{playersBean.showSelectedPlayer(t)}"/>
  </h:column>
...
```

Since the `showSelectedPlayer` method receives the selected row, it can process it further with no other requirements. The complete example is available in the code bundle of this chapter, and is named `ch6_8_1`.

Generally speaking, selecting one item from a bunch of items is a job for a group of radio buttons. In a JSF table, items are rows, and adding a radio button per row will result in a column as shown in the following screenshot:

| Select | Ranking | Name | Age | Birthplace |
|--------|---------|------|-----|------------|
| ○ | 3 | DAVID FERRER | 31 | Javea, Spain |
| ○ | 2 | NOVAK DJOKOVIC | 26 | Belgrade, Serbia |
| ○ | 10 | JO-WILFRIED TSONGA | 28 | Le Mans, France |
| ● | 1 | RAFAEL NADAL | 27 | Manacor, Mallorca, Spain |
| ○ | 7 | TOMAS BERDYCH | 28 | Valasske Mezirici, Czech |
| ○ | 6 | ROGER FEDERER | 32 | Basel, Switzerland |

However, adding radio buttons in the `<h:column>` tag using the `<h:selectOneRadio>` tag doesn't behave as expected. The main functionality of radio buttons doesn't work; selecting one radio will not deselect the rest of radios in the group. It is now acting more like a group of checkboxes. You can fix this issue by implementing a deselection mechanism through JavaScript. Moreover, at this point, you can set a JSF hidden field with the value of the selected row. For example, if the table is populated by `Map`, you use the following code:

```
<script type="text/javascript">
//<![CDATA[
```

```
    function deselectRadios(id, val) {

      var f = document.getElementById("hashMapFormId");
      for (var i = 0; i < f.length; i++)
      {
        var e = f.elements[i];
        var eid = e.id;
        if (eid.indexOf("radiosId") !== -1) {
          if (eid.indexOf(id) === -1) {
            e.checked = false;
          } else {
            e.checked = true;
            document.getElementById("hashMapFormId:
              selectedRowId").value = val;
          }
        }
      }
    }
  //]]>
</script>
```

First, you need to find the form containing the radios by the ID. Afterwards, iterate through the form's children, and identify each radio by a fixed part of its ID. Check only the radio that was selected by the user, and uncheck the rest of them. Next, populate a hidden field with the value of the selected row. The ID of the selected radio and the row value are provided as arguments, as follows (in this case, the table is populated from Map):

```
<h:dataTable value="#{playersBean.dataHashMap.entrySet()}"
  var="t">
  <h:column>
    <f:facet name="header">Select</f:facet>
    <h:selectOneRadio id="radiosId"
      onclick="deselectRadios(this.id, '#{t.key}');">
      <f:selectItem itemValue="null"/>
    </h:selectOneRadio>
  </h:column>
  ...
```

Besides the hidden field for storing the selected row information, you need a button labeled **Show Hash Map Selection**, as shown in the following code:

```
<h:inputHidden id="selectedRowId"
  value="#{playersBean.selectedPlayerKey}"/>
<h:commandButton value="Show Hash Map Selection"
  action="#{playersBean.showSelectedPlayer()}" />
```

The following `showSelectedPlayer` method is ready to process the selected row:

```
public void showSelectedPlayer() {
  Players player = dataHashMap.get(selectedPlayerKey);

  if (player != null) {
    logger.log(Level.INFO, "Selected player:{0}",
      player.getPlayer());
  } else {
    logger.log(Level.INFO, "No player selected!");
  }
}
```

Done! The complete example is available in the code bundle of this chapter and is named `ch6_8_2`.

If you feel that using a hidden field is not a very elegant approach, then you can replace its role by using the `valueChangeListener` attribute of the `<h:selectOneRadio>` tag.

In the code bundle of this chapter, you can find an example that uses the `valueChangeListener` attribute named `ch6_8_3`.

# Selecting multiple rows

Multiple selection is commonly achieved using groups of checkboxes. One of the most convenient approaches for multiple selections consists of using a special property for tracking the row selection status. This property can be named `selected` and it should be of type `boolean` (default `false`). You can define it in the POJO class as follows:

```
public class Players {
...
  private boolean selected;
  ...
  public boolean isSelected() {
    return selected;
  }

  public void setSelected(boolean selected) {
    this.selected = selected;
  }
}
...
```

If your POJO class is an entity class, then define this new property as transient, using the `@Transient` annotation or transient modifier. This annotation will tell JPA that this property doesn't participate in persistence and his values are never stored in the database.

Next, assign a checkbox to each row (`<h:selectBooleanCheckbox>`). Using the `value` attribute and the `selected` property, you can easily track the selection status, as shown in the following code:

```
<h:dataTable value="#{playersBean.dataHashSet}" var="t">
  <h:column>
    <f:facet name="header">Select</f:facet>
    <h:selectBooleanCheckbox value="#{t.selected}" />
  </h:column>
. . .
```

So the `<h:selectBooleanCheckbox>` tag will do the hard work for us (we just exploit its natural behavior), therefore, all you need is a button labeled **Show Selected Players**, as shown in the following line:

```
<h:commandButton value="Show Selected Players"
    action="#{playersBean.showSelectedPlayers()}" />
```

The `showSelectedPlayers` method has an easy task. It can iterate the collection and check the status of the `selected` property for each item; this is a good chance to reset the selected items as well. For example, you can extract the selected items in a separate list, as follows:

```
. . .
HashSet<Players> dataHashSet = new HashSet<>();
List<Players> selectedPlayers  = new ArrayList<>();
. . .
public void showSelectedPlayers() {
  selectedPlayers.clear();
  for (Players player : dataHashSet) {
    if(player.isSelected()){
      logger.log(Level.INFO, "Selected player: {0}",
        layer.getPlayer());
      selectedPlayers.add(player);
      player.setSelected(false);
    }
  }

  //the selected players were extracted in a List ...
}
```

The complete example is available in the code bundle of this chapter, and is named `ch6_8_4`.

If you don't want to use an extra property, such as `selected`, you can use a `Map<String, Boolean>` map. The code is pretty straightforward; therefore, a quick look over the complete code, `ch6_8_5`, will clarify things instantly.

# Nesting tables

It's most likely that you won't need to display a table inside another table, but there are cases when this workaround can be useful in obtaining a clear presentation of the data. For example, nested collections can be presented as nested tables as follows:

```
HashMap<Players, HashSet<Trophies>> dataHashMap = new HashMap<>();
```

Here, players are stored in `HashMap` as keys, and each player has a collection (`HashSet`) of trophies. Each `HashSet` value is a value in `HashMap`. Therefore, you need to display the table of players; however, you need to display each player's trophies. This can be achieved as shown in the following code:

```
<h:dataTable value="#{playersBean.dataHashMap.entrySet()}"
  var="t">
  <h:column>
    <f:facet name="header">Ranking</f:facet>
    #{t.key.ranking}
  </h:column>
  <h:column>
    <f:facet name="header">Name</f:facet>
    #{t.key.player}
  </h:column>
    ...
  <h:column>
    <f:facet name="header">Trophies 2013</f:facet>
    <h:dataTable value="#{t.value}" var="q" border="1">
    <h:column>
      #{q.trophy}
    </h:column>
    </h:dataTable>
  </h:column>
</h:dataTable>
```

A possible output for the preceding code can be seen in the following screenshot:

| Ranking | Name | Born | Trophies 2013 |
|---------|------|------|---------------|
| 2 | NOVAK DJOKOVIC | 21.05.1987 | Beijing |
| | | | ATP World Tour Masters 1000 Paris |
| | | | Dubai |
| | | | Barclays ATP World Tour Finals |
| | | | ATP World Tour Masters 1000 Monte Carlo |
| | | | Australian Open |
| | | | ATP World Tour Masters 1000 Shanghai |

The complete application is named `ch6_9`, and is available in the code bundle of this chapter.

# Paginating tables

When you need to display large tables (with many rows), it can be useful to implement a pagination mechanism. There are many advantages, such as its fancy look, the clear presentation of data, saving space in web pages, and lazy loading.

In a standard version of such a table, we should be able to navigate to the first page, last page, next page, previous page, and in some tables, to select the number of rows displayed on one page.

When you bind a table to its backing bean, you have access to three handy properties, which are listed as follows:

- `first`: This property represents the first row number that is displayed in the current table page (it starts from the default value 0). The value for this property can be specified using the `first` attribute of the `<h:dataTable>` tag. In the JSF API, this is accessible through the `HtmlDataTable.getFirst` and `HtmlDataTable.setFirst` methods.

- `rows`: This property represents the number of rows displayed in a single page, starting from `first`. The value for this property can be specified using the `rows` attribute of the `<h:dataTable>` tag. In the JSF API, this is accessible through the `HtmlDataTable.getRows` and `HtmlDataTable.setRows` methods.

- `rowCount`: This property represents the total number of rows, from all pages, starting from row 0. There is no attribute for this property. In the JSF API, this is accessible through the `HtmlDataTable.getRowCount` method. Setting the row count can be accomplished through the data model, as you will see later. By default, is determined by JSF.

In the following screenshot, these properties can be seen in detail:

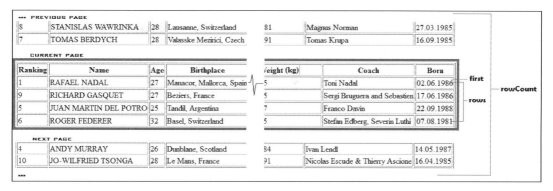

The preceding information is very useful for to implementing the pagination mechanism. First, we bind the table, and set the first row number and the number of rows per page, as follows:

```
<h:dataTable value="#{playersBean.dataHashSet}"
  binding="#{playersBean.table}"
  rows="#{playersBean.rowsOnPage}" first="0" var="t">
...
```

Based on some arithmetic and EL condition's support, we can conclude the following:

- The first row number, the row number per page, and the total row count are accessible via the following code:

```
<b>FIRST:</b> #{playersBean.table.first}
<b>ROWS:</b> #{playersBean.table.rows}
<b>ROW COUNT:</b> #{playersBean.table.rowCount}
```

- Navigate to the first page by using the following code:

```
public void goToFirstPage() {
    table.setFirst(0);
}
```

   A button that accomplishes this navigation can be disabled by an EL condition, as shown in the following code:

```
<h:commandButton value="First Page"
  action="#{playersBean.goToFirstPage()}"
  disabled="#{playersBean.table.first eq 0}" />
```

- Navigate to the next page by using the following code:

```
public void goToNextPage() {
   table.setFirst(table.getFirst() + table.getRows());
}
```

A button that accomplishes this navigation can be disabled by an EL condition, as shown in the following code:

```
<h:commandButton value="Next Page"
   action="#{playersBean.goToNextPage()}"
   disabled="#{playersBean.table.first +
   playersBean.table.rows ge playersBean.table.rowCount}" />
```

- Navigate to the previous page by using the following code:

```
public void goToPreviousPage() {
   table.setFirst(table.getFirst() - table.getRows());
}
```

A button that accomplishes this navigation can be disabled by an EL condition, as shown in the following code:

```
<h:commandButton value="Previous Page"
   action="#{playersBean.goToPreviousPage()}"
   disabled="#{playersBean.table.first eq 0}" />
```

- Navigate to the last page by using the following code:

```
public void goToLastPage() {
   int totalRows = table.getRowCount();
   int displayRows = table.getRows();
   int full = totalRows / displayRows;
   int modulo = totalRows % displayRows;

   if (modulo > 0) {
      table.setFirst(full * displayRows);
   } else {
      table.setFirst((full - 1) * displayRows);
   }
}
```

A button that accomplishes this navigation can be disabled by an EL condition, as shown in the following code:

```
<h:commandButton value="Last Page"
   action="#{playersBean.goToLastPage()}"
   disabled="#{playersBean.table.first +
   playersBean.table.rows ge playersBean.table.rowCount}" />
```

- Display the **current page** of the **total pages** message by using the following code:

```
<h:outputText value="#{(playersBean.table.first div
  playersBean.table.rows) + 1}">
    <f:converter converterId="javax.faces.Integer"/>
</h:outputText>
of
<h:outputText value="#{playersBean.table.rowCount mod
  playersBean.table.rows eq 0 ? (playersBean.table.rowCount
  div playersBean.table.rows) :
  ((playersBean.table.rowCount div playersBean.table.rows)
  + 1)-(((playersBean.table.rowCount div
  playersBean.table.rows) + 1) mod 1)}">
    <f:converter converterId="javax.faces.Integer"/>
</h:outputText>
```

Merging all these chunks of code in a sample application (see the application `ch6_10_1`), will result in something like the following screenshot:

| Ranking | Name | Age | Birthplace | Residence | Height (cm) | Weight (kg) | Coach | Born |
|---|---|---|---|---|---|---|---|---|
| 4 | ANDY MURRAY | 26 | Dunblane, Scotland | London, England | 190 | 84 | Ivan Lendl | 14.05.1987 |
| 8 | STANISLAS WAWRINKA | 28 | Lausanne, Switzerland | St. Barthelemy, Switzerland | 183 | 81 | Magnus Norman | 27.03.1985 |
| 7 | TOMAS BERDYCH | 28 | Valasske Mezirici, Czech | Monte Carlo, Monaco | 196 | 91 | Tomas Krupa | 16.09.1985 |
| 3 | DAVID FERRER | 31 | Javea, Spain | Valencia, Spain | 175 | 73 | Jose Francisco Altur | 01.04.1982 |

1 of 3 | First Page | Previous Page | Next Page | Last Page | **FIRST: 0 ROWS: 4 ROW COUNT: 10**

The biggest issue here is that even if the data is displayed in pages, they are still loaded in the memory as a bulk. In this case, pagination is just a *slicer* of the collection, which has only visual effect. In reality, the pagination is the effect of **lazy loading**, which represents a technique for querying only a portion of data from a database (instead of slicing the data in memory, you slice it from the database directly). There are many kinds of querying in a database, but in Java web/enterprise applications, EJB/JPA is the most used. EJB and JPA are large technologies that can't be covered here, but with some assumptions it will be very easy to understand the upcoming example.

> If you feel that EJB/JPA are not good choices, you should can take into account the fact that the `<h:dataTable>` tag also supports `java.sql.ResultSet`, `javax.servlet.jsp.jstl.Result`, and `javax.sql.CachedRowSet`. So, for tests, you can use plain JDBC as well.

Instead of the `Players` POJO class, this time you will use a `Players` JPA entity that is bounded to a table named PLAYERS. This table contains the data that should be displayed in the JSF table and it was created in Apache Derby RDBMS, in the APP database (if you have NetBeans 8.0 with GlassFish 4.0, then this RDBMS and the APP database are out of the box). The idea is to query this table to obtain only the rows from `first` to `first + rows`, which is exactly the amount of rows displayed per page. This can be easily accomplished by JPA using the `setFirstResult` and `setMaxResults` methods of a query (the `loadPlayersAction` method was defined in a EJB component, named `PlayersSessionBean`), as shown in the following code:

```
public HashSet<Players> loadPlayersAction(int first, int max) {

    Query query = em.createNamedQuery("Players.findAll");
    query.setFirstResult(first);
    query.setMaxResults(max);

    return new HashSet(query.getResultList());
}
```

So, passing the right `first` and `max` arguments will return the needed rows!

But pagination works if we know the total number of rows, since without this we can't calculate the number of pages, or the last page, and so on. In JPA, we can do this easily (the `countPlayersAction` method was defined in a EJB component, named `PlayersSessionBean`) by using the following code:

```
public int countPlayersAction() {
    Query query = em.createNamedQuery("Players.countAll");
    return ((Long)query.getSingleResult()).intValue();
}
```

Knowing the total number of rows (without actually extracting the data from the database) is great, but we need to tell JSF that number! Since `HtmlDataTable` doesn't provide a `setRowCount` method, we have to take another approach into account. One solution is to extend the `DataModel` class (or one of its subclasses) and provide the row count explicitly; since we are using `HashSet`, we can extend the `CollectionDataModel` class of JSF 2.2 as follows:

```
public class PlayersDataModel extends CollectionDataModel {

    private int rowIndex = -1;
    private int allRowsCount;
    private int pageSize;
```

```java
private HashSet hashSet;

public PlayersDataModel() {}

public PlayersDataModel(HashSet hashSet, int allRowsCount,
  int pageSize)
{
  this.hashSet = hashSet;
  this.allRowsCount = allRowsCount;
  this.pageSize = pageSize;
}

@Override
public boolean isRowAvailable() {
  if (hashSet == null) {
    return false;
  }

  int c_rowIndex = getRowIndex();
  if (c_rowIndex >= 0 && c_rowIndex < hashSet.size()) {
    return true;
  } else {
    return false;
  }
}

@Override
public int getRowCount() {
  return allRowsCount;
}

@Override
public Object getRowData() {
  if (hashSet == null) {
    return null;
  } else if (!isRowAvailable()) {
    throw new IllegalArgumentException();
  } else {
    int dataIndex = getRowIndex();
    Object[] arrayView = hashSet.toArray();
    return arrayView[dataIndex];
```

```
      }
    }

    @Override
    public int getRowIndex() {
      return (rowIndex % pageSize);
    }

    @Override
    public void setRowIndex(int rowIndex) {
      this.rowIndex = rowIndex;
    }

    @Override
    public Object getWrappedData() {
      return hashSet;
    }

    @Override
    public void setWrappedData(Object hashSet) {
      this.hashSet = (HashSet) hashSet;
    }
  }
```

So, creating a `PlayersDataModel` class can be accomplished in the following manner:

```
...
@Inject
private PlayersSessionBean playersSessionBean;
private int rowsOnPage;
private int allRowsCount = 0;
...
@PostConstruct
public void initHashSet() {
  rowsOnPage = 4; //any constant in [1, rowCount]
  allRowsCount = playersSessionBean.countPlayersAction();
  lazyDataLoading(0);
}
...
private void lazyDataLoading(int first) {
  HashSet<Players> dataHashSet =
    playersSessionBean.loadPlayersAction(first, rowsOnPage);
  playersDataModel = new PlayersDataModel(dataHashSet,
    allRowsCount, rowsOnPage);
}
```

Finally, each time a page navigation is detected in the table, we just need to call the following method:

```
lazyDataLoading(table.getFirst());
```

The complete example is available in the code bundle of this chapter, and is named ch6_10_2.

# Generating tables with the JSF API

JSF tables can be programmatically generated as well. The JSF API provides comprehensive support to accomplish such tasks. First, you *prepare* the place where the generated table will be added, as follows:

```
<h:body>
  <h:form id="tableForm">
    <h:panelGrid id="myTable">
    </h:panelGrid>
    <h:commandButton value="Add Table"
      action="#{playersBean.addTable()}"/>
  </h:form>
</h:body>
```

The idea is simple: when the button labeled **Add Table** is clicked, the generated table should be attached in the <h:panelGrid> tag identified by the myTable ID.

Before creating a JSF table in a programmatic fashion, you need to know how to create a table, a header/footer, a column, and so on. Let's have a short overview as follows—the code is self-explanatory and straightforward, since JSF provides very intuitive methods:

1. Let's create the simplest table, <h:dataTable value="..." var="t" border="1"> using the following code:

```
public HtmlDataTable createTable(String exp, Class<?> cls) {
  HtmlDataTable table = new HtmlDataTable();
  table.setValueExpression("value",
    createValueExpression(exp, cls));
  table.setVar("t");
  table.setBorder(1);

  return table;
}
```

2. Now, we will create a column with a header, a footer, and a possible converter, as follows:

```java
public HtmlColumn createColumn(HtmlDataTable table,
  String header_name, String footer_name, String exp,
  Class<?> cls, Class<?> converter) {

  HtmlColumn column = new HtmlColumn();
  table.getChildren().add(column);

  if (header_name != null) {
    HtmlOutputText header = new HtmlOutputText();
    header.setValue(header_name);
    column.setHeader(header);
  }

  if (footer_name != null) {
    HtmlOutputText footer = new HtmlOutputText();
    footer.setValue(footer_name);
    column.setFooter(footer);
  }

  HtmlOutputText output = new HtmlOutputText();
  output.setValueExpression("value",
    createValueExpression(exp, cls));
  column.getChildren().add(output);

  if (converter != null) {
    if (converter.getGenericInterfaces()[0].
      equals(Converter.class)) {
      if (converter.equals(DateTimeConverter.class)) {
        DateTimeConverter dateTimeConverter = new
          DateTimeConverter();
        dateTimeConverter.setPattern("dd.MM.yyyy");
        output.setConverter(dateTimeConverter);
      }
      //more converters ...
    } else {
      //the passed class is not a converter!
    }
  }

  return column;
}
```

3. Now, attach the table in DOM (in order to do that, you need to find the desired parent component) using the following code:

```java
public void attachTable(HtmlDataTable table,
  String parent_id) throws NullPointerException {
  UIComponent component = findComponent(parent_id);
  if (component != null) {
    component.getChildren().clear();
    component.getChildren().add(table);
  } else {
    throw new NullPointerException();
  }
}
```

The findComponent method uses the JSF visit method, which is very useful for traversing a tree of components, which is shown in the following code:

```java
private UIComponent findComponent(final String id) {
  FacesContext context = FacesContext.getCurrentInstance();
  UIViewRoot root = context.getViewRoot();
  final UIComponent[] found = new UIComponent[1];
  root.visitTree(new FullVisitContext(context),
    new VisitCallback() {

    @Override
    public VisitResult visit(VisitContext context,
      UIComponent component) {
      if (component.getId().equals(id)) {
        found[0] = component;
        return VisitResult.COMPLETE;
      }
      return VisitResult.ACCEPT;
    }
  });
  return found[0];
}
```

In Mojarra, the FullVisitContext method comes from the com.sun.faces.component.visit package. In MyFaces, this class comes from the org.apache.myfaces.test.mock.visit package. Both the implementations extend javax.faces.component.visit.VisitContext.

4. The necessary expressions are then added as shown in the following code (you saw another example of this in *Chapter 2, Communication in JSF*):

```
private ValueExpression createValueExpression(String exp,
  Class<?> cls) {
FacesContext facesContext =
  FacesContext.getCurrentInstance();
ELContext elContext = facesContext.getELContext();
return facesContext.getApplication().
  getExpressionFactory().
  createValueExpression(elContext, exp, cls);
}
```

5. Finally, merge these methods in a helper class, `TableHelper`.

Remember the button labeled **Add Table**? Well, when that button is clicked, the `addTable` method is called. This method exploits the `TableHelper` class for programmatically creating a table, as shown in the following code:

```
public void addTable() {

  TableHelper tableHelper = new TableHelper();
  HtmlDataTable tableHashSet = tableHelper.createTable
    ("#{playersBean.dataHashSet}", HashSet.class);
  tableHelper.createColumn(tableHashSet, "Ranking",
    null, "#{t.ranking}", Integer.class, null);
  tableHelper.createColumn(tableHashSet, "Name",
    null, "#{t.player}", String.class, null);
  tableHelper.createColumn(tableHashSet, "Age",
    null, "#{t.age}", Byte.class, null);
  tableHelper.createColumn(tableHashSet, "Birthplace",
    null, "#{t.birthplace}", String.class, null);
  tableHelper.createColumn(tableHashSet, "Residence",
    null, "#{t.residence}", String.class, null);
  tableHelper.createColumn(tableHashSet, "Height (cm)",
    null, "#{t.height}", Short.class, null);
  tableHelper.createColumn(tableHashSet, "Weight (kg)",
    null, "#{t.weight}", Byte.class, null);
  tableHelper.createColumn(tableHashSet, "Coach",
    null, "#{t.coach}", String.class, null);
  tableHelper.createColumn(tableHashSet, "Born",
    null, "#{t.born}", java.util.Date.class,
    DateTimeConverter.class);
  tableHelper.attachTable(tableHashSet, "myTable");
}
```

Done! The complete application is available in the code bundle of this chapter, and is named `ch6_11`.

A programmatically generated table would be an apt approach for generating tables with variable number of columns, or dynamic columns. Let's suppose that we have two JPA entities, `Players` and `Trophies`. The first entity should produce a table with nine columns, while `Trophies` should produce a table with three columns. Moreover, the column names (headers) differ. It may sound complicated, but actually is more simple than you would have expected.

Think that each table is mapped by a JPA entity, which means that we can write specific queries by indicating the entity name. Moreover, each entity can be passed through Java's reflection mechanism to extract the field's names (we are focusing on the `private` fields), which gave us the column headers. (If you alter the column names using `@Column(name="alias_name")`, then the process will be a little tricky to reflect the alias names.) So, we can use the following code (the package name is fixed):

```
@Inject
//this is the EJB component that queries the database
private QueryBean queryBean;
HashSet<Object> dataHashSet = new HashSet<>();
...
public void addTable(String selectedTable) {

  try {
    dataHashSet.clear();

    dataHashSet = queryBean.populateData(selectedTable);

    String tableToQuery = "book.ejbs." + selectedTable;

    Class tableClass = Class.forName(tableToQuery);
    Field[] privateFields = tableClass.getDeclaredFields();

    TableHelper tableHelper = new TableHelper();
    HtmlDataTable tableHashSet = tableHelper.createTable
      ("#{playersBean.dataHashSet}", HashSet.class);

    for (int i = 0; i < privateFields.length; i++) {
      String privateField = privateFields[i].getName();
      if ((!privateField.startsWith("_")) &&
        (!privateField.equals("serialVersionUID"))) {
        tableHelper.createColumn(tableHashSet, privateField,
          null, "#{t."+privateField+"}",
          privateFields[i].getType(), null);
```

```
      }
    }

    tableHelper.attachTable(tableHashSet, "myTable");

  } catch (ClassNotFoundException ex) {
    Logger.getLogger(PlayersBean.class.getName()).
      log(Level.SEVERE, null, ex);
  }
```

So, as long as we pass the table name (entity name) to this method, it will return the corresponding data. For the complete example, check the application named ch6_12 in the code bundle of this chapter.

# Filtering tables

Filtering data is a very useful facility in a table. It allows the user to *see* only the set of data that matches a certain set of rules (criteria); most commonly, filter by column(s). For example, the user may need to see all players younger than 26 years, which is a filter applied in the column labeled **Age**.

Basically, a filter can have only visual effect, without modifying the filtered data (using some CSS, JS code, or duplicating the filter results in a separate collection and displaying that collection), or by removing the unnecessary items for the initial collection (which requires restoring its content when the filter is removed).

In JSF, we can write a nice filter by playing with some CSS code, which can be used to hide/show rows of a table; this is not a recommended approach in production, since all the data is still available in the source page, but it might be useful when you don't need anything fancy. The idea is to hide all of the table's rows that do not match the filter criteria, and for this, we can exploit the rowClasses attribute of the <h:dataTable> tag. This attribute's value is represented by a string of CSS classes separated by a comma; JSF iterates the CSS classes and applies them sequentially and repeatedly over rows.

Consider the following two CSS classes:

```
.rowshow
{
  display:visible;
}

.rowhide
{
  display:none;
}
```

Now, a filter can use the `rowshow` CSS class to display a row containing valid data, and the `rowhide` CSS class to hide the rest of the rows. For example, iterating over a collection of five elements can reveal the following string of CSS classes:

```
rowshow, rowhide, rowshow, rowhide, rowhide
```

So, only the first and the third row will be visible.

Let's have a look at the steps involved in the writing of such a filter:

1.  A convenient way to add a filter selection per column consists of using the `<h:selectOneMenu>` tag. For example, we add a filter selection in the **Age** column, as follows:

```
. . .
<h:column>
  <f:facet name="header">
    Age<br/>
    <h:selectOneMenu value="#{playersBean.criteria}">
      <f:selectItem itemValue="all" itemLabel="all" />
      <f:selectItem itemValue="&lt;26" itemLabel="&lt;26" />
      <f:selectItem itemValue="&gt;=26" itemLabel="&gt;=26" />
    </h:selectOneMenu>
    <h:commandButton value="Go!"
      action="#{playersBean.addTableFilter()}"/>
  </f:facet>
  <h:outputText value="#{t.age}"/>
</h:column>
. . .
```

2.  The `addTableFilter` method is called when the button labeled **Go!** is clicked. It checks the value of the `criteria` property, and if the value equals `<26` or `>=26`, then it iterates over the table rows and builds the corresponding string of CSS classes. Otherwise, if the `criteria` property is equal to `all`, the filter is removed, as shown in the following code:

```
public void addTableFilter() {

  if (!criteria.equals("all")) {
    String c = "";
    for (int i = 0; i < table.getRowCount(); i++) {
      table.setRowIndex(i);
      Players player = (Players) table.getRowData();
      if (criteria.equals("<26")) {
        if (player.getAge() >= 26) {
```

```
        c = c + "rowhide,";
      } else {
        c = c + "rowshow,";
      }
    }
    if (criteria.equals(">=26")) {
      if (player.getAge() < 26) {
        c = c + "rowhide,";
      } else {
        c = c + "rowshow,";
      }
    }
  }

  String css = "rowshow";
  if (!c.isEmpty()) {
    css = c.substring(0, c.length() - 1);
  }

  rowsOnPage = table.getRowCount();
  table.setRowClasses(css);
  table.setFirst(0);
} else {
  removeTableFilter();
}
}
```

3.  The following `removeTableFilter` method will restore the CSS class; therefore, all data will be visible again:

```
public void removeTableFilter() {
  String css = "rowshow";
  rowsOnPage = 4;  //any constant in [1, rowCount]
  table.setRowClasses(css);
  table.setFirst(0);
}
```

For the complete example, check the application named ch6_13_1 in the code bundle of this chapter.

It's important to notice that the number of rows per page is modified when the filter is applied. Actually, when the filter results are displayed, the rows per page become equal to table row count, and when the filter is removed, they take a value anything from 1 to row count. The conclusion is that the filtered data is displayed in a table without pagination.

In some cases, like filtering by age, you can apply a sort before generating the string of CSS classes. This will help you to display the filter results, without affecting data, and with pagination available. A complete example can be found in the code bundle of this chapter, named ch6_13_2.

You can obtain the same results by removing from the initial collection the items that do not match the filter criteria. For example, notice that before applying a filter, you need to restore the initial data of the collection—the initHashSet method can do that:

```java
public void addTableFilter() {

    initHashSet();

    Iterator<Players> i = dataHashSet.iterator();
    while (i.hasNext()) {
      Players player = i.next();
      if (criteria.equals("<26")) {
        if (player.getAge() >= 26) {
          i.remove();
        }
      }
      if (criteria.equals(">=26")) {
        if (player.getAge() < 26) {
          i.remove();
        }
      }
    }

    table.setFirst(0);
}
```

If you want to apply a chain of filters, then restore the data before entering in the chain. A complete example can be found in the code bundle of this chapter named ch6_13_3.

Since collections that feed tables are usually populated from databases, you can apply filters directly on databases. A common case is represented by tables with a lazy loading mechanism; since you have only a slice of data in memory, you need to apply the filter on the database instead of filtering the collection that populates the table. This means that the filtration process is accomplished through SQL queries. For example, our filter can be modeled through SQL queries, by performing the following steps (this example is based on the lazy loading application presented earlier in this chapter):

1. You pass the filter criteria to the EJB component (`copy_criteria` acts as a flag—you don't want to count the number of rows each time the user navigates through table pages using the same filter), as shown in the following code:

```
@Inject
private PlayersSessionBean playersSessionBean;
private PlayersDataModel playersDataModel;
private String criteria = "all";
private String copy_criteria = "none";
private int allRowsCount = 0;
...
private void lazyDataLoading(int first) {
  if (!copy_criteria.equals(criteria)) {
    allRowsCount =
      playersSessionBean.countPlayersAction(criteria);
    copy_criteria = criteria;
  }

  HashSet<Players> dataHashSet =
    playersSessionBean.loadPlayersAction(first, rowsOnPage,
      criteria);
  playersDataModel = new PlayersDataModel(dataHashSet,
    allRowsCount, rowsOnPage);
}
```

2. Count the number of rows returned by the filter as follows:

```
public int countPlayersAction(String criteria) {

  if (criteria.equals("all")) {
    Query query = em.createNamedQuery("Players.countAll");
    return ((Long) query.getSingleResult()).intValue();
  }

  if (criteria.equals("<26")) {
```

```
    Query query = em.createQuery("SELECT COUNT(p) FROM
      Players p WHERE p.age < 26");
    return ((Long) query.getSingleResult()).intValue();
  }

  if (criteria.equals(">=26")) {
    Query query = em.createQuery("SELECT COUNT(p) FROM
      Players p WHERE p.age >= 26");
    return ((Long) query.getSingleResult()).intValue();
  }

  return 0;
}
```

3.  Finally, round off by applying the filter criteria using SQL queries as follows:

```
public HashSet<Players> loadPlayersAction(int first,
  int max, String criteria) {

  if (criteria.equals("all")) {
    Query query = em.createNamedQuery("Players.findAll");
    query.setFirstResult(first);
    query.setMaxResults(max);
    return new HashSet(query.getResultList());
  }

  if (criteria.equals("<26")) {
    Query query = em.createQuery("SELECT p FROM Players
      p WHERE p.age < 26");
    query.setFirstResult(first);
    query.setMaxResults(max);
    return new HashSet(query.getResultList());
  }

  if (criteria.equals(">=26")) {
    Query query = em.createQuery("SELECT p FROM Players p
      WHERE p.age >= 26");
    query.setFirstResult(first);
    query.setMaxResults(max);
    return new HashSet(query.getResultList());
  }

  return null;
}
```

Done! The complete example is available in the code bundle of this chapter and it is named ch6_13_4.

# Styling tables

Almost all JSF UI components support the `style` and `styleClass` attributes for creating custom designs using CSS. But the `<h:dataTable>` tag supports attributes, such as `captionClass`, `captionStyle`, `columnClasses`, `rowClasses`, `headerClass`, and `footerClass`. Therefore, we should have no problem in adding a CSS style to every single part of a table (header, footer, caption, and so on). Obviously, there are plenty of examples that can be built, but let's see three of the most impressive and used ones.

## Alternate row colors with the rowclasses attribute

The `rowClasses` attribute is used to indicate a string of CSS classes separated by a comma. The string is parsed by JSF, and the styles are applied sequentially and repeatedly to rows. For example, you can color the even rows with one color, and the odd rows with some other color, as follows:

```
<h:dataTable value="#{playersBean.data}" rowClasses="even, odd"
  var="t">
. . .
```

Here, `even` and `odd` are the following CSS classes:

```
.odd {
  background-color: gray;
}

.even{
  background-color: darkgray;
}
```

A possible output can be seen in the following screenshot:

| Ranking | Name | Age | Birthplace | t (kg) | Coach | Born |
|---|---|---|---|---|---|---|
| 2 | NOVAK DJOKOVIC | 26 | Belgrade, Serbia | | Boris Becker, Marian Vajda | 21.05.1987 |
| 1 | RAFAEL NADAL | 27 | Manacor, Mallorc | | Toni Nadal | 02.06.1986 |
| 7 | TOMAS BERDYCH | 28 | Valasske Mezirici, | | Tomas Krupa | 16.09.1985 |
| 8 | STANISLAS WAWRINKA | 28 | Lausanne, Switzer | | Magnus Norman | 27.03.1985 |
| 4 | ANDY MURRAY | 26 | Dunblane, Scotlan | | Ivan Lendl | 14.05.1987 |
| 5 | JUAN MARTIN DEL POTRO | 25 | Tandil, Argentina | | Franco Davin | 22.09.1988 |
| 10 | JO-WILFRIED TSONGA | 28 | Le Mans, France | | Nicolas Escude & Thierry Ascione | 16.04.1985 |
| 6 | ROGER FEDERER | 32 | Basel, Switzerland | | Stefan Edberg, Severin Luthi | 07.08.1981 |
| 9 | RICHARD GASQUET | 27 | Beziers, France | | Sergi Bruguera and Sebastien | 17.06.1986 |
| 3 | DAVID FERRER | 31 | Javea, Spain | | Jose Francisco Altur | 01.04.1982 |

You can obtain the same effect for columns, by using the `columnClasses` attribute instead of the `rowClasses` attribute.

The complete example is named `ch6_14_1`.

# Highlighting rows on mouse hover

Highlighting rows on mouse hover is a nice effect that can be accomplished with a piece of JavaScript. The idea is to set the `onmouseover` and `onmouseout` attributes, as shown in the following self-explanatory code:

```
...
<script type="text/javascript">
  //<![CDATA[
    function onmouseOverOutRows() {
      var rows = document.getElementById('playersTable').
        getElementsByTagName('tr');
      for (var i = 1; i < rows.length; i++) {
        rows[i].setAttribute("onmouseover",
          "this.bgColor='#00cc00'");
        rows[i].setAttribute("onmouseout",
          "this.bgColor='#ffffff'");
      }
    }
  //]]>
</script>
...

<h:body onload="onmouseOverOutRows();">
  <h:dataTable id="playersTable" value="#{playersBean.data}"
    var="t">
...
```

The complete example is named `ch6_14_2`.

Another approach does not involve using the JavaScript code. In this case, you can try CSS pseudo-classes, as follows:

```
tbody tr:hover {
  background-color: red;
}
```

Done! The complete application is named `ch6_14_3`.

# Highlighting rows on mouse click

Highlighting rows with a mouse click can be done with another piece of JavaScript code. You have to add the `onclick` attribute to each row and control the color alternation when the user clicks repeatedly on the same row, as shown in the following code:

```
<script type="text/javascript">
  //<![CDATA[
    function onClickRows() {
      var rows = document.getElementById('playersTable').
        getElementsByTagName('tr');
      for (var i = 1; i < rows.length; i++) {
        rows[i].setAttribute("onclick", "changeColor(this);");
      }
    }

    function changeColor(row) {
      var bgcolor = row.bgColor;
      if (bgcolor === "") {
        row.bgColor = "#00cc00";
      } else if (bgcolor === "#00cc00") {
        row.bgColor = "#ffffff";
      } else if (bgcolor === "#ffffff") {
        row.bgColor = "#00cc00";
      }
    }
  //]]>
</script>
...
<h:body onload="onClickRows();">
  <h:dataTable id="playersTable" value="#{playersBean.data}"
    var="t">
...
```

The complete example is named ch6_14_4 in the code bundle of this chapter.

# Summary

Tabular data is very commonly used in web applications, and this chapter is a tribute to the powerful JSF DataTable component (`<h:dataTable>`). JSF 2.2 brought even more power by allowing developers to render more collections than before, by adding the new `CollectionDataModel` class. This chapter covers the most common tasks that a table should accomplish, such as sorting, filtering, lazy loading, and CSS support. Notice that a cool and comprehensive extension of the `<h:dataTable>` tag is provided by PrimeFaces (`http://primefaces.org/`) under the tag named `<p:dataTable>` (`http://www.primefaces.org/showcase/ui/datatableHome.jsf`).

In the next chapter, we will be covering the AJAX technique for JSF applications.

# 7
# JSF and AJAX

JSF and AJAX have been a great team for a long time. The potential of this combination has been heavily exploited by many JSF extensions (Ajax4Jsf, OmniFaces, PrimeFaces, RichFaces, ICEfaces, and so on) that provide many AJAX built-in components, extend AJAX default capabilities, increase AJAX security and reliability, and add more control to developers who need to manipulate the *bowels* of AJAX mechanism.

By default, JSF contains a JavaScript library that encapsulates AJAX methods for dealing with AJAX requests or responses. This library can be loaded in the following two ways:

- Using the `<f:ajax>` tag, the built-in AJAX library is loaded implicitly.
- Using `jsf.ajax.request()`, the AJAX library is loaded explicitly and developers have access to AJAX code. This approach is commonly used when the default AJAX behavior must be altered. It should be performed only by developers with high expertise, because modifying the default AJAX behavior may lead to undesirable issues and gaps.

In this chapter, you will learn the following topics:

- A brief overview of the JSF-AJAX lifecycle
- A simple JSF-AJAX example
- How the `execute`, `render`, `listener`, and `event` attributes work
- Monitoring AJAX state on client
- Monitoring AJAX errors on client
- Grouping components under the `<f:ajax>` tag
- Updating input fields with AJAX after a validation error
- Mixing AJAX and flow scope
- How postback and AJAX work together

- How to determine whether a request is AJAX or non-AJAX
- How AJAX and `<f:param>` work
- Queue control for AJAX requests
- How `jsf.js` can be loaded explicitly
- How to write an AJAX progress bar / indicator

# A brief overview of the JSF-AJAX lifecycle

AJAX's request-response cycle is characterized by **partial processing** and **partial rendering** stages; this means that AJAX partially affects the current view. As such, requests are not typical JSF requests, they follow a different lifecycle dictated by the `javax.faces.context.PartialViewContext` class. The methods of this class know how to deal with AJAX requests, which means that they are responsible for solving partial processing and rendering of the component tree.

The kernel of an AJAX request is represented by two attributes of the `<f:ajax>` tag: `execute` and `render`. The `execute` attribute indicates the components that should be processed on the server (partial processing), while the `render` attribute indicates the components that should be rendered (or re-rendered) on the client (partial rendering).

In the upcoming sections, you will see many examples of how these attributes works.

# A simple JSF-AJAX example to get started

The simplest JSF-AJAX example can be written in a matter of a few seconds. Let's consider a JSF form with an input text and a button that sends the user input to the server. The user input (a string) is converted by the server to uppercase and is displayed to the user in an output text component. Next, you can ajaxify this scenario as shown in the following example code:

```
<h:form>
  <h:inputText id="nameInputId" value="#{ajaxBean.name}"/>
  <h:commandButton value="Send" action="#{ajaxBean.ajaxAction()}">
    <f:ajax/>
  </h:commandButton>
  <h:outputText id="nameOutputId" value="#{ajaxBean.name}"/>
</h:form>
```

The presence of the `<f:ajax>` tag is sufficient to transform this request into an AJAX request. Well, it is true that this request is not very useful because we did not specify which components should be executed and what components should be re-rendered. But the good part is that you will not receive any errors; JSF will use the default values for the `execute` and `render` attributes, which ask JSF to process the element that triggered the request and to re-render nothing.

 When the `execute` or `render` attribute is missing, JSF will process the element that triggered the request and re-render nothing.

Adding the `execute` attribute with the value of the `inputText` ID (`nameInputId`) tag will tell JSF to pass to the server the user input. This means that the user input will be available in the `ajaxAction` method and will be converted to uppercase. You can check the effect of this method in the application server log because it is not visible on the client side, since the `render` attribute still defaults to nothing. Therefore, you need to add the `render` attribute and indicate the IDs of the components that should be re-rendered; in this case, the output text with the ID `nameOutputId`:

```
<h:form>
  <h:inputText id="nameInputId" value="#{ajaxBean.name}"/>
  <h:commandButton value="Send" action="#{ajaxBean.ajaxAction()}">
    <f:ajax execute ="nameInputId" render="nameOutputId"/>
  </h:commandButton>
  <h:outputText id="nameOutputId" value="#{ajaxBean.name}"/>
</h:form>
```

Done! This is a simple and functional AJAX application. You can find the complete code in the code bundle of this chapter, named `ch7_1`.

# The JSF-AJAX attributes

In this section, you will see what the main attributes supported by `<f:ajax>` are. We start with `execute` and `render`, continue with `listener` and `event`, and finish with `onevent` and `onerror`.

# The execute and render attributes

In the previous example, the `execute` and `render` attributes affect a single component indicated by its ID. When multiple components are affected, we can specify a list of IDs separated by space, or we can use the following keywords:

- `@form`: This keyword refers to all component IDs in the form that contains the AJAX component. If it is present in the `execute` attribute, then the entire `<h:form>` is submitted and processed. In case of the `render` attribute, the entire `<h:form>` is rendered.

- `@this`: This keyword refers to the ID of the element that triggers the request (default when `execute` is missing). For the `execute` attribute, `@this` will submit and process only the component that contains the AJAX component, while for the `render` attribute, it will render only the component that contains the AJAX component.

- `@none`: No component will be processed/re-rendered. But for the `execute` attribute, JSF will still execute the lifecycle, including its phase listeners; while for the `render` attribute, JSF will perform the *Render Response* phase, including firing any `preRenderView` events. This is the default value for the `render` attribute.

- `@all`: This keyword represents all components IDs. For `execute`, all components in a page are submitted and processed—like a full page submit. For the `render` attribute, JSF will render all components in the page; this will update the page, but will allow preserving some client-side states outside the JSF.

Depending on the application's needs, these keywords and component IDs can be mixed to obtain cool AJAX requests. For example, go through the following AJAX requests:

- Process and re-render the current form using the following code:

  ```
  <f:ajax execute="@form" render="@form"/>
  ```

- Process form, re-render none, as follows:

  ```
  <f:ajax execute="@form" render="@none"/>
  ```

- Process the element that triggers the request and re-renders the form, as follows:

  ```
  <f:ajax execute="@this" render="@form"/>
  ```

- Process the form and re-render all as follows:

```
<f:ajax execute="@form" render="@all"/>
```

- Process the form and re-render the components with IDs `nameInputId` `phoneInputId` inside the form as follows:

```
<f:ajax execute="@form" render="nameInputId phoneInputId"/>
```

We can continue with many other examples, but I think you got the idea.

> The keywords (`@form`, `@this`, `@all`, and `@none`) and component IDs can be mixed in the same value of the `render` and `execute` attribute. Don't forget to separate them with spaces.

The complete application can be seen in the code bundle of this chapter, and is named as `ch7_2`.

A special case consists in re-rendering components outside the form that contains the AJAX element that triggers the request. Take a look at the following example:

```
<h:message id="msgId" showDetail="true" showSummary="true"
                      for="nameId" style="color: red;"/>
<h:form>
 <h:inputText id="nameId" value="#{ajaxBean.name}"
                          validator="nameValidator"/>
 <h:commandButton value="Submit">
  <f:ajax execute="@form" listener="#{ajaxBean.upperCaseName()}"
          render="@form :msgId :trackRequestId:trackId"/>
 </h:commandButton>
</h:form>
<h:form id="trackRequestId">
 Request number: <h:outputText id="trackId"
  value="#{ajaxBean.request}"/>
</h:form>
```

> Use the : notation for updating components outside the form, which contains the element that triggers the AJAX request. This notation represents the default separator returned by the `UINamingContainer.getSeparatorChar` method. This can be specified via the `javax.faces.SEPARATOR_CHAR` context parameter.

The complete application can be found in the code bundle of this chapter, and is named `ch7_3`.

# The listener attribute

Another important attribute of `<f:ajax>` is named `listener`. This attribute indicates a server-side method that should be executed when an AJAX request is fired by a client action. For example, you can do this using the following code:

```
<h:form>
  <h:inputText value="#{ajaxBean.name}"/>
  <h:commandButton value="Send"
    action="#{ajaxBean.upperCaseName()}">
  <f:ajax execute="@form" render="@form"/>
  </h:commandButton>
</h:form>
```

Well, using the `listener` attribute you can transform the preceding code into the following code:

```
<h:form>
  <h:inputText value="#{ajaxBean.name}"/>
  <h:commandButton value="Send">
    <f:ajax listener="#{ajaxBean.upperCaseName()}"
          execute="@form" render="@form"/>
  </h:commandButton>
</h:form>
```

An obvious question arises here. What is the difference between these two and why should I use `listener` and not `action`? Well, there are a few differences between these two, and the following are the most important ones:

- A server-side method called through the `action` attribute can return `String` representing a navigation case (outcome), while a server-side method called through `listener` cannot provide a navigation case.

- If the client disables JavaScript in the browser configuration, the `listener` attribute will not work anymore—the server-side method will not be called. The `action` attribute still works.

- Components that do not support the `action` attribute can use `listener` instead.

- The server-side method called through the `listener` attribute accepts an argument of type `AjaxBehaviorEvent`, which represents the component behavior specific to AJAX. This is not accepted in case of the `action` attribute. For example, refer to the following code:

```
<h:form>
  <h:inputText value="#{ajaxBean.name}"/>
  <h:commandButton value="Send">
```

```
    <f:ajax listener="#{ajaxBean.upperCaseName}"
        execute="@form" render="@form"/>
  </h:commandButton>
</h:form>
...


public void upperCaseName(AjaxBehaviorEvent event){
  ...
}
```

> Remember that the client behavior (the ClientBehavior interface)
> is responsible for generating reusable JavaScript code that can be
> added to JSF components. The AJAX (<f:ajax>) is a client-side
> behavior, which means it is always attached as a behavior to another
> UI component(s). You can find more details about ClientBehavior
> in the *Working with client behavior functionality* section in *Chapter 5, JSF
> Configurations Using XML Files and Annotations – Part 2*.

The complete application can be found in the code bundle of this chapter, and is
named ch7_4.

# The event attribute

Each AJAX request is fired by an event indicating a user or programmatic
action. JSF defines default events based on the parent components; according to
documentation "The default event is action for ActionSource components such as
<h:commandButton>, and valueChange for EditableValueHolder components such
as <h:inputText>". Most of the time, the default events are exactly what you need,
but in case that you want to explicitly set an event for a component, you can use the
event attribute. Some of the most common values for this attribute are click, focus,
blur, keyup, and mouseover.

> Do not confuse these events with JavaScript events, which are prefixed
> with the on notation (onclick, onkeyup, onblur, and so on). The
> JavaScript events are *behind* AJAX events; or, with other words, AJAX
> events are based on JavaScript events. For example, AJAX click event
> is based on the onclick JavaScript event.

In the following code, the event that triggers the AJAX action is `keyup`:

```
<h:form>
  <h:inputText value="#{ajaxBean.name}">
  <f:ajax event="keyup" listener="#{ajaxBean.upperCaseName()}"
    render="@this"/>
  </h:inputText>
</h:form>
```

The complete application can be found in the code bundle of this chapter, and is named `ch7_5`.

# The onevent attribute – monitoring AJAX state on client

During an AJAX request, JSF is capable of calling a client-defined JavaScript method and passing an object named `data` to it, containing information about the current state of the request. The JavaScript function is called when the request begins, completes, and succeeds.

The `data` objects encapsulate the following properties:

- `type`: This property gives the type of the AJAX call, `event`
- `status`: This property returns the `begin`, `complete`, or `success` status (can be used to implement an indeterminate progress bar).

 When the `status` property has the value `begin`, which means that the AJAX request has not been sent yet. When it equals `complete`, it means that the AJAX response has successfully reached to the client, but it hasn't been processed yet. If the received response is successfully processed (without errors), the `status` value becomes `success`.

- `source`: This property returns the DOM element representing the source of the AJAX event
- `responseXML`: This is the AJAX response in XML format
- `responseText`: This is the AJAX response in text format
- `responseCode`: This is the AJAX response code

You need to indicate the name of the JavaScript method through the `onevent` attribute (in `jsf.js`, the JavaScript method representing implementation of this attribute is named `addOnEvent(callback)`):

```
<h:commandButton value="Submit">
  <f:ajax onevent="ajaxMonitoring" execute="@form"
         listener="#{ajaxBean.upperCaseName()}" render="@form"/>
</h:commandButton>
```

Next, the `ajaxMonitoring` function can use the `data` object and its properties to accomplish different client-side tasks. For example, the following implementation feeds up some `div` tags with details about the AJAX request:

```
<script type="text/javascript">
  function ajaxMonitoring(data) {
    document.getElementById("statusId").innerHTML += data.status +
      " | ";
    document.getElementById("responseCodeId").innerHTML +=
    status.responseCode + "| ";
    if(data.status === "complete") {
      document.getElementById("typeId").innerHTML += data.type;
      document.getElementById("sourceId").innerHTML +=
        data.source;
  ...
</script>
```

In the following figure, you can see a possible output:

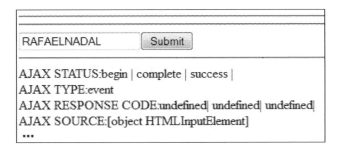

The complete application can be found in the code bundle of this chapter, and is named `ch7_21`.

# The onerror attribute – monitoring AJAX errors on client

In the preceding section, you saw how to monitor the state of AJAX requests using a client-defined JavaScript function and the data object. Based on the same technique, we can obtain information about the possible errors that can occur during AJAX requests. The passed data object encapsulates the following properties (notice that this is the same data object from the preceding section; therefore you still have access to those properties): description, errorName, and errorMessage.

The data.type property will be error and the data.status property will be one of the following:

- serverError: This is the response of the AJAX request that contains an error
- malformedXML: This is an XML well-formed error
- httpError: This is a valid HTTP error
- emptyResponse: This is a server-side code that did not provide a response

The name of the JavaScript method is indicated through the onerror attribute (in jsf.js, the JavaScript method representing implementation of this attribute is named addOnError (callback)). So at this point, we can update the application from the previous section to report errors on the client as well, as shown in the following code (note that onevent and onerror calls the same method, ajaxMonitoring; however this is not mandatory as you can use separate JavaScript methods as well):

```
<script type="text/javascript">
  function ajaxMonitoring(data) {
    document.getElementById("statusId").innerHTML += data.status +
      " | ";
    if(data.status === "serverError" || data.status
      === "malformedXML" ||
      data.status === "httpError" || data.status
      === "emptyResponse"){
      document.getElementById("descriptionId").innerHTML +=
        data.description;
      document.getElementById("errorNameId").innerHTML +=
        data.errorName;
      document.getElementById("errorMessageId").innerHTML +=
        data.errorMessage;
    }
    document.getElementById("responseCodeId").innerHTML +=
        status.responseCode + "| ";
    if (data.status === "complete") {
      document.getElementById("typeId").innerHTML += data.type;
```

```
        document.getElementById("sourceId").innerHTML +=
          data.source +
        "<br/><xmp>" + new XMLSerializer().
          serializeToString(data.source) +
        "</xmp>";
        document.getElementById("responseXMLId").innerHTML +=
        data.responseXML + "<br/><xmp>" + new
        XMLSerializer().serializeToString(data.responseXML)
          + "</xmp>";
        document.getElementById("responseTextId").innerHTML +=
          "<xmp>" +
        data.responseText + "</xmp>";
    }
   }
</script>
```

Now, you can test this code by adding an intentional error, such as calling nonexistent server-side method, as shown in the following code:

```
<h:commandButton value="Submit">
  <f:ajax onevent ="ajaxMonitoring" onerror="ajaxMonitoring"
          execute="@form" listener="#{ajaxBean.unexistedMethod()}"
          render="@form"/>
</h:commandButton>
```

A possible output is shown in the following screenshot:

The complete application can be found in code bundle of this chapter, and is named ch7_6.

# Grouping components under <f:ajax> tag

Sometimes, it may be useful to group multiple components under the same
<f:ajax> tag. For example, the following code snippet groups two <h:inputText>
components under the same <f:ajax> tag (you can nest other components as well):

```
<f:ajax event="click" execute="submitFormId" render="submitFormId">
  <h:form id="submitFormId">
    Name:
    <h:inputText id="nameId" value="#{ajaxBean.name}"
                          validator="nameValidator"/>
    <h:message id="msgNameId" showDetail="true" showSummary="true"
                          for="nameId" style="color: red;"/>
    Surname:
    <h:inputText id="surnameId" value="#{ajaxBean.surname}"
                          validator="nameValidator"/>
    <h:message id="msgSurnameId" showDetail="true"
       showSummary="true"
                          for="surnameId" style="color: red;"/>
  </h:form>
</f:ajax>
```

So, how does it work? When you click either of the input components, an AJAX
request is fired for the input component and one for the form (two requests in our
example) and all the components in the form are re-rendered. Since the click
event will generate AJAX requests/responses, you will not be able to enter keys
in those <h:inputText> unless you are using the *Tab* key to gain focus in each
<h:inputText> component.

> The components grouped under <f:ajax> can still use inner
> (or locally used) <f:ajax> tags. In this case, the effect is
> cumulative. Of course, you have to be extra careful when you
> use this technique, because undesired behaviors may occur.

The complete application can be found in the code bundle of this chapter, and is
named ch7_7.

# Updating input fields with AJAX after validation error

Updating input fields with AJAX after validation error is a very old, well-known, and annoying issue for JSF developers. When an AJAX request fails in the validation phase, there is no built-in way to update the input fields with some valid values because JSF does not allow access to the model value after a validation error (usually, you want to clear up those fields or provide some default values, or even some old values provided by the same user). Of course, JSF developers found different workarounds, or used other libraries, such as PrimeFaces or OmniFaces, but a JSF solution was required.

Starting with JSF 2.2, all components that should be re-rendered (components indicated in the `render` attribute) will be reset if we set the `resetValues` attribute to `true`. The easiest way to understand this is to proceed with a comparison test. First, let's use an AJAX request without `resetValues`:

```
<h:form>
  <h:message id="msgId" showDetail="true" showSummary="true"
    for="nameId" style="color: red;"/>
  <h:inputText id="nameId" value="#{ajaxBean.name}"
                         validator="nameValidator"/>
  <h:commandButton value="Submit">
    <f:ajax execute="@form" resetValues="false"
      listener="#{ajaxBean.upperCaseName()}" render="nameId
        msgId"/>
  </h:commandButton>
</h:form>
```

Let's suppose that a valid value for our input field is an alphanumeric string (with respect to the [^a-zA-Z0-9] pattern). In the following screenshot, on the left-hand side, you can see the AJAX result after inserting a valid value, and on the right-hand side, you can see the AJAX result after inserting an invalid value:

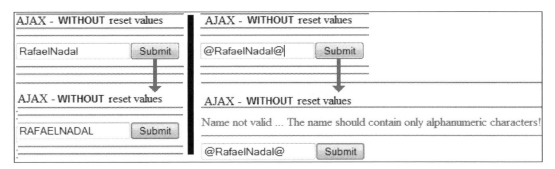

As you can see in the preceding screenshot, on the right-hand side, the invalid value was not reset. The invalid value retains and is very annoying.

Next, we proceed with the same case, but we add the `resetValues` attribute:

```
<h:form>
  <h:message id="msgId" showDetail="true" showSummary="true"
    for="nameId"
  style="color: red;"/>
  <h:inputText id="nameId" value="#{ajaxBean.name}"
                          validator="nameValidator"/>
  <h:commandButton value="Submit">
    <f:ajax execute="@form" resetValues="true"
      listener="#{ajaxBean.upperCaseName()}" render="nameId
      msgId"/>
  </h:commandButton>
</h:form>
```

Now, we repeat the test. In the following screenshot, on the left-hand side, the submitted value is valid, while on the right-hand side, it is invalid:

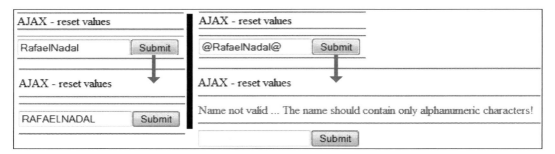

Now, when the submitted value was invalid, the input field was reset (in this case, cleared).

From this example, you may misunderstand that `resetValues` works as a clear (empty) field's action. Well, it does not! When an input field is reset, the valid value that replaces the invalid one is related to the managed bean (the renderer will pick up the value from the bean). If the managed bean is in the request scope, the replacer (valid value) will be the one used for initialization of corresponding property (which may be anything, not just an empty string). But, if the managed bean is in view scope, then the replacer will be the currently valid value of the corresponding property, which may be the initialization value, or the previous valid value inserted by the user (of course, altered or not altered in a server-side method).

Keep this note in mind while testing the complete application available in the code bundle of this chapter, named `ch7_8_1`. By default, this application comes with a request scoped managed bean, but you can easily transform it into a view scoped for more tests.

Besides the `resetValues` attribute for AJAX requests, JSF 2.2 comes with a tag, named `<f:resetValues>`, for non-AJAX requests. Basically, this is an action listener that can be easily attached to any `ActionSource` instance (for example, `<h:commandButton>`). The effect will consist of resetting all components that are given in its `render` attribute (use only component IDs, not keywords such as `@form`, `@all`, and so on):

```
<h:commandButton value="Submit"
  action="#{nonAjaxBean.upperCaseName()}">
  <f:resetValues render="nameId" />
</h:commandButton>
```

The complete application can be found in the code bundle of this chapter, and is named `ch7_8_2`. This tag is not recognized in all JSF 2.2 (Mojarra and MyFaces) versions, therefore you have to test it in order to be sure that you can use it.

# The Cancel and Clear buttons

Buttons of type **Cancel** (which resets the form's fields to the initial state or to the most recent valid state) and **Clear** (which clears up the form's fields) are not very popular in web applications, but sometimes they can be useful to end users. When implementing the **Cancel/Clear** buttons, you need to find a way to skip the *Process Validation* phase (which is needed for the **Submit** button). The motivation is simple: when a user cancels/clears a form's values, we certainly don't need valid values in order to accomplish these tasks; therefore, no validation is needed.

In non-AJAX requests, a common technique consists of using the `immediate="true"` attribute, which, for command components (for example, `<h:commandButton>`), will transfer the invocation of action in *Apply Request Values* phase. This attribute is available for AJAX requests as well, but AJAX provides a better solution for these kinds of tasks. Instead of using `immediate="true"`, we can use the `@this` keyword. Furthermore, we can use the `resetValues` feature to simplify and fortify the **Cancel/Clear** buttons.

Now, let's look at some scenarios. We will keep things simple, therefore we need a form with a single input field and three buttons: **Submit**, **Cancel**, and **Clear**. The validator will allow only alphanumeric characters (with respect to the `[^a-zA-Z0-9]` pattern).

# Value submitted to a view scoped managed bean

In this case, run the following code:

```
<h:form>
  <h:message id="msgId" showDetail="true" showSummary="true"
    for="nameId" style="color: red;"/>
  <h:inputText id="nameId" value="#{ajaxBean.name}"
                        validator="nameValidator"/>
  <h:commandButton value="Submit">
    <f:ajax execute="@form" resetValues="true"
      listener="#{ajaxBean.upperCaseName()}" render="nameId
      msgId"/>
  </h:commandButton>
  <h:commandButton value="Cancel">
    <f:ajax execute="@this" render="@form"/>
  </h:commandButton>
  <h:commandButton value="Clear">
    <f:ajax execute="@this" render="@form"
                        listener="#{ajaxBean.cancelName()}"/>
  </h:commandButton>
</h:form>
```

Press the **Submit** button. In case of an invalid value, you will see a specific error message (`<h:message>`), and `resetValues` will reset the input field to the initial value (empty string or some suggestion) or the most recent valid value.

Press the **Cancel** button. Since we are using `execute="@this"`, the input field will not be processed on the server; therefore no validation happens. The re-render process will have the same effect as `resetValues` for the input field, but will clear the `<h:message>` tag as well.

Press the **Clear** button. This button uses `execute="@this"`, too. But, instead of resetting the input field to `resetValues`, it clears up the input field and `<h:message>`. For this, an additional method is needed in the managed bean as follows:

```
private String name = "RafaelNadal";
...
public void cancelName() {
  name = "";
}
```

The complete application can be found in the code bundle of this chapter, which is named `ch7_9_1`.

As a simple tip and trick, for the **Clear** button you may want to use a place holder as follows:

```
xmlns:f5="http://xmlns.jcp.org/jsf/passthrough"
...
<h:inputText id="nameId" value="#{ajaxBean.name}"
  validator="nameValidator"  f5:placeholder
    ="Enter your name ..."/>
```

# Value submitted to a request scoped managed bean

Since the submitted value is not persisted across multiple AJAX requests, the `resetValues` method and the **Cancel** button will reset the input field to the initialization value (empty string or suggestion). The **Cancel** button will also reset the `<h:message>` tag. The **Clear** button will clear up input text and `<h:message>`. Of course, under some circumstances (such as using an empty string for initialization), the **Cancel** and **Clear** buttons will do the same thing; therefore, you can drop one of them.

The complete application can be seen in the code bundle of this chapter, and is named `ch7_9_2`.

> More examples of how to use `resetValues` and implement the
> **Cancel** and **Clear** buttons can be found in the source code that
> accompanies this book. A set of examples using the `keyup` event
> in an input field with cancel/clear facilities contain the following
> applications: `ch7_9_3`, `ch7_9_4`, `ch7_9_5`, and `ch7_9_6`.

Everything seems to work pretty straightforward, but there is an issue that we have to fix. Let's take a closer look at the following code (there is nothing tricky in it):

```
<h:form>
  Name:
  <h:inputText id="nameId" value="#{ajaxBean.name}"
                         validator="nameValidator"/>
  <h:message id="msgNameId" showDetail="true" showSummary="true"
                         for="nameId" style="color: red;"/>
  Surname:
  <h:inputText id="surnameId" value="#{ajaxBean.surname}"
                         validator="nameValidator"/>
  <h:message id="msgSurnameId" showDetail="true"
    showSummary="true"
                         for="surnameId" style="color: red;"/> ..

  <h:commandButton value="Submit">
    <f:ajax execute="@form"
```

```
            listener="#{ajaxBean.upperCaseNameAndSurname()}"
            render="@form"/>
    </h:commandButton>
    <h:commandButton value="Cancel">
      <f:ajax execute="@this" render="@form"/>
    </h:commandButton>
    <h:commandButton value="Clear/Reset">
      <f:ajax execute="@this" render="@form"
            listener="#{ajaxBean.cancelNameAndSurname()}"/>
    </h:commandButton>
</h:form>
```

Let's focus on the submit process. When we submit a valid name and surname, the form is re-rendered and everything looks as expected, but if one value (or both) is invalid, then the input fields are not reset and the corresponding error messages appear. This is normal since the resetValues method is not present; therefore, the first thought would be to add resetValues="true" to <f:ajax> that corresponds to the **Submit** button. However, this will not work as expected, because nothing happens in case of invalid values. While you may think that the input fields will be reset for invalid values, you will be surprised to see that everything remains unchanged and the invalid values are still there after re-render. The cause seems to be the presence of @form in the render attribute of the **Submit** button. If you replace this with the components IDs that should be re-rendered (nameId, msgNameId, surnameId, and msgSurnameId), the resetValues method works perfectly.

But, what you can do if there are many input fields and you don't want to list all the components IDs? Or you just want to use the @form keyword in the render attribute? In this case, you should be aware that the invalid input fields will not be automatically reset (the resetValues method is useless) and the end user should manually cancel/clear input fields by clicking on the **Cancel** or **Clear** button. While the **Cancel** button works fine, there is a big *Oops!* for the **Clear** button because JSF will not clear the input fields that are not executed (listed in the execute attribute) and are re-rendered (listed in the render attribute), unless you submit only valid values. In other words, if the name is valid and the surname is not (or any other combination involving invalid values), then after submit and clear, the input field for the name is not cleared.

One solution to this problem is given on OmniFaces (https://code.google. com/p/omnifaces/), which provides an action listener named org.omnifaces. eventlistener.ResetInputAjaxActionListener (http://showcase.omnifaces. org/eventlisteners/ResetInputAjaxActionListener). This listener is capable of fixing the **Clear** button and other issues of the same category:

```
<h:commandButton value="Clear/Reset">
    <f:ajax execute="@this" render="@form"
```

```
          listener="#{ajaxBean.cancelNameAndSurname()}"/>
    <f:actionListener type="org.omnifaces.eventlistener.
              ResetInputAjaxActionListener"/>
  </h:commandButton>
```

The complete application can be found in the code bundle of this chapter, which is named `ch7_9_7`.

# Mixing AJAX and flow scope

AJAX requests are usually associated with beans in view scope (`@ViewScoped`), which means that data can be persisted (stored) over multiple AJAX requests as long as the current view is not destroyed by a navigation case (or other causes). A flow is defined as a collection of logical related pages/views; therefore AJAX cannot survive across flow transitions.

For better understanding, we will adapt the application developed in *Chapter 3, JSF Scopes – Lifespan and Use in Managed Beans Communication* (the `ch3_7_3` application, which you need to be familiar with) to support AJAX requests in the `registration.xhtml` view (the first page in flow). The main idea is to write a view scoped bean that may populate the player name and surname defined in the flow scoped bean, `RegistrationBean`. The view-scoped bean, named `ViewRegistrationBean`, will randomly generate a name-surname pair and will present them as a suggestion to the end user. The user can provide the name and surname or he can choose to use the suggested ones. So, the flow-scoped bean looks like the following code:

```
import javax.faces.flow.FlowScoped;
import javax.inject.Named;

@Named
@FlowScoped(value = "registration")
public class RegistrationBean {

  private String playerName ="";
  private String playerSurname="";

  //getters and setters

  public void credentialsUpperCase(){
    playerName = playerName.toUpperCase();
    playerSurname = playerSurname.toUpperCase();
  }

  public String getReturnValue() {
```

```
      return "/done";
   }

   public String registrationAction() {
      return "confirm";
   }
}
```

Notice that the getReturnValue method represents a flow return (exits flow), while the registrationAction method navigates to the next page in the flow. Both of them will break down the current view.

Next, the view-scoped bean is the method annotated with @PostConstruct that will help us to see if AJAX uses the same instance of this bean over multiple requests:

```
@Named
@ViewScoped
public class ViewRegistrationBean implements Serializable {

   @Inject
   RegistrationBean registrationBean;
   private String playerNameView = "nothing";
   private String playerSurnameView = "nothing";
   private static final Map<Integer, String> myMap = new
      HashMap<>();
   static {
         myMap.put(1, "Nadal Rafael");
         myMap.put(2, "Federer Roger");
         ...
   }

   @PostConstruct
   public void init() {
      Random r = new Random();
      int key = 1 + r.nextInt(9);
      String player = myMap.get(key);
      String[] fullname = player.split(" ");

      playerNameView = fullname[0];
      playerSurnameView = fullname[1];
      playerNameView = playerNameView.toUpperCase();
      playerSurnameView = playerSurnameView.toUpperCase();
   }

   public String getPlayerNameView() {
```

```
      return playerNameView;
   }

   public void setPlayerNameView(String playerNameView) {
      this.playerNameView = playerNameView;
   }

   public String getPlayerSurnameView() {
      return playerSurnameView;
   }

   public void setPlayerSurnameView(String playerSurnameView) {
      this.playerSurnameView = playerSurnameView;
   }

   public void generateCredentials() {
      registrationBean.setPlayerName(playerNameView);
      registrationBean.setPlayerSurname(playerSurnameView);
   }
}
```

We can easily monitor the values of name and surname by displaying them in
registration.xhtml using the following code:

```
Your registration last credentials (in <b>flow</b>):
<h:outputText id="credentialsFlowId"
                value="#{registrationBean.playerName}
                    #{registrationBean.playerSurname}"/>
<hr/>
Random credentials (in <b>view</b>) [as long as we are in this view
this value won't change]:
<h:outputText id="credentialsViewId"
                value="#{viewRegistrationBean.playerNameView}
                    #{viewRegistrationBean.playerSurnameView}"/>
```

Now, two buttons will fire AJAX requests. One button will call the server-side
method credentialsUpperCase (from flow-scoped bean, RegistrationBean)
and the other one will call the server-side method generateCredentials
(from view-scoped bean, ViewRegistrationBean). In both cases, we will
re-render the player name and surname from the beans as follows:

```
<h:form>
   Name: <h:inputText value="#{registrationBean.playerName}"/>
   Surname: <h:inputText
      value="#{registrationBean.playerSurname}"/>
```

```
    <h:commandButton value="Register To Tournament (AJAX call a
      method of a
    flow bean)" action="#{registrationBean.credentialsUpperCase()}">
    <f:ajax execute="@form"
            render="@form :credentialsFlowId :credentialsViewId"/>
    </h:commandButton>
    <h:commandButton value="Register To Tournament (AJAX call a
      method of a
    view bean)"
      action="#{viewRegistrationBean.generateCredentials()}">
    <f:ajax execute="@this"
            render="@form :credentialsFlowId :credentialsViewId"/>
    </h:commandButton>
  </h:form>
```

Now, the end user can register to the tournament in two ways: by manually inserting the name and surname through the input fields and register by pressing the first button (the result will be the inserted name and surname in uppercase), or he/she can choose to use the suggested name and surname and register by pressing the second button (the result will be the random name and surname in uppercase).

A few important things can be noticed here, which are listed as follows:

- Firing AJAX requests, by pressing the first button, will put the submitted name and surname in the flow scope (manually entered or imported from random suggestion)

- Firing AJAX requests, by pressing the second button, will assign the suggested name and surname to their counterparts in the flow-scoped bean. It will not generate new names and surnames for each request, since we are in the same view across multiple AJAX requests, and the init method is called only when a new instance of the ViewRegistrationBean bean is created.

- If we exit and re-enter in the flow, the persisted name and surname lose their values. When we exit from the flow, we reach the flow-scope boundaries, which means a new RegistrationBean instance must be created when entering in the flow again. Moreover, this outcome will change the current view; therefore, a new instance of ViewRegistrationBean is also needed.

- When we navigate to the next page in the flow, the submitted name and surname have the same values because they were persisted in flow scope; while the suggested name and surname are randomly generated again, the outcome has changed the view, even if we are in the same flow, as shown in the following screenshot:

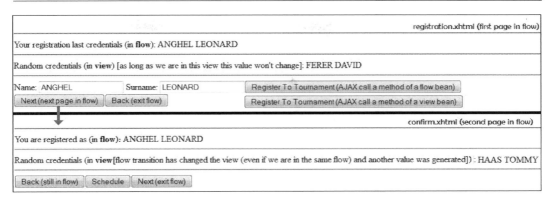

Now you know how AJAX works with flow scope combined with view scope. The complete application can be found in the code bundle of this chapter, which is named `ch7_10`.

# Postback and AJAX

Throughout this book, we have mentioned the postback request several times. For those who are not familiar with it, or just need a quick reminder, let's say that JSF recognizes the initial request and the postback request.

**Initial request** (for example, HTTP GET) is the first request that the browser sends for loading the page. You can obtain such a request by accessing the application URL in a browser or by following a link (it can be a link to any page of the application). Moreover, the initial request happens in page_B when page_A contains a redirection (`faces-redirect=true`) to page_B (this is not true for forwarding mechanism). This kind of request is processed in *Restore View* phase and *Render Response* phase.

**Postback request** happens when we click on a button/link for submitting a form. Unlike the initial request, the postback request passes through all the phases.

JSF provides a method named `isPostback` that returns a Boolean value: it returns `true` for postback request and `false` for initial request. Speaking in the code lines, we can:

- Check the initial/postback request in a managed bean using the following code:

```
FacesContext facesContext =
  FacesContext.getCurrentInstance();
logger.log(Level.INFO, "Is postback: {0}",
  facesContext.isPostback());
```

- Check the initial/postback request in the page using the following code:

```
Is postback ? <h:outputText
  value="#{facesContext.postback}"/>
```

For example, you can check the initial/postback request for AJAX with a simple application. The JSF page is as follows:

```
<h:form>
  <h:commandButton value="Click Me!">
    <f:ajax listener="#{ajaxBean.requestAction()}"
      render=":postbackId"/>
  </h:commandButton>
</h:form>
<h:panelGrid id="postbackId" columns="1">
  <h:outputText value="Is postback ?: #{facesContext.postback}"/>
  <h:outputText value="REQUEST NUMBER: #{ajaxBean.request_number}"/>
</h:panelGrid>
```

The managed bean is as follows:

```
@Named
@ViewScoped
public class AjaxBean implements Serializable{

    private static final Logger logger =
            Logger.getLogger(AjaxBean.class.getName());
    private int request_number = 1;

    public int getRequest_number() {
      FacesContext facesContext = FacesContext.getCurrentInstance();
      logger.log(Level.INFO, "Is postback (getRequest_number
        method): {0}",
        facesContext.isPostback());
      return request_number;
    }

    public void setRequest_number(int request_number) {
      this.request_number = request_number;
    }

    public void requestAction(){
      FacesContext facesContext = FacesContext.getCurrentInstance();
      logger.log(Level.INFO, "Is postback (requestAction method):
        {0}", facesContext.isPostback());
      request_number ++;
    }
}
```

The code is very simple; therefore we can jump directly to inspect the initial/postback requests, as follows:

- **First request**: The first page of the application is loaded by accessing the application URL. The client side indicates an initial request as it is shown in the following screenshot on the left-hand side, and the server side indicates the same, as shown in the same screenshot on the right-hand side:

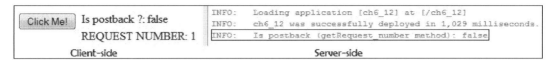

- **Second request**: The **Click Me!** button is clicked for the first time (the result is `true` for the second time, third time, and so on). The client side (in the browser) indicates a postback request as it is shown in the following screenshot on the left-hand side, and the server side indicates the same as shown in the same screenshot on the right-hand side:

It would be useful to know when the request is initial or postback. For example, you may want to accomplish a task a single time, at initial request (for example, the initialization tasks), or every time, except for the first time (for example, display a message, which is not proper to appear when a page is displayed as a result of the initial request).

# Postback request's conditional rendering/executing

We can use initial/postback request detection to conditionally render UI components (of course, you can use it for partial processing also). Take a look at the following code:

```
<h:form id="ajaxFormId">
  <h:commandButton id="buttonId" value="Click Me!">
    <f:ajax listener="#{ajaxBean.requestAction()}"
      render="#{facesContext.postback eq true ?
    ':postbackId': 'ajaxFormId'}"/>
  </h:commandButton>
  Is postback ? <h:outputText value="#{facesContext.postback}"/>
</h:form>
```

```
<h:panelGrid id="postbackId" columns="1">
  <h:outputText value="REQUEST NUMBER:
    #{ajaxBean.request_number}"/>
</h:panelGrid>
```

So, let's see how it works! When the page is loaded, we have an initial request (#{facesContext.postback} returns false), which means that the server response will contain something like the following code snippet (we need to focus on the <f:ajax> component):

```
<input id="ajaxFormId:buttonId" type="submit"
       name="ajaxFormId:buttonId" value="Click Me!"
       onclick="mojarra.ab(this,event,'action',0,'ajaxFormId');
       return false" />
```

On the server side, the log line from the getRequest_number method will also reveal an initial request. Moreover, notice that the reported request number is 1, which is the initial value of the request_number property.

Next, let's click once on the **Click Me!** button. Now, the AJAX request will look like the following line of code:

```
ajaxFormId=ajaxFormId&javax.faces.ViewState
   =411509096033316844%3A7611114960827713853&javax.faces.source
   =ajaxFormId%3AbuttonId&javax.faces.partial.event
   =click&javax.faces.partial.execute
   =ajaxFormId%3AbuttonId%20ajaxFormId%3AbuttonId&
   javax.faces.partial.render
   =ajaxFormId&javax.faces.behavior.event
   =action&javax.faces.partial.ajax=true
```

The highlighted code provides important information! This is a postback request, but the render attribute contains the ID of the <h:form> component, not the ID of the <h:panelGrid> component (as you may have thought); this happens because the #{facesContext.postback} expression was evaluated to false in the previous request. So, with the first click on our button, AJAX will not re-render the <h:panelGrid> component. Meanwhile, on the server side, the request_number property was successfully incremented to 2; however for the end user, it still appears as 1.

Now, the server response for this AJAX will contain the following code:

```
<input id="ajaxFormId:buttonId" type="submit"
       name="ajaxFormId:buttonId" value="Click Me!"
       onclick="mojarra.ab(this,event,'action',0,'postbackId');
       return false">
```

Note that the `postbackId`, which is the `<h:panelGrid>` ID, is present in the response. The next click (the second click) on the button will generate the next AJAX request:

```
ajaxFormId=ajaxFormId&javax.faces.ViewState
    =270275638491205347%3A7563196939691682163&javax.faces.source
    =ajaxFormId%3AbuttonId&javax.faces.partial.event
    =click&javax.faces.partial.execute
    =ajaxFormId%3AbuttonId%20ajaxFormId%3AbuttonId
    &javax.faces.partial.render=postbackId
    &javax.faces.behavior.event=action&javax.faces.partial.ajax=true
```

Now, when the AJAX request completes, the `<h:panelGrid>` component will be re-rendered. The `request_number` property reaches the value 3, and it will be displayed on the client side. Further AJAX requests will be the postback requests.

In the following screenshot, you can see the initial request, first click on the button and second click from client and server sides:

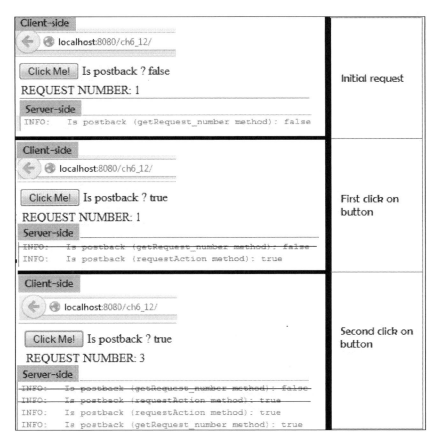

It would be helpful to know this behavior of AJAX with initial/postback requests—it is not a bug. Of course, once you know this *issue*, there are many workarounds depending on what you really want to accomplish.

Further, you can try to test the `execute` attribute in a similar approach.

The complete application can be found in the code bundle of this chapter, which is named `ch7_11`.

# Is it a non-AJAX request?

JSF can answer this question by inspecting request headers or checking the `PartialViewContext.isAjaxRequest` method. The request headers that provide information about the request type are `Faces-Request` and `X-Requested-With`. For an AJAX request, the `Faces-Request` header will have the value `partial/ajax`, while the `X-Requested-With` request type will have the value `XMLHttpRequest` (in JSF 2.2, `X-Requested-With` doesn't seem to work; however, for the sake of completeness, you can test them again). In the following screenshot, you can see the headers of a typical JSF 2.2 AJAX request:

```
     •••
          Cookie  JSESSIONID=fe2076c64ad212a2ca7c33ff7808
  Faces-Request  partial/ajax
            Host  localhost:8080
     •••
```

In a managed bean, you can determine the type of the request, as shown in the following code:

```java
public void requestTypeAction() {

    FacesContext facesContext = FacesContext.getCurrentInstance();
    ExternalContext externalContext = facesContext.getExternalContext();
    Map<String, String> headers = externalContext.getRequestHeaderMap();
    logger.info(headers.toString());

    //determination method 1
    PartialViewContext partialViewContext =
                    facesContext.getPartialViewContext();
    if (partialViewContext != null) {
      if (partialViewContext.isAjaxRequest()) {
          logger.info("THIS IS AN AJAX REQUEST (DETERMINATION 1)
              ...");
      } else {
```

```
            logger.info("THIS IS A NON-AJAX REQUEST(DETERMINATION
                1)...");
        }
    }


    //determination method 2
    String request_type_header_FR = headers.get("Faces-Request");
    if (request_type_header_FR != null) {
        if (request_type_header_FR.equals("partial/ajax")) {
            logger.info("THIS IS AN AJAX REQUEST (DETERMINATION 2)
                ...");
        } else {
            logger.info("THIS IS A NON-AJAX REQUEST(DETERMINATION
                2)...");
        }
    }


    //determination method 3
    String request_type_header_XRW = headers.get
        ("X-Requested-With");
    if (request_type_header_XRW != null) {
        if (request_type_header_XRW.equals("XMLHttpRequest")) {
            logger.info("THIS IS AN AJAX REQUEST (DETERMINATION 3)
                ...");
        } else {
            logger.info("THIS IS A NON-AJAX REQUEST(DETERMINATION
                3)...");
        }
    }
}
```

Alternatively, on a JSF page, you can write the following code:

```
AJAX/NON-AJAX:
#{facesContext.partialViewContext.ajaxRequest ? 'Yes' : 'No'}
FACES-REQUEST HEADER:
    #{facesContext.externalContext.requestHeaderMap
    ['Faces-Request']}
X-REQUESTED-WITH HEADER:
    #{facesContext.externalContext.requestHeaderMap
    ['X-Requested-With']}
```

The complete application can be found in the code bundle of this chapter, which is named ch7_12.

# AJAX and <f:param>

The <f:param> tag can be used to pass request parameters to a managed bean. Since we have discussed this tag in detail in *Chapter 2, Communication in JSF*, we can continue here with an example of using it inside <f:ajax>:

```
<h:form>
  <h:inputText id="nameInputId" value="#{ajaxBean.name}"/>
  <h:commandButton value="Send" action="#{ajaxBean.ajaxAction()}">
    <f:ajax execute ="nameInputId" render="nameOutputId">
      <f:param name="surnameInputId" value="Nadal"/>
    </f:ajax>
  </h:commandButton>
  <h:outputText id="nameOutputId" value="#{ajaxBean.name}"/>
</h:form>
```

Remember that the parameter that was passed is available in the request parameter map:

```
FacesContext fc = FacesContext.getCurrentInstance();
Map<String, String> params =
            fc.getExternalContext().getRequestParameterMap();
logger.log(Level.INFO, "Surname: {0}",
    params.get("surnameInputId"));
```

> Keep in mind that <f:param> can be used with buttons and links only. Trying to add <f:param> in inputs will not work. Further details are available in *Chapter 2, Communication in JSF*.

The complete application can be found in the code bundle of this chapter, which is named ch7_13.

# Queue control for AJAX requests

Queuing AJAX requests on the client side is a common practice meant to ensure that only one request is processed at a time. The goal of this approach is to protect the server from being overwhelmed and the client browser from blocking or receiving AJAX responses in an undefined order. While AJAX queuing is available in JSF 2.0, queue control for AJAX is available starting with JSF 2.2.

In order to provide AJAX queue control, JSF 2.2 introduced an attribute named `delay` for the `<f:ajax>` tag. The value of this attribute is a string that represents a number of milliseconds (defaults to `none`). During this time interval, only the most recent request is actually sent to the server, while the rest of them are ignored. In other words, JSF will wait *n* milliseconds until the most recent AJAX request is executed. By default, it will not wait.

Here is an example of using the default `delay` attribute, and an explicit delay of 1000 milliseconds. In order to point out the delay effect, we've built a simple application that sends an AJAX request (submit an input text value) on the `keyup` event, and waits for a suggestion text as a server response. In the following screenshot, you can compare the number of entered keys until the server responds with the first suggestion text. In both the cases, this is the first triggered AJAX request. It is obvious that in the second case, a number of seven requests (keystrokes) were not sent because they were fired during the1000 milliseconds range. Generally speaking, every time a new key is entered, prior AJAX requests are removed, and only the last request is taken into account.

| No delay (default) |
| --- |
| **Type a tennis player name:** |
| n |
| Nadal Rafael |
| Explicit delay (1000 miliseconds or 1 second): |
| **Type a tennis player name:** |
| nadal ra |
| Nadal Rafael |

The complete application can be found in the code bundle of this chapter, and is named `ch7_14`. You may also want to check out the *Customizing jsf.js* section, where you'll see the `delay` attribute at work.

You can disable the effect of the `delay` attribute by setting its value to `none`. This is the default value.

# Explicit loading of jsf.js

The AJAX mechanism used by JSF is encapsulated in a JavaScript file, named `jsf.js`. This file is available in the `javax.faces` library. When we are using `<f:ajax>`, this file is loaded behind the scene without any explicit requirements.

However, `jsf.js` can be loaded explicitly with any of the following methods:

- Using the `<h:outputScript>` component as follows:

  ```
  <h:outputScript name="jsf.js" library="javax.faces"
  target="head"/>
  ```

- Using the `@ResourceDependency` keyword as follows:

  ```
  @ResourceDependency(name="jsf.js" library="javax.faces"
  target="head")
  ```

Focusing on `<h:outputScript>`, you can attach AJAX to a component as shown in the following example code:

```
<h:form prependId="false">
  <h:outputScript name="jsf.js" library
   ="javax.faces" target="head"/>
  <h:inputText id="nameInId" value="#{ajaxBean.name}"/>
  <h:outputText id="nameOutId" value="#{ajaxBean.name}"/>
  <h:commandButton id="submit" value="Send"
                 action="#{ajaxBean.upperCaseAction()}"
                 onclick="jsf.ajax.request(this, event,
                   {execute:'nameInId',render:'nameOutId'});
                   return false;" />
</h:form>
```

The `jsf.ajax.request` method defined in `jsf.js` is capable of dealing with AJAX requests. It takes the following three parameters:

- `source`: This is the DOM element (for example, `<h:commandButton>`, `<h:commandLink>`, and so on) that triggers the AJAX request (this is a mandatory parameter)
- `event`: This is an optional parameter representing the DOM event that triggers the request
- `options`: This is an optional parameter that can contain the values: `execute`, `render`, `onevent`, `onerror`, `delay`, and `params`.

The complete application for explicitly loading the `jsf.js` file is available in the code bundle of this chapter, which is named `ch7_15`.

# Depicting the params value

While the `execute`, `render`, `delay`, `onevent`, and `onerror` values are very well known from previous sections, the `params` value is something new, so let's give it some attention. The `params` value is actually an object that allows us to add supplementary parameters into the request.

For example, the following code is a fancy solution for sending a JavaScript JSON object to a managed bean. The code is straightforward as follows:

```
<script type="text/javascript">
  var myJSONObject =
    [{
      "name": "Rafael",
      "surname": "Nadal",
      "age": 27,
      "isMarried": false,
      "address": {
                 "city": " Mallorca",
                 "country": "Spain"
                 },
      "websites": ["http://www.rafaelnadal.com",
                   "http://rafaelnadalfans.com/"]
    },
    ...
    }]
</script>
...
<h:form prependId="false">
  <h:outputScript name="jsf.js" library="javax.faces"
    target="head"/>
    Data type (e.g. JSON): <h:inputText id="typeInId"
                                        value="#{ajaxBean.type}"/>
  <h:commandButton id="submit" value="Send"
                   action="#{ajaxBean.processJSONAction()}"
                   onclick='jsf.ajax.request(this, event, {execute:
                   "typeInId", render: "typeOutId playersId",
                     params: JSON.stringify(myJSONObject)});
                   return false;' />
  <h:outputText id="typeOutId" value="#{ajaxBean.type}"/>
  <h:dataTable id="playersId" value="#{ajaxBean.players}" var="t">
  ...
  </h:dataTable>
</h:form>
```

On the server side, the `params` value is available in the request parameter map as follows:

```
FacesContext facesContext = FacesContext.getCurrentInstance();
String json = facesContext.getExternalContext().
              getRequestParameterMap().get("params");
JsonArray personArray;
try (JsonReader reader = Json.createReader(new StringReader(json))) {
    personArray = reader.readArray();
    }
...
```

The complete application can be found in the code bundle of this chapter, and is named `ch7_16`.

# Non-UICommand components and jsf.ajax. request

The `<f:ajax>` tag is far more popular than `jsf.ajax.request`. This is absolutely normal, since `<f:ajax>` fits more natural in *context* and is much more easy to use and understand. Moreover, `<f:ajax>` supports the `listener` attribute, which allows us to call the server-side methods even when the `<f:ajax>` tag is nested in other components than in `UICommand`. By default, `jsf.ajax.request` cannot do that!

For example, let's say that we have a table (`<h:dataTable>`) that displays a `Map` object containing several tennis players (the `Map` key is an integer of type: 1, 2,3, ... *n*, and the `Map` value is the player name):

```
private Map<Integer, String> myMap = new HashMap<>();
...
myMap.put(1, "Nadal Rafael");
myMap.put(2, "Federer Roger");
...
```

Next, we want to add a column labeled **Delete** that contains a delete icon for each row, as shown in the following screenshot:

We want to capture the client-side onclick event and trigger an AJAX request using jsf.ajax.request for each icon. The idea is to send the player number (1, 2, 3, ... *n*) to a server-side method named deletePlayerAction. This method will find and delete the record from the Map object and when the table is re-rendered, the corresponding row will disappear. So, the code can be written as follows:

```
<h:form prependId="false">
  <h:outputScript name="jsf.js" library="javax.faces"
    target="head"/>
  <h:dataTable id="playersTableId"
               value="#{ajaxBean.myMap.entrySet()}" var="t">
    <h:column>
      <f:facet name="header">
        Delete
      </f:facet>
      <h:graphicImage value="./resources/default/imgs/delete.png"
                  onclick="jsf.ajax.request(this, event,
                      {execute: '@this', render:
                      'playersTableId',
                      params: '#{t.key}'});"/>
    </h:column>

    ...
  </h:dataTable>
</h:form>
```

We can use the params value to send the player number to delete; this will be available through the request parameter map. But the big issue here is that we can't call the server-side method, deletePlayerAction, because we don't have a UICommand component (such as a button) and jsf.ajax.request doesn't have a listener value for the options parameter.

Well, the solution comes from the JSF extensions such as PrimeFaces (check <p:remoteCommand>), OmniFaces (check <o:commandScript>), or RichFaces (check <a4j:jsfFunction>), but you can also solve the problem through pure JSF. First, you need to add a UICommand component that is not visible, such as a <h:commandLink> tag, as added in the following code snippet:

```
<h:form prependId="false">
  <h:commandLink id="commandDeleteId" immediate="true"
              action="#{ajaxBean.deletePlayerAction()}"
              style='display: none;'/>
  <h:outputScript name="jsf.js" library="javax.faces"
    target="head"/>
```

Next, we bind the AJAX request to this `UICommand` component, as shown in the following code snippet:

```
<h:graphicImage value="./resources/default/imgs/delete.png"
                onclick="jsf.ajax.request('commandDeleteId',
                  event, {'javax.faces.behavior.event': 'action',
                execute: '@this', render:
                  'playersTableId', params: '#{t.key}'});"/>
```

At this moment, when we click on a delete icon, the server-side method is executed. The code of this method is pretty simple, which is as follows:

```
public void deletePlayerAction() {
    FacesContext facesContext = FacesContext.getCurrentInstance();
    String nr = facesContext.getExternalContext().
                    getRequestParameterMap().get("params");

    if(nr!=null){
        myMap.remove(Integer.valueOf(nr));
    }
}
```

Done! The complete application can be found in the code bundle of this chapter, which is named `ch7_17`.

Of course, as the section name suggests, this was an example of using `jsf.ajax.request`, not the best solution to this scenario. Nevertheless, there are simple solutions for this, such as using a `<h:commandLink>` tag in conjunction with the icon and ajaxify the link (proposed by Michael Muller at `http://blog.mueller-bruehl.de/tutorial-web-development/`), The following code snippet shows this approach:

```
<h:form id="playersFormId">
  <h:dataTable id="playersTableId"
    value="#{ajaxBean.myMap.entrySet()}" var="t">
  <h:column>
    <f:facet name="header">Delete</f:facet>
    <h:commandLink id="commandDeleteId" immediate="true"
      action="#{ajaxBean.deletePlayerAction(t.key)}">
    <f:ajax render="playersFormId:playersTableId"/>
    <h:graphicImage value=
      "#{resource['default:imgs/delete.png']}"/>
    </h:commandLink>
  </h:column>
  . . .
```

The complete example can be found in the code bundle of this chapter named `ch7_18`.

# Customizing jsf.js

The biggest advantage of explicitly loading jsf.js is the fact that we can customize the AJAX mechanism by altering the default code. First, we need to isolate the default jsf.js file in a separate place—you can easily save it in a folder such as resources/default/js in the web pages folder. Afterwards, you can edit the JavaScript file and perform the desired modifications. Of course, modify this code only if you really know what you are doing, because you may cause undesired issues! It is not recommended that you modify the code, unless you really need to.

As an example, we can modify the Mojarra, the jsf.js code to see how the AJAX queue works. More precisely, to see how requests are added in queue and removed from queue depending on the delay value, perform the following steps:

1.  In jsf.js, find the enqueue function. This function is called by JSF to add an AJAX request in queue:

    ```
    this.enqueue = function enqueue(element) {
      // Queue the request
      queue.push(element);
    };
    ```

2.  Modify this function to call a JavaScript custom function and pass to it the AJAX queue:

    ```
    this.enqueue = function enqueue(element) {
      // Queue the request
      queue.push(element);
      monitorQueue(queue);
    };
    ```

3.  Do the same thing in the dequeue function. This function is called by JSF to remove an AJAX request from the queue:

    ```
    this.dequeue = function dequeue() {
      ...
      // return the removed element
      try {
          return element;
          } finally {
              element = null; // IE 6 leak prevention
          }
    };
    ```

4. Modify this function to call the same JavaScript custom function:

```
this.dequeue = function dequeue() {
    ...
    monitorQueue(queue);
    // return the removed element
    try {
        return element;
    } finally {
        element = null; // IE 6 leak prevention
    }
};
```

At this point, a JavaScript custom function will be called every time an AJAX request is added/removed in/from the queue and the current queue will be passed in. Each entry in the queue is an AJAX request; therefore, we can loop the queue and extract information about each of them:

```
<script type="text/javascript">
    function monitorQueue(q) {
        document.getElementById("ajaxqueueId").innerHTML = "";
        if (q.length > 0)
        {
        //<![CDATA[
        var report = "";
        document.getElementById("ajaxqueueId").innerHTML =
            "<b>TOTAL REQUESTS: </b>" + q.length + "<hr/>";
        for (var i = 0; i < q.length; i++) {
          var request = q[i];
          report += (i + 1) + ".<b>Request Type:</b> " +
            request.xmlReq + " <b>Source Id:</b> " +
            request.context.sourceid + "  <b>URL: </b> " +
            request.url + " <b>Taken Off Queue ?</b>: " +
            request.fromQueue + "<hr/>";
        }

        document.getElementById("ajaxqueueId").innerHTML += report;
        //]]>
        }
    }
</script>
```

Each request object has a suit of properties, which can be easily seen in the following code (this is extracted directly from the `jsf.js` source code):

```
var AjaxEngine = function AjaxEngine(context) {

    var req = {};                       // Request Object
    req.url = null;                     // Request URL
    req.context = context;              // Context of request and
                                        //    response
    req.context.sourceid = null;        // Source of this request
    req.context.onerror = null;         // Error handler for request
    req.context.onevent = null;         // Event handler for request
    req.xmlReq = null;                  // XMLHttpRequest Object
    req.async = true;                   // Default - Asynchronous
    req.parameters = {};                // Parameters For GET or POST
    req.queryString = null;             // Encoded Data For GET or POST
    req.method = null;                  // GET or POST
    req.status = null;                  // Response Status Code From
                                        //    Server
    req.fromQueue = false;              // Indicates if the request was
                                        //    taken off the queue
    ...
```

All you have to do now is to trigger some AJAX requests and monitor the queue report generated in the `monitorQueue` function. As you can see in the following code, each button has a different `delay` value:

```
<h:body>
    <h:outputScript name="js/jsf.js" library="default"
      target="head"/>
    <hr/>
    MONITOR AJAX QUEUE
    <hr/>
    <h:form prependId="false">
        <h:commandButton id="button_1_Id" value="Send 1 (no delay)"
          action="#{ajaxBean.ajaxAction()}"
            onclick='jsf.ajax.request(this,
          event, {execute: "@this", render: "@this"});
          return false;' />
        <h:commandButton id="button_2_Id" value="Send 2 (delay:600)"
          action="#{ajaxBean.ajaxAction()}"
            onclick='jsf.ajax.request(this,
          event, {delay: 600, execute: "@this", render: "@this"});
          return false;' />
```

```
    <h:commandButton id="button_3_Id" value="Send 3 (delay:1000)"
      action="#{ajaxBean.ajaxAction()}"
        onclick='jsf.ajax.request(this,
      event, {delay: 1000, execute: "@this", render: "@this"});
      return false;' />
  </h:form>
  AJAX QUEUE CONTENT:
  <div id="ajaxqueueId"></div>
</h:body>
```

As you can see, all AJAX requests are referring the same server-side method, ajaxAction. This method can easily simulate some business logic by sleeping for a random number of milliseconds for each request, as shown in the following code:

```
public void ajaxAction() {
    Random rnd = new Random();
    int sleep=1000 + rnd.nextInt(4000);
    try {
        //sleep between 1 and 5 seconds
        Thread.sleep(sleep);
    } catch (InterruptedException ex) {
        Logger.getLogger(AjaxBean.class.getName()).
                        log(Level.SEVERE,null, ex);
    };
}
```

Once you know how to monitor the queue content, you can go further and alter its content by queuing only certain requests, changing their priority of execution, accepting a limited number of entries in queue, and so on.

The complete application can be found in the code bundle of this chapter, and is named ch7_19.

# AJAX and the progress bar/indicator

While testing on localhost, AJAX requests seem pretty fast, but in real production environments they cannot be solved as fast because many aspects slow down the process (Internet connection speed, number of concurrent users, and so on).

A common practice consists of using a progress bar/indicator that signals the user that requests are being processed and he/she should wait until the AJAX response is received and rendered accordingly. For example, PrimeFaces provides a cool determinate progress bar for upload tasks (<p:fileUpload>) and an indeterminate progress indicator for any other AJAX request (check <p:ajaxStatus>). RichFaces also have similar capabilities.

In the next chapter, you will see how to implement a progress bar for upload tasks. Without writing a custom component, such as `<p:ajaxStatus>`, we can easily implement a progress indicator using the `onevent` attribute, the `data` object, and a small piece of CSS, as shown in the following code:

```
<script type='text/javascript'>
  function progressIndicator(data) {
  if (data.status === "begin") {
      document.getElementById("progressDivId").style.display =
        "block";
  }
    if (data.status === "complete") {
      document.getElementById("progressDivId").style.display =
        "none";
    }
  }
</script>
. . .
<h:body>
  <h:panelGrid columns="2">
    <h:form>
      <h:inputText id="nameInputId" value="#{ajaxBean.name}"/>
      <h:commandButton value="Send"
        action="#{ajaxBean.ajaxAction()}">
      <f:ajax onevent="progressIndicator" execute ="nameInputId"
          render="nameOutputId"/>
      </h:commandButton>
      <h:outputText id="nameOutputId" value="#{ajaxBean.name}"/>
    </h:form>

  <div id="progressDivId" style="display:none;">
    <img src="resources/default/imgs/ajax.gif"/>
  </div>
  </h:panelGrid>
</h:body>
```

In the following screenshot, you can see an example of running the complete application, named `ch7_20` in the code bundle of this chapter:

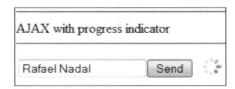

# Summary

In this chapter, we covered the AJAX support in JSF 2.2 Core. Besides common tasks such as using `render`, `execute`, `listener`, and other attributes, you learned how to use AJAX with JSF 2.2 flow scope, how to use the JSF 2.2 `delay` attribute, and how to update input fields with AJAX after validation error, using the new JSF 2.2 `resetValues` attribute and the `<f:resetValues>` tag. Moreover, you saw how to use postback with AJAX, how to determine if a request is AJAX or non-AJAX, customize jsf.js, how to write a progress bar/indicator, how to create the **Cancel/Clear** buttons, how to monitor AJAX queue, and so on.

In conclusion, JSF framework (including major extensions, such as PrimeFaces, OmniFaces, RichFaces, ICEfaces, and so on) has the most comprehensive and easy-to-use AJAX capabilities.

See you in the next chapter, where we will cover the JSF 2.2 support for HTML5 and the new upload mechanism.

# 8
# JSF 2.2 – HTML5 and Upload

This chapter can be read in two parts. The first part will present the JSF 2.2 support for HTML5, while the second part discusses the new **upload** component of JSF 2.2. Apparently, these two parts are not related, but as you will see, the upload component of JSF 2.2 can be spiced up with HTML5 features and the new pass-through attributes can be very helpful to extend the upload component of JSF 2.2 with HTML5 upload component facilities.

## Working with HTML5 and JSF 2.2

Everybody involved in web application development is enthusiastic to explore and use HTML5, which comes with a suite of new components and features, such as `<audio>`, `<video>`, `<keygen>`, and so on. Starting with version 2.2, JSF developers can interact with HTML5 using the following:

- Pass-through attributes
- Pass-through elements (HTML-friendly markup)

 Although pass-through elements and pass-through attributes are inspired by HTML5, they are JSF elements that might be used with other HTML versions as well.

These mechanisms are the alternative to writing custom render kits. This is a great solution, because HTML5 is in the developing stage, which means that writing and adapting render kits to constant HTML5 changes can be a real challenge.

If you want to use HTML5 with JSF 2.0, then you need to write custom render kits for supporting the new components and attributes.

# Pass-through attributes

Starting with JSF 2.2, we have attributes that are processed by JSF components on the server side and **pass-through attributes** that are processed at runtime on the client side.

A handy HTML5 element that can be used for exemplifying pass-through attributes is the `<input>` element. Among the new supported features, we have new values for `type` attribute (such as, `email`, `tel`, `color`, and `reset`) and the new attribute, `placeholder` (a text used as a hint in empty fields).

In pure HTML5, such an element can be as shown in the following code:

```
<input placeholder="Enter player e-mail" type="email">
```

The same thing can be obtained with pass-through attributes in five different ways:

- Place the pass-through attributes in the new namespace `http://xmlns.jcp.org/jsf/passthrough` (any JSF developer is familiar with namespaces and prefixed elements. There is no trick to use this namespace or prefixed attributes). Let's see how to obtain the preceding HTML5 element using JSF pass-through attributes, as follows:

```
<html xmlns="http://www.w3.org/1999/xhtml"
      xmlns:h="http://xmlns.jcp.org/jsf/html"
      xmlns:f5="http://xmlns.jcp.org/jsf/passthrough"
      xmlns:f="http://xmlns.jcp.org/jsf/core">

 ...
 <h:body>
  <h:inputText value="#{playersBean.email}"
               f5:type="email" f5:placeholder="Enter player
e-mail"/>
 ...
```

> When this book was written, there was still a debate about which is the proper prefix for this namespace. Initially, p was chosen, but this is recognized as the prefix of PrimeFaces; therefore, another prefix had to be used. So, when you read this book, feel free to replace f5 (used here) with the one that wins this debate and becomes more popular.

- Use `<f:passThroughAttribute>` nested in `<h:inputText>`, as follows:

```
<h:inputText value="#{playersBean.email}">
 <f:passThroughAttribute name="placeholder"
                          value="Enter player e-mail" />
 <f:passThroughAttribute name="type" value="email" />
</h:inputText>
```

- Pass-through attributes might come from a managed bean also. Place them in a `Map<String, String>`, where the map key is the attribute name and the map value is the attribute value, as follows:

```
private Map<String, String> attrs = new HashMap<>();
...
attrs.put("type", "email");
attrs.put("placeholder", "Enter player e-mail");
```

  Further, use `<f:passThroughAttributes>` tag, as shown in the following code:

```
<h:inputText value="#{playersBean.email}">
 <f:passThroughAttributes value="#{playersBean.attrs}" />
</h:inputText>
```

- Using Expression Language 3 (part of Java EE 7), multiple attributes can also be directly defined, as follows (practically, you define a `Map<String, String>` via EL 3):

```
<h:inputText value="#{playersBean.email}">
 <f:passThroughAttributes value='#{{"placeholder":"Enter player
e-mail", "type":"email"}}' />
</h:inputText>
```

  The complete example is available in the code bundle of this chapter and is named `ch8_1`.

- Pass-through attributes can be added programmatically. For example, you can generate an HTML5 input element and add it into a form, as follows:

```
<h:body>
 <h:form id="playerForm">
 ...
 </h:form>
</h:body>
```

```
    . . .
    FacesContext facesContext = FacesContext.getCurrentInstance();
    UIComponent formComponent = facesContext.getViewRoot().
                                        findComponent("playerForm");

    HtmlInputText playerInputText = new HtmlInputText();
    Map passThroughAttrs = playerInputText.getPassThroughAttributes();
    passThroughAttrs.put("placeholder", "Enter player email");
    passThroughAttrs.put("type", "email");

    formComponent.getChildren().add(playerInputText);
    . . .
```

The complete example is available on the code bundle of this chapter and is named ch8_1_2.

# Pass-through elements

JSF developers hide HTML code behind JSF components. For web designers, the JSF code may look pretty strange, but the generated HTML is more familiar. In order to alter the generated HTML, web designers have to modify the JSF code, which can be difficult for them. But JSF 2.2 comes with friendly markup for HTML5, known as **pass-through elements**. Using this feature, web designers can write pure HTML code and JSF developers can come over and link the HTML elements to the server side by adding/replacing the necessary attributes. JSF recognizes such attributes if they are in the http://xmlns.jcp.org/jsf namespace. For example, we can write a JSF page without any JSF tag, as follows:

```
<html xmlns="http://www.w3.org/1999/xhtml"
      xmlns:jsf="http://xmlns.jcp.org/jsf">

  <head jsf:id="head">
   <title></title>
  </head>

  <body jsf:id="body">
   <form jsf:id="form">
     Name:<input type="text" jsf:value="#{playersBean.playerName}"/>
     Surname:<input type="text" jsf:value="#{playersBean.
playerSurname}"/>
     <button jsf:action="#{playersBean.playerAction()}">Show</button>
   </form>
  </body>
</html>
```

JSF scans the HTML elements for attributes in the namespace `http://xmlns.jcp.org/jsf`. For such elements, JSF will determine the element type and will add the corresponding JSF component instead (`<h:head>` for `<head>` and `<h:inputText>` for `<input>`). JSF will add the components in the component tree, which will be rendered as HTML code to the client. This JSF component will be linked to the particular element and will receive the attributes as "normal" attributes or as pass-through attributes, depending on their origins. The correspondence between JSF components and HTML elements is available at `http://docs.oracle.com/javaee/7/api/javax/faces/view/facelets/TagDecorator.html`. For HTML elements that don't have a direct correspondent (for example `<div>` and `<span>`), JSF will create a special component, component-family, such as `javax.faces.Panel`, and render-type `javax.faces.passthrough.Element` as detailed at `http://docs.oracle.com/javaee/7/javaserverfaces/2.2/vldocs/facelets/jsf/element.html`.

The complete example is available in the code bundle of this chapter and is named `ch8_1_3`.

Since JSF replaces the HTML elements with JSF components, we can use these components at full capacity, meaning that we can use them as in JSF. For example, we can use validators, converters, and `<f:param>`, as follows:

```
<html xmlns="http://www.w3.org/1999/xhtml"
      xmlns:jsf="http://xmlns.jcp.org/jsf"
      xmlns:f="http://xmlns.jcp.org/jsf/core">

<head jsf:id="head">
 <title></title>
</head>
<body jsf:id="body">
 <form jsf:id="form">
  Name:
  <input type="text" jsf:value="#{playersBean.playerName}">
   <f:validator validatorId="playerValidator"/>
  </input>
  <!-- or, like this -->
 <input type="text" jsf:value="#{playersBean.playerName}"
                    jsf:validator="playerValidator"/>
  Surname:
  <input type="text" jsf:value="#{playersBean.playerSurname}">
   <f:validator validatorId="playerValidator"/>
  </input>
```

```
       <!-- or, like this -->
       <input type="text" jsf:value="#{playersBean.playerSurname}"
                           jsf:validator="playerValidator"/>
       <button jsf:action="#{playersBean.playerAction()}">Show
        <f:param id="playerNumber" name="playerNumberParam" value="2014"/>
       </button>
      </form>
    </body>
  </html>
```

The complete example is available in the code bundle of this chapter and is named ch8_1_4.

# JSF 2.2 – HTML5 and Bean Validation 1.1 (Java EE 7)

The Bean Validation 1.1 (see http://docs.oracle.com/javaee/7/tutorial/doc/
partbeanvalidation.htm) can be the perfect choice for validating user inputs in a
JSF 2.2/HTML5 application. For example, we can validate the submitted name and
surname in PlayersBean, as follows—we don't accept null values, empty values, or
values shorter than three characters:

```
@Named
@RequestScoped
public class PlayersBean {

    private static final Logger logger = Logger.getLogger(PlayersBean.
class.getName());

    @NotNull(message = "null/empty values not allowed in player name")
    @Size(min = 3,message = "Give at least 3 characters for player
name")
    private String playerName;
    @NotNull(message = "null/empty values not allowed in player
surname")
    @Size(min = 3,message = "Give at least 3 characters for player
surname")
    private String playerSurname;
    ...
```

JSF can interpret empty string submitted values as `null` if you set the following context parameter in `web.xml`:

```
<context-param>
 <param-name>
  javax.faces.INTERPRET_EMPTY_STRING_SUBMITTED_VALUES_AS_NULL
 </param-name>
 <param-value>true</param-value>
</context-param>
```

So in this case, there is no need to use the `<f:validator>` or `validator` attribute. Check out the complete application named `ch8_2`.

 OmniFaces provides an HTML5 render kit that extends support for HTML5 specific attributes. You may want to check it out at `http://showcase.omnifaces.org/`.

# JSF 2.2 upload feature

JSF developers have waited a long time for a built-in upload component. Until JSF 2.2, the workarounds consisted of using JSF extensions, such as PrimeFaces, RichFaces, and third-party libraries such as Apache Commons FileUpload.

JSF 2.2 comes with an input component dedicated for upload tasks (that renders an HTML `input` element of type `file`). This component is represented by the `<h:inputFile>` tag and it can be used as any other JSF component. The entire list of supported attributes is available at `http://docs.oracle.com/javaee/7/javaserverfaces/2.2/vldocs/facelets/h/inputFile.html`, but the most important ones are as follows:

- `value`: This represents the file to be uploaded as a `javax.servlet.http.Part` object.

- `required`: This is a Boolean value. If it is `true`, the user must provide a value to submit.

- `validator`: This indicates a validator for this component.

- `converter`: This indicates a converter for this component.

- `valueChangeListener`: This indicates a method that will be called when the component's value is changed.

The `<h:inputFile>` component is based on Servlet 3.0, which is part of Java EE since version 6. Servlet 3.0 provides an upload mechanism based on the `javax.servlet.http.Part` interface and the `@MultipartConfig` annotation. A simple Servlet 3.0 for upload files looks like the following code—keep in mind this servlet because we will use it in the last section of this chapter:

```
@WebServlet(name = "UploadServlet", urlPatterns = {"/UploadServlet"})
@MultipartConfig(location="/folder", fileSizeThreshold=1024*1024,
                 maxFileSize=1024*1024*3,
maxRequestSize=1024*1024*3*3)
public class UploadServlet extends HttpServlet {

  @Override
  protected void doPost(HttpServletRequest request,
                        HttpServletResponse response)
    throws ServletException, IOException {

    for (Part part : request.getParts()) {
        String filename = "";
        for (String s: part.getHeader("content-disposition").
split(";")) {
            if (s.trim().startsWith("filename")) {
                filename = s.split("=")[1].replaceAll("\"", "");
            }
        }
        part.write(filename);
    }
  }
}
```

 If you take a quick look over the JSF 2.2 `FacesServlet` source code, you will notice that it was annotated with `@MultipartConfig` especially for handling multipart data.

If you are not familiar with uploading files using Servlet 3.0, then you can try the tutorial at `http://docs.oracle.com/javaee/6/tutorial/doc/glrbb.html`.

On the client side, you can use a `<form>` tag and an HTML5 input of type `file`:

```
<form action="UploadServlet" enctype="multipart/form-data"
method="POST">
  <input type="file" name="file">
  <input type="Submit" value="Upload File">
</form>
```

Basically, JSF 2.2 upload component is just a wrapper of this example.

# A simple JSF 2.2 upload example

In this section, we will cover the fundamental steps of a JSF 2.2 upload application. Even if this is a simple example, you will see that further examples are based on this one. So in order to use the `<h:inputFile>` component, you need to focus on the client side and on the server side:

On the client side, we need to perform the following steps:

1. First, the `<h:form>` encoding must be set to multipart/form-data, which will help the browser to build the POST request accordingly, as shown in the following code:

```
<h:form id="uploadFormId" enctype="multipart/form-data">
```

2. Second, the `<h:inputFile>` must be configured to respect your needs, Here, we provide a simple case, as follows:

```
<h:inputFile id="fileToUpload" required="true"
             requiredMessage="No file selected ..."
             value="#{uploadBean.file}"/>
```

3. Further, you need a button (or a link) to start the upload process, as follows:

```
<h:commandButton value="Upload" action="#{uploadBean.upload()}"/>
```

Optionally, you can add some tags for handling upload messages, as shown in the following code:

```
<h:messages globalOnly="true" showDetail="false"
            showSummary="true" style="color:red"/>
<h:form id="uploadFormId" enctype="multipart/form-data">
 <h:inputFile id="fileToUpload" required="true"
              requiredMessage="No file selected ..."
              value="#{uploadBean.file}"/>
 <h:commandButton value="Upload" action="#{uploadBean.upload()}"/>
 <h:message showDetail="false" showSummary="true"
            for="fileToUpload" style="color:red"/>
</h:form>
```

On the server side, we need to perform the following steps:

1. Usually, the `value` attribute of `<h:inputFile>` contains an EL expression of type #{*upload_bean.part_object*}. If you replace *upload_bean* with `uploadBean` and *part_object* with `file`, you will obtain #{uploadBean.file}. The `file` object is used to store the uploaded data as an instance of `javax.servlet.http.Part` in the `UploadBean` bean. All you have to do is to define the `file` property in the same manner as any other property, as shown in the following code:

```
import javax.servlet.http.Part;
...
private Part file;
...
public Part getFile() {
 return file;
}

public void setFile(Part file) {
 this.file = file;
}
...
```

 The uploaded data can be read through the `getInputStream` method of `Part`.

2. When the button labeled **Upload** is clicked, the `upload` method is called. When this method is called, the `file` object is already populated with the uploaded bytes; therefore, you can obtain the data as a stream (use the `getInputStream` method) and process it accordingly. For example, you can use the `Scanner` API to extract the data into a `String`, as follows:

```
public void upload() {
  try {
      if (file != null) {
          Scanner scanner = new Scanner(file.getInputStream(),
                             "UTF-8").useDelimiter("\\A");
          fileInString = scanner.hasNext() ? scanner.next() : "";

          FacesContext.getCurrentInstance().addMessage(null,
              new FacesMessage("Upload successfully ended!"));
      }
  } catch (IOException | NoSuchElementException e) {
```

```
                FacesContext.getCurrentInstance().addMessage(null,
                        new FacesMessage("Upload failed!"));
        }
    }
```

The complete application is available in the code bundle of this chapter and is named `ch8_3`. In this case, the uploaded data is converted into string and displayed in a log; therefore, try to upload readable information, such as plain text files.

# Using multiple <h:inputFile> elements

If you ask yourself whether you can use more than one `<h:inputFile>` element in a `<h:form>` form, the answer is yes. Specify an ID for each `<h:inputFile>` element and associate it with a unique `Part` instance. In order to use two `<h:inputFile>` elements, the `<h:form>` form will change to the following code—you can easily extrapolate this example for three, four, or more `<h:inputFile>` elements:

```
<h:form id="uploadFormId" enctype="multipart/form-data">
 <h:inputFile id="fileToUpload_1" required="true"
            requiredMessage="No file selected ..."
            value="#{uploadBean.file1}"/>
 <h:inputFile id="fileToUpload_2" required="true"
            requiredMessage="No file selected ..."
            value="#{uploadBean.file2}"/>
 ...
 <h:message showDetail="false" showSummary="true"
           for="fileToUpload_1" style="color:red"/>
 <h:message showDetail="false" showSummary="true"
           for="fileToUpload_2" style="color:red"/>
 ...
 <h:commandButton value="Upload" action="#{uploadBean.upload()}"/>
</h:form>
```

Now, on the server side, you need two `Part` instances, defined as follows:

```
...
private Part file1;
private Part file2;
...
//getter and setter for both, file1 and file2
...
```

In the `upload` method, you need to process both `Part` instances:

```
. . .
if (file1 != null) {
    Scanner scanner1 = new Scanner(file1.getInputStream(),
                      "UTF-8").useDelimiter("\\A");
    fileInString1 = scanner1.hasNext() ? scanner1.next() : "";
    FacesContext.getCurrentInstance().addMessage(null, new
        FacesMessage("Upload successfully ended for file 1!"));
}

if (file2 != null) {
    Scanner scanner2 = new Scanner(file2.getInputStream(),
                      "UTF-8").useDelimiter("\\A");
    fileInString2 = scanner2.hasNext() ? scanner2.next() : "";
    FacesContext.getCurrentInstance().addMessage(null, new
        FacesMessage("Upload successfully ended for file 2!"));
}
. . .
```

Done! The complete application is available in the code bundle of this chapter and is named `ch8_4`.

# Extracting info about a file to be uploaded

Filename, size, and content type are the most common types of information needed when uploading a file. In JSF, this information is available on both the client side and the server side. Let's consider the following `<h:inputFile>` element:

```
<h:form id="formUploadId" enctype="multipart/form-data">
 <h:inputFile id="fileToUpload" value="#{uploadBean.file}"
              required="true" requiredMessage="No file selected ...">
 . . .
 </h:inputFile>
</h:form>
```

Now you will see how to extract the information about the file selected for upload.

On the client side, we need to perform either of the following steps:

- Extracting the filename, size (in bytes), and the content type on the client side can be accomplished in a JavaScript function, as follows:

  ```
  var file = document.getElementById('formUploadId:fileToUpload').
  files[0];
  . . .
  ```

```
alert(file.name);
alert(file.size);
alert(file.type);
```

- Another approach is to use EL in a JSF page, as follows (of course, this works after the file is uploaded):

```
// the id of the component, formUploadId:fileToUpload
#{uploadBean.file.name}

// the uploaded file name
#{uploadBean.file.submittedFileName}

// the uploaded file size
#{uploadBean.file.size}

// the uploaded file content type
#{uploadBean.file.contentType}
```

On the server side, we need to perform either of the following steps:

- Extracting the filename, size (in bytes), and the content type on server side can be accomplished through several methods of the `Part` interface, as follows:

```
...
private Part file;
...
System.out.println("File component id: " + file.getName());
System.out.println("Content type: " + file.getContentType());
System.out.println("Submitted file name:" +
 file.getSubmittedFileName());
System.out.println("File size: " + file.getSize());
...
```

 If the string returned by this method represents the entire path instead of the filename, then you have to isolate the filename as a substring of this string.

- The filename can be obtained from the `content-disposition` header as well using the following code:

```
private String getFileNameFromContentDisposition(Part file) {

  for (String content:file.getHeader("content-disposition").
split(";")) {
        if (content.trim().startsWith("filename")) {
            return content.substring(content.indexOf('=') +
                                    1).trim().replace("\"", "");
```

```
        }
    }

    return null;
}
```

An example of the `content-disposition` header can be seen in the following screenshot:

```
uploadFormId
----------------------------41184676334
Content-Disposition: form-data; name="uploadFormId:fileToUpload"; filename="RafaelNadal.jpg"
Content-Type: image/jpeg
```

This is very easy to understand if you inspect the POST request (you can do this with Firebug or any other specialized tool). In the preceding screenshot, you can see the relevant chunk of request that is depicted in the `getFileNameFromContentDisposition` method.

The complete application is available in the code bundle of this chapter and is named `ch8_5`.

# Writing uploaded data to a disk

In the previous examples, the uploaded data was converted to `String` and displayed on a console. Normally, when you upload a file, you want to save its content on a disk in a specific location (let's say, the `D:\files` folder). For this, you can use `FileOutputStream`, as follows:

```
try (InputStream inputStream = file.getInputStream();
    FileOutputStream outputStream = new FileOutputStream("D:" +
    File.separator + "files" + File.separator +
      getSubmittedFileName())) {

  int bytesRead = 0;
  final byte[] chunck = new byte[1024];
  while ((bytesRead = inputStream.read(chunck)) != -1) {
        outputStream.write(chunck, 0, bytesRead);
  }

  FacesContext.getCurrentInstance().addMessage(null, new
        FacesMessage("Upload successfully ended!"));
  } catch (IOException e) {
        FacesContext.getCurrentInstance().addMessage(null, new
                        FacesMessage("Upload failed!"));
  }
```

If you want buffered I/O, then add `BufferedInputStream` and `BufferedOutputStream` into your code.

The complete application is available in the code bundle of this chapter and is named ch8_6. If you prefer to obtain the filename from the `content-disposition` header, you better check the application ch8_7.

Another approach consists of using the `Part.write` method. In this case, you have to indicate the location where the file should be saved through the `<multipart-config>` tag (http://docs.oracle.com/javaee/7/tutorial/doc/servlets011.htm). Moreover, you can set the maximum file size, request size, and the file size threshold; these configurations should be added in `web.xml`, as follows:

```
<servlet>
 <servlet-name>Faces Servlet</servlet-name>
 <servlet-class>javax.faces.webapp.FacesServlet</servlet-class>
 <load-on-startup>1</load-on-startup>
 <multipart-config>
  <location>D:\files</location>
  <max-file-size>1310720</max-file-size>
  <max-request-size>20971520</max-request-size>
  <file-size-threshold>50000</file-size-threshold>
 </multipart-config>
</servlet>
```

 If you don't specify a location, the default one will be used. The default location is "".

The uploaded file will be saved in the indicated location under the name passed to the `Part.write` method, as shown in the following code:

```
try {
    file.write(file.getSubmittedFileName());
    FacesContext.getCurrentInstance().addMessage(null, new
                FacesMessage("Upload successfully ended!"));
    } catch (IOException e) {
      FacesContext.getCurrentInstance().addMessage(null, new
                FacesMessage("Upload failed!"));
    }
```

The complete application is available in the code bundle of this chapter and is named ch8_8.

# Upload validator

In most cases, you need to restrict the user upload based on certain constraints. Commonly, you will limit the filename length, file size, and file content type. For example, you may want to reject the following:

- Files that have names bigger than 25 characters
- Files that are not PNG or JPG images
- Files that are bigger than 1 MB in size

For this, you can write a JSF validator, as follows:

```
@FacesValidator
public class UploadValidator implements Validator {

  private static final Logger logger =
        Logger.getLogger(UploadValidator.class.getName());

  @Override
  public void validate(FacesContext context, UIComponent component,
                       Object value) throws ValidatorException {

    Part file = (Part) value;

    //VALIDATE FILE NAME LENGTH
    String name = file.getSubmittedFileName();
    logger.log(Level.INFO, "VALIDATING FILE NAME: {0}", name);
    if (name.length() == 0) {
       FacesMessage message = new FacesMessage("Upload Error: Cannot
                                      determine the file name !");
       throw new ValidatorException(message);
    } else if (name.length() > 25) {
      FacesMessage message = new FacesMessage("Upload Error:
                                   The file name is to long !");
      throw new ValidatorException(message);
    }

    //VALIDATE FILE CONTENT TYPE
    if ((!"image/png".equals(file.getContentType())) &&
                     (!"image/jpeg".equals(file.getContentType())))) {
       FacesMessage message = new FacesMessage("Upload Error: Only
                         images can be uploaded (PNGs and JPGs) !");
```

```
        throw new ValidatorException(message);
    }

    //VALIDATE FILE SIZE (not bigger than 1 MB)
    if (file.getSize() > 1048576) {
        FacesMessage message = new FacesMessage("Upload Error: Cannot
                                  upload files larger than 1 MB !");
        throw new ValidatorException(message);
    }
  }
}
```

Next, add the validator to the `<h:inputFile>` element, as follows:

```
<h:inputFile id="fileToUpload" required="true"
             requiredMessage="No file selected ..."
             value="#{uploadBean.file}">
 <f:validator validatorId="uploadValidator" />
</h:inputFile>
```

Now, only the files that meet our constraints will be uploaded. For each rejected file, you will see an info message that will signal if the filename or its size is too big, or whether the file is a PNG or JPG image.

The complete application is available in the code bundle of this chapter and is named `ch8_9`.

# Ajaxify the upload

A JSF upload can take advantages of the AJAX mechanism by combining the `<h:inputFile>` tag with `<f:ajax>` or the `<h:commandButton>` tag (upload initialization) with `<f:ajax>`. In the first case, a common ajaxified upload will look like the following code:

```
<h:form enctype="multipart/form-data">
 <h:inputFile id="fileToUpload" value="#{uploadBean.file}"
             required="true" requiredMessage="No file selected ...">
  <!-- <f:ajax listener="#{uploadBean.upload()}"
             render="@all"/> use @all in JSF 2.2.0 -->
  <f:ajax listener="#{uploadBean.upload()}"
```

```
                   render="fileToUpload"/> <!-- works in JSF 2.2.5 -->
    </h:inputFile>
    <h:message showDetail="false" showSummary="true"
             for="fileToUpload" style="color:red"/>
    </h:form>
```

 The render attribute should contain the IDs of components to re-render after upload. In JSF 2.2.0, you need to use @all instead of IDs because there is a bug associated that was fixed in the later versions. For example, in JSF 2.2.5 everything works as expected.

The complete application is available in the code bundle of this chapter and is named ch8_10.

In the second case, place <f:ajax> in <h:commandButton>, as follows:

```
<h:form enctype="multipart/form-data">
 <h:inputFile id="fileToUpload" value="#{uploadBean.file}"
             required="true" requiredMessage="No file selected ..."/>
 <h:commandButton value="Upload" action="#{uploadBean.upload()}">
  <!-- <f:ajax execute="fileToUpload"
             render="@all"/> use @all in JSF 2.2.0 -->
  <f:ajax execute="fileToUpload"
             render="fileToUpload"/> <!-- works in JSF 2.2.5 -->
 </h:commandButton>
 <h:message showDetail="false" showSummary="true"
             for="fileToUpload" style="color:red"/>
</h:form>
```

The complete application is available in the code bundle of this chapter and is named ch8_11.

# Uploading images with preview

A nice feature of the upload components is that they allow us to preview images before they are uploaded. In the following screenshot, you can see what we will develop next:

So when the user browses an image, you need to proceed with a behind the scene auto AJAX upload, which should cause the user to see the image preview immediately after he/she chooses the image from the local machine. The POST request generated by AJAX will populate the server-side Part object (let's call it file). When AJAX completes, you need to re-render a component capable of displaying an image, such as <h:graphicImage>. This component will call a servlet using a GET request. The managed bean responsible with upload should be session scoped; therefore, the servlet will be able to extract the bean instance from the session and use the file object representing the image. Now, the servlet can pass the image bytes directly to the response output stream, or create a thumbnail of the image and send a small number of bytes. Further, when the user clicks the button that initializes the upload, you need to write the file object on the disk.

This is the main idea. Next, you will implement it and spice it up with some validation capabilities, a cancel button, and some image information displayed next to the preview.

In order to achieve this, you need to perform the following steps:

1.  Write an auto upload based on AJAX, as follows:

```
<h:form enctype="multipart/form-data">
 <h:inputFile id="uploadFileId" value="#{uploadBean.file}"
         required="true" requiredMessage="No file selected ...">
  <f:ajax render=":previewImgId :imgNameId :uploadMessagesId"
         listener="#{uploadBean.validateFile()}"/>
 </h:inputFile>
</h:form>
```

2.  AJAX will call the validateFile method. This server-side method is capable of validating the filename, length, size, and the content type. The validateFile method is defined as follows:

```
...
private Part file;
...
public void validateFile() {

  //VALIDATE FILE NAME LENGTH
  String name = file.getSubmittedFileName();
  if (name.length() == 0) {
      resetFile();

      FacesContext.getCurrentInstance().addMessage(null, new
FacesMessage("Upload
```

```
                    Error: Cannot determine the file name !"));
    } else if (name.length() > 25) {
      resetFile();
      FacesContext.getCurrentInstance().addMessage(null, new
      FacesMessage("Upload Error: The file name is to long !"));
    } else //VALIDATE FILE CONTENT TYPE
    if ((!"image/png".equals(file.getContentType())) &&
          (!"image/jpeg".equals(file.getContentType()))) {
        resetFile();
        FacesContext.getCurrentInstance().addMessage(null, new
        FacesMessage("Upload Error: Only images can be uploaded
              (PNGs and JPGs) !"));
    } else //VALIDATE FILE SIZE (not bigger than 1 MB)
    if (file.getSize() > 1048576) {
        resetFile();
        FacesContext.getCurrentInstance().addMessage(null, new
        FacesMessage("Upload Error: Cannot upload files larger than
            1 MB !"));
    }
}
```

3.  If the constraints are violated, then the resetFile method is called. This is a
    simple method that resets the file object to its initial state. Moreover, it calls
    the delete method, which deletes the underlying storage for the file item
    (including temporary files on the disk).The resetFile method is defined
    as follows:

```
public void resetFile() {
  try {
      if (file != null) {
          file.delete();
      }
  } catch (IOException ex) {
    Logger.getLogger(UploadBean.class.getName()).
                          log(Level.SEVERE, null, ex);
  }
  file = null;
}
```

4. When the AJAX request is complete, it will re-render the components with IDs: `previewImgId`, `imgNameId`, and `uploadMessagesId`. The following code reveals the components having the `previewImgId` and `imgNameId` IDs—here the `uploadMessagesId` ID corresponds to a `<h:messages>` component:

```
...
<h:panelGrid columns="2">
 <h:graphicImage id="previewImgId"
                 value="/PreviewServlet/#{header['Content-
Length']}"
                 width="#{uploadBean.file.size gt 0 ? 100 : 0}"
                 height="#{uploadBean.file.size gt 0 ? 100 : 0}"/>
 <h:outputText id="imgNameId" value="#{uploadBean.file.
submittedFileName}
  #{empty uploadBean.file.submittedFileName ? '' : ','}
  #{uploadBean.file.size} #{uploadBean.file.size gt 0 ? 'bytes' :
''}"/>
</h:panelGrid>
...
```

5. The value of `<h:graphicImage>` accesses `PreviewServlet`. This servlet can serve the image for preview through the response output stream. In order to avoid the caching mechanism, you need to provide a URL with a random part (the request content length can be a convenient choice). This technique will load the correct image every time, instead of loading the same image for all requests. The relevant part of the servlet is as follows:

```
protected void processRequest(HttpServletRequest request,
                              HttpServletResponse response)
  throws ServletException, IOException {

  //decorate with buffers if you need to
  OutputStream out = response.getOutputStream();

  response.setHeader("Expires", "Sat, 6 May 1995 12:00:00 GMT");
  response.setHeader("Cache-Control","no-store,no-cache,must-
revalidate");
  response.addHeader("Cache-Control", "post-check=0, pre-check=0");
  response.setHeader("Pragma", "no-cache");

  int nRead;
  try {
      HttpSession session = request.getSession(false);
      if (session.getAttribute("uploadBean") != null) {
          UploadBean uploadBean = (UploadBean)
```

```
                session.getAttribute("uploadBean");
        if (uploadBean.getFile() != null) {
            try (InputStream inStream =
                        uploadBean.getFile().getInputStream()) {
                byte[] data = new byte[1024];
                while ((nRead =inStream.
                    read(data, 0, data.length)) != -1) {
                    out.write(data, 0, nRead);
                }
            }
        }
    }
} finally {
    out.close();
}
}
```

6.  The preceding code will send all bytes of the uploaded image to the response output stream. A common technique consists of scaling down the image to obtain a thumbnail that contains a smaller number of bytes. In Java, scaling an image can be accomplished in many ways, but a quick approach can be seen in the following code:

```
protected void processRequest(HttpServletRequest request,
                            HttpServletResponse response)
throws ServletException, IOException {

OutputStream out = response.getOutputStream();

response.setHeader("Expires", "Sat, 6 May 1995 12:00:00 GMT");
response.setHeader("Cache-Control","no-store,no-cache,must-
revalidate");
response.addHeader("Cache-Control", "post-check=0, pre-check=0");
response.setHeader("Pragma", "no-cache");

try {
    HttpSession session = request.getSession(false);
    if (session.getAttribute("uploadBean") != null) {
        UploadBean uploadBean = (UploadBean)
                        session.getAttribute("uploadBean");
        if (uploadBean.getFile() != null) {
            BufferedImage image = ImageIO.read(uploadBean.
                getFile().getInputStream());
            BufferedImage resizedImage = new BufferedImage(100,
                100, BufferedImage.TYPE_INT_ARGB);
```

```
                    Graphics2D g = resizedImage.createGraphics();
                    g.drawImage(image, 0, 0, 100, 100, null);
                    g.dispose();
                    ImageIO.write(resizedImage, "png", out);
            }
        }
    } finally {
        out.close();
    }
}
```

7. Further, you add two buttons: one button labeled **Upload** and another one labeled **Cancel**. The first one will initialize the upload, and the second one will cancel the upload, as shown in the following code:

```
<h:form>
  <h:commandButton value="Upload Image"
                   action="#{uploadBean.saveFileToDisk()}"/>
  <h:commandButton value="Cancel" action="#{uploadBean.
resetFile()}"/>
</h:form>
```

8. When the button labeled **Upload** is clicked, the saveFileToDisk method will save the uploaded data to the disk, as shown in the following code:

```
public void saveFileToDisk() {

  if (file != null) {
      //decorate with buffers if you need too
      try (InputStream inputStream = file.getInputStream();
          FileOutputStream outputStream = new
            FileOutputStream("D:" + File.separator + "files" +
            File.separator + getSubmittedFileName())) {

          int bytesRead;
          final byte[] chunck = new byte[1024];
          while ((bytesRead = inputStream.read(chunck)) != -1) {
                outputStream.write(chunck, 0, bytesRead);
          }

          resetFile();

          FacesContext.getCurrentInstance().addMessage(null, new
                    FacesMessage("Upload successfully ended!"));
      } catch (IOException e) {
```

```
                    FacesContext.getCurrentInstance().addMessage(null,
                                new FacesMessage("Upload failed!"));
            }
        }
    }
```

Done! The complete application, without thumbnail, is available in the code bundle of this chapter and is named `ch8_13`. The complete application, with thumbnail, is named `ch8_12`.

The validation process can be eliminated from the server side and can be accomplished on the client side also. Such an example can be found in the code bundle of this chapter and is named `ch8_14`. The JavaScript code is pretty straightforward, as follows:

```
<script type="text/javascript">
function validateFile() {
 // <![CDATA[
 document.getElementById('formSaveId:uploadHiddenId').value = false;
 document.getElementById('validationId').innerHTML = "";

 var file= document.getElementById('formUploadId:fileToUpload').
files[0];

 document.getElementById('fileNameId').innerHTML =
                        "<b>File Name:</b> " + file.name;
 if (file.size > 1048576)
     fileSize = (Math.round(file.size * 100 /
                    (1048576)) / 100).toString() + 'MB';
 else
     fileSize = (Math.round(file.size * 100
                    / 1024) / 100).toString() + 'KB';

 document.getElementById('fileSizeId').innerHTML =
                        "<b>File Size:</b> " + fileSize;
 document.getElementById('fileContentTypeId').innerHTML =
                        "<b>File Type:</b> " + file.type;

 //VALIDATE FILE NAME LENGTH
 if (file.name.length === 0) {
     clearUploadField();
     document.getElementById('validationId').innerHTML =
```

```
        "<ul><li>Upload Error: Cannot determine the file name !</li></
ul>";
      return false;
  }

  if (file.name.length > 25) {
      clearUploadField();
      document.getElementById('validationId').innerHTML =
          "<ul><li>Upload Error: The file name is to long !</li></
ul>";
      return false;
  }

  //VALIDATE FILE CONTENT TYPE
   if (file.type !== "image/png" && file.type !== "image/jpeg") {
      clearUploadField();
      document.getElementById('validationId').innerHTML =
         "<ul><li>Upload Error: Only images can be uploaded
                                  (PNGs and JPGs) !</li></ul>";
      return false;
  }


  //VALIDATE FILE SIZE (not bigger than 1 MB)
  if (file.size > 1048576) {
      clearUploadField();
      document.getElementById('validationId').innerHTML =
        "<ul><li>Upload Error: Cannot upload files
                                  larger than 1 MB !</li></ul>";
      return false;
  }

  document.getElementById('formSaveId:uploadHiddenId').value = true;
  return true;
  //]]>
}

function clearUploadField() {

  document.getElementById('previewImgId').removeAttribute("src");
  document.getElementById('imgNameId').innerHTML = "";
```

```
document.getElementById('uploadMessagesId').innerHTML = "";
var original = document.getElementById("formUploadId:fileToUpload");
var replacement = document.createElement("input");

replacement.type = "file";
replacement.id = original.id;
replacement.name = original.name;
replacement.className = original.className;
replacement.style.cssText = original.style.cssText;
replacement.onchange = original.onchange;
// ... more attributes

original.parentNode.replaceChild(replacement, original);
}

</script>
```

# Uploading multiple files

By default, JSF 2.2 does not provide support for uploading multiple files, but with some adjustments, we can easily achieve this goal. In order to have multiple file uploads, you need to focus on two aspects, which are listed as follows:

- Making multiple file selections possible
- Uploading all the selected files

Regarding the first task, the multiple selection can be activated using an HTML5 input file attribute (`multiple`) and the JSF 2.2 pass-through attribute feature. When this attribute is present and its value is set to `multiple`, the file chooser can select multiple files. So, this task requires some minimal adjustments:

```
<html xmlns="http://www.w3.org/1999/xhtml"
      xmlns:h="http://xmlns.jcp.org/jsf/html"
      xmlns:f5="http://xmlns.jcp.org/jsf/passthrough">
...
<h:form id="uploadFormId" enctype="multipart/form-data">
 <h:inputFile id="fileToUpload" required="true" f5:multiple="multiple"
     requiredMessage="No file selected ..." value="#{uploadBean.
file}"/>
 <h:commandButton value="Upload" action="#{uploadBean.upload()}"/>
</h:form>
```

The second task is a little bit tricky, because when multiple files are selected, JSF will overwrite the previous `Part` instance with each file in the uploaded set. This is normal, since you use an object of type `Part`, but you need a collection of `Part` instances. Fixing this issue requires us to focus on the renderer of the file component. This renderer is named `FileRenderer` (an extension of `TextRenderer`), and the `decode` method implementation is the key for our issue (the bold code is very important for us), as shown in the following code:

```
@Override
public void decode(FacesContext context, UIComponent component) {

    rendererParamsNotNull(context, component);

    if (!shouldDecode(component)) {
        return;
    }

    String clientId = decodeBehaviors(context, component);

    if (clientId == null) {
        clientId = component.getClientId(context);
    }

    assert(clientId != null);
    ExternalContext externalContext = context.getExternalContext();
    Map<String, String> requestMap =
                    externalContext.getRequestParameterMap();

    if (requestMap.containsKey(clientId)) {
        setSubmittedValue(component, requestMap.get(clientId));
    }

    HttpServletRequest request = (HttpServletRequest)
                            externalContext.getRequest();
    try {
        Collection<Part> parts = request.getParts();
        for (Part cur : parts) {
            if (clientId.equals(cur.getName())) {
                component.setTransient(true);
                setSubmittedValue(component, cur);
            }
```

```
        }
    } catch (IOException ioe) {
            throw new FacesException(ioe);
    } catch (ServletException se) {
            throw new FacesException(se);
    }
}
```

The highlighted code causes the override `Part` issue, but you can easily modify it to submit a list of `Part` instances instead of one `Part`, as follows:

```
try {
    Collection<Part> parts = request.getParts();
    List<Part> multiple = new ArrayList<>();
    for (Part cur : parts) {
            if (clientId.equals(cur.getName())) {
                component.setTransient(true);
                multiple.add(cur);
            }
    }
    this.setSubmittedValue(component, multiple);
} catch (IOException | ServletException ioe) {
    throw new FacesException(ioe);
}
```

Of course, in order to modify this code, you need to create a custom file renderer and configure it properly in `faces-config.xml`.

Afterwards, you can define a list of `Part` instances in your bean using the following code:

```
...
private List<Part> files;

public List<Part> getFile() {
 return files;
}

public void setFile(List<Part> files) {
 this.files = files;
}
...
```

Each entry in the list is a file; therefore, you can write them on the disk by iterating the list using the following code:

```
...
for (Part file : files) {
  try (InputStream inputStream = file.getInputStream();
       FileOutputStream
       outputStream = new FileOutputStream("D:" + File.separator +
         "files" + File.separator + getSubmittedFileName())) {

       int bytesRead = 0;
       final byte[] chunck = new byte[1024];
       while ((bytesRead = inputStream.read(chunck)) != -1) {
              outputStream.write(chunck, 0, bytesRead);
       }

       FacesContext.getCurrentInstance().addMessage(null, new
        FacesMessage("Upload successfully ended: " +
          file.getSubmittedFileName()));
  } catch (IOException e) {
         FacesContext.getCurrentInstance().addMessage(null, new
                                 FacesMessage("Upload failed !"));
  }
}
...
```

The complete application is available in the code bundle of this chapter and is named ch8_15.

# Upload and the indeterminate progress bar

When users upload small files, the process happens pretty fast; however, when large files are involved, it may take several seconds, or even minutes, to end. In this case, it is a good practice to implement a progress bar that indicates the upload status. The simplest progress bar is known as an indeterminate progress bar, because it shows that the process is running, but it doesn't provide information for estimating the time left or the amount of processed bytes.

In order to implement a progress bar, you need to develop an AJAX-based upload. The JSF AJAX mechanism allows us to determine when the AJAX request begins and when it completes. This can be achieved on the client side; therefore, an indeterminate progress bar can be easily implemented using the following code:

```
<script type="text/javascript">
 function progressBar(data) {
  if (data.status === "begin") {
     document.getElementById("uploadMsgId").innerHTML="";
     document.getElementById("progressBarId").
               setAttribute("src", "./resources/progress_bar.gif");
  }

  if (data.status === "complete") {
     document.getElementById("progressBarId").removeAttribute("src");
  }
 }
</script>
...
<h:body>
 <h:messages id="uploadMsgId" globalOnly="true" showDetail="false"
                             showSummary="true" style="color:red"/>
 <h:form id="uploadFormId" enctype="multipart/form-data">
  <h:inputFile id="fileToUpload" required="true"
     requiredMessage="No file selected ..." value="#{uploadBean.
file}"/>
  <h:message showDetail="false" showSummary="true"
     for="fileToUpload" style="color:red"/>
  <h:commandButton value="Upload" action="#{uploadBean.upload()}">
   <f:ajax execute="fileToUpload" onevent="progressBar"
                          render=":uploadMsgId @form"/>
  </h:commandButton>
 </h:form>
 <div>
  <img id="progressBarId" width="250px;" height="23"/>
 </div>
</h:body>
```

A possible output is as follows:

The complete application is available in the code bundle of this chapter and is named `ch8_16`.

# Upload and the determinate progress bar

A determinate progress bar is much more complicated. Usually, such a progress bar is based on a listener capable to monitor the transferred bytes (if you have worked with Apache Commons' `FileUpload`, you must have had the chance to implement such a listener). In JSF 2.2, `FacesServlet` was annotated with `@MultipartConfig` for dealing multipart data (upload files), but there is no progress listener interface for it. Moreover, `FacesServlet` is declared `final`; therefore, we cannot extend it.

Well, the possible approaches are pretty limited by these aspects. In order to implement a server-side progress bar, we need to implement the upload component in a separate class (servlet) and provide a listener. Alternatively, on the client side, we need a custom POST request that tricks `FacesServlet` that the request is formatted by `jsf.js`.

In this section, you will see a workaround based on HTML5 XMLHttpRequest Level 2 (can upload/download streams as `Blob`, `File`, and `FormData`), HTML5 progress events (for upload it returns total transferred bytes and uploaded bytes), HTML5 progress bar, and a custom Servlet 3.0. If you are not familiar with these HTML5 features, then you have to check out some dedicated documentation.

After you get familiar with these HTML5 features, it will be very easy to understand the following client-side code. First we have the following JavaScript code:

```
<script type="text/javascript">
  function fileSelected() {
    hideProgressBar();
    updateProgress(0);
    document.getElementById("uploadStatus").innerHTML = "";
    var file = document.getElementById('fileToUploadForm:
```

```
                                        fileToUpload').files[0];
    if (file) {
        var fileSize = 0;
        if (file.size > 1048576)
            fileSize = (Math.round(file.size * 100 / (1048576)) /
                                        100).toString() + 'MB';
        else
            fileSize = (Math.round(file.size * 100 / 1024) /
                                        100).toString() + 'KB';

        document.getElementById('fileName').innerHTML = 'Name: ' +
                                                        file.name;
        document.getElementById('fileSize').innerHTML = 'Size: ' +
                                                        fileSize;
        document.getElementById('fileType').innerHTML = 'Type: ' +
                                                        file.type;

    }
}

function uploadFile() {
 showProgressBar();
 var fd = new FormData();
 fd.append("fileToUpload", document.getElementById('fileToUploadForm:
                                        fileToUpload').files[0]);

 var xhr = new XMLHttpRequest();
 xhr.upload.addEventListener("progress", uploadProgress, false);
 xhr.addEventListener("load", uploadComplete, false);
 xhr.addEventListener("error", uploadFailed, false);
 xhr.addEventListener("abort", uploadCanceled, false);
 xhr.open("POST", "UploadServlet");
 xhr.send(fd);
}

function uploadProgress(evt) {
 if (evt.lengthComputable) {
     var percentComplete = Math.round(evt.loaded * 100 / evt.total);
                updateProgress(percentComplete);
 }
}

function uploadComplete(evt) {
 document.getElementById("uploadStatus").innerHTML = "Upload
                successfully completed!";
```

```
}

function uploadFailed(evt) {
 hideProgressBar();
 document.getElementById("uploadStatus").innerHTML = "The upload
   cannot be complete!";
}

function uploadCanceled(evt) {
 hideProgressBar();
 document.getElementById("uploadStatus").innerHTML = "The upload was
                   canceled!";
}

var updateProgress = function(value) {
    var pBar = document.getElementById("progressBar");
    document.getElementById("progressNumber").innerHTML=value+"%";
    pBar.value = value;
}

function hideProgressBar() {
  document.getElementById("progressBar").style.visibility = "hidden";
  document.getElementById("progressNumber").style.visibility =
"hidden";
 }

function showProgressBar() {
  document.getElementById("progressBar").style.visibility = "visible";
  document.getElementById("progressNumber").style.visibility =
"visible";
 }
</script>
```

Further, we have the upload component that uses the preceding JavaScript code:

```
<h:body>
 <hr/>
 <div id="fileName"></div>
 <div id="fileSize"></div>
 <div id="fileType"></div>
 <hr/>
 <h:form id="fileToUploadForm" enctype="multipart/form-data">
  <h:inputFile id="fileToUpload" onchange="fileSelected();"/>
  <h:commandButton type="button" onclick="uploadFile()"
   value="Upload" />
```

```
    </h:form>
    <hr/>
    <div id="uploadStatus"></div>
     <table>
      <tr>
       <td>
        <progress id="progressBar" style="visibility: hidden;"
                                    value="0" max="100"></progress>
       </td>
       <td>
        <div id="progressNumber" style="visibility: hidden;">0 %</div>
       </td>
      </tr>
     </table>
    <hr/>
    </h:body>
```

A possible output can be seen in the following screenshot:

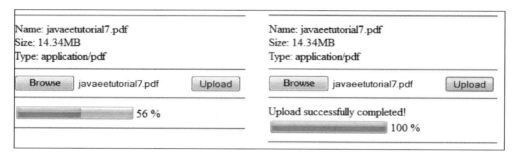

The servlet behind this solution is `UploadServlet` that was presented earlier. The complete application is available in the code bundle of this chapter and is named `ch8_17`.

 For multiple file uploads and progress bars, you can extend this example, or choose a built-in solution, such as PrimeFaces Upload, RichFaces Upload, or jQuery Upload Plugin.

# Summary

In this chapter, you saw how to exploit HTML5 through JSF 2.2 using the pass-through attribute and the pass-through elements techniques. Moreover, in the second part of this chapter, you saw how to work with the new JSF 2.2 upload component (simple upload, multiple file uploads, upload images with preview, and indeterminate/determinate progress bars for upload).

See you in the next chapter, where we will go further with a great feature of JSF 2.2, that is, stateless views.

# 9
# JSF State Management

Commonly, the JSF applications' performance is directly related to CPU memory, serialization/deserialization tasks, and network bandwidth. When these variables start to become the source of headache, or errors of type `ViewExpiredException` or `NotSerializableException` occur, it is time to find out about JSF's managing view state feature and how it can be finely tuned to increase the performance. Therefore, in this chapter, we will discuss about JSF saving the view state (JSF's partial saving view state feature, JSF saving the view state on server/client, logical and physical views, and so on) and JSF 2.2 stateless views.

## JSF saving the view state

First, you have to know that JSF saves and restores the view state between requests using the `ViewHandler`/`StateManager` API. JSF does this during its lifecycle, the view state is saved in the session (or on the client machine) at the end of a request and is restored at the beginning of a request.

JSF uses this technique because it needs to preserve the views state over the HTTP protocol, which is a stateless protocol. Since JSF is stateful, it needs to save the state of views in order to perform the JSF lifecycle over multiple requests from the same user. Each page has a view state that acts as a ping-pong ball between the client and the server. A view is basically a component tree that may be dynamically changed (altered) during HTTP GET and POST requests. Each request will successfully go through the JSF lifecycle only if the component tree was previously saved and is fully capable to provide the needed information, that is, Faces Servlet succeeds to call the needed view handler implementations to restore or build the view. So, when the component tree is programmatically changed (for example, from backing beans or static components) it can't be successfully recreated from scratch (or rebuilt). The only solution is to use the existing state saved at the *Render Response* phase. Trying to recreate it from scratch will make the programmatic changes useless, since they would no longer be available.

Keep in mind that the component tree is just a hand of UI components hierarchically and logically related. The view state maintains the tree structure and the components state (selected/deselected, enabled/disabled, and so on). Therefore, the component tree contains only references to backing beans properties/actions through EL expressions, and does not store the model values.

# JSF partial saving view state

Starting with JSF 2.0, the performance of managing the state was seriously increased by adding the partial state saving feature. Basically, JSF will not save the entire component tree, only a piece of it. Obviously this will require less memory. In other words, this means that instead of saving the entire component tree (the whole view, `<html>`), now, for every request during restore view, JSF will recreate the entire component tree from scratch and initialize the components from their tag attributes. In this way, JSF will save only the things that are deserved to be saved. These are the things that are susceptible to changes (for example, `<h:form>`) that cannot be recreated from scratch and/or represent inland details of components. These details are: dynamic (programmatic) changes that alter the component tree, different kinds of values that were determined for some components (usually at first postback), and values that were changed for components but have not been submitted (for example, moving a slider or checking a checkbox). On the other hand, the things that cannot be changed by the client will not be saved.

# Partial state saving and tree visiting

In JSF 2.0, the JSF partial state saving feature raised a question similar to how a JSF implementation should visit all the components in the component tree and ask them for their state (partial)? The answer in JSF 2.1 (and earlier versions) was specific to this implementation: Mojarra used a tree visiting algorithm, while MyFaces used a so-called "facets + children" traversal. But, technically speaking, these two approaches are pretty different, because Mojarra provides a pluggable algorithm, while MyFaces doesn't. Moreover, the Mojarra approach is in context (before children are visited, the parent component can choose to use a context/scope), while the MyFaces approach follows a pointer design. Furthermore, the Mojarra algorithm can visit virtual components. (These kinds of components are obtained by looping components such as `UIData`.) On the other hand, from the saving state perspective, using a context/scope and looping virtual components is not desirable, even if affecting the visiting process can be major and useful.

In order to solve this problem, JSF 2.1 offers some hints, which can be considered deprecated starting with JSF 2.2. Starting with JSF 2.2, tree visiting is fully capable of partial state saving; thanks to the `StateManagementStrategy.saveView` and `StateManagementStrategy.restoreView` methods. These two methods are meant to replace their counterparts from the `StateManager` class, and their implementations are now mandatory to use the visit API. (A good point to start studying may be the `UIComponent.visitTree` method.) As a JSF developer, you will probably never interact with this feature, but for the sake of completeness, it may be good to be aware of it.

# JSF saving view state on the server or client

Saving the view state can be accomplished on the server that hosts the application, or on the client machine. We can easily choose between the client and the server by adding the context parameter named `javax.faces.STATE_SAVING_METHOD` to the `web.xml` file. The value of this method can be `server` or `client` as shown in the following code:

```xml
<context-param>
  <param-name>javax.faces.STATE_SAVING_METHOD</param-name>
  <param-value>server</param-value>
</context-param>
```

Starting with JSF 2.2, the values of this context parameter are case insensitive.

Saving the state on the server means to save it in a session with a special ID known as the view state ID that refers to the state stored in the server memory. This is sent to the client as the value of a hidden input field named, `javax.faces.ViewState`. This can be easily tested by running the `ch9_1_1` application, which produces the HTML code that contains this field, as shown in the following screenshot:

```
<input name="javax.faces.ViewState" id="j_id1:javax.faces.ViewState:0"
            value="-1266465715138344142:-8894012522559559935" autocomplete="off" type="hidden">
```

If the state is saved on the client, JSF stores it as the value of the same hidden input field. This value is a base64 encrypted string representing the serialization of the state. Running the `ch9_1_2` application will produce the following output:

```
<input name="javax.faces.ViewState" id="j_id1:javax.faces.ViewState:0"
value="3WVFO4C4pJZA+r1gV0X+pSxm0b6g3eeGChl+dNEU48DJ15o3OUyLwEos5ejIJu18MjPQcn  ...
/1h3yLZ82Xv6TnUt6wsrGGvhL+IVIZwqlEHSiQ6cdWAl4aMC62OsSPB9G047vrOy0fNSqgxD63ibxA/
/NGbGoGq2r3r0sS4QO7qyjNQ0epMl4qKjKKTnc8icqbPzki1bRW4lxOITKAe8HVQhTv9KzQ6SmIXga  ...
0wcZlO0HoaNgH+77w58gysT1XThJGyrifCeIuKL8bW0EMEiUgYJ05YqMPBw+gktPIG02JeyD4Xga
cPQbEg2ClCKOUtgKVUokxPCrVdQCjAvvO/b3j7g==" autocomplete="off" type="hidden">
```

Specifying where the view state will be saved is a piece of cake, but choosing between saving the view state on a client or on a server can be a difficult choice, because each has its own advantages and disadvantages. Both have a cost, and everybody wants to pay a lower price. Choosing the client will increase network traffic because the serialized state will generate a larger value for the `javax.faces.ViewState` input field. Moreover, encoding/decoding the view state and possible trespasser attacks are also important drawbacks of this approach. On the other hand, the server uses less memory because nothing is stored in the session. Moreover, storing the view state on the client will also be a good solution to prevent losing it when the server is down, and to prevent `ViewExpiredException` that occurs when the session has expired, or when the maximum number of opened views was reached. Saving the state on the server has an opposite effect: the network traffic is lower, the usage of memory by the server increases, and the server failures will result in loss of the state and possible `ViewExpiredException` instances.

> Usually, developers prefer to have a lower network traffic and use more memory on the server, because memory is easy to provide to an application server. But this is not a rule; you just have to think what's cheaper for you. Some heavy benchmarks can also provide compelling indications about storing the state on the client or on the server.

In order to make the right choice, do not forget that JSF 2.0 comes, by default, with partial state saving, which will be reflected in a smaller size of the `javax.faces.ViewState` input field (the state saved on the client) or in less memory needed (the state saved on the server). You can disable partial state saving by adding the following `context` parameter in `web.xml`:

```
<context-param>
 <param-name>javax.faces.PARTIAL_STATE_SAVING</param-name>
 <param-value>false</param-value>
</context-param>
```

For a simple visual test, you can choose to save the state on the client and run the same application twice (you can use the application named, ch9_1_2): first time, enable partial state saving, and second time, disable it—the result shown in the following screenshot speaks for itself:

```
Partial State Saving Enabled (default starting with JSF 2.0)
```
```
<input name="javax.faces.ViewState" id="j_id1:javax.faces.ViewState:0"
value="hsRadMlUhXPzPKxW9mVTMbUF2hI4htAPlK8djgzIjhGzjI9D46yNteB8KWqZA1Vu70BuI6pVxFFVbMJKq    ...
/MuFIo3JztmvseeOVpm+poRXevR7m7hrZYNqvw7hZHohcQkUM4TeOwdhFrq0CjFp4b8KanTdZVLNuFAE1lUq5
+P06HWDvXOaF6fv6WNfplIlwthJXZLwhF8jfC/SmMuA2Sq7sCY=" autocomplete="off" type="hidden">
```

```
Partial State Saving Disabled
```
```
<input name="javax.faces.ViewState" id="j_id1:javax.faces.ViewState:0"
value="nafxvLIJjEusI+PFSH2neoXnBdMOmyvrCWFblxTFl5wySBk+j2thnBrOrFc3hpCQXkSp4Z/z7ylw2ILQNiM4C   ...
/X1rQp2M+5E3OL2oftH9LTeJl+hyjramrPF8rYwvgdyss0Y6Yv9ZWzFnQSKvxe+FQ1XeZRFJREAgLxVLHzhKdqXpV
/lSiCi3ZMmEte2OgbRskFK1dJP3fnRR3uQpcrma9kKryGbykuHwTjpS29t6moI8lq6Lcn132sHp1iO5jwaplqITyscQ1
ZxEq1K64PKqtLcGTLjTgg2eddBvCczx0PUgE4l2j9cmcgAIfaiUjfNIksQVMPDJ6/F6NFKPVS1CkgYC+qVBlfziq8tZ6V
/9i9NF9U6Gla0ox8CIXO/u4pUhYvuhG2HTLWR5U2Z6f97EKMCP8+Meu4gjwMZcPfoD6ndv/8zdG+kKzz07ryOxk
/mODvWscYC1sKzy2jIiFa21C05SYK6h7OsNLuLAMENtqMASI4ca2+MUh4T3Ft10HcMaXDvIkjDbJ0EgykylPVxEGT   ...
/PjfQRqvJb5dJdc83Y3H75WIsL67JoVV2I74N8S4nF4ntK3P+EpMu9j0NCHbLfEqxspc6v0e9uxCMUChZEtHBUfv8l
/9VzXvY6G4Y2Qjs9pL0UCHG+IZnYO1P9lI2OKwT5K7ioccea3K2Fs66ETYUPHgbipw5Pnd7Fvvekih4cJP0Lt7cxIo6
H1byRWRbNMx6ek7Q/rB6uppvMuB0jju6sIF6y437ce+lcfiYoAbQ2Yxyey8O1tSWl0uvaLUCjOa+z2aYraQxEI+wa
/4dq3O5r6k6x9sjz+CDlciqJPIgnrBjIrzTbvWzK07DsVAtFKp7OYEx0zIne8voKbWP9QU4QKB1Kq5JOWFLt2ED1If
/6jZvuSXAglbptbDRhEq6+gcMaOeyKMvetmHR7ZwGxm+2RQxrT9IzzgRZOescmCbSB+kK4gkyE+9iij2m2EKFWI
/spIQ3j1nnj/zW1/NNH5kgY2q/nfFg22fqefLaIUqzX6MYIYOJOm4ePd/rtNW7X8cx58aUbG2/9AvhTucyy9xvi5sPc
/vGNrLv+ifhBy7maZmUfO0Ul+jywMaopY3RI5umi5YZz0/uLKzGOoSmQqxDEq1Cm9
/xtI4Hv6UHrW1GxkYr7jUSE3u3+29Y4sqQdTdXnOA7Z123Rnp0aKwUGu9bnuorBoRFr+eYTyw4IgujsnVvC16Q2
nvW543QddInIIHmSDUvNo4++I3Le8b2cHkIm+Tu+x5TLLXxDcSzJVEAOSvqjyuxiL9GtlF7jgCevQgZhXXsUt1TKl
/FcmTRt9AJ9HBaAZqKVc+XZAVGyQre9SCOdT5uMBMkXoOYyKiwf2RpyquN2ep5HLvgiSzmiLJTjQ4K+gzc567A/1
/drVz5Rx9Ub7Q74lRVW7BuaNqcHeAnhoR8Ec8xvPBU3r
ii9nICftAfIvTVYI3TDw4UB7HWDTD00lpsuCn1Ik/oEA1m8=" autocomplete="off" type="hidden">
```

Furthermore, in the same application, you can use partial state saving for some views and full state saving for other views. Skip the `javax.faces.PARTIAL_STATE_SAVING` context parameter and use the `javax.faces.FULL_STATE_SAVING_VIEW_IDS` context parameter. The value of this context parameter contains a list of view IDs for which the partial state saving will be disabled. The IDs should be comma separated, as shown in the following code (suppose you have three pages: `index.xhtml`, `done.xhtml`, and `error.xhtml`, partial state saving is used only for `index.xhtml`):

```
<context-param>
  <param-name>javax.faces.FULL_STATE_SAVING_VIEW_IDS</param-name>
  <param-value>/done.xhtml,/error.xhtml</param-value>
</context-param>
```

Programmatically, you can check if the state is saved on the client as follows:

- In view/page the code is as follows:

```
#{facesContext.application.stateManager.
                    isSavingStateInClient(facesContext)}
```

- In backing bean, the code is as follows:

```
FacesContext facesContext = FacesContext.getCurrentInstance();
Application application = facesContext.getApplication();
StateManager stateManager = application.getStateManager();
logger.log(Level.INFO, "Is view state saved on client ? {0}",
            stateManager.isSavingStateInClient(facesContext));
```

# JSF logical and physical views

So far, so good! We know that JSF can store a full or partial view state on server or on client with some advantages and disadvantages. Further, you have to know that JSF differentiates views in logical views (specific to the GET requests) and physical views (specific to the POST requests). Each GET request generates a new logical view. By default, JSF Mojarra (the reference implementation of JSF) manages 15 logical views, but this number can be adjusted through the context parameter, `com.sun.faces.numberOfLogicalViews`, as shown in the following code:

```
<context-param>
  <param-name>com.sun.faces.numberOfLogicalViews</param-name>
  <param-value>2</param-value>
</context-param>
```

You can easily perform a test of this setting by starting the browser and opening the `ch9_2` application three times, in three different browser tabs. Afterwards, come back to the first tab and try to submit the form. You will see a `ViewExpiredException` because the first logical view was removed from the logical views map, as shown in the following screenshot:

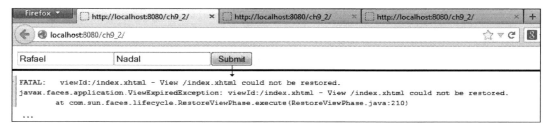

If you open the application in one or two tabs, this error will not occur.

There is another story with the POST requests (non-AJAX), because, in this case, JSF (Mojarra implementation) will store every single form in the session until the maximum size is reached. A POST request creates a new physical view (except AJAX requests which use the same physical view repeatedly) and JSF Mojarra can store 15 physical views per logical view (`Map<LogicalView, Map<PhysicalView, and ViewState>>`). Obviously, a physical view can contain multiple forms.

You can control the number of physical views through the context parameter named `com.sun.faces.numberOfViewsInSession`. For example, you can decrease its value to 4 as shown in the following code:

```
<context-param>
  <param-name>com.sun.faces.numberOfViewsInSession</param-name>
  <param-value>4</param-value>
</context-param>
```

This small value allows you to perform a quick test. Open the application named `ch9_3` in the browser and submit that form four times. Afterwards, press the browser's back button four times, to return to the first form and try to submit it again. You will see an exception, because this physical view was removed from the physical view's map. This will not happen if you submit the form less than four times.

> In case you need more than 15 logical/physical views, then you can increase their number or choose to save the state on the client. Saving the state on the client is recommended since it will totally eliminate this problem.

In case of navigation between pages, JSF doesn't store anything in the session for the GET requests, but will save the state of forms for the POST requests.

# Saving the state in a database – an experimental application

Combining the client saving state and complex views can really stress up the network bandwidth. The root of this drawback is represented by the size of the serialized state that should be passed between the client and the server at each request-response cycle. Usually, this string increases the server's response size significantly. An interesting idea is to save the view state in a database and send to the client only an identifier to the corresponding record. In this section, you will see how to accomplish this task using a MongoDB database and a custom implementation of saving the client view state. The implementation is tight coupled to JSF Mojarra (there are `com.sun.faces.*` specific dependencies requiring Mojarra). So, since it is not utilizing the standard API methods, this approach won't work in MyFaces.

> If you are not familiar with MongoDB (or NoSQL database systems), you can use SQL RDBMSs (for example, MySQL) and plain JDBC.

In order to pass the client view state into a database, you have to be aware of how JSF deals with it by default, and perform the corresponding adjustments. The magic of saving the state begins in the `ViewHandler`/`StateManager` pair of classes, which guides the tasks of saving/restoring the views between requests. Both of them use a helper class, named `ResponseStateManager`, which knows how to determine where the state should be saved (based on the default settings or on `web.xml` explicit settings) and delegates the saving/restoring task to one of the two helper classes, named `ClientSideStateHelper` and `ServerSideStateHelper`.

Getting more in details, when the view state should be saved, the `StateManager.writeState` method is called from the `ViewHandler.renderView` method. In the `StateManager.writeState` method, JSF will obtain an instance of `ResponseStateManager`. This object can inspect each rendering-technology-specific request, because it knows the rendering technology used. The instance of `ResponseStateManager` comes from the `RenderKit` class (by calling the `RenderKit` method, named `getResponseStateManager`) and delegates the writing task to the `ResponseStateManager.writeState` method. In the `ResponseStateManager` constructor, JSF will determine where the view state should be saved (on the client or the server), and indicates that the writing task should happen in one of the two helper classes, which are responsible for effectively writing the view state.

On the way back, during restore view, the `ViewHandler` uses the `ResponseStateManager` class to test if the request is an initial request or a postback request. In case of a postback request, JSF will call the `ViewHandler.restoreView` method.

Since we are interested in saving view state on the client, we will focus on the `ClientSideStateHelper` class, which defines the following important methods:

- `writeState`: This method generates the hidden input field and populates its value with the encrypted version of the serialization view state
- `getState`: This method inspects the incoming request parameters for the standardized state parameter name and decrypts the string

So, we need to write our helper class, named `CustomClientSideStateHelper`. The `writeState` method is a convenient point to start. The idea is to modify the default method for sending the encrypted state into a MongoDB database, instead of sending it to the client. The client will receive the primary key used for storing the state in the database. The modifications are highlighted in the following code:

```
@Override
public void writeState(FacesContext ctx, Object state,
            StringBuilder stateCapture) throws IOException {

    if (stateCapture != null) {
        doWriteState(ctx,state,new StringBuilderWriter(stateCapture));
    } else {
        ResponseWriter writer = ctx.getResponseWriter();

        writer.startElement("input", null);
        writer.writeAttribute("type", "hidden", null);
        writer.writeAttribute("name",
```

```
                                ResponseStateManager.VIEW_STATE_PARAM, null);
        if (webConfig.isOptionEnabled(EnableViewStateIdRendering)) {
            String viewStateId = Util.getViewStateId(ctx);
            writer.writeAttribute("id", viewStateId, null);
        }
        StringBuilder stateBuilder = new StringBuilder();
        doWriteState(ctx,state,new StringBuilderWriter(stateBuilder));

        WriteStateInDB writeStateInDB = new WriteStateInDB();
        String client_id =
            writeStateInDB.writeStateDB(stateBuilder.toString());

        if (client_id != null) {
            writer.writeAttribute("value", client_id, null);
        } else {
            writer.writeAttribute("value",
                                    stateBuilder.toString(), null);
        }
        if (webConfig.isOptionEnabled(AutoCompleteOffOnViewState)) {
            writer.writeAttribute("autocomplete", "off", null);
        }
        writer.endElement("input");

        writeClientWindowField(ctx, writer);
        writeRenderKitIdField(ctx, writer);
    }
}
```

Further, a subsequent client request will pass the primary key to the default
getState method. Therefore, you need to write a custom getState method
that will extract the corresponding state from the database by its ID (primary key):

```
@Override
public Object getState(FacesContext ctx, String viewId)
                                                throws IOException {

    String stateString = ClientSideStateHelper.getStateParamValue(ctx);

    if (stateString == null) {
        return null;
    }

    if ("stateless".equals(stateString)) {
```

```
        return "stateless";
    } else {
        WriteStateInDB writeStateInDB = new WriteStateInDB();
        stateString = writeStateInDB.readStateDB(stateString);
        if (stateString == null) {
            return null;
        }
    }

    return doGetState(stateString);
}
```

# Writing the custom ResponseStateManager class

At this point, we can save/restore the client view state using a MongoDB database. Looking forward, we need to tell JSF to use our `CustomClientSideStateHelper` class instead of the default `ClientSideStateHelper` class. This task can be easily accomplished if we write a custom implementation of the `ResponseStateManager` class. This will be almost the same as the Mojarra implementation, but with a small adjustment in the constructor (notice how we slipped the `CustomClientSideStateHelper` class here) as shown in the following code:

```
public class CustomResponseStateManager extends ResponseStateManager {

    private StateHelper helper;

    public CustomResponseStateManager() {
      WebConfiguration webConfig = WebConfiguration.getInstance();
      String stateMode =
            webConfig.getOptionValue(StateSavingMethod);
      helper = ((StateManager.STATE_SAVING_METHOD_CLIENT.
    equalsIgnoreCase(stateMode)
        ? new CustomClientSideStateHelper()
        : new ServerSideStateHelper()));
    }
    . . .
```

Following the same reasoning, we need to tell JSF to use our custom
`ResponseStateManager` class. Remember that JSF obtains an instance of this
class through the default `RenderKit` class; therefore, we can easily write our
custom `RenderKit` class and override the `getResponseStateManager` method,
which is responsible for creating an instance of the `ResponseStateManager` class.
In order to write a custom `RenderKit` class, we will extend the wrapper class,
`RenderKitWrapper`, which represents a simple implementation of the `RenderKit`
abstract class and spares us the implementation of all the methods as shown in the
following code:

```
public class CustomRenderKit extends RenderKitWrapper {

  private RenderKit renderKit;
  private ResponseStateManager responseStateManager =
                            new CustomResponseStateManager();

  public CustomRenderKit() {}

  public CustomRenderKit(RenderKit renderKit) {
    this.renderKit = renderKit;
  }

  @Override
  public synchronized ResponseStateManager getResponseStateManager() {

    if (responseStateManager == null) {
        responseStateManager = new CustomResponseStateManager();
    }
    return responseStateManager;
  }


  @Override
  public RenderKit getWrapped() {
    return renderKit;
  }
}
```

The custom `RenderKit` class must be appropriately configured in the `faces-config.xml` file as follows:

```
<render-kit>
 <render-kit-class>
   book.beans.CustomRenderKit
 </render-kit-class>
</render-kit>
```

Done! Now, the default `StateManager` class will require a `ResponseStateManager` instance from our `RenderKit` class, which will provide an instance of the `CustomResponseStateManager` class. Further, the `CustomResponseStateManager` class will use `CustomClientSideStateHelper` for saving/restoring the client state.

# Adding MongoDB in equation

The missing part of the preceding section is the `WriteStateInDB` class. This is a class capable of writing/reading data from a MongoDB (Version 2.2.2 or later) database using the MongoDB Java Driver (Version 2.8.0 or later), and is listed in the following code (for those who are familiar with the MongoDB Java Driver, this is a very simple code):

```
public class WriteStateInDB {

 private DBCollection dbCollection;

 public WriteStateInDB() throws UnknownHostException {
  Mongo mongo = new Mongo("127.0.0.1", 27017);
  DB db = mongo.getDB("jsf_db");
  dbCollection = db.getCollection(("jsf"));
 }

 protected String writeStateDB(String state) {

 //TTL Index
 BasicDBObject index = new BasicDBObject("date", 1);
 BasicDBObject options = new BasicDBObject("expireAfterSeconds",
                                 TimeUnit.MINUTES.toSeconds(1));
         dbCollection.ensureIndex(index, options);

 BasicDBObject basicDBObject = new BasicDBObject();
 basicDBObject.append("date", new Date());
 basicDBObject.append("state", state);

 dbCollection.insert(basicDBObject);
```

```
    ObjectId id = (ObjectId) basicDBObject.get("_id");

    return String.valueOf(id);

  }

  protected String readStateDB(String id) {

    BasicDBObject query = new BasicDBObject("_id", new ObjectId(id));
    DBObject dbObj = dbCollection.findOne(query);
    if (dbObj != null) {
        return dbObj.get("state").toString();
    }
    return null;

  }
}
```

Moreover, this class exploits a great facility of MongoDB, named TTL (`http://docs.mongodb.org/manual/tutorial/expire-data/`), which is capable of automatically removing the data after a specified number of seconds or at a specific clock time. This is useful for cleaning up the database for the expired sessions (orphans). In this demo, each state will be deleted after 60 seconds from the insertion of data into the database, but setting the time to 30 minutes can be more realistic. Of course, even so, you are under the risk of deleting the states that are currently active; therefore, supplementary checks or an alternative solution is needed. Unfortunately, we can't provide more details regarding MongoDB, since this is beyond the scope of this book. Therefore you have to go for a research (`http://www.mongodb.org/`). In the following screenshots, you can see a simple test that reveals the page size difference between the default client view state saving (1.3 KB) and the customized client view state. The default approach is as follows:

The custom approach is as follows:

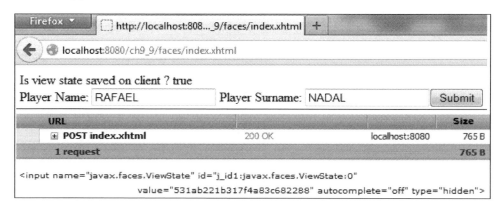

Of course, this approach brings into discussion the main drawback represented by the need of hitting the database for each save/restore state (caching can solve this).

The complete application is named `ch9_9`. In order for it to work, you need to install MongoDB 2.2.2 (or later). The application comes with the MongoDB Java Driver Version 2.8.0, but you can provide a more recent one.

As a final note to this section, keep in mind that a custom `StateManager` class can be written by extending the wrapper class, `StateManagerWrapper`, as shown in the following code (starting with JSF 2.0, we can use this wrapper class to easily decorate the `StateManager` class):

```
public class CustomStateManager extends StateManagerWrapper {

  private StateManager stateManager;

  public CustomStateManager() {
  }

  public CustomStateManager(StateManager stateManager) {
   this.stateManager = stateManager;
  }

  @Override
```

```
   // ... override here the needed methods


   @Override
   public StateManager getWrapped() {
    return stateManager;
   }
  }
```

The custom state manager should be configured in the `faces-config.xml` file as follows:

```
<application>
 <state-manager>
   book.beans.CustomStateManager
 </state-manager>
</application>
```

# Handling ViewExpiredException

When a user session expires (for any reason) `ViewExpiredException` occurs. The scenario behind this exception is based on the following steps:

- The user view state is saved on the server (the `javax.faces.STATE_SAVING_METHOD` context parameter's value is server).

- The user receives the view state ID as the value of the hidden input field, `javax.faces.ViewState`. This points out the view state saved on the server.

- The user session expires (for example, timeout session) and the view state is removed from the server session, but the user still has the view state ID.

- The user sends a POST request, but the view state ID indicates an unavailable view state; therefore, `ViewExpiredException` occurs.

In order to deal with this exception, you have two choices: to avoid it or to treat it. Suppose that you are in view **A** and you click on the **Logout** button that invalidates the session and redirects control to view **B** (when the session is invalidated the state is automatically removed from the session). Since this is a POST non-AJAX request, the user can press the browser back button, which will load the view **A** again. Now, he can click on the **Logout** button again, but this time, instead of view **B**, he/she will see `ViewExpiredException`, because, most probably, view **A** is not requested to the server again, and is loaded from the browser cache. Since it is loaded from the cache, the `javax.faces.ViewState` view state ID is the same as it was at first logout; therefore, the associated state is not available anymore. The flow is shown in the following screenshot:

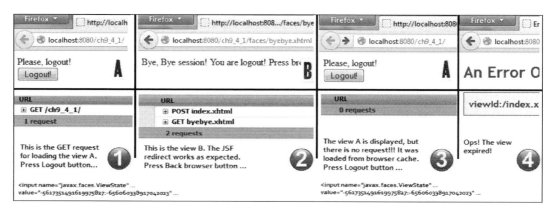

Obviously, this is not the desired behavior. You have to tell the browser to make a new request to the server instead of loading the view **A** from the cache. This can be accomplished by a filter that sets the right headers in order to disable browser caching. The filter will be applied to the `Faces Servlet` class as shown in the following code:

```
@WebFilter(filterName = "LogoutFilter", servletNames = {"Faces
Servlet"})
public class LogoutFilter implements Filter {
...
@Override
public void doFilter(ServletRequest request, ServletResponse response,
            FilterChain chain) throws IOException, ServletException {

  HttpServletRequest requestHTTP = (HttpServletRequest) request;
  HttpServletResponse responseHTTP = (HttpServletResponse) response;
  try {
      String resourceURI = requestHTTP.getContextPath() +
            requestHTTP.getServletPath() +
```

```
                    ResourceHandler.RESOURCE_IDENTIFIER;
        String requestURI = requestHTTP.getRequestURI();

        if (!requestURI.startsWith(resourceURI)) {
            responseHTTP.setHeader("Expires",
                                    "Sat, 6 May 1995 12:00:00 GMT");
            responseHTTP.setHeader("Cache-Control",
                                    "no-store,no-cache,must-revalidate");
            responseHTTP.addHeader("Cache-Control",
                                    "post-check=0, pre-check=0");
            responseHTTP.setHeader("Pragma", "no-cache");
        }
        chain.doFilter(request, response);
    } catch (IOException | ServletException t) {
    }
}
```

Now, repeat the scenario and note that instead of `ViewExpiredException`, view **A** receives a new view state ID in `javax.faces.ViewState`.

You can see two examples in the code bundle of this chapter. One is named `ch9_4_1`, and the other one is named `ch9_4_2`.

The preceding solution may be a little bit confusing to the user, since it doesn't provide any explicit information about what is happening. Moreover, a session may expire for many other reasons; therefore it would be a better idea to display an error page to the user instead of using a filter to prevent browser cache. The error page can be the login page or just an intermediary page containing a link to the login page. This can be accomplished by adding in the `web.xml` file as shown in the following code:

```
<error-page>
 <exception-type>
   javax.faces.application.ViewExpiredException
 </exception-type>
 <location>/faces/expired.xhtml</location>
</error-page>
```

A simple `expired.xhtml` will be as follows:

```
<h:body>
 Your session expired ...
 <h:link value="Go to Login Page ..." outcome="index" />
</h:body>
```

The complete example is named `ch9_5` and is available in the code bundle of this book.

There is at least one more approach that comes from JSF 1.2 that works in JSF 2.2 also. You can try to set the following `context` parameter:

```
<context-param>
 <param-name>
  com.sun.faces.enableRestoreView11Compatibility
 </param-name>
 <param-value>true</param-value>
</context-param>
```

Well, this can be interpreted as: when the current view expires, generate a brand new one and do not throw `ViewExpiredException`.

The complete example is named `ch9_6` and is available in the code bundle of this book.

More details about this exception (including how you can deal with it in AJAX environments) are available in the *Configuring the view handler* and *Configuring the global exception handler* sections in *Chapter 5, JSF Configurations Using XML Files and Annotations – Part 2*.

# Server-state serialization in a session

On the server side, the state can be stored as a shallow copy or as a deep copy. In a shallow copy, the state is not serialized in the session (JSF stores only pointers to the state in a session and only the container deals with serialization stuff), which requires less memory and allows you to inject EJBs in the view scoped beans (use this technique carefully, since the changes that affect objects in one copy will be reflected in the rest of the copies). The deep copy represents a full serialization of the state in a session, which requires more memory and doesn't allow injecting EJBs.

 By default, JSF Mojarra uses shallow copy, while JSF MyFaces uses deep copy. Anyway, perform a quick test to be sure which is the default.

We can easily alter the default behavior by explicitly setting the `javax.faces.SERIALIZE_SERVER_STATE` context parameter in `web.xml`. This context parameter was introduced starting with JSF 2.2 and represents the standard context parameter for setting the server state serialization in Mojarra and MyFaces. You can indicate that the shallow copy should be used as follows:

```
<context-param>
 <param-name>javax.faces.SERIALIZE_SERVER_STATE</param-name>
 <param-value>false</param-value>
</context-param>
```

In order to avoid exceptions of type, `java.io.NotSerializableException` (and warnings of type `Setting non-serializable attribute value ...`), keep in mind that serializing the state in a session implies serializable backing beans. (They import `java.io.Serializable` and their properties are serializable. Special attention to nested beans, EJBs, streams, JPA entities, connections, and so on.) This is also true when you are storing the view state in the client since the entire state should be serializable. When a bean property should not (or cannot) be serialized, just declare it `transient` and do not forget that it will be `null` at deserialization.

In addition to the preceding note, a common case implies `java.io.NotSerializableException`, when the state is saved on the client. But when switching the state on the server, this exception miraculously disappears on Mojarra, while it is still present in MyFaces. This can be confusing, but is perfectly normal if you are using Mojarra implementation, the state should be fully serializable while saving it on the client (and it is not, since this exception occurred), while this is not true on the server, where Mojarra by default doesn't serialize the state in a session. On the other hand, MyFaces defaults to serialize the state; therefore, the exception persists.

Sometimes, you may optimize memory usage and save server resources by redesigning the application state, which contains view or session or application backing beans (don't cache the data that can be queried from a database and try to reduce the number of such beans). Besides managing the view state, this is also an important aspect that reflects directly in performance. When more memory is needed, the container may choose to serialize the parts of the application state, which means that you have to pay the price of deserialization also. While the price of saving in the session is represented by memory, the price of serialization/deserialization is represented by the time and insignificant disk space (at least it should be insignificant).

# JSF 2.2 is stateless

The notion of being stateless is pretty confusing, because every application must maintain some kind of state (for example, for runtime variables). Generically speaking, a stateless application will follow the rule of a state per request, which means that a state's lifecycle is the same as the request-response lifecycle. This is an important issue in web applications, where we need to use session/application scope that, obviously, breaks down the notion of stateless.

Even so, one of the most popular features of JSF 2.2 consists of stateless views (and is actually available starting with Version 2.1.19). The idea behind this concept assumes that JSF will not save/restore the view state between requests and will prefer to recreate the view state from the XHTML tags on every request. The goal is to seriously increase performances: the gain time used for the save/restore view state, more efficient usage of server memory, more support for clustered environments, and the prevention of `ViewExpiredExceptions`. So, JSF developers have certain requirements of the stateless feature.

Nevertheless, it seems that the stateless feature doesn't affect too much of the time used for saving/restoring the view state (this is not expensive, especially when the state is saved on a server session and is not going to be serialized) and memory performances. On the other hand, when an application is deployed on several computers (in clustered environments), the stateless feature can be a real help because we don't need session replication (refers to replicating the data stored in a session across different instances) and/or sticky sessions (refers to the mechanism used by the load balancer to improve efficiency of persistent sessions in a clustered configuration) anymore. For stateless applications, the nodes do not need to share states, and client postback requests can be resolved by different nodes. This is a big achievement, because in order to resolve many requests, we can add new nodes without worrying about sharing the state. In addition, preventing `ViewExpiredException` is also a big advantage.

 Stateless views can be used to postpone session creation or dealing with big (complex) component trees that implies an uncomfortable state.

Starting with JSF 2.2, the developers can choose between saving the view state and creating stateless views in the same application, which means that the application can use dynamic forms in some views (stateful) and create/recreate them for every request in other views (stateless). For a stateless view, the component tree cannot be dynamically generated/changed (for example, JSTL and bindings are not available in the stateless mode) and resubmitting forms will probably not work as expected. Moreover, some of the JSF components are stateful, which will lead to serious issues in a stateless view. But, it is not so easy to nominate those components and the issues, since their behavior is dependent on the environment (context). Some specific tests may be helpful.

In order to write a JSF stateless application, you have to design everything to work only with the request scoped bean. In some cases, we can use different tricks to accomplish this task, like using hidden fields and special request parameters for emulating a session. While session and application beans will break down the idea of stateless (even if it is possible to use), the view bean will act as request beans.

Programmatically speaking, defining a view as stateless is a piece of cake: just add the attribute named, `transient` to the `<f:view>` tag and set its value to `true`. Note that in order to have a stateless view, the presence of `<f:view>` tag is mandatory, even if it doesn't have any other use. Each stateless view of an application needs this setting because there isn't a global setting for indicating that the stateless effect should be applied at the application level.

```
<f:view transient="true">
 ...
</f:view>
```

When a view is stateless, the `javax.faces.ViewState` value will be `stateless`, as shown in the following screenshot:

```
<input name="javax.faces.ViewState" id="j_id1:javax.faces.ViewState:0'
     value="stateless" autocomplete="off" type="hidden">
```

# The view scoped beans and the stateless feature

In a stateless environment, the view scoped beans act as request scoped beans. Besides the fact that you can't create/manipulate views dynamically, this is one of the big disadvantages that comes with the stateless feature, because it will affect AJAX-based applications that usually use view scoped beans. You can easily test this behavior with a set of beans with different scopes (the complete application is named `ch9_7`). The view scoped bean can be defined as follows:

```
@Named
@ViewScoped
public class TimestampVSBean implements Serializable{

 private Timestamp timestamp;

 public TimestampVSBean() {
  java.util.Date date = new java.util.Date();
  timestamp = new Timestamp(date.getTime());
 }

 public Timestamp getTimestamp() {
  return timestamp;
 }

 public void setTimestamp(Timestamp timestamp) {
  this.timestamp = timestamp;
 }
}
```

Just change the scope to request, session, and application to obtain the other three beans.

Next, we will write a simple stateless view as follows:

```
<f:view transient="true">
 <h:form>
  <h:commandButton value="Generate Timestamp"/>
 </h:form>
 <hr/>
 Request Scoped Bean:
 <h:outputText value="#{timestampRSBean.timestamp}"/>
 <hr/>
 View Scoped Bean:
 <h:outputText value="#{timestampVSBean.timestamp}"/>
 [keep an eye on this in stateless mode]
 <hr/>
 Session Scoped Bean:
 <h:outputText value="#{timestampSSBean.timestamp}"/>
 <hr/>
 Application Scoped Bean:
 <h:outputText value="#{timestampASBean.timestamp}"/>
 <hr/>
</f:view>
```

Afterwards, just submit this form several times (click on the **Generate Timestamp** button) and notice that the timestamp generated by the view scoped bean changes at every request as shown in the following screenshot:

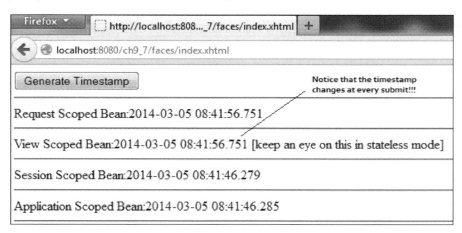

The request, session, and application scopes work as expected!

# Detecting stateless views programmatically

Programmatically speaking, you can detect if a view is stateless by using the following options:

- In view or page, enter the following code:

```
<f:view transient="true">
  Is Stateless (using transient) ? #{facesContext.viewRoot.
transient}

    ...
</f:view>
```

- In view or page, enter the following code. This works only for the `postback` **requests:**

```
Is Stateless (using stateless) ?
#{facesContext.postback ? facesContext.renderKit.
responseStateManager.
          isStateless(facesContext, null) : 'Not postback yet!'}
```

- In backing bean, enter the following code:

```
FacesContext facesContext = FacesContext.getCurrentInstance();
UIViewRoot uiViewRoot = facesContext.getViewRoot();
logger.log(Level.INFO, "Is stateless (using isTransient) ? {0}",
                              uiViewRoot.isTransient());
logger.log(Level.INFO, "Is stateless (using isStateless) ?
{0}", facesContext.getRenderKit().getResponseStateManager().
isStateless(facesContext, null));
```

 Notice that the `isStateless` method can be used only on the `postback` requests.

The complete application is named `ch9_8`.

# JSF security notes

Dissertations about JSF saving state also imply some aspects regarding JSF security. It appears that saving the JSF state on the client is less secure than saving the JSF state on the server. For the most common security concerns (for example, XSS, CSRF, SQL injection, and phishing), JSF provides implicit protection.

# Cross-site request forgery (CSRF)

CSRF and phishing attacks can be prevented by saving state on the server. JSF 2.0 comes with implicit protection against CSRF attacks based on the value of the `javax.faces.ViewState` hidden field. Starting with JSF 2.2, this protection was seriously fortified by creating a powerful and robust value for this field.

# Cross-site scripting (XSS)

XSS attacks are implicitly prevented by JSF through the `escape` attribute, which is set to `true` by default (`<h:outputText/>`, `<h:outputLabel/>`). The following are the examples:

```
<p>Hi, <h:outputText value="#{loginbean.name}" /></p>
<p>Hi, #{loginbean.name}</p>
```

The preceding examples are XSS protected because they are both escaped.

But, if you write the following example, then an XSS attack is possible:

```
<p>Hi, <h:outputText value="#{loginbean.name}" escape="false" /></p>
```

In order to allow HTML tags, you have to focus on a specialized tool, which will be able to parse the HTML code.

 In the stateless mode, the `escape` attribute should always be set to `true`, because an XSS gap can facilitate an easy way for CSRF attacks.

# SQL injection

SQL injection is usually an attack that speculates SQL queries that are created based on user inputs/selections. JSF itself cannot prevent these kinds of attacks, because it is not implicated in generating and executing SQL transactions. On the other hand, you can use JSF to filter/validate user inputs or selections, which may prevent such attacks. Outside JSF, it is a good technique to prevent these attacks consisting of writing parameterized queries instead of embedding user inputs in the statements and be extra careful at filtering escape characters and type handling.

# Summary

I hope you found this as an interesting dissertation about the JSF state. This was a controversial subject for a long time, and starting with JSF 2.2, the stateless views pour more gas on the fire of this controversy. Nevertheless, choosing the right way of managing states is a serious decision that affects the applications' performance; therefore, choose wisely and try to be documented about the existing benchmarks and workarounds regarding the JSF state.

See you in the next chapter, where we will discuss about custom and composite components in JSF.

# 10
# JSF Custom Components

JSF is a component-based framework, and JSF custom components are the major proof that sustain JSF flexibility and extensibility. In order to write custom components or extend the existing ones, JSF provides a powerful API that allows us to develop two types of components: **custom components,** and, from JSF 2.0 onwards, **composite components**. A custom component implementation is responsible for providing an **aspect** (optional for non-UI components, such as custom validators, converters, and renderers) and a **behavior**. Usually the decision to write custom components and the skills for accomplishing it belong to advanced JSF developers.

Before you decide to write a custom component, which can be a time-consuming task, you have to overview the following bullets (especially the first bullet):

- Check the Internet (for example, `http://jsfcentral.com/`) to make sure the component doesn't exist yet. Many JSF extensions, such as PrimeFaces, ICEfaces, OmniFaces, and RichFaces, already come with hundreds of custom components.

- Make sure that you need a custom component and not just a Facelet template (see *Chapter 12, Facelets Templating*) or some custom logic over the existing components.

- Try to redesign the application goals to use the existing components (sometimes you can combine several existing components to obtain the desired aspect and behavior).

- Take a closer look at non-JSF components, such as jQueryUI, ComponentJS, and AmplifyJS (as you are not forced to solely use JSF components in your JSF applications!).

If your application has some specific goals that just cannot be solved by any of the preceding bullets, it is time to start coding your own components.

In the first part of this chapter, you will see how to write noncomposite custom components, and in the second part you will learn about composite components. The noncomposite components have been available for a long time in JSF, and the technique of writing such components is based on writing several Java classes. The new concept, which came along with composite components, is available from JSF 2 onwards, and the idea behind it is to replace the Java classes with XHTML pages.

# Building noncomposite custom components

Let's jump directly to the cool stuff and say that in JSF 2.0 a custom component was made available to page authors by configuring it in a Facelet tag library (`*taglib.xml`).

Moreover, when the component is mapped in a JAR, a special entry in `web.xml` is needed to point to the `*taglib.xml` file. See the application named `ch10_3`.

As of JSF 2.2, we don't need these files anymore. A JSF 2.2 simple custom component contains a single class, and it may look like the following code:

```
@FacesComponent(value = "components.WelcomeComponent", createTag =
true)
public class WelcomeComponent extends UIComponentBase {

    @Override
    public String getFamily() {
        return "welcome.component";
    }

    @Override
    public void encodeBegin(FacesContext context) throws IOException {

        String value = (String) getAttributes().get("value");
        String to = (String) getAttributes().get("to");

        if ((value != null) && (to != null)) {
            ResponseWriter writer = context.getResponseWriter();
            writer.writeAttribute("id", getClientId(context), null);
            writer.write(value + ", " + to);
        }
    }
}
```

Most of the hard work is accomplished by the @FacesComponent annotation (javax.faces.component.FacesComponent). All we need to do is set the createTag element to true, and JSF should create the tag for us. Further, we can easily exploit our custom components, as shown in the following code:

```
<?xml version='1.0' encoding='UTF-8' ?>
<!DOCTYPE html PUBLIC "-//W3C//DTD XHTML 1.0 Transitional//EN"
"http://www.w3.org/TR/xhtml1/DTD/xhtml1-transitional.dtd">
<html xmlns="http://www.w3.org/1999/xhtml"
      xmlns:h="http://xmlns.jcp.org/jsf/html"
      xmlns:t="http://xmlns.jcp.org/jsf/component">
    <h:head>
        <title></title>
    </h:head>
    <h:body>
        <t:welcomeComponent value="Welcome" to="Rafael Nadal"/>
    </h:body>
</html>
```

Notice that the default namespace of the component is http://xmlns. jcp.org/jsf/component. This is true for all components that don't have an explicit namespace.

The complete application is named ch10_1.

The entire list of elements supported by JSF 2.2 @FacesComponent is as follows:

- createTag: This can be set to true or false. When it is set to true, JSF will generate the tag for us (to be more specific, JSF will create, at runtime, a Facelet tag handler that extends ComponentHandler). This element can be used only in JSF 2.2.

- tagName: This allows us to indicate the tag name. When createTag is set to true, JSF will use this name for the generated tag. This element can only be used in JSF 2.2.

- namespace: This allows us to indicate the tag namespace. When createTag is set to true, JSF will use this namespace for the generated tag. When namespace is not specified, JSF will use the http://xmlns.jcp.org/jsf/ component namespace. This element can be used only in JSF 2.2.

- value: This element comes from JSF 2.0 and indicates the **component type**. The component type can be used as the argument of the Application. createComponent(java.lang.String) method for creating instances of the Component class. As of JSF 2.2, if the value element is missing or is null, JSF will obtain it by calling the getSimpleName method on the class to which @FacesComponent is attached and lowercasing the first character.

By the component type, we understand a small chunk of data, specific to each `UIComponent` subclass, that can be used in conjunction with an `Application` instance to programmatically obtain new instances of those subclasses. Moreover, each `UIComponent` subclass belongs to a component family (for example `javax.faces.Input`). This is important when we write a custom component and declare it under a certain family, because we can exploit the renderer specific to that family of components. Next to the component family, we can use the **renderer type** property to select a `Renderer` instance from a `RenderKit` collection (for example, an input field belongs to the `javax.faces.Input` family and to the `javax.faces.Text` renderer type).

Each custom component must extend `UIComponent` or one of its subtypes, such as `UIComponentBase`, which is actually just a default implementation of all abstract methods of `UIComponent`. Anyway, there is one exception represented by the `getFamily` method that must be overridden even when you extend `UIComponentBase`. As a common practice, when a custom component needs to accept end user inputs, it will extend `UIInput`, and when it needs to act as a command, it will extend `UICommand`.

Further, let's modify our application as follows to indicate a custom namespace and tag name:

```
@FacesComponent(value = "components.WelcomeComponent", createTag
= true, namespace = "http://atp.welcome.org/welcome", tagName =
"welcome")
public class WelcomeComponent extends UIComponentBase {
. . .
}
```

Next, the component will be used as follows:

```
<html xmlns="http://www.w3.org/1999/xhtml"
      xmlns:h="http://xmlns.jcp.org/jsf/html"
      xmlns:t="http://atp.welcome.org/welcome">
. . .
   <t:welcome value="Welcome" to="Rafael Nadal"/>
```

The complete application is named `ch10_2`. Moreover, the JSF 2.0 version of this application (containing the `*taglib.xml` descriptor and the specific entry in `web.xml`) is named `ch10_3`.

# Writing a custom tag handler

Notice that `*taglib.xml` is still needed in some cases. For example, if you decide to write a custom tag handler for your component, then you still need this file to configure the handler class. In this rare case, you will extend the `ComponentHandler` class and override the desired methods. Most developers exploit the `onComponentCreated` and `onComponentPopulated` methods. The first one is called after the component has been created but before it has been populated with children, and the second one is called after the component has been populated with children. As of JSF 2.2, a new method was added for developers who wish to take over the task of instantiating the `UIComponent`. This method is named `createComponent`. If it returns `null`, then this method will be required to create the component by `TagHandlerDelegate` instead. Since this is a pretty rare case, we do not insist on it, and we just provide a simple stub of `ComponentHandler`:

```
public class WelcomeComponentHandler extends ComponentHandler {

  private static final Logger logger =
          Logger.getLogger(WelcomeComponentHandler.class.getName());

  public WelcomeComponentHandler(ComponentConfig config) {
    super(config);
  }

  @Override
  public UIComponent createComponent(FaceletContext ctx) {
    logger.info("Inside 'createComponent' method");
    return null;
  }

  @Override
  public void onComponentCreated(FaceletContext ctx,
              UIComponent c, UIComponent parent) {
    logger.info("Inside 'onComponentCreated' method");
    super.onComponentCreated(ctx, c, parent);
  }

  @Override
  public void onComponentPopulated(FaceletContext ctx,
              UIComponent c, UIComponent parent) {
    logger.info("Inside 'onComponentPopulated' method");
    super.onComponentPopulated(ctx, c, parent);
  }
}
```

In order to indicate that our class handler should be used, we need to configure it in the *taglib.xml file, as shown in the following code:

```
<handler-class>book.beans.WelcomeComponentHandler</handler-class>
```

The complete example is named ch10_24_1. Another stub that can be used as a starting point can be found in ch10_24_2. The latter one defines the minimum implementation for a custom ComponentHandler, a custom TagHandlerDelegateFactory, and a custom TagHandlerDelegate.

# Dissecting a custom component

So far you can see that our component class overrides the encodeBegin method. This method belongs to a set of four methods used for rendering a component where each component can render itself (the setRendererType method gets a null value for its argument) or delegate the rendering process to a Renderer class (built-in or user defined). These methods are as follows:

- decode: In order to parse the input values and save them into the component, each request passes through the decode method. Usually, when this method is overridden, the developer extracts the needed values from the request map (or from the Map attributes using the UIComponent.getAttributes method) and sets them into the component by calling the setSubmittedValue(*value*) method.

- encodeBegin: This method starts the rendering process of the custom component. It writes to the response stream obtained through the FacesContext.getResponseWriter method. This method is overridden when we need to encode child components, but we want to output a response to the user before that.

>  The ResponseWriter object (FacesContext.getResponseWriter) contains special methods for generating a markup, such as startElement, writeAttribute, writeText, and endElement.

- encodeChildren: This method renders the custom component children. It is very rarely overridden; however, if you want to alter the default recursive process of encoding component children, then go ahead and override it.

- encodeEnd: Probably this is the most overridden method. As its name suggests, this method is called at the end. Here, we write the custom markup to the response stream. When the custom component accepts end user inputs, the encodeEnd is preferred against encodeBegin because in the case of encodeBegin, the inputs may not be passed yet through a potential attached converter.

> The four methods we just discussed are available for all custom components and for all renderers. In both cases, they have the same name, and the difference between them consists of one argument. When they are overridden in a custom component class, they get a single argument representing FacesContext. On the other hand, when they are overridden in a custom renderer, they get as arguments the FacesContext instance and the corresponding custom component (UIComponent).

So we are at a point where we can conclude that a custom component is based on a subclass of UIComponent and it can render itself or delegate this task to a Renderer class, which is capable of rendering UIComponent instances and decoding the POST requests for obtaining user inputs.

An important aspect of custom components involves managing their state. You should already be familiar with the concept of states from *Chapter 9, JSF State Management*. For this reason, we can say that JSF 2.0 comes with the StateHelper interface, which basically allows us to store, read, and remove data across multiple requests (postbacks). This means we can use it to preserve states of the components.

It can be a little tricky to understand how to use the StateHelper methods in conjunction with custom components, but a common example can be useful to clear things up. Let's consider the following custom component usage:

```
<t:temperature unitto="Celsius" temp="100" />
```

In the custom component class, we can easily map these attribute names and default values, as shown in the following code:

```
// Attribute name constant for unitto
private static final String ATTR_UNITTO = "unitto";
// Default value for the unitto attribute
private static final String ATTR_UNITTO_DEFAULT = "Fahrenheit";
// Attribute name constant for temp
private static final String ATTR_TEMP = "temp";
// Default value for the temp attribute
private static final Float ATTR_TEMP_DEFAULT = 0f;
```

Next, we want to preserve the value of `unitto` under the constant `ATTR_UNITTO` (for `temp` it is exactly the same). For this, we use the `StateHelper.put` method, as shown in the following code:

```
public void setUnitto(String unitto) {
  getStateHelper().put(ATTR_UNITTO, unitto);
}
```

These examples use the `Object put(Serializable key, Object value)` method, but `StateHelper` also has a method `Object put(Serializable key, String mapKey, Object value)`, which can be used to store values that would otherwise be stored in a `Map` instance variable. Moreover, `StateHelper` has a method named `void add(Serializable key, Object value)` that can be used to preserve values which would otherwise be stored in a `List` instance variable.

Next, you can retrieve the value stored under the `ATTR_UNITTO` constant, as shown in the following code:

```
public String getUnitto() {
  return (String) getStateHelper().eval(ATTR_UNITTO, ATTR_UNITTO_
DEFAULT);
}
```

The `Object eval(Serializable key, Object defaultValue)` method will search for the `ATTR_UNITTO` constant. If it can't find it, then the default value (`ATTR_UNITTO_DEFAULT`) is returned. This is a very useful approach because it spears us to perform `null` value checks. Besides this method, `StateHelper` also has the `Object eval(Serializable key)` and `Object get(Serializable key)` methods.

In order to remove an entry from `StateHelper`, we can call `Object remove(Serializable key)` or `Object remove(Serializable key, Object valueOrKey)`.

At this moment, we have plenty of information that can be translated into code, so let's write a custom component to exemplify the above knowledge. Let's name it the Temperature custom component. Basically, the next custom component will expose a public web service as a JSF component. The web service is capable of converting the temperature from Celsius to Fahrenheit and vice versa for which we need to pass the temperature value and the conversion unit as arguments. Based on these two arguments, we can intuit that the corresponding JSF tag will look like the following code:

```
<t:temperature unitto="celsius/fahrenheit" temp="number_of_degrees" />
```

We can start by implementing a helper class to deal with the web service underlying the communication tasks. The name of this class is `TempConvertClient`, and it can be seen in the complete application named `ch10_4`. It's relevant part is the declaration of the following method:

```
public String callTempConvertService(String unitto, Float temp) {
...
}
```

# Custom component implementation

Now we can focus on the important part for us, the custom component implementation. For this we can follow the ensuing steps:

1. Write a class annotated with `@FacesComponent`.
2. Use `StateHelper` to preserve the component's attribute values over multiple requests.
3. Call the `callTempConvertService` method.
4. Render the result.

The first three steps can be coded as follows:

```
@FacesComponent(value = TempConvertComponent.COMPONENT_TYPE, createTag
= true, namespace = "http://temp.converter/", tagName = "temperature")
public class TempConvertComponent extends UIComponentBase {

 public TempConvertComponent() {
  setRendererType(TempConvertRenderer.RENDERER_TYPE);
 }

 public static final String COMPONENT_FAMILY =
                          "components.TempConvertComponent";
 public static final String COMPONENT_TYPE =
                          "book.beans.TempConvertComponent";
 private static final String ATTR_UNITTO = "unitto";
 private static final String ATTR_UNITTO_DEFAULT = "fahrenheit";
 private static final String ATTR_TEMP = "temp";
 private static final Float ATTR_TEMP_DEFAULT = 0f;
 public String getUnitto() {
  return (String) getStateHelper().
          eval(ATTR_UNITTO, ATTR_UNITTO_DEFAULT);
 }

 public void setUnitto(String unitto) {
```

```
    getStateHelper().put(ATTR_UNITTO, unitto);
  }

  public Float getTemp() {
    return (Float) getStateHelper().eval(ATTR_TEMP, ATTR_TEMP_DEFAULT);
  }

  public void setTemp(Float temp) {
    getStateHelper().put(ATTR_TEMP, temp);
  }

  public String getTempConvert() {
    TempConvertClient tempConvertClient = new TempConvertClient();
    return String.format("%.1f", Float.valueOf(tempConvertClient.
              callTempConvertService(getUnitto(), getTemp())));
  }

  @Override
  public String getFamily() {
    return TempConvertComponent.COMPONENT_FAMILY;
  }
}
```

For step number four there is a hint in the preceding code. If you look carefully at the class constructor, you can see that the rendering tasks are delegated to an external class (renderer). This class will render a simple styled HTML `div` containing the web service response as follows:

```
@ResourceDependencies({
  @ResourceDependency(name="css/temp.css",library="default",target="head")
})
@FacesRenderer(componentFamily = TempConvertComponent.COMPONENT_
FAMILY, rendererType = TempConvertRenderer.RENDERER_TYPE)
public class TempConvertRenderer extends Renderer {

public static final String RENDERER_TYPE =
              "book.beans.TempConvertRenderer";

public TempConvertRenderer() {
}

@Override
```

```java
public void encodeEnd(FacesContext context, UIComponent uicomponent)
                                            throws IOException {

    ResponseWriter responseWriter = context.getResponseWriter();
    TempConvertComponent component = (TempConvertComponent) uicomponent;

    String unit = component.getUnitto();

    responseWriter.startElement("div", component);
    responseWriter.writeAttribute("class", "tempClass", null);
    responseWriter.writeAttribute("id", component.getClientId(), "id");
    responseWriter.write("&deg;");
    if (unit.equals("fahrenheit")) {
        responseWriter.write("F ");
    } else {
        responseWriter.write("C ");
    }
    responseWriter.write(component.getTempConvert());
    responseWriter.endElement("div");
    }
}
```

 The @ResourceDependency and @ResourceDependencies annotations are used for linked external resources (for example, JavaScript, and CSS) in custom components and renderers.

In order to register this class as a `Renderer` class, you need to annotate it with @FacesRenderer or configure it in `faces-config.xml`, as shown in the following code:

```xml
<application>
 <render-kit>
  <renderer>
   <component-family>
    components.TempConvertComponent
   </component-family>
   <renderer-type>book.beans.TempConvertRenderer</renderer-type>
   <renderer-class>book.beans.TempConvertRenderer</renderer-class>
  </renderer>
 </render-kit>
</application>
```

Another important characteristic of a `Renderer` class consists of the fact that it must define a public zero-argument constructor.

Notice that the `<renderer-type>` tag corresponds to the `renderedType` element and the `<component-family>` tag corresponds to the `componentFamily` element. Moreover, the value of `componentFamily` is the same as the value returned by the component's `getFamily` method. A `RenderKit` can provide a `Renderer` instance based on this information.

Of course, in this example you can implement the rendering process in the custom component class also, since there is no real justification for writing a separate class. Usually, you will want to write a separate renderer class when you need to support multiple client devices and you need special renderers to be registered through a `RenderKit` collection.

The following is an example of code that uses our custom component (the code is self explanatory):

```
<html xmlns="http://www.w3.org/1999/xhtml"
      xmlns:h="http://xmlns.jcp.org/jsf/html"
      xmlns:t="http://temp.converter/"
      xmlns:f="http://xmlns.jcp.org/jsf/core">
...
  <h:form>
   Convert to:
   <h:selectOneMenu value="#{tempBean.unitto}">
    <f:selectItem itemValue="fahrenheit" itemLabel="fahrenheit" />
    <f:selectItem itemValue="celsius" itemLabel="celsius" />
   </h:selectOneMenu>
   Insert value:
   <h:inputText value="#{tempBean.temp}"/>
   <h:commandButton value="Convert">
    <f:ajax execute="@form" render=":tempId" />
   </h:commandButton>
  </h:form>

  <t:temperature id="tempId"
             unitto="#{tempBean.unitto}" temp="#{tempBean.temp}" />
```

Alternatively, we can provide the conversion unit and temperature as constants (if one, or both attributes are missing, then the default value(s) will be used):

```
<t:temperature id="tempId" unitto="celsius" temp="10" />
```

The `TempBean` is just a simple backing bean, as shown in the following code:

```
@Named
@SessionScoped
public class TempBean implements Serializable {

  private String unitto = "fahrenheit";
  private Float temp = 0f;
  ...
  //getters and setters
}
```

The complete application is in the code bundle of this chapter under the name `ch10_4`. In the following screenshot, you can see the result of running this application:

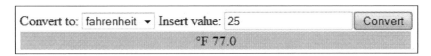

So, our custom component just renders a `div` block containing the result of the temperature conversion. Further, we want to write a custom component that, besides this `div`, will render the user interface for collecting data (conversion unit and temperature) and submit it through AJAX. In other words, the content of the preceding form will be a part of the custom component.

This time we need to deal with user inputs directly into the custom component, which means that our custom component can extend `UIInput` instead of `UIComponentBase`. This major change will bring us the advantages of an `UIInput` component. We can submit the custom component value (using the `setSubmittedValue` method during the decoding process) and obtain the resultant value (using the `getValue` method during the encoding (rendering) process).

The big problem is that our custom component value is made up of two values: the conversion unit and the temperature value. There are a few workarounds to solve this kind of issue. In this case, we can simply concatenate these values into one, such as the one shown in the following example (*conversion_unit/temperature*):

```
<t:temperature value="celsius/1" />
```

Now we can write the custom component class, as shown in the following code:

```
@FacesComponent(createTag = true, namespace = "http://temp.
converter/", tagName = "temperature")
public class TempConvertComponent extends UIInput
                                implements NamingContainer {

  public TempConvertComponent() {
    setRendererType(TempConvertRenderer.RENDERER_TYPE);
  }

  public String getTempConvert(String unitto, float temp) {
    TempConvertClient tempConvertClient = new TempConvertClient();
    return String.format("%.1f",
      tempConvertClient.callTempConvertService(unitto, temp));
  }
}
```

Notice that we don't need to specify the component family anymore and the getFamily method is inherited from the UIInput class. Going further, we need to write the renderer class.

If you want to allow the component to render itself, use setRendererType(null) and override the corresponding methods in the component class.

We need to render four HTML tags (the drop-down list, the input field, the button for submit, and the result div). For this, we can override the encodeEnd method, as shown in the following code:

```
@Override
public void encodeEnd(FacesContext context, UIComponent uicomponent)
                                                throws IOException
{

  TempConvertComponent component = (TempConvertComponent) uicomponent;

  String clientId = component.getClientId(context);
  char separator = UINamingContainer.getSeparatorChar(context);
  encodeSelectOneMenu(context,
                   component, clientId + separator + "selectonemenu");
  encodeInput(context, component, clientId + separator + "inputfield");
  encodeButton(context, component, clientId + separator + "button");
  encodeResult(context, component, clientId + separator + "div");
}
```

The identifier of each component was obtained from the client ID of the main component (using the `getClientId` method) concatenated with the char naming container separator and a string hinting the component type.

 In this example, the `NamingContainer` interface (implemented by `UINamingContainer`) is queried for obtaining the separator used to separate segments of client ID, but its main purpose is to ensure the uniqueness of the components declared within it.

Next, the method that renders the drop-down component is as follows:

```
private void encodeSelectOneMenu(FacesContext context,
TempConvertComponent component, String clientId) throws IOException {

String cv = String.valueOf(component.getValue());
String unitto = cv.substring(0, cv.indexOf("/"));

ResponseWriter responseWriter = context.getResponseWriter();
responseWriter.startElement("span", component);
responseWriter.write("Convert to:");
responseWriter.endElement("span");
responseWriter.startElement("select", component);
responseWriter.writeAttribute("name", clientId, "clientId");
responseWriter.writeAttribute("size", 1, "size");
responseWriter.startElement("option", component);
responseWriter.writeAttribute("value", "fahrenheit", "value");
if (unitto.equals("fahrenheit")) {
    responseWriter.writeAttribute("selected", "selected",
"selected");
    }
responseWriter.writeText("fahrenheit", "fahrenheit");
responseWriter.endElement("option");
responseWriter.startElement("option", component);
responseWriter.writeAttribute("value", "celsius", "value");
if (unitto.equals("celsius")) {
    responseWriter.writeAttribute("selected", "selected",
"selected");
}
responseWriter.writeText("celsius", "celsius");
responseWriter.endElement("option");
responseWriter.endElement("select");
}
```

The first two lines of this code are important where we extract the conversion unit part from the component value, and select the corresponding item in the drop-down component.

Next, we render the input field, as shown in the following code:

```
private void encodeInput(FacesContext context, TempConvertComponent
component, String clientId) throws IOException {

  String cv = String.valueOf(component.getValue());
  String temp = cv.substring(cv.indexOf("/") + 1);

  ResponseWriter responseWriter = context.getResponseWriter();
  responseWriter.startElement("span", component);
  responseWriter.write("Insert value:");
  responseWriter.endElement("span");
  responseWriter.startElement("input", component);
  responseWriter.writeAttribute("name", clientId, "clientId");
  responseWriter.writeAttribute("value", temp, "value");
  responseWriter.writeAttribute("type", "text", "type");
  responseWriter.endElement("input");
}
```

Now we will extract the temperature value from the component value. To accomplish this, we render the button labeled **Convert**, which is responsible to submit the user input via AJAX as follows:

```
private void encodeButton(FacesContext context, TempConvertComponent
component, String clientId) throws IOException {

  ResponseWriter responseWriter = context.getResponseWriter();
  responseWriter.startElement("input", component);
  responseWriter.writeAttribute("type", "Submit", null);
  responseWriter.writeAttribute("name", clientId, "clientId");
  responseWriter.writeAttribute("value", "Convert", null);
  responseWriter.writeAttribute("onclick",
    "jsf.ajax.request(this,event,{execute:'" + "@form" + "',"
+ "render:'" + "@form" + "'," + "});"
+ "return false;", null);
  responseWriter.endElement("input");
}
```

After the user inputs are submitted, we need to render the result obtained from the web service:

```
private void encodeResult(FacesContext context, TempConvertComponent
component, String clientId) throws IOException {

  String cv = String.valueOf(component.getValue());
  String unitto = cv.substring(0, cv.indexOf("/"));
  String temp = cv.substring(cv.indexOf("/") + 1);
  String result = component.getTempConvert(unitto, Float.
valueOf(temp));

  ResponseWriter responseWriter = context.getResponseWriter();
  responseWriter.startElement("div", component);
  responseWriter.writeAttribute("class", "tempClass", null);
  responseWriter.writeAttribute("name", clientId, "clientId");
  responseWriter.write("&deg;");
  if (unitto.equals("fahrenheit")) {
      responseWriter.write("F ");
  } else {
      responseWriter.write("C ");
  }
  responseWriter.write(result);
  responseWriter.endElement("div");
}
```

The backing bean, `TempBean`, is pretty simple, as shown in the following code:

```
@Named
@SessionScoped
public class TempBean implements Serializable {

  private String value = "celsius/0";

  public String getValue() {
   return value;
  }

  public void setValue(String value) {
   this.value = value;
  }
}
```

The final step involves decoding the user input and submitting it to the component, as shown in the following code:

```
@Override
public void decode(FacesContext context, UIComponent uicomponent) {

  TempConvertComponent component = (TempConvertComponent) uicomponent;
  Map requestMap = context.getExternalContext().
getRequestParameterMap();
  String clientId = component.getClientId(context);
  char separator = UINamingContainer.getSeparatorChar(context);
  String temp = ((String)
               requestMap.get(clientId+ separator + "inputfield"));
  String unitto = ((String)
               requestMap.get(clientId + separator +
"selectonemenu"));
  component.setSubmittedValue(unitto+"/"+temp);
}
```

Done! Now you can see both the tests, as shown in the following code:

```
Specified unit and temperature from bean:
<h:form id="tempForm1">
 <t:temperature id="temp1" value="#{tempBean.value}" />
 <h:message for="temp1"/>
</h:form>
<hr/>
Specified unit and temperature as constants:
<h:form id="tempForm2">
 <t:temperature id="temp2" value="celsius/1" />
 <h:message for="temp2"/>
</h:form>
```

The complete application is present in the code bundle of this chapter under the name ch10_5.

# Building composite components

Maybe the idea behind composite components originates from the fact that JSF page authors and JSF component authors have different perspectives regarding components. While JSF page authors perceive components as tags that can be used in XHTML pages, JSF component authors see components as a mixture of `UIComponent`, `UIComponentBase`, `NamingContainer`, `Renderer`, `Validator`, and `Converter` elements—these are elements that shape up a JSF component. Based on this, it seems that custom components can be written only by JSF component authors, since they have knowledge about these JSF elements and Java language. This fact, however, has begun to change as of JSF 2 and composite components, which are practically custom components written in XHTML pages using markup tags. This means that JSF page authors can start writing their components without having the same level of knowledge and skills as dedicated JSF component authors—at least, simple, composite components.

For example, the skeleton of a JSF 2.2 composite component looks as shown in the following code:

```
<?xml version='1.0' encoding='UTF-8' ?>
<!DOCTYPE html PUBLIC "-//W3C//DTD XHTML 1.0 Transitional//EN"
"http://www.w3.org/TR/xhtml1/DTD/xhtml1-transitional.dtd">
<html xmlns="http://www.w3.org/1999/xhtml"
      xmlns:cc="http://xmlns.jcp.org/jsf/composite">

 <!-- INTERFACE -->
 <cc:interface>
 </cc:interface>

 <!-- IMPLEMENTATION -->
 <cc:implementation>
 </cc:implementation>
</html>
```

The structure is pretty simple! As you can see, there are two main tags that belong to the `http://xmlns.jcp.org/jsf/composite` library. The first tag demarcates the interface section and represents the component use contract. Here, we can define the component's attributes that may be changed by the end user (in principle, anything that can be used by the page author). The second tag marks the implementation section, which contains the component itself. This will be rendered to the end user. Moreover, in this section, we define the component behavior based on the attributes defined in the interface section (the use contract implementation).

Composite components are basically XHTML pages stored in libraries under the resources folder (placed as a top-level folder under the web application root or under the META-INF folder in JARs). Remember that a library is just a subfolder of the resources folder. Based on this, a composite component path is of type http://xmlns.jcp.org/jsf/composite/*library_name*.

So, let's have a quick test. Remember that the first custom component developed in this chapter, WelcomeComponent, was built from a class annotated with @FacesComponent. In that class, we have overridden the encodeBegin method for rendering the component. Well, now let's see the same component, but this time as a composite component. We store this page under resources/customs/welcome.xhtml, as shown in the following code:

```xml
<?xml version='1.0' encoding='UTF-8' ?>
<!DOCTYPE html PUBLIC "-//W3C//DTD XHTML 1.0 Transitional//EN"
"http://www.w3.org/TR/xhtml1/DTD/xhtml1-transitional.dtd">
<html xmlns="http://www.w3.org/1999/xhtml"
      xmlns:cc="http://xmlns.jcp.org/jsf/composite">

 <!-- INTERFACE -->
 <cc:interface>
  <cc:attribute name="value"/>
  <cc:attribute name="to"/>
 </cc:interface>

 <!-- IMPLEMENTATION -->
 <cc:implementation>
  <p>#{cc.attrs.value}, #{cc.attrs.to}</p>
 </cc:implementation>
</html>
```

It is very simple to make the analogy between the custom component and the composite version of it. The important thing here is to notice how attributes were declared using the <cc:attribute> tag. Besides the name, an attribute can have a type, can be required or not, can have a default value, can target component(s), and so on (during this chapter, you will have the chance to explore different kinds of attributes). As a general rule, JSF determines if the attribute is MethodExpression (or it has a special name such as actionListener, valueChangeListener, action, and so on) or ValueExpression.

The first case is a little bit tricky; JSF will try to match the attribute with the components from the implementation based on the list of IDs defined in the `targets` attribute (the list of IDs are separated by space and relative to top-level component). If the `targets` attribute is not present, then JSF will take the value of the `name` attribute as the client ID (relative to the top-level component) and try to find the corresponding component in the implementation section. Well, in the simple case, the attribute is a `ValueExpression`, and JSF will just store the attribute in the attributes map that is accessible via `UIComponent.getAttributes`.

In the implementation section, the attributes are used via the `#{cc}` implicit object.

> It may be useful to know that JSF will implicitly create a top-level component for all the components that form a composite component. This component is the parent of all components in the page and is named `UINamingContainer` (available through the `UIComponent.getNamingContainer` method). Now the `#{cc}` implicit object actually refers to this top-level component and can be used to obtain various information, but it is especially used for obtaining the client ID (`#{cc.clientId}`) and for accessing the composite component attributes (`#{cc.attrs}`).

Now it's time to test our composite component. This is very easy—just import the composite namespace, set a prefix, and start using it, as shown in the following code:

```
<?xml version='1.0' encoding='UTF-8' ?>
<!DOCTYPE html PUBLIC "-//W3C//DTD XHTML 1.0 Transitional//EN"
"http://www.w3.org/TR/xhtml1/DTD/xhtml1-transitional.dtd">
<html xmlns="http://www.w3.org/1999/xhtml"
      xmlns:h="http://xmlns.jcp.org/jsf/html"
      xmlns:t="http://xmlns.jcp.org/jsf/composite/customs">
 <h:head>
  <title></title>
 </h:head>
 <h:body>
  <t:welcome value="Welcome" to="Rafael Nadal"/>
 </h:body>
</html>
```

Learning the techniques for writing composite components can be achieved by a lot of practice. This is why, in the upcoming sections you will see several types of composite components that explore different kinds of implementations.

The complete application is named `ch10_6`.

# Developing the Temperature composite component

Starring: backing component

Remember the Temperature custom component that we implemented in the preceding section? Well, we are sure you do. So let's see how to develop a composite component that looks and behaves the same. The composite component page can be named `temperature.xhtml`, and we can store it in the `temperature` folder under the `resources` folder. First, let's see it in the following code; afterwards we can dissect it:

```
<?xml version='1.0' encoding='UTF-8' ?>
<!DOCTYPE html PUBLIC "-//W3C//DTD XHTML 1.0 Transitional//EN"
"http://www.w3.org/TR/xhtml1/DTD/xhtml1-transitional.dtd">
<html xmlns="http://www.w3.org/1999/xhtml"
      xmlns:cc="http://xmlns.jcp.org/jsf/composite"
      xmlns:h="http://xmlns.jcp.org/jsf/html"
      xmlns:f="http://xmlns.jcp.org/jsf/core">

<!-- INTERFACE -->
<cc:interface componentType="book.beans.TempConvertComponent">
 <cc:attribute name="value" type="java.lang.String"
                                          default="celsius/0"/>
</cc:interface>

<!-- IMPLEMENTATION -->
<cc:implementation>
 <h:outputStylesheet name="temperature/temp.css" />
 <div id="#{cc.clientId}">
  <h:outputLabel for="selectonemenu" value="Convert to:"/>
  <h:selectOneMenu id="selectonemenu" binding="#{cc.unittoI}">
   <f:selectItem itemValue="fahrenheit" itemLabel="fahrenheit" />
   <f:selectItem itemValue="celsius" itemLabel="celsius" />
  </h:selectOneMenu>
  <h:outputLabel for="inputfield" value="Insert value:"/>
  <h:inputText id="inputfield" binding="#{cc.temptI}"/>
  <h:commandButton id="button" value="Convert">
   <f:ajax execute="@form" render="@form"/>
  </h:commandButton>
  <h:panelGroup id="div" layout="block" class="tempClass">
```

```
    <h:outputText value="&deg; #{cc.unittoI.value eq
      'fahrenheit' ? 'F ': 'C ' } #{cc.getTempConvert()}"/>
   </h:panelGroup>
  </div>
 </cc:implementation>
</html>
```

In the interface section, we have defined the attribute named `value`, which is specific to an `UIInput` component. Further, we indicate that the accepted value is of type `String` and the default value, applicable when the attribute is missing, is `celsius/0`. Usually, the `type` attribute is used to link the element(s) to the bean's properties (for its value, use the fully qualified name, as shown in the preceding code).

The implementation section is more interesting, because here we need to define the subcomponents of our component: the drop-down menu, the input field, the submit button, and the result div (notice that JSF generates an HTML `<div>` from `<h:panelGroup layout="block"/>`). When your composite component contains multiple components, it is a good practice to place them inside a `<div>` or a `<span>` tag with the ID set to `#{cc.clientId}`. This ID is the client identifier of the composite itself and is useful when the page author needs to refer to the entire composite component via a simple ID.

External resources, such as CSS and JS, don't need any special treatment. You can place them under the same library with composite components or under any other library, and you can load them using `<h:outputScript>` and `<h:outputStylesheet>`.

After a quick look, an obvious question arises: where is the implementation of the `getTempConvert` method and the backing beans properties used for linking these components according to the `binding` attribute? Well, all these are in a Java class, known as **backing component** (do not confuse this with the backing bean!). Yes, I know that earlier I said composite components don't need Java code, but sometimes they do, like in this case, where we need to write the code for calling the web service! In order to write a backing component, you need to keep in mind the following steps:

1. Annotate the backing component with `@FacesComponent`

2. Extend `UINamingContainer` or implement `NamingContainer` and override the `getFamily` method as follows:

   ```
   @Override
   public String getFamily() {
     return UINamingContainer.COMPONENT_FAMILY;
   }
   ```

3. Link the composite component with the backing component by adding the `componentType` attribute to the `<cc:interface>` tag. The value of this attribute is the component-type (this tells JSF to create an instance of the class indicated here):

```
@FacesComponent(value = "component type value")
...
<cc:interface componentType="component type value">
```

 A backing component can define getters for exposing its properties via the `#{cc}` implicit object (`#{cc}` has access to action methods also). On the other hand, the `<cc:attribute>` attributes are available in a backing component via the `UIComponent.getAttributes` method.

Keeping these in mind, the backing component for our composite component is as follows:

```
@FacesComponent(value = "book.beans.TempConvertComponent",
                                         createTag = false)
public class TempConvertComponent extends UIInput implements
NamingContainer {

  private UIInput unittoI;
  private UIInput temptI;

  public TempConvertComponent() {
  }

  public UIInput getUnittoI() {
   return unittoI;
  }

  public void setUnittoI(UIInput unittoI) {
   this.unittoI = unittoI;
  }

  public UIInput getTemptI() {
   return temptI;
  }

  public void setTemptI(UIInput temptI) {
   this.temptI = temptI;
  }

  public String getTempConvert() {
```

```
    TempConvertClient tempConvertClient = new TempConvertClient();
    return String.format("%.1f",
    tempConvertClient.callTempConvertService(String.valueOf(unittoI.
    getValue()), Float.valueOf(String.valueOf(temptI.getValue()))));
}


  @Override
  public void decode(FacesContext context) {
    this.setSubmittedValue(temptI.getSubmittedValue() + "/" +
                                   unittoI.getSubmittedValue());

  }

  /*
   * you can override getSubmittedValue instead of decode
  @Override
  public Object getSubmittedValue() {
    return temptI.getSubmittedValue() + "/" + unittoI.
getSubmittedValue();
  }
  */


  @Override
  public void encodeBegin(FacesContext context) throws IOException {

    if (getValue() != null) {
        String cv = String.valueOf(getValue());
        String unitto = cv.substring(0, cv.indexOf("/"));
        String temp = cv.substring(cv.indexOf("/") + 1);
        if (temptI.getValue() == null) {
            temptI.setValue(temp);
        }
        if (unittoI.getValue() == null) {
            unittoI.setValue(unitto);
        }
    }
    super.encodeBegin(context);
  }

  @Override
  public String getFamily() {
    return UINamingContainer.COMPONENT_FAMILY;
  }
}
```

The story of our backing component is pretty clear. In the `encodeBegin` method, we ensure that the component value is parsed and each subcomponent (the dropdown and the input field) received the correct part of the value. When the user submits the data, we deal with it in the `encode` method, where we take the value of the dropdown and of the input field and build a string of type *conversion_unit/temperature*. This becomes the submitted value.

This is a good time to point out how JSF chooses the top-level component. JSF tries to do the following:

- Locate the `componentType` attribute in the `<cc:interface>` tag. If it is present, then the backing component is instantiated and used as a top-level component. This is the case with the Temperature composite component.

- Locate a `UIComponent` implementation that fits the composite component page. This can be a Groovy script with the same name and location as the composite component page (of course, with the `.groovy` extension).

- Locate a Java class named *component_library_name.composite_component_page_name* and instantiate it as a top-level component. This approach spears us to use `@FacesComponent`.

- Generate a component with the component type `javax.faces.NamingContainer`.

The complete application is named `ch10_8`. Based on the knowledge introduced through this didactical example, you can check out another example, named Timezone, as shown in the following screenshot. The complete application is named `ch10_25`.

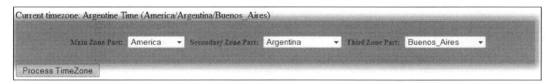

# Transforming a jQuery component into composite component

Starring: JavaScript closures

The jQuery UI is a great collection of user interface interactions, effects, widgets, and themes built on top of the jQuery JavaScript library. In this section, you will see how to expose a jQuery component as a JSF composite component. More precisely, we will transform the jQuery range slider (`https://jqueryui.com/slider/#range`), as shown in the following screenshot:

**Ranged Slider**

Range Value: 90 - 290

The main code behind this component is listed as follows:

```html
<!doctype html>
<html lang="en-US">
 <head>
  <meta charset="utf-8">
  <title>Range Slider with jQuery UI</title>
  <link rel="stylesheet" type="text/css" media="all"
                                      href="css/styles.css">
  <link rel="stylesheet" type="text/css" media="all" href="https://
ajax.googleapis.com/ajax/libs/jqueryui/1.8.16/themes/base/jquery-ui.
css">
  <script type="text/javascript" src="https://ajax.googleapis.com/
ajax/libs/jquery/1.9.1/jquery.min.js"></script>
  <script type="text/javascript" src="https://ajax.googleapis.com/
ajax/libs/jqueryui/1.10.3/jquery-ui.min.js"></script>
 </head>

 <body>
  <div id="w">
   <div id="content">
    <h2>Ranged Slider</h2>
    <div id="rangedval">
     Range Value: <span id="rangeval">90 - 290</span>
    </div>
    <div id="rangeslider"></div>
   </div>
  </div>
  <script type="text/javascript">
  $(function(){
  $('#rangeslider').slider({
    range: true,
    min: 0,
    max: 100,
    values: [ 5, 20 ],
    slide: function( event, ui ) {
     $('#rangeval').html(ui.values[0]+" - "+ui.values[1]);
    }
```

```
        });
      });
    </script>
  </body>
</html>
```

The JSF composite component should look like the following code (the important part is highlighted):

```
<h:form id="sliderFormId">
 <h:panelGrid columns="1">
  <t:range-slider id="sliderId" min="#{sliderBean.min}"
         max="#{sliderBean.max}" leftside="#{sliderBean.leftside}"
         rightside="#{sliderBean.rightside}"/>
  <h:commandButton value="Send" action="#{sliderBean.
sliderListener()}">
    <f:ajax execute="@form" render="@form"/>
  </h:commandButton>
 </h:panelGrid>
</h:form>
```

We can start by defining the composite component attributes. These will allow the end user to set the minimum (`min` attribute), maximum (`max` attribute) and the initial range (`leftside` and `rightside` attributes). These attributes will be declared in the interface section, as shown in the following code:

```
<!-- INTERFACE -->
<cc:interface>
 <cc:attribute name="min" type="java.lang.Integer"
                      default="0" required="true"/>
 <cc:attribute name="max" type="java.lang.Integer"
                      default="1000" required="true"/>
 <cc:attribute name="leftside" type="java.lang.Integer"
                      default="450" required="true"/>
 <cc:attribute name="rightside" type="java.lang.Integer"
                      default="550" required="true"/>
</cc:interface>
```

The implementation section can be divided into three logical parts. In the first part we define the external resources (CSS and JS files). Notice that `<h:outputScript>` and `<h:outputStylesheet>` cannot load such resources for an absolute URL (`http://...`), so you need to have these resources on your local machine:

```
<!-- IMPLEMENTATION -->
<cc:implementation>
 <h:outputStylesheet name="range-slider/css/styles.css"/>
```

```
<h:outputStylesheet name="range-slider/css/jquery-ui.css"/>
<h:outputScript target="head" name="range-slider/js/jquery.min.js"/>
<h:outputScript target="head" name="range-slider/js/jquery-ui.min.
js"/>
...
```

In the second part, we render the divs that expose the range slider. For this, we follow the exact model of the original component, but we add our attributes, `leftside` and `rightside`, as shown in the following code:

```
<div id="#{cc.clientId}:w" class="w">
  <div id="#{cc.clientId}:content" class="content">
    <div id="#{cc.clientId}:rangedval" class="rangedval">
     Range Value: <span id="#{cc.clientId}:rangeval">
                   #{cc.attrs.leftside} - #{cc.attrs.rightside}</span>
    </div>
    <div id="#{cc.clientId}:slider">
    </div>
  </div>
  <h:inputHidden id="leftsideId" value="#{cc.attrs.leftside}"/>
  <h:inputHidden id="rightsideId" value="#{cc.attrs.rightside}"/>
</div>
```

While the `min` and `max` attributes can be set to certain values, we are especially interested in the `leftside` and `rightside` attributes, which should be treated as the end user inputs. For this, we have added two hidden fields (one for `leftside` and one for `rightside`) that can easily transport this information to the server.

In the third part, we need to adapt the JavaScript code, which represents the component engine. This code has to be correctly generated when multiple range sliders are added in the same page, so we need to modify it as follows to fit the correct IDs and attribute values:

```
<script type="text/javascript">
$(function() {
  var rangeval = "${cc.clientId}:rangeval".replace(/:/g, "\\:");
  var slider = "${cc.clientId}:slider".replace(/:/g, "\\:");
  $('#' + slider).slider({
    range: true,
    min: #{cc.attrs.min},
    max: #{cc.attrs.max},
    values: [#{cc.attrs.leftside}, #{cc.attrs.rightside}],
    slide: function(event, ui) {
    $('#' + rangeval).html(ui.values[0] + " - " + ui.values[1]);
    $("#${cc.clientId}:leftsideId".
        replace(/:/g, "\\:")).val(ui.values[0]);
```

```
    $("#${cc.clientId}:rightsideId".
        replace(/:/g, "\\:")).val(ui.values[1]);
    }
  });
  });
</script>
</cc:implementation>
```

A common issue of combining JSF and jQuery involves using the colon (:). While JSF uses it as a separator of ID segments, the jQuery selector has other jobs for it. In order to work in jQuery, we need to escape the colon. This can be easily accomplished if you use a PrimeFaces method, as shown in the following code:

```
escadpeClientId:function(a){return"#"+a.
replace(/:/g,"\\:")}
```

Done! Now you can test the composite component in your page. The complete application is named `ch10_11`.

Well, if you add multiple range sliders in the page, you will see that the preceding JavaScript code will be generated and added each time. The size of this code is insignificant, and the chances that you'll need multiple range sliders in the same page are pretty small, so it will not be a big issue. But, when such an issue arises, you need to know that there are a few workarounds for it.

For example, we can take out JavaScript from the composite component and place it into the page, or as a component should be self contained it would be better to place the code in a separate JavaScript file and reference it in the composite component with `<h:outputScript>`. After that, we parameterize the JavaScript code with the desired attributes, and call it from the composite component. So, the parameterized version might look like the following code (place this in a file named `slider.js`):

```
var rangeslider = {
init: function(clientId, min, max, leftside, rightside) {
var rangeval = (clientId + ":rangeval").replace(/:/g, "\\:");
var slider = (clientId + ":slider").replace(/:/g, "\\:");
 $('#' + slider).slider({
   range: true,
   min: min,
   max: max,
   values: [parseInt(leftside), parseInt(rightside)],
   slide: function(event, ui) {
```

```
    $('#' + rangeval).html(ui.values[0] + " - " + ui.values[1]);
    $("#" + (clientId + ":leftsideId").
            replace(/:/g, "\\:")).val(ui.values[0]);
    $("#" + (clientId + ":rightsideId").
            replace(/:/g, "\\:")).val(ui.values[1]);
    }
   });
  }
 };
```

Further, we adapt the composite component implementation section for calling the following reusable JavaScript code:

```
<cc:implementation>
 . . .
 <h:outputScript target="head" name="range-slider/js/slider.js"/>
 . . .
 <script>
  rangeslider.init('#{cc.clientId}', '#{cc.attrs.min}',
   '#{cc.attrs.max}', '#{cc.attrs.leftside}', '#{cc.attrs.
rightside}');
 </script>
</cc:implementation>
```

Probably you already know that you just saw a technique of JavaScript closures. The idea is to speculate the fact that JavaScript is a dynamic language that lets us modify the DOM at runtime. Using the JSF client identifier and this JavaScript capability can help us to solve the issue of repeating code for multiple components. Sometimes, a good practice is to place the entire composite component inside a `div` element whose ID is the JSF client identifier. Moreover, you can identify and manage each `div` content directly from JavaScript.

The complete application for this example is named `ch10_9`. If you want to place the JavaScript code directly into the page, check the application named `ch10_26`. Besides this application, another complete example of using JavaScript closures is named `ch10_7`. In this example, a composite component encapsulates an HTML5 SSE (Server-sent Events) example. For those who are not familiar with SSE, a good starting point is the tutorial at `http://www.html5rocks.com/en/tutorials/eventsource/basics/`.

# Writing the HTML5 date picker as a composite component

Starring: `<cc:clientBehavior>` and `<cc:insertChildren />`

In this section, you will see how to transform the HTML5 date picker component into a composite component. There are a few attributes that allow us to customize the native date picker component. The following is a list of three examples:

- The code for the simplest case is as follows:

```
<input id="exId" type="date" value="" />
```

- The code for the constrained date picker is as follows:

```
<input id="exId" type="date" value="2015-01-05"
              min="2015-01-01" max="2015-01-31" />
```

- The code for the date picker with data list is as follows:

```
<input id="exId" type="date" value="" list="listId" />
<datalist id="listId">
 <option label="Day 1" value="2015-01-01"/>
 <option label="Day 2" value="2015-01-02" />
 <option label="Day 3" value="2015-01-03" />
</datalist>
```

Our composite component should reflect these forms, so it might look like the following code:

```
Date-time without data-list:
<h:form>
 <t:datetime value="#{dateTimeBean.date}"
             min="#{dateTimeBean.min}" max="#{dateTimeBean.max}">
  <f:ajax event="change" execute="@form"
                          listener="#{dateTimeBean.selectedDate()}"/>
 </t:datetime>
</h:form>
```

Alternatively, use a data list, as shown in the following code:

```
Date-time with data-list:
<h:form>
 <t:datetime list="listId" value="#{dateTimeBean.date}">
 <f:ajax event="change" execute="@form"
                 listener="#{dateTimeBean.selectedDate()}"/>
</t:datetime>
<t:datalist id="listId">
```

```
<t:option label="Day 1" value="2015-01-01"/>
<t:option label="Day 2" value="2015-01-02"/>
<t:option label="Day 3" value="2015-01-03"/>
</t:datalist>
```

So, let's focus on the interface definition. First, we have a set of attributes that are very easy to define, such as value, list, step, required, and readonly:

```
<cc:attribute name="value" type="java.util.Date" required="true" />
<cc:attribute name="list" type="java.lang.String" default="" />
<cc:attribute name="step" type="java.lang.String" default="1" />
<cc:attribute name="required" type="java.lang.String"
  default="false" />
<cc:attribute name="readonly" type="java.lang.String"
  default="false" />
```

This was easy! Now we need to take a closer look at the min and max attributes, which delimitate the range of selection. Practically, they are just some dates, but NOT instances of java.util.Date, because their format is specific to HTML 5 (y-m-d), not to Java. This means that we need some Java code for accomplishing the conversion from Java date format to HTML5 date format. We need a backing component to do this (notice that we can't use any converter here):

```
@FacesComponent(value = "datetime")
public class DateTimeComponent extends UINamingContainer {

  private static final DateTimeFormatter HTML5_FORMAT =
                DateTimeFormat.forPattern("yyyy-MM-dd");
  private String minHTML5Date = "";
  private String maxHTML5Date = "";

  public String getMinHTML5Date() {
   return minHTML5Date;
  }

  public String getMaxHTML5Date() {
   return maxHTML5Date;
  }

  @Override
  public void encodeBegin(FacesContext context) throws IOException {

   Date min = (Date) getAttributes().get("min");
   if (min != null) {
       DateTime minDateTime = new DateTime(min);
       minHTML5Date = HTML5_FORMAT.print(minDateTime);
```

```
      }
    Date max = (Date) getAttributes().get("max");
    if (max != null) {
        DateTime maxDateTime = new DateTime(max);
        maxHTML5Date = HTML5_FORMAT.print(maxDateTime);
    }
    super.encodeBegin(context);
  }
}
```

Of course, we don't forget to indicate the backing component in the interface and the restriction selection attributes, which can now be declared as `java.util.Date`, as shown in the following code:

```
<cc:interface componentType="datetime">
 <cc:attribute name="min" type="java.util.Date" />
 <cc:attribute name="max" type="java.util.Date" />
...
```

We need to do one more thing in the interface. When the end user selects a date, we want it to be submitted via AJAX to a backing bean. For this, we need to allow him/her to attach a client behavior (we spoke about client behavior several times in this book, but a perfect tutorial can be found at DZone, http://java. dzone.com/articles/jsf-2-client-behaviors), and for this we need the `<cc:clientBehavior>` tag, as shown in the following code. The `name` attribute contains the name of the event that will listen (for example, `change` here) and the `targets` attribute indicates the component(s) from the implementation, which will support the declared JavaScript event via the `event` attribute (do not use the prefix on for JavaScript events).

```
<cc:clientBehavior name="change" targets="#{cc.id}" event="change" />
```

So far, the interface is ready! Going further, we need an implementation. This is pretty simple and is based on JSF 2.2 pass-through elements, as shown in the following code:

```
<cc:implementation>
 <div id="#{cc.clientId}:dt">
  <input jsf:id="#{cc.id}" type="date" jsf:value="#{cc.attrs.value}"
        jsf:readonly="#{cc.attrs.readonly != 'false' ? 'true':
'false'}"
        min="#{cc.minHTML5Date}" max="#{cc.maxHTML5Date}"
        jsf:required="#{cc.attrs.required != 'false' ? 'true':
'false'}"
        step="#{cc.attrs.step}" list="#{cc.attrs.list}">
  <f:convertDateTime pattern="yyyy-MM-dd" />
```

```
      </input>
    </div>
  </cc:implementation>
```

In order to have an easy way to reference `<datalist>`, we used `#{cc.id}`. If the component is used multiple times in a page, then you have to specify a unique ID for each use. Nevertheless, if you need a clean solution that avoids nonunique IDs in the rendered XHTML document, you might require some additional ID resolving to be done (with JavaScript or in a backing component for instance).

At this moment, we can use our composite component, except the data list (see the preceding HTML5 `<datalist>`). For this, we need to write two more composite components. As you can see, a data list is just a set of several options (items) and each option has two attributes, named `label` and `value`. So, we can easily encapsulate an option in a composite component, as shown in the following code:

```
<!-- INTERFACE -->
<cc:interface>
 <cc:attribute name="label" type="java.lang.String" default="" />
 <cc:attribute name="value" type="java.lang.String" default="" />
</cc:interface>

<!-- IMPLEMENTATION -->
<cc:implementation>
 <option value="#{cc.attrs.value}" label="#{cc.attrs.label}" />
</cc:implementation>
```

Now we need to nest several options in `<datalist>`, but this is inappropriate here, because the number of options is indeterminate. Fortunately, for these kinds of situations, JSF provides the `<cc:insertChildren>` tag, which is used to insert the child component within a parent component (the child components will be automatically re-parented by JSF). Knowing this, we can write the following composite component for `<datalist>`:

```
<!-- INTERFACE -->
<cc:interface>
</cc:interface>

<!-- IMPLEMENTATION -->
<cc:implementation>
 <datalist id="#{cc.id}">
  <cc:insertChildren />
 </datalist>
</cc:implementation>
```

Use the `<datalist>` tag only in `<cc:implementation>` and be careful to avoid duplicate ID errors. In order to avoid this, it is recommended that you use this tag only once. To find out the number of children, use `#{cc.childCount}`.

Done! Now you can try to test the complete application named `ch10_12`.

 For the sake of completeness, you can treat the case when the browser doesn't support HTML5 by getting back to the jQuery UI version of this component. This can be accomplished via the Modernizr library (`http://modernizr.com/`), which is able to detect this kind of issue. From our point of view, such browsers will be obsolete in the future, so we don't think the effort to add this check and fallback is justified.

# Decorating an image with actions

Starring: `<cc:actionSource>`, Java `enum` types

Composite components are amazing because they can transform simple things into a real powerful component. For example, in this section we will decorate a simple image to become a composite component with AJAX and action capabilities by adding action and action listener support. Moreover, we will force the page author to use only a range of values for a certain attribute.

First, we take care of the interface section, and we can start by declaring an attribute that represents the image location, as shown in the following code:

```
<cc:attribute name="src" required="true"/>
```

After this quick warm up, we can declare the `action` attribute. The page author will use this attribute to indicate an `action` method of a backing bean. Notice that the `action` method signature must be declared here, as shown in the following code:

```
<cc:attribute name="action" method-signature="void action()"/>
```

When you write a method signature, you need to indicate the return type (`void` in this case), the method name and the argument types. For example, an `action` method that returns `String` and gets two `Integer` arguments will be declared as follows:

```
method-signature="java.lang.String
myMethod(java.lang.Integer, java.lang.Integer)"
```

Furthermore, we add support for the `<f:actionListener>` tag. For this, we use the `<cc:actionSource>` tag as follows:

```
<cc:actionSource name="imgActionListener" targets="#{cc.
clientId}:imgForm:imgAction"/>
```

The value of the `name` attribute will be used by the page authors as the value for the `<f:actionListener>` `for` attribute. The `targets` attribute points the component(s) from the implementation section, which receives this capability.

 The `<cc:actionSource>` tag specifies the implementation of `ActionSource2`.

Next, we declare a client behavior using the `<cc:clientBehavior>` tag as follows:

```
<cc:attribute name="item" targets="#{cc.clientId}:
    imgForm:imgAction" required="true"/>
```

As the final touch, we add an attribute that will accept only a range of values, as shown in the following code:

```
<cc:attribute name="item" targets="#{cc.clientId}:
    imgForm:imgAction" required="true"/>
```

The interface section is ready, so let's focus on the implementation section. For a better understanding, let's have a look at it as follows:

```
<cc:implementation>
 <h:outputStylesheet library="default" name="css/styles.css" />
 <ui:param name="range" value="#{cc.attrs.item}" /> <!-- or c:set -->
 <ui:fragment rendered="#{range == 'item_1' or
                          range == 'item_2' or range == 'item_3'}">
  <div id="#{cc.clientId}:img">
   <h:form id="imgForm">
    <h:commandLink id="imgAction" immediate="true"
       action="#{cc.attrs.action}" styleClass="linkopacity">
     <h:inputHidden id="itemId" value="#{cc.attrs.item}"/>
     <h:graphicImage value="#{cc.attrs.src}"/>
    </h:commandLink>
   </h:form>
  </div>
 </ui:fragment>
</cc:implementation>
```

There are a few interesting points here! Let's dissect the code from the inside to the outside in the following points:

- First, the image is loaded in JSF classic style through the `<h:graphicImage>` tag. Nothing fancy here!

- The `<h:graphicImage>` tag is nested in a `<h:commandLink>` tag, which supports action and action listener capabilities. Notice that this component is targeted from the interface section. Moreover, we nest a hidden field here (`<h:inputHidden>`) that associates (holds) a value with our image. This value comes from a range of allowed values via the `item` attribute.

- The `<h:commandLink>` tag is nested in a `<h:form>` tag and everything is added into a `<div>` tag. Notice that, usually, it is not a good practice to add `<h:form>` in a composite component, since the page author may want to use the composite component in his/her `<h:form>`. This will lead to nested forms, which leads to invalid HTML code.

- In order to restrict an attribute value to a range of values, you may think of using Java enum types. The problem is that you cannot do that in the interface section, but you can add a check in the implementation section. For example, we choose not to render the composite component when the value of the `item` attribute is different from `item_1`, `item_2`, and `item_3`.

The composite component is ready for testing. A perfect example can be seen in the code bundle of this chapter under the name `ch10_18`. Based on the same principle, we have written another example under the name `ch10_13`.

# Working with composite facets

Starring: `<cc:facet>`, `<cc:renderFacet>`, and `<cc:insertFacet>`

A composite component contains the facets definition in the interface section. For this, we need to use the `<cc:facet>` tag and to specify at least the facet name through the `name` attribute, as shown in the following code:

```
<cc:facet name="name" />
<cc:facet name="surname" />
```

Once the facets are declared in the interface section, they can be used in the implementation section via the `<cc:renderFacet>` tag. For this tag, we need to specify which facet to be rendered, by setting the value of the `name` attribute in agreement with the corresponding facet defined in the interface section, as shown in the following code:

```
<cc:renderFacet name="name" required="true"/>
<cc:renderFacet name="surname" required="true"/>
```

That's all! You can see a complete example in the code bundle of this chapter under the name ch10_14.

Besides `<cc:renderFacet>`, a composite component supports the `<cc:insertFacet>` tag. Now things become more interesting, because a common question is, what is the difference between them? The best answer will come from an example. Let's take a simple composite component that uses `<cc:renderFacet>`, as shown in the following code:

```
<!-- INTERFACE -->
<cc:interface>
 <cc:facet name="header" />
</cc:interface>

<!-- IMPLEMENTATION -->
<cc:implementation>
 <cc:renderFacet name="header"/>
 <!-- this will not render -->
 <!-- <cc:insertFacet name="header"/> -->
</cc:implementation>
```

This will render correctly through the following usage:

```
...
xmlns:q="http://xmlns.jcp.org/jsf/composite/renderfacet"
...
<q:renderfacet>
 <f:facet name="header">
  Render Facet
 </f:facet>
</q:renderfacet>
```

However, replacing `<cc:renderFacet>` with `<cc:insertFacet>` will not work. Nothing will be rendered.

Now let's take a look at the following composite component that uses `<cc:insertFacet>`:

```
<!-- INTERFACE -->
<cc:interface>
 <cc:facet name="header" />
</cc:interface>

<!-- IMPLEMENTATION -->
<cc:implementation>
 <h:dataTable border="1">
```

```
  <cc:insertFacet name="header"/>
  <!-- this will not render -->
  <!-- <cc:renderFacet name="header"/> -->
</h:dataTable>
</cc:implementation>
```

The following code snippet will render the desired result:

```
<t:insertfacet>
 <f:facet name="header">
  Insert Facet
 </f:facet>
</t:insertfacet>
```

But again, replacing `<cc:insertFacet>` with `<cc:renderFacet>` will not work. Nothing will be rendered.

So, we can conclude that `<cc:renderFacet>` is useful for rendering facets as child components of the composite component. This means that `<cc:renderFacet>` allows us to render facets when the parent component doesn't support facets; the facet name can be any accepted string. On the other hand, `<cc:insertFacet>` allows us to render facets only in components that support facets. Here, the facet name must exist in the facet map of the top-level component. The facet is inserted as a facet child of the component in which this element is nested.

The complete application is named `ch10_17`.

# Validating/converting inputs inside composite components

Starring: `<cc:editableValueHolder>`

Let's take a quick look at a simple composite component in the following code, especially at the highlighted parts:

```
<!-- INTERFACE -->
<cc:interface>
 <cc:attribute name="name" type="java.lang.String" required="true"/>
 <cc:attribute name="surname" type="java.lang.String"
  required="true" />
 <cc:editableValueHolder name="playerId" targets="nameId surnameId"/>
 <cc:attribute name="action"
```

```
                    method-signature="void action()" required="true" />
</cc:interface>

<!-- IMPLEMENTATION -->
<cc:implementation>
 <h:messages/>
 <h:outputLabel for="nameId" value="Player Name:"/>
 <h:inputText id="nameId" value="#{cc.attrs.name}" />
 <h:outputLabel for="surnameId" value="Player Surname:"/>
 <h:inputText id="surnameId" value="#{cc.attrs.surname}" />
 <h:commandButton id="button" value="Submit" action="#{cc.attrs.
action}">
  <f:ajax execute="@form" render="@form"/>
 </h:commandButton>
</cc:implementation>
```

Now we write a page that uses this component and attaches a custom converter and a custom validator to it as follows:

```
<h:form id="playerFormId">
 <t:player name="#{playerBean.name}" surname="#{playerBean.surname}"
           action="#{playerBean.playerAction()}">
  <f:converter converterId="playerConverter" for="playerId"/>
  <f:validator validatorId="playerValidator" for="playerId"/>
 </t:player>
</h:form>
```

Everything works as expected, thanks to `<cc:editableValueHolder>`. In this case, this tag tells JSF that any converter/validator that has the value of the `for` attribute equal to `playerId` should be applied to the targeted components, `nameId` and `surnameId`. Generally speaking, `< cc:editableValueHolder>` indicates the components that implement `EditableValueHolder`, so any attached objects suitable for implementations of `EditableValueHolder` may be attached to the composite component.

The complete application is named `ch10_10`.

As you know, `EditableValueHolder` is an extension of `ValueHolder`. Besides `<cc:editableValueHolder>`, JSF defines a tag named `<cc:valueHolder>`, which indicates the components that implement `ValueHolder`.

# Checking the presence of an attribute

Sometimes you need to render a composite component only if a certain attribute is present in the author page. For example, the following composite component checks for the presence of the mandatory attribute:

```
<!-- INTERFACE -->
<cc:interface>
 <cc:attribute name="value" required="true"/>
 <cc:attribute name="mandatory" type="java.lang.Boolean"/>
</cc:interface>

<!-- IMPLEMENTATION -->
<cc:implementation>
 <h:panelGroup rendered="#{not empty cc.attrs.mandatory}">
  <h:inputText value="#{cc.attrs.value}"
               required="#{cc.attrs.mandatory}"/>
 </h:panelGroup>
</cc:implementation>
```

Now the composite component will be rendered only if the mandatory attribute is present, as shown in the following code:

```
<t:attrcheck value="some_text" mandatory="false"/>
```

The complete application is named ch10_22.

# Composite components' pitfalls

In the next part of this chapter, we will discuss a few pitfalls of composite components, such as: null values within composite component attributes, hidden pass-through attributes in composite components, number of children of composite components, and rendered top-level component in <h:panelGrid>.

# Null values within a composite component's attributes

As of version 2.2, JSF can determine the right type of a composite component attributes even when that value is null. This is an issue in version 2.1.

Let's have a simple composite component, as shown in the following code:

```
<!-- INTERFACE -->
<cc:interface>
 <cc:attribute name="value"/>
 <cc:editableValueHolder name="test"/>
</cc:interface>

<!-- IMPLEMENTATION -->
<cc:implementation>
 <h:inputText id="test" value="#{cc.attrs.value}"/>
</cc:implementation>
```

Also, a simple page that uses this composite component is as follows:

```
<h:form>
 <t:nullTest value="#{dummyBean.dummy}">
  <f:validator for="test" binding="#{dummyBean.dummyValidator}"/>
 </t:nullTest>
 <h:commandButton value="Send"/>
</h:form>
```

Now if you supply a `null` value from this component, it will work correctly in JSF 2.2, but will not work in JSF 2.1. The complete example is named `ch10_19`.

# Hiding pass-through attributes in composite components

A composite component can hide pass-through attributes. For example, let's take a simple composite component as follows:

```
<!-- INTERFACE -->
<cc:interface componentType="book.beans.PtaComponent">
 <cc:attribute name="value"/>
</cc:interface>

<!-- IMPLEMENTATION -->
<cc:implementation>
 <h:inputText value="#{cc.attrs.value}"/>
</cc:implementation>
```

Next, let's use this composite component in a page by adding two pass-through attributes to it as follows:

```
<h:form>
 <t:pta value="leoprivacy@yahoo.com">
  <f:passThroughAttribute name="placeholder"
                            value="Type an e-mail address" />
  <f:passThroughAttribute name="type" value="email" />
 </t:pta>
 <h:commandButton value="Submit"/>
</h:form>
```

At this moment, if you check the list of attributes (using the `UIComponent.getAttributes` method) and the list of pass-through attributes (using the `UIComponent.getPassThroughAttributes` method), you will notice that the `placeholder` and `type` attributes are in the list of pass-through attributes. We can easily move them into the attributes list by encapsulating them into the composite component, as shown in the following code:

```
<!-- INTERFACE -->
<cc:interface componentType="book.beans.PtaComponent">
 <cc:attribute name="value"/>
 <cc:attribute name="placeholder"/>
 <cc:attribute name="type"/>
</cc:interface>

<!-- IMPLEMENTATION -->
<cc:implementation>
 <h:inputText value="#{cc.attrs.value}">
  <f:passThroughAttribute name="placeholder"
                            value="#{cc.attrs.placeholder}" />
  <f:passThroughAttribute name="type" value="#{cc.attrs.type}" />
 </h:inputText>
</cc:implementation>
```

Also, you can use the composite component in the page, as follows:

```
<h:form>
 <t:pta value="leoprivacy@yahoo.com"
        placeholder="Type an e-mail address" type="email" />
 <h:commandButton value="Submit"/>
</h:form>
```

Done! Now the `placeholder` and `type` attributes are not present in the pass-through attributes list. They were added in the attributes list returned by the `getAttributes` method.

The complete application is named `ch10_16`.

# Counting the children of a composite component

Suppose that you have a composite component that accepts children via the `<cc:insertChildren/>` tag. Sometimes you may need to render a certain message when the list of children is empty, and for this you may think of writing a composite component implementation, as shown in the following code:

```
<!-- IMPLEMENTATION -->
<cc:implementation>
 <div id="#{cc.clientId}">
  <ul>
   <cc:insertChildren/>
   <h:panelGroup rendered="#{cc.childCount == 0}">
    The list of names is empty!
   </h:panelGroup>
  </ul>
 </div>
</cc:implementation>
```

Now if the composite component is used as follows, you may think that the message **The list of names is empty!** will be rendered:

```
<t:iccc/>
```

Well, you are right! But, the same message, next to the list content, will be rendered when the component is used as follows:

```
<t:iccc>
 <li>Mike</li>
 <li>Andrew</li>
</t:iccc>
```

In order to solve this issue, you can use the following code:

```
<cc:implementation>
 <div id="#{cc.clientId}">
  <ul>
   <cc:insertChildren/>
```

```
    <c:if test="#{cc.childCount == 0}">
     The list of names is empty!
    </c:if>
   </ul>
  </div>
 </cc:implementation>
```

Done! The complete application is named `ch10_20`.

# Top-level component's pitfall

Remember that we have said earlier in this chapter that each composite component receives `UINamingContainer` as the top-level component. Well, it is important to not forget this when you define a composite component, as shown in the following code:

```
<!-- INTERFACE -->
<cc:interface>
 <cc:attribute name="labelvalue"/>
 <cc:attribute name="imgvalue"/>
</cc:interface>

<!-- IMPLEMENTATION -->
<cc:implementation>
 <h:outputLabel for="img" value="#{cc.attrs.labelvalue}"/>
 <h:graphicImage id="img" value="#{cc.attrs.imgvalue}"/>
</cc:implementation>
```

And, you try to use it, as shown in the following code:

```
<h:panelGrid columns="2" border="1">
 <t:pg labelvalue="SMILEY"
        imgvalue="#{resource['default/images:smiley.gif']}"/>
 <t:pg labelvalue="SAD SMILE"
        imgvalue="#{resource['default/images:sad_smile.gif']}"/>
</h:panelGrid>
```

If you forgot about the top-level component, you probably expect to see something like the left-hand side of the following screenshot, while in reality, you will see something like the right-hand side of the following screenshot:

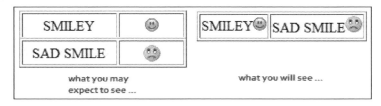

This is normal, since `<h:panelGrid>` perceives the composite component as a whole. All components that define the composite component are the children of the top-level component and are invisible to `<h:panelGrid>`.

The complete example is named `ch10_15`.

# Distributing composite components as JARs in JSF 2.2

As of JSF 2, we can add composite components in custom tag libraries (taglibs). After placing the composite component artifacts in the correct folders, we need to write a file of type (this filename should be suffixed with `taglib.xml`), as shown in the following code:

```
<facelet-taglib version="2.0">
 <namespace>http://some/namespace</namespace>
 <composite-library-name>
  library_name
 </composite-library-name>
</facelet-taglib>
```

Based on this file's content, and more precisely on `<composite-library-name>`, JSF 2 detects the composite components belonging to this library. This means that the composite components mapped in this JAR must come from this library only.

As of JSF 2.2, this restriction doesn't exist anymore, and we can add, in the same JAR, composite components that come from different libraries.

Let's see an example! Suppose that we want to add in the same JAR the Temperature component (developed in application `ch10_8`) and the Range-slider component (developed in application `ch10_11`). The JAR will be named `jsfcc.jar`. The steps for accomplishing this are as follows:

1. Create an empty JAR named `jsfcc.jar`.

2. In `jsfcc.jar`, create the folder `META-INF/resources`.

3. Copy the libraries that contain the composite components in `META-INF/resources` (copy the `resources/temperature` folder from the application `ch10_8` and `resources/range-slider` from the application `ch10_11`).

4. For the Temperature composite component, copy the classes `book.beans.TempConvertClient.class` and `book.beans.TempConvertComponent.class` under the JAR root.

5.  Create an empty `faces-config.xml` file and place it under the `META-INF` folder as follows:

```xml
<?xml version="1.0"?>
<faces-config xmlns="http://xmlns.jcp.org/xml/ns/javaee"
 xmlns:xsi="http://www.w3.org/2001/XMLSchema-instance"
        xsi:schemaLocation="http://xmlns.jcp.org/xml/ns/javaee
        http://xmlns.jcp.org/xml/ns/javaee/web-facesconfig_2_2.xsd"
        version="2.2">
</faces-config>
```

6.  Create the following `cc.taglib.xml` file and place it under the `META-INF` folder. Notice that we don't need a `<composite-library-name>` tag, and we have configured both composite components under the same namespace, `http://jsf/cc/packt/taglib`. Using this example, it is very easy to define more components as follows:

```xml
<facelet-taglib version="2.2"
      xmlns="http://xmlns.jcp.org/xml/ns/javaee"
      xmlns:xsi="http://www.w3.org/2001/XMLSchema-instance"
      xsi:schemaLocation="http://xmlns.jcp.org/xml/ns/javaeehttp://
xmlns.jcp.org/xml/ns/javaee/web-facelettaglibrary_2_2.xsd"

 <namespace>http://jsf/cc/packt/taglib</namespace>
 <tag>
  <tag-name>range-slider</tag-name>
   <component>
    <resource-id>
     resources/range-slider/range-slider.xhtml
    </resource-id>
   </component>
 </tag>
 <tag>
  <tag-name>temperature</tag-name>
   <component>
    <resource-id>
     resources/temperature/temperature.xhtml
    </resource-id>
   </component>
 </tag>
</facelet-taglib>
```

7. In the following screenshot, you can see how the JAR structure should look:

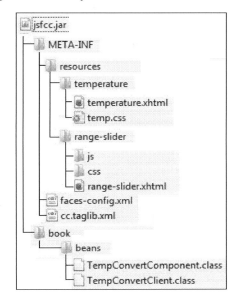

Specially for testing `jsfcc.jar`, you can run the application `ch10_21`. Notice that even if NetBeans doesn't recognize the tags of the composite components, they work like a charm.

# Adding composite components programmatically

The last section in this chapter discusses adding composite components programmatically. Before JSF 2.2, there wasn't any official API for instantiating composite components as a Java instance via user code. But, there were at least two facile options for unofficially accomplishing this:

- Using the `Components.includeCompositeComponent` method available in OmniFaces from JSF Version 1.5 onwards (`https://code.google.com/p/omnifaces/`).

- Using the `Components.includeCompositeComponent` source code as an inspiration to write your own implementation. This kind of implementation is listed in the complete application named `ch10_23`. In that application, you can see how to programmatically add in a page the Welcome and Temperature composite components (you need to pass to the `addCompositeComponent` method the following data: the composite component parent, the library name and path, and a unique ID).

As of JSF 2.2, we can use an explicit API for instantiating composite components programmatically. The core of this API is based on the new `createComponent` method added in the `ViewDeclarationLanguage` class. The signature of this method is as follows:

```
public UIComponent createComponent(FacesContext context, String
taglibURI, String tagName, Map<String,Object> attributes)
```

Besides `FacesContext`, you need to pass the tag library URI, the tag name, and the tag's attributes, or `null`, if there are no attributes. For example, the Welcome component can be added via this API as follows (we append the Welcome component to a `<h:panelGroup>` with the `welcomeId` ID):

```
public void addWelcomeCompositeComponent() {
  FacesContext context = FacesContext.getCurrentInstance();
  ViewDeclarationLanguage vdl = context.getApplication().
   getViewHandler().getViewDeclarationLanguage(context,
   context.getViewRoot().getViewId());

  Map<String, Object> attributes = new HashMap<>();
  attributes.put("value", createValueExpression("#{welcomeBean.value}",
   java.lang.String.class).getExpressionString());
  attributes.put("to", createValueExpression("#{welcomeBean.to}",
   java.lang.String.class).getExpressionString());

  UINamingContainer welcomeComponent = (UINamingContainer)
   vdl.createComponent(context, "http://xmlns.jcp.org/jsf/composite/
    customs", "welcome", attributes);
  UIComponent parent = context.getViewRoot().
findComponent("welcomeId");
  welcomeComponent.setId(parent.getClientId(context) + "_" +
"welcomeMsgId");
  parent.getChildren().add(welcomeComponent);
}
```

The complete application is named `ch10_27_1`.

A side-effect of this API includes the fact that it allows us to add regular components also. For example, you can append an `UIOutput` component to `<h:panelGroup>` with the `myPlayerId` ID, as follows:

```
public void addComponent() {
  FacesContext context = FacesContext.getCurrentInstance();
```

```
ViewDeclarationLanguage vdl = context.getApplication().
 getViewHandler().getViewDeclarationLanguage(context,
 context.getViewRoot().getViewId());

Map<String, Object> attributes = new HashMap<>();
 attributes.put("value", createValueExpression("#{playersBean.
player}", java.lang.String.class).getExpressionString());
 UIOutput outputTextComponent = (UIOutput) vdl.
createComponent(context,
   "http://java.sun.com/jsf/html", "outputText", attributes);

UIComponent parent = context.getViewRoot().
findComponent("myPlayerId");
 outputTextComponent.setId(parent.getClientId(context) +
  "_" + "nameId_"+ new Date().getTime());
 parent.getChildren().clear();
 parent.getChildren().add(outputTextComponent);
}
```

The complete application is named `ch10_27_2`. In *Chapter 12, Facelets Templating,* you can see an example of adding `<ui:include>` using this API.

# Summary

In this chapter, you saw at work one of the greatest facilities of JSF. The custom and composite components feature represents the way how JSF expresses the respect for its developers. Writing custom/composite components is definitely a mandatory test of each JSF developer, since the difference between an ordinary and an extraordinary component resides in his skills. I hope that, next to many other books and tutorials about JSF custom/composite components, you have found this chapter as an interesting dissertation about this wide topic.

As a final note of this chapter, we have to apologize to all JSP fans who felt ignored in this chapter by the fact that we did not mention anything about writing custom/composite components compatible with JSP. As you know, such components can be made compatible with JSP via tag classes (not tag handlers), but JSP was deprecated as of JSF 2. I think that this is a plausible excuse for not covering or even mentioning JSP.

See you in the next chapter, where we will explore the new JSF 2.2 themes!

# 11
# JSF 2.2 Resource Library Contracts – Themes

Starting with version 2.0, JSF developers exploit Facelets as the default **View Declaration Language (VDL)**. Facelets provide many advantages, but we are especially interested in using **Facelet templates**, which represent a mix of XHTML and other resources such as CSS, JS, and images. A Facelet template acts as a base (or a model) for the application pages. Practically, it represents a piece of reusable code that serves as a consistent and standard look and feel for the application pages. In the final chapter of this book, we will get more into the details of Facelets and templating, while in this chapter we will focus on the new JSF 2.2 feature known as **Resource Library Contracts**.

This new feature fortifies and simplifies the implementation of **themes** (such as PrimeFaces or RichFaces) by allowing us to easily decorate and use Facelet templates over the entire application in a reusable and flexible approach.

In this chapter, you will see how to do the following:

- Work with contracts
- Style the JSF tables and UI components using contracts
- Style contracts across different kinds of devices
- Write contracts for composite components
- Write a theme switcher
- Configure contracts in XML
- Package contracts in JARs

Further, keep in mind to correctly interpret the *contracts* word in the current context. It can be used to define the concepts such as the `contracts` folder, the `contracts` attribute, or the `<contracts>` tag. Sometimes, it may get confusing.

# Working with contracts

Contracts consist of templates and CSS files that are grouped under the `contracts` folder. In order to define contracts, we need to respect some conventions under the root directory of Web application. The most important conventions (for example, names, structure, and content) concern folders that are involved in the defining of contracts. All contracts are stored under a special folder—named `contracts`—placed directly under the Web root of the application, or under the `META-INF` folder that resides in a JAR file.

We can alter the location and the name of this folder via `WEBAPP_CONTRACTS_DIRECTORY_PARAM_NAME` context parameter. The value of this context parameter must not start with a slash (/), though it may contain a slash. The runtime will interpret this value as a path relative to the Web root of the application.

Commonly, under the `contracts` folder, we define a subfolder for each contract (the subfolder's name represents the contract's name), which contains the contract's artifacts such as the CSS, JS, images, and XHTML templates (you can separate resources such as CSS, JS, and images from the XHTML templates by adding them into representative subfolders).

In the following screenshot, you can see the folder structure for two contracts (`rafa1` and `rafa2`) in the same application, named `ch11_1`:

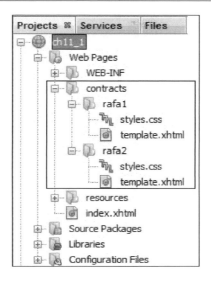

In our example, the source code for `rafa1/template.xhtml` and `rafa2/template.xhtml` is identical (of course, this is not mandatory); however, they just use different CSS files. These XHTML files serve as templates for the application pages. The listing of `rafa1/template.xhtml` is as follows:

```
<?xml version='1.0' encoding='UTF-8' ?>
<!DOCTYPE html PUBLIC "-//W3C//DTD XHTML 1.0 Transitional//EN"
   "http://www.w3.org/TR/xhtml1/DTD/xhtml1-transitional.dtd">
<html xmlns="http://www.w3.org/1999/xhtml"
  xmlns:h="http://xmlns.jcp.org/jsf/html"
  xmlns:ui="http://xmlns.jcp.org/jsf/facelets">
  <h:head>
  <title></title>
  </h:head>
  <h:body>
    <h:outputStylesheet name="styles.css"/>
    <div class="header">
      <ui:insert name="header"/>
    </div>
    <div class="content">
      <ui:insert name="content"/>
    </div>
    <div class="footer">
      <ui:insert name="footer"/>
    </div>
  </h:body>
</html>
```

Further, you can use the contracts directly in the application web pages, thanks to the new JSF 2.2 attribute of the `<f:view>` tag named `contracts` (this has to be placed in the template client). The value of this attribute should be the contract name that you want to use. For example, if you want to use the contract named `rafa2`, you can write this in the `index.xhtml` page as follows:

```
<?xml version='1.0' encoding='UTF-8' ?>
<!DOCTYPE html PUBLIC "-//W3C//DTD XHTML 1.0 Transitional//EN"
  "http://www.w3.org/TR/xhtml1/DTD/xhtml1-transitional.dtd">
<html xmlns="http://www.w3.org/1999/xhtml"
  xmlns:h="http://xmlns.jcp.org/jsf/html"
  xmlns:f="http://xmlns.jcp.org/jsf/core"
  xmlns:ui="http://xmlns.jcp.org/jsf/facelets">
  <h:head>
    <title></title>
  </h:head>
  <h:body>
    <f:view contracts="rafa2"><!-- switch to rafa1 to see
      first theme -->
    <ui:composition template="/template.xhtml">
      <ui:define name="header">
        <p>Rafael Nadal photos - header</p>
      </ui:define>
      <ui:define name="content">
        <h:graphicImage
          value="#{resource['default/images:RafaelNadal.jpg']}"/>
      </ui:define>
      <ui:define name="footer">
        <p>Rafael Nadal photos - footer</p>
      </ui:define>
    </ui:composition>
    </f:view>
  </h:body>
</html>
```

In order to use the contract named `rafa1`, you just need to specify this name as the value of the `contracts` attribute.

The complete application is named `ch11_1`.

# Styling tables with contracts

Now that you know how to write and use contracts, you can try to play around with this great feature for creating different kinds of styles/themes for your pages. Most of the time, creating cool themes involves two things: having a cool and flexible templating mechanism and having solid knowledge of CSS and JS.

For example, we can try to write two cool themes for the JSF tables. First, we'll define two contracts named `tableBlue` and `tableGreen`. The XHTML template, in both the cases, will have the following code:

```
<?xml version='1.0' encoding='UTF-8' ?>
<!DOCTYPE html PUBLIC "-//W3C//DTD XHTML 1.0 Transitional//EN"
  "http://www.w3.org/TR/xhtml1/DTD/xhtml1-transitional.dtd">
<html xmlns="http://www.w3.org/1999/xhtml"
  xmlns:h="http://xmlns.jcp.org/jsf/html"
  xmlns:ui="http://xmlns.jcp.org/jsf/facelets">
  <h:head>
    <title></title>
  </h:head>
  <h:body>
    <h:outputStylesheet name="styles.css"/>
    <div class="content">
      <ui:insert name="content"/>
    </div>
  </h:body>
</html>
```

Now, you can use the `tableBlue` or `tableGreen` contract, as shown in the following code:

```
...
  <h:body>
    <f:view contracts="tableBlue">
      <ui:composition template="/template.xhtml">
        <ui:define name="content">
          <h:dataTable value="#{playersBean.data}" var
            ="t" border="1">
            <h:column>
              <f:facet name="header">
                Ranking
              </f:facet>
```

```
        #{t.ranking}
      </h:column>
      ...
    </h:dataTable>
  </ui:define>
</ui:composition>
</f:view>
</h:body>
...
```

The result will be as shown in the following screenshot:

| Ranking | Name | Ranking | Name |
|---------|------|---------|------|
| 2 | NOVAK DJOKOVIC | 2 | NOVAK DJOKOVIC |
| 1 | RAFAEL NADAL | 1 | RAFAEL NADAL |
| 7 | TOMAS BERDYCH | 7 | TOMAS BERDYCH |

As you can see, there is no need to specify a class or a style attribute for
<h:dataTable>. The idea is pretty simple; JSF renders <h:dataTable> using HTML
tags such as <table>, <tr>, <td>, <tbody>, <thead>, and <tfoot>. So, if we write a
CSS style sheet that customizes the aspect of these HTML tags, then we will obtain
the desired results. For <h:dataTable>, a basic CSS may contain the following classes
(content matches the value of the name attribute of the <ui:define> component):

```
.content {}
.content table {}
.content table td,.content table th {}
.content table thead th {}
.content table thead th:first-child {}
.content table tbody td {}
.content table tbody .alt td {}
.content table tbody td:first-child {}
.content table tbody tr:last-child td {}
```

Sometimes, you may need to add pagination to your tables. JSF doesn't provide
attributes for this task (unlike the <p:dataTable> tag in PrimeFaces). But, as
an example, you may fix this issue if you write a footer, like the following code
snippet—of course, the <div> content should be dynamically generated and
controlled (for more details, see *Chapter 6, Working with Tabular Data*):

```
  ...
  <f:facet name="footer">
    <div id="paging">
```

```
<ul>
  <li>
    <a href="#">
      <span>Previous</span>
    </a>
  </li>
  ...
  </ul>
 </div>
 </f:facet>
</h:dataTable>
```

Now, you need to add a few CSS classes to control the pagination aspect, as follows:

```
.content table tfoot td div {}
.content table tfoot td {}
.content table tfoot td ul {}
.content table tfoot li {}
.content table tfoot li a {}
.content table tfoot ul.active,.content table tfoot ul a:hover {}
```

The result is shown in the following screenshot:

Special thanks to Eli Geske, the author of *Learning DHTMLX Suite UI* (`http://www.packtpub.com/learning-dhtmlx-suite-ui/book`). His free online CSS3 table generator (you can find HTML Table Style Generator at `http://tablestyler.com/`) was really useful to accomplish the result in this section.

The complete application is named `ch11_3`.

# Styling UI components with contracts

Based on the preceding example, we can write styles/themes for all the JSF UI components. In this section, you can see an example that focuses on JSF UI components that usually appear in forms such as `<h:inputText>`, `<h:inputTextarea>`, `<h:selectOneMenu>`, `<h:selectManyCheckbox>`, and so on. Practically, we want to obtain something like the following screenshot (this is just a sample form):

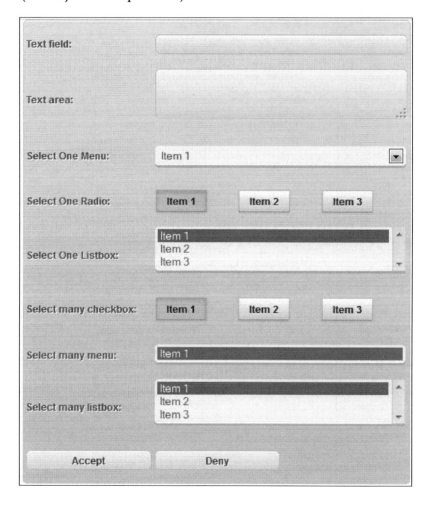

We start by defining a new contract named `jsfui`. The template is pretty simple, as follows:

```xml
<?xml version='1.0' encoding='UTF-8' ?>
<!DOCTYPE html PUBLIC "-//W3C//DTD XHTML 1.0 Transitional//EN"
  "http://www.w3.org/TR/xhtml1/DTD/xhtml1-transitional.dtd">
<html xmlns="http://www.w3.org/1999/xhtml"
  xmlns:h="http://xmlns.jcp.org/jsf/html"
  xmlns:ui="http://xmlns.jcp.org/jsf/facelets">
  <h:head>
    <title></title>
  </h:head>
  <h:body>
    <h:outputStylesheet name="styles.css"/>
    <div class="content">
      <ui:insert name="content"/>
    </div>
  </h:body>
</html>
```

Now, we just need to write the CSS classes that correspond to the HTML elements rendered by JSF, as follows:

```css
.content input[type=text] {}        /* <h:inputText> */
.content input[type=submit] {}      /* <h:commandButton> */
.content textarea {}                /* <h:inputTextarea> */
.content label {}                   /* <h:outputLabel> */
.content select {}                  /* <h:selectOneMenu>,
                                       <h:selectOneListbox>,
                                       <h:selectManyMenu>,
                                       <h:selectManyListbox> */
.content input[type=radio] {}       /* <h:selectOneRadio> */
.content input[type=checkbox] {}    /* <h:selectManyCheckbox> */
```

You can easily add CSS classes for the rest of UI components. Further, you can write JSF forms with a custom theme, just by specifying the theme name as the value of the `contracts` attribute:

```
...
<f:view contracts="jsfui">
<ui:composition template="/template.xhtml">
<ui:define name="content">
...
```

The complete application is named `ch11_2`.

# Styling contracts across different devices

In the preceding examples, we saw how to write the JSF contracts and how to use them by explicitly setting them by name in the `contracts` attribute of the `<f:view>` tag. Sometimes, you may need to dynamically set a contract (theme); for example, you may need to choose the right contract based on the device type that should display the application (PC, tablet, smartphone, mobile phone, and so on). In this case, you need to provide the `contracts` attribute value from a managed bean.

It is beyond the scope of this book to provide a powerful code (or algorithm) for detecting device types, resolutions, and so on. With minimum involvement in the mobile area, we will try to write a JSF application capable of choosing the right contract depending on the device type. Practically, we will define the following four contracts (do not consider the following associations between resolutions and devices as a certified or authorized decision):

- `contracts/browserpc`: This contract applies to PCs (it will be the default)
- `contracts/Device640`: This contract applies to tablets (we suppose that, for any kind of tablet, a resolution of 640 pixels width is a reasonable choice)
- `contracts/Device480`: This contract applies to smartphones (we suppose that, for any kind of smartphone, a resolution of 480 pixels width is a reasonable choice)
- `contracts/Device320`: This contract applies to normal mobile phones (we suppose that, for any kind of mobile phone, a resolution of 320 pixels width is a reasonable choice)

Now, we will write a simple managed bean that will detect the device type based on the helper class named `UAgentInfo` (visit `http://blog.mobileesp.com/`). Basically, this class detects different kinds of devices based on the HTTP request headers, `User-Agent` and `Accept`. Based on this detection, we can set a managed bean property with the name of the correct contract. The managed bean code is as follows:

```
@Named
@SessionScoped
public class ThemeBean implements Serializable {

  private String theme = "browserpc";

  public String getTheme() {
    return theme;
  }

  public void setTheme(String theme) {
```

```
        this.theme = theme;
    }

  publicThemeBean() {
    Map<String, String>getRequestMap
      = FacesContext.getCurrentInstance()
      .getExternalContext().getRequestHeaderMap();
    String userAgent = getRequestMap.get("User-Agent");
    String httpAccept = getRequestMap.get("Accept");

    UAgentInfo detector = new UAgentInfo(userAgent, httpAccept);

    if (detector.isMobilePhone) {
      if ((detector.detectSmartphone())) {
        System.out.println("SMARTPHONE THEME!");
        theme = "Device480";
      } else {
        System.out.println("SIMPLE MOBILE THEME!");
        theme = "Device320";
      }
    } else {
      if (detector.detectTierTablet()) {
        System.out.println("TABLET THEME!");
        theme = "Device640";
      } else {
        System.out.println("BROWSER THEME!");
        theme = "browserpc";
      }
    }
  }
}
```

Each of these contracts contains an XHTML template and a CSS file named `styles.
css`. Each CSS file contains classes for styling the output for a resolution type. The
template is the same for all contracts and is pretty simple, as follows:

```
<?xml version='1.0' encoding='UTF-8' ?>
<!DOCTYPE html PUBLIC "-//W3C//DTD XHTML 1.0 Transitional//EN"
  "http://www.w3.org/TR/xhtml1/DTD/xhtml1-transitional.dtd">
<html xmlns="http://www.w3.org/1999/xhtml"
  xmlns:h="http://xmlns.jcp.org/jsf/html"
  xmlns:ui="http://xmlns.jcp.org/jsf/facelets">
  <h:head>
    <title></title>
    <meta http-equiv="X-UA-Compatible"
      content="IE=edge,chrome=1"/>
```

```
    <meta name="HandheldFriendly" content="true"/>
    <meta name="viewport" content="width=device-width, initial-
      scale=1,maximum-scale=1,user-scalable=no"/>
  </h:head>
  <h:body>
    <h:outputStylesheet name="styles.css"/>
    <div class="content">
      <ui:insert name="content"/>
    </div>
  </h:body>
</html>
```

Let's take a simple page, as shown in the following screenshot. (The JSF code is straightforward and you can see it in the complete application named `ch11_4`.) This view is for desktop browsers.

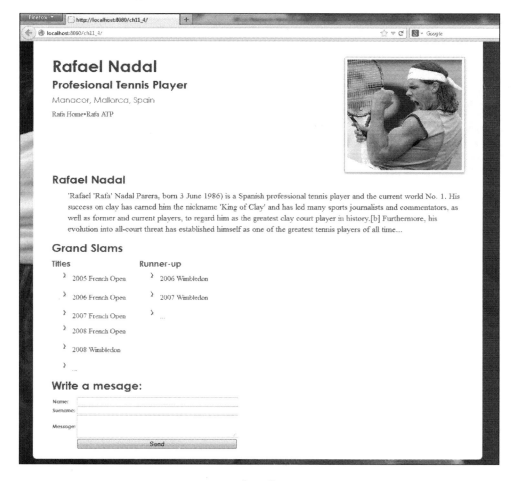

The relevant JSF code for this page consists of adding the right contract:

```
<h:body>
  <f:view contracts="#{themeBean.theme}">
  <ui:composition template="/template.xhtml">
  <ui:define name="content">
...
```

Done! Now, you can easily perform some test using a mobile emulator, such as Opera Mobile Operator. In the following screenshot, you can see the same page as that on a Samsung Galaxy Tab, at a resolution of 1024x600 (PPI: 240):

Further, the same page can be rendered for mobile phone devices: shown on the left is Motorola Atrix4G at a resolution of 540x960 (PPI: 267) and on the right is a Nokia N9 mobile phone at resolution of 320x480 (PPI: 252):

Notice that we can reduce the preceding example to a single contract and without a managed bean, by using responsive CSS. Instead of using four contracts (`browserpc`, `Device640`, `Device480`, and `Device320`), you can use a single contract; let's name it `alldevices`. We place two CSS files under the `alldevices` contract: a general CSS file (`styles.css`) and the responsive CSS file (`responsive.css`). Further, we modify the `template.xhtml` file to load both the CSS files using the following code:

```
<h:body>
  <h:outputStylesheet name="styles.css"/>
  <h:outputStylesheet name="responsive.css"/>
  ...
</h:body>
```

In the final step, we set this contract on the JSF page of the application, as follows:

```
<f:view contracts="alldevices">
  <ui:composition template="/template.xhtml">
  <ui:define name="content">
...
```

Done! The complete application is named ch11_5.

Another approach consists of writing a custom RenderKitFactory class, a custom RenderKit class and a set of custom Renderers classes—one for each device. For example, using these artifacts, the application named ch11_15 shows you how to render, for different devices, the Temperature custom component developed in *Chapter 10, JSF Custom Components*.

# Writing contracts for composite components

In this section, you will see how to write contracts for composite components. For this, we will use the Temperature composite component developed in *Chapter 10, JSF Custom Components*. The implementation section in the code is given as follows:

```
<cc:implementation>
  <div id="#{cc.clientId}:tempconv_main">
    <h:outputLabel id="tempconv_smlabel"
      for="tempconv_selectonemenu" value="Convert to:"/>
    <h:selectOneMenu id="tempconv_selectonemenu"
      binding="#{cc.unittoI}">
      <f:selectItem itemValue="fahrenheit" itemLabel
        ="fahrenheit" />
      <f:selectItem itemValue="celsius" itemLabel="celsius" />
    </h:selectOneMenu>
    <h:outputLabel id="tempconv_iflabel"
      for="tempconv_inputfield" value="Insert value:"/>
    <h:inputText id="tempconv_inputfield"
      binding="#{cc.temptI}"/>
    <h:commandButton id="tempconv_button" value="Convert">
      <f:ajax execute="@form" render="@form"/>
    </h:commandButton>
    <h:panelGroup id="tempconv_result" layout="block">
      <h:outputText value="&deg;
        #{cc.unittoI.valueeq 'fahrenheit' ? 'F ':   'C ' }
        #{cc.getTempConvert()}"/>
    </h:panelGroup>
  </div>
</cc:implementation>
```

The IDs of subcomponents are used to define the CSS file used for styling the composite component. Therefore, we need to write the following CSS classes. Notice how we exploit CSS wildcards to find the subcomponents.

```
.content {}
.content *[id*='tempconv_main'] {}
.content *[id*='tempconv_result'] {}
.content *[id*='tempconv_inputfield'] {}
.content *[id*='tempconv_button'] {}
.content *[id*='tempconv_inputfield']:hover {}
.content *[id*='tempconv_inputfield']:active {}
.content *[id*='tempconv_smlabel'] {}
.content *[id*='tempconv_iflabel'] {}
.content *[id*='tempconv_selectonemenu'] {}
```

Further, we place this CSS file under the same contract with the following XHTML template:

```
<?xml version='1.0' encoding='UTF-8' ?>
<!DOCTYPE html PUBLIC "-//W3C//DTD XHTML 1.0 Transitional//EN"
  "http://www.w3.org/TR/xhtml1/DTD/xhtml1-transitional.dtd">
<html xmlns="http://www.w3.org/1999/xhtml"
  xmlns:h="http://xmlns.jcp.org/jsf/html"
  xmlns:ui="http://xmlns.jcp.org/jsf/facelets">
  <h:head>
    <title></title>
  </h:head>
  <h:body>
    <h:outputStylesheet name="styles.css"/>
    <div class="content">
      <ui:insert name="content"/>
    </div>
  </h:body>
</html>
```

Finally, use the composite component as follows:

```
...
<f:view contracts="tempStyleGray">
  <ui:composition template="/template.xhtml">
    <ui:define name="content">
      <h3>Composite component with contract:</h3>
      <h:form id="tempForm">
       <t:temperature id="temp" value="#{tempBean.value}" />
      </h:form>
    </ui:define>
  </ui:composition>
</f:view>
...
```

Notice that we have defined two contracts: `tempStyleGray` (first bar in the following screenshot) and `tempStyleGreen` (second bar in the following screenshot):

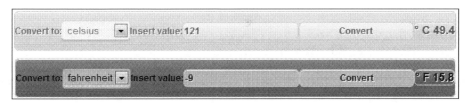

The complete application is named `ch11_6`.

# Writing a theme switcher

If you are a PrimeFaces fan, then I'm sure you have seen the PrimeFaces theme switcher. Basically, a theme switcher is represented by a drop-down menu that contains themes' names and thumbnails. End users can switch between application's themes just by selecting it from the list.

In this section, you will see how to develop a theme switcher using the JSF 2.2 contracts. The goal is to obtain a theme switcher so that:

- It can be added as a JAR in any JSF 2.2 application
- It can automatically detect and list the themes of an application
- It can give a nice look and feel, as shown in the following screenshot (shown on the left-hand side is the PrimeFaces theme switcher, and on the right-hand side is our theme switcher)

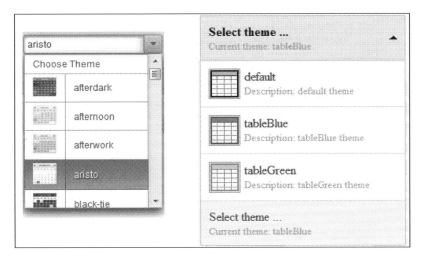

Obviously, this kind of a drop-down menu cannot be generated using the built-in `<h:selectOneMenu>` tag. In order to customize a drop-down menu with images and description, we can write a dedicated `Renderer`, or try to use a JavaScript plugin capable of rendering it like in the preceding screenshot. Well, the second option is much easier to accomplish and doesn't require us to reinvent the wheel. Practically, we can use a free and cool jQuery plugin named **ddSlick** (`http://designwithpc.com/Plugins/ddSlick`), which is a free light-weight jQuery plugin that allows you to create a custom drop-down menu with images and description. There are many other such plugins that do the same thing.

Basically, this plugin is capable of transforming a simple drop-down menu (defined using `<select>` and `<option>`) into a fancy drop-down menu that contains images and descriptions. For this, we start with a pure HTML5 `<select>` tag, as shown in the following code snippet:

```
<select id="demo-htmlselect">
  <option value="0" data-imagesrc="http://..."
    data-description="Description ...">text</option>
  <option value="1" data-imagesrc="http://..."
    data-description="Description ...">text</option>
  ...
</select>
```

When this `<select>` tag passes through ddSlick, it will result in the desired drop-down menu. Basically, ddSlick will render the `<select>` tag as a `<ul>` tag and each `<option>` tag as `<li>`. The images and descriptions are rendered using `<img>` and `<small>`, while the option's text is rendered using `<label>`. Moreover, an input hidden will be generated for each `<option>` value. The HTML5 attributes `data-imagesrc` and `data-description` are used to tell ddSlick what images and descriptions to use for each `<option>`.

It is important to understand how ddSlick works, because we will wrap it into a composite component named `ThemeSwitcher`. The interface section is very simple and contains a single attribute named `theme`. This attribute represents the selected theme, as follows:

```
<!-- INTERFACE -->
<cc:interfacecomponentType="book.beans.ThemeSwitcherComponent">
<cc:attribute name="theme" default=""
  type="java.lang.String" required="true"/>
</cc:interface>
```

In the implementation section, we accomplish several tasks. First, we load the JavaScript libraries needed by our component:

```
<!-- IMPLEMENTATION -->
<cc:implementation>
  <h:outputScript library="themeswitcher"
    name="js/jquery.min.js"/>
  <h:outputScript library="themeswitcher"
    name="js/modernizr-2.0.6-development-only.js"/>
  <h:outputScript library="themeswitcher"
    name="js/jquery-ui.min.js"/>
  <h:outputScript library="themeswitcher"
    name="js/prettify.js"/>
  <h:outputScript library="themeswitcher"
    name="js/ddslick.js"/>
  ...
```

Further, we define HTML's `<select>` component encapsulated in `<h:form>` (ideally, this component is not used in `<h:form>` with other components; therefore, we don't have to worry about the nested forms):

```
<div id="#{cc.clientId}:themeswitcher">
  <h:form id="themeswitcherForm">
    <!--<h:outputScript name="jsf.js"
      library="javax.faces" target="head"/> -->
    <select id="#{cc.clientId}:
      themeswitcherForm:themeswitcher_content">
      <ui:repeat value="#{cc.contracts}" var="t">
        <option value="#{t}" data-imagesrc
          ="#{request.contextPath}#{request.servletPath}/
          javax.faces.resource/#{t}.png?con=#{t}" data-description
          ="Description: #{t} theme">#{t}
        </option>
      </ui:repeat>
      <option selected="true" style="display:none;
        " data-description="Current theme: #{cc.attrs.theme}">
        Select theme ...
      </option>
    </select>
    <h:inputHidden id="selectedTheme" value="#{cc.attrs.theme}"/>
  </h:form>
</div>
```

The contracts are automatically detected and added as `<option>` using the `<ui:repeat>` component. The selected theme (`<option>`) is submitted to a managed bean using a hidden field, `<h:inputHidden>`. After submission (via AJAX or non-AJAX), the entire page is loaded and the `contracts` attribute (of `<f:view>`) will receive and apply the selected theme. For this, we need a little JavaScript code. First, we call the `ddslick` method, which will do the magic of transforming the boring drop-down menu into a cool one. Further, we indicate a JavaScript callback method, which will be automatically called when a theme is selected. In this method, we refresh the value of the hidden field, and submit the form (via AJAX or non-AJAX):

```
<cc:implementation>
...
<script type="text/javascript">
  $(document).ready(function() {

    var themeForm = ("#{cc.clientId}:themeswitcherForm").
      replace(/:/g, "\\:");
    var themeSelectElem =
      ("#{cc.clientId}:themeswitcherForm:themeswitcher_content").
      replace(/:/g, "\\:");
    var themeHiddenElem =
      ("#{cc.clientId}:themeswitcherForm:selectedTheme").
      replace(/:/g, "\\:");

    $('#' + themeSelectElem).ddslick({
      onSelected: function(data) {
        if (data.selectedData.text !== "Select theme ...") {
          setTheme(data);
        }
      }
    });

  // callback function
    functionsetTheme(data) {
      $('#' + themeHiddenElem).val(data.selectedData.text);
      //jsf.ajax.request(this, null, {execute:
        '#{cc.clientId}:themeswitcherForm:selectedTheme',
        render: "@all"});
      $('#' + themeForm).submit(); // without AJAX
    }
  });

</script>
</cc:implementation>
```

It was very handy to work with this callback method to submit the selected theme, since ddSlick provides this feature out of the box. There are many other possibilities such as writing a value change listener, firing a custom event, and so on.

I'm sure that you notice that our composite components indicate the presence of a backing component. This component is responsible to detect the application's contracts and add their names into List. This list is transformed in `<option>` by `<ui:repeat>`. Its code is pretty straightforward, which is as follows:

```
@FacesComponent(value = "book.beans.ThemeSwitcherComponent",
  createTag = false)
public class ThemeSwitcherComponent extends
  UIComponentBase implements NamingContainer {

    private List<String> contracts = new ArrayList<>();

    public List<String>getContracts() {
      return contracts;
    }

    publicThemeSwitcherComponent() throws IOException {
      FacesContextfacesContext
        = FacesContext.getCurrentInstance();
      ExternalContextexternalContext
        = facesContext.getExternalContext();
      Path path = Paths.get(((ServletContext)
        externalContext.getContext()).getRealPath("/contracts"));
      try (DirectoryStream<Path> ds
        = Files.newDirectoryStream(path)) {
        for (Path file : ds) {
          if (Files.readAttributes(file,
            BasicFileAttributes.class).isDirectory()) {
              contracts.add(file.getFileName().toString());
          }
        }
      } catch (IOException e) {
        throw e;
      }
    }

    @Override
    public String getFamily() {
      returnUINamingContainer.COMPONENT_FAMILY;
    }
}
```

A developer who wants to use this ThemeSwitcher component must add, in each contract, a PNG image with the same name as the contract (recommended size is 40 x 40 pixels). By convention, for each contract, the ThemeSwitcher component will look for such an image to display it next to the theme name and description. You can improve this backing component to ensure that such images exist. Moreover, you can extend its functionality in order to allow the user of the component to provide custom descriptions.

Done! The complete application is named ch11_10.

The ThemeSwitcher composite component was packaged as a JAR file and used as an example in the ch11_7 application as follows:

```
<html ...
  xmlns:t="http://jsf/cc/packt/taglib">
  ...
  <h:body>
    <f:view contracts="#{themeSwitcherBean.theme}">
    <t:themeswitcher theme="#{themeSwitcherBean.theme}"/>
  ...
```

The ThemeSwitcherBean source code is very simple, as follows:

```
@Named
@RequestScoped
public class ThemeSwitcherBean {

  private String theme = "tableBlue";

  public String getTheme() {
    return theme;
  }

  public void setTheme(String theme) {
    this.theme = theme;
  }
}
```

The output of the `ch11_7` application is shown in the following screenshot:

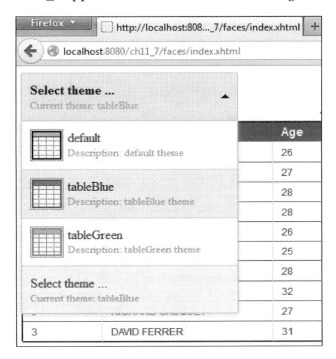

If you decide to programmatically alter the `contracts` attribute value of `<f:view>`, you don't need this bean anymore. Moreover, if you consider a disadvantage in loading this jQuery plugin, you can write pure JavaScript code. Or, if you want a JavaScript code, a custom renderer can be a good choice.

A `ThemeSwitcher` component example, based on pure JavaScript, is developed in the application named `ch11_11` and is exemplified as a JAR file in the application named `ch11_12`. The example modifies the free JavaScript UI library named `iconselect. js` (`http://bug7a.github.io/iconselect.js/`) and uses the complete rewritten iScroll 4 library (`http://cubiq.org/iscroll-4`). Both of these libraries are pure JavaScript; they don't use additional libraries such as jQuery. Moreover, they are very small, free to be copied, modified, distributed, adapted, and commercially used.

The composite component that wraps these libraries can be used as shown in the following code. Notice that you can customize the aspect (which is a grid) and you can optionally specify which contracts to be ignored (not listed in theme switcher).

```
<t:themeswitcher theme="#{themeSwitcherBean.theme}"
  ignore="default" columns="1" rows="1"/>
```

The output is as shown in the following screenshot:

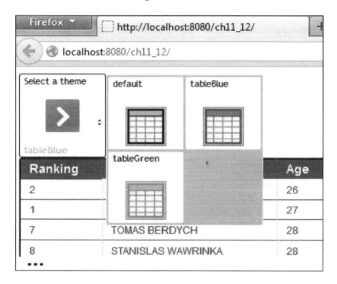

If you don't want any JavaScript code, you can write a custom `Renderer` code or extend the existing `MenuRenderer` code (Mojarra or MyFaces implementation) or write a composite component that uses the JSF UI components to create a nice theme switcher. Writing a custom `Renderer` code (or extending the `MenuRenderer` code) doesn't seem to be an easy job, and I don't know if it deserves the effort. But writing a composite component based on JSF UI components is pretty simple. You can see such an implementation in the application named `ch11_13` and exemplified as a JAR file in the application named `ch11_14`. In this example, the themes are listed in a `<h:dataTable>` component, as you can see in the following screenshot:

# Configuring contracts in XML

Contracts can be associated with the JSF pages, as you saw in the previous sections. As an alternative, we can accomplish the same thing by configuring contracts in the `faces-config.xml` file. For example, let's suppose that we have three contracts: `default`, `tableGreen`, and `tableBlue`. Their association with different pages is as follows:

- The `default` contract is associated with the `tables/defaultTablePage.xhtml` page

- The `tableGreen` contract is associated with the `greenTablePage.xhtml` page

- The `tableBlue` contract is associated with the `blueTablePage.xhtml` page

In `faces-config.xml`, we can do these associations using a few tags—the following example code speaks for itself:

```
<application>
  <resource-library-contracts>
    <contract-mapping>
      <url-pattern>/blueTablePage.xhtml</url-pattern>
      <contracts>tableBlue</contracts>
    </contract-mapping>
    <contract-mapping>
      <url-pattern>/greenTablePage.xhtml</url-pattern>
      <contracts>tableGreen</contracts>
    </contract-mapping>
```

```
    <contract-mapping>
      <url-pattern>/tables/*</url-pattern>
      <contracts>default</contracts>
    </contract-mapping>
  </resource-library-contracts>
</application>
```

 As a note, take a quick look at the third association. Notice how you can associate a contract with all the XHTML pages from a folder using the * wildcard. Do not try to use EL in `<contracts>`. It will not work!

The complete application is named `ch11_8`.

# Packaging contracts in JARs

In order to distribute contracts, you can place them into a JAR file. This is a very simple job that can be accomplished in just three steps, which are as follows:

1.  Consider an empty JAR file.
2.  Create, in JAR, a folder named `META-INF`.
3.  Copy the `contracts` folder from your application into `META-INF`.

For example, a JAR file that contains the `default`, `tableGreen`, and `tableBlue` contract folders has the structure shown in the following screenshot:

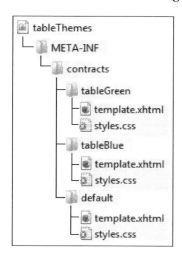

A complete example that uses this JAR file is named `ch11_9`.

# Summary

I hope that you have enjoyed this penultimate chapter.

The JSF 2.2 Resource Library Contracts is one of the big ticket features. For a long time, JSF developers requested for a mechanism that allows writing and using themes in JSF, just like in other systems. As you just saw, JSF 2.2 contracts open a door in this direction and encourage developers to write and use themes. Of course, there are many other things that should be added, such as a theme repository, administration console for themes, switch between themes on the fly, and so on. But, this is a good start!

See you in the final chapter where we will discuss about Facelets.

# 12
# Facelets Templating

In this chapter, we will cover several aspects of Facelets templating and some related aspects.

JSF is defined as a component-based application development framework. When we say Facelets, we mean friendly page development, reusability of code, templating, composition components, custom logic tags, expression functions, high-performance rendering, optimized compilation time, and so on. But what actually is Facelets? Well, Facelets represents a **VDL (View Declaration Language)**, and initially, it was created as an alternative to JSP. During JSF 1.1 and 1.2, this view handler can be used only after a separate download and configuration, while JSP was the default view handler. Things started to change with JSF 2.0, when the mismatch between JSF and JSP allowed Facelets to become the standard and default VDL, while JSP was deprecated. Starting with JSF 2.2, this concept was seriously fortified and Facelets was boosted with new features and capabilities.

# A brief overview of the Facelets tags

**Templating** is a concept based on code reusability. Templates, or tiles, represent the portions of reusable code that can be puzzled together to obtain JSF pages. In order to accomplish this, we exploit a handful of tags from `http://xmlns.jcp.org/jsf/facelets` namespace.

Usually, prefixed with `ui`, these tags are listed as follows:

- The `<ui:composition>` tag (`TagHandler`): This defines a page composition that can use a template (any content outside of this tag is ignored). The `template` attribute is optional and is used for indicating a template to which the enclosed content should be applied. Multiple compositions can use the same template, thus encapsulating and reusing the layout. Facelets will paste the enclosed content into the component's hierarchy, usually under `UIViewRoot`. The `<ui:composition>` tag is used in the following manner:

  ```
  <ui:composition template="template_path">
  ```

- The `<ui:define>` tag (`TagHandler`): This defines the content that is inserted into a page by a template. It may appear in the `<ui:composition>`, `<ui:component>`, `<ui:decorate>`, and `<ui:fragment>` tags and it has a matching `<ui:insert>` tag, which is capable of inserting the defined content into a page. Most commonly, it appears in the `<ui:composition>` tag. The `<ui:define>` tag is used in the following manner:

  ```
  <ui:define name="ui_insert_name">
  ```

- The `<ui:insert>` tag (`TagHandler`): This inserts the content into a template. Usually, that content is defined by the `<ui:define>` tag in a `<ui:composition>`, `<ui:component>`, `<ui:decorate>`, or `<ui:fragment>` tag. This tag indicates the exact place where the content will be inserted. When the `name` attribute is missing, Facelets will add the body content of this tag to the view. The `<ui:insert>` tag is used in the following manner:

  ```
  <ui:insert name="ui_insert_name">
  ```

- The `<ui:include>` tag (`TagHandler`): This is used to encapsulate and reuse content from multiple pages. The included content can be plain XHTML and XHTML pages that have either a `<ui:composition>` tag or a `<ui:component>` tag. This tag can be easily combined with `<ui:param>` to provide parameters to the included pages, but is also combined with the `<ui:fragment>`, `<ui:decorate>`, and `<ui:insert>` tags. This is one of the most used tags since it sustains the idea of reusing templated code. The `<ui:include>` tag is used in the following manner:

  ```
  <ui:include src="filename_to_include_path">
  ```

  Starting with JSF 2.2, the `UIViewRoot.restoreViewScopeState(FacesCont ext context, Object state)` method was added to allow the use of view scoped beans for EL expressions in the template from which the component tree is built. This means that the following code is useful:

  ```
  <ui:include src="#{viewScopedBean.includeFileName}"/>
  ```

- The `<ui:param>` tag (`TagHandler`): This passes parameters to an included file or a template. It is used in the `<ui:include>`, `<ui:composition>`, or `<ui:decorate>` tags. A parameter is characterized by a name-value pair—both can be string literals or EL expressions. In the included file or template, the parameter is available via EL. The `<ui:param>` tag is used in the following manner:

  ```
  <ui:param name="param_name" value="param_value">
  ```

- The `<ui:repeat>` tag (`ComponentHandler`): This is used as an alternative for loop tags such as `<c:forEach>` and `<h:dataTable>`. Since `<ui:repeat>` is a component handler, while `<c:forEach>` is a tag handler, you have to pay attention when you choose between them! The `<ui:repeat>` tag is used in the following manner:

```
<ui:repeat value="some_collection" var="var_name">
```

- The `<ui:debug>` tag (`ComponentHandler`): This defines a debug component in the component tree capable to capture debugging information such as component tree, scoped variables, and view state. By default, this information appears in a debug pop-up window when you press *Ctrl + Shift + D* (in Windows OS). You can alter the *D* key by explicitly setting another keyboard using the optional `hotkey` attribute. The `<ui:debug>` tag is used in the following manner:

```
<ui:debug hotkey="key" />
```

- The `<ui:component>` tag (`ComponentHandler`): This is similar to `<ui:composition>`, only that it defines a component directly into the component tree without an associated template. The `<ui:component>` tag is used in the following manner:

```
<ui:component>
```

- The `<ui:fragment>` tag (`ComponentHandler`): Again, this is similar to `<ui:component>` tag, but doesn't ignore the content outside this tag. Its main skill consists of the `rendered` attribute, which is very useful for deciding if the enclosed content will be displayed or not. This tag doesn't produce client-side effects, which makes it a great alternative to `<h:panelGroup>`, which has the client side effect of producing the `<span>` or `<div>` tags. If you want to work with `<h:panelGroup>` without producing the `<span>` or `<div>` tags, then skip adding an explicit ID to it. An `<h:panelGroup>` tag produces a `<span>` tag if it has an explicit ID, and a `<div>` tag if it has an explicit ID and the value of the `layout` attribute set to the `block` value. The `<ui:fragment>` tag is used in the following manner:

```
<ui:fragment>
```

- The `<ui:decorate>` tag (`TagHandler`): This is similar to the `<ui:composition>` tag, but doesn't ignore the content outside this tag. This is a nice feature, since it allows us to apply any element in the page to a template. The `template` attribute is mandatory. The `<ui:decorate>` tag is used in the following manner:

```
<ui:decorate template="template_path">
```

- The `<ui:remove>` tag: This removes the content from a page. The `<ui:remove>` tag is used in the following manner:

  ```
  <ui:remove>
  ```

You can read about further details of these tags at http://docs.oracle.com/javaee/7/javaserverfaces/2.2/vdldocs/facelets/ui/tld-summary.html.

# Creating a simple template – PageLayout

When these eleven tags combine their skills, we can create amazing templates. For example, let's suppose that we want to create the template from the following diagram and we name it `PageLayout`:

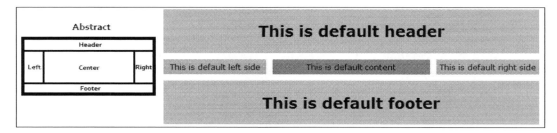

 Notice that with just a few clicks, NetBeans can generate the code behind several templates of Facelets, including the preceding abstractization. But, this time we will write it manually, in order to exemplify the Facelets tags. While NetBeans provides a compact code, based on a single XHTML page, we will write an expanded approach using six XHTML pages. In this way, you will have two ways of writing this kind of template.

As you can see, there are five distinctive sections: **Header**, **Footer**, **Left**, **Center**, and **Right**. For each of these sections, we will write a separate XHTML page. The header is generated in the `topDefault.xhtml` page, that simply uses the `<ui:composition>` tag to provide the default content as follows:

```
<?xml version='1.0' encoding='UTF-8' ?>
<!DOCTYPE html PUBLIC "-//W3C//DTD XHTML 1.0 Transitional//EN"
   "http://www.w3.org/TR/xhtml1/DTD/xhtml1-transitional.dtd">
<html xmlns="http://www.w3.org/1999/xhtml"
   xmlns:ui="http://xmlns.jcp.org/jsf/facelets"
   xmlns:h="http://xmlns.jcp.org/jsf/html">

<h:body>
```

```
    <ui:composition>
      <h1>This is default header</h1>
    </ui:composition>
  </h:body>
</html>
```

The same approach can be used for the remaining four sections. Just replace the default header text and create the following XHTMLs: `bottomDefault.xhtml` for the footer, `contentDefault.xhtml` for the center, `leftDefault.xhtml` for the left-hand side, and `rightDefault.xhtml` for the right-hand side.

These five XHTMLs are like five pieces of the puzzle and they serve as the default content for our template. Now, we can compose the puzzle (this is known as the template file or simply the template) by writing an XHTML page that uses the `<ui:insert>` and `<ui:include>` tags as shown in the following code—this is `layout.xhtml`:

```
<?xml version='1.0' encoding='UTF-8' ?>
<!DOCTYPE html PUBLIC "-//W3C//DTD XHTML 1.0 Transitional//EN"
  "http://www.w3.org/TR/xhtml1/DTD/xhtml1-transitional.dtd">
<html xmlns="http://www.w3.org/1999/xhtml"
  xmlns:ui="http://xmlns.jcp.org/jsf/facelets"
  xmlns:h="http://xmlns.jcp.org/jsf/html">

  <h:head>
    <meta http-equiv="Content-Type" content="text/html;
      charset=UTF-8" />
    <h:outputStylesheet name="css/default.css"/>
    <h:outputStylesheet name="css/cssLayout.css"/>
    <title>My Template</title>
  </h:head>

  <h:body>
    <div id="top">
      <ui:insert name="top">
        <ui:include src="/template/default/topDefault.xhtml" />
      </ui:insert>
    </div>
    <div>
      <div id="left">
        <ui:insert name="left">
          <ui:include src="/template/default/leftDefault.xhtml" />
```

```
        </ui:insert>
      </div>
      <div id="right">
        <ui:insert name="right">
          <ui:include src="/template/default/
            rightDefault.xhtml" />
        </ui:insert>
      </div>
      <div id="content">
        <ui:insert name="content">
          <ui:include src="/template/default/
            contentDefault.xhtml" />
        </ui:insert>
      </div>
    </div>
    <div id="bottom">
      <ui:insert name="bottom">
        <ui:include src="/template/default/bottomDefault.xhtml" />
      </ui:insert>
    </div>
  </h:body>
</html>
```

Each section was represented by an `<ui:insert>` tag and the default content was included using `<ui:include>`. Some `<div>` tags and CSS were used for arranging and styling the pieces of the puzzle in the main template file.

Now, the template, as shown in the following code, is ready to be used in `index.xhtml`; this is known as the **template client**:

```
<?xml version='1.0' encoding='UTF-8' ?>
<!DOCTYPE html PUBLIC "-//W3C//DTD XHTML 1.0 Transitional//EN"
  "http://www.w3.org/TR/xhtml1/DTD/xhtml1-transitional.dtd">
<html xmlns="http://www.w3.org/1999/xhtml"
  xmlns:h="http://xmlns.jcp.org/jsf/html"
  xmlns:ui="http://xmlns.jcp.org/jsf/facelets">
  <h:head>
    <title></title>
  </h:head>
  <h:body>
    <ui:composition template="template/layout.xhtml" />
  </h:body>
</html>
```

At this moment, we can alter the default content of our template using the
`<ui:define>` tag, for example, if we want to replace the text that appears in the
center section. This is the default content, with the **Rafael Nadal Home Page** text,
as shown in the following code:

```
...
<ui:composition template="template/layout.xhtml">
  <ui:define name="content">
    Rafael Nadal Home Page
  </ui:define>
</ui:composition>
...
```

In the same way, you can redefine the content for the remaining four sections.
The complete application is named `ch12_1`.

This is a pretty simple template that can serve us as support for presenting the rest
of Facelets tags. We will continue with several punctual examples for `<ui:param>`,
`<ui:decorate>`, `<ui:fragment>`, `<ui:repeat>`, and so on.

# Passing parameters via <ui:param>

The `<ui:param>` tag is a tag handler that is capable of sending parameters
to an included file or to a template. A quick example will make you understand
how `<ui:param>` works. In the following code, we are in the template client,
`index.xhtml`, and we send a parameter to the template file, `layout.xhtml`:

```
<ui:composition template="template/layout.xhtml">
  <ui:param name="playername" value="Rafael " />
</ui:composition>
```

We can also access this parameter in `layout.xhtml` using its name via EL. We
can do that anywhere in the template file; for example, we can use this parameter
for creating a new parameter to be sent to an included file, in this case, to the
`contentDefault.xhtml` file, as shown in the following code:

```
<div id="content">
  <ui:insert name="content">
    <ui:include src="/template/default/contentDefault.xhtml">
      <ui:param name="playernamesurname"
        value="#{playername} Nadal" />
    </ui:include>
  </ui:insert>
</div>
```

From the same template, we can send parameters to different included pages. Besides the `playernamesurname` parameter, let's send one to the `topDefault.xhtml` page using the following code:

```
<ui:insert name="top">
  <ui:include src="/template/default/topDefault.xhtml">
    <ui:param name="headertext" value="This is default header
      (passed through ui:param)" />
  </ui:include>
</ui:insert>
```

Next, send one parameter to the `bottomDefault.xhtml` page using the following code:

```
<ui:insert name="bottom">
  <ui:include src="/template/default/bottomDefault.xhtml">
    <ui:param name="footertext" value="This is default footer
      (passed through ui:param)" />
  </ui:include>
</ui:insert>
```

Now, the `playernamesurname` parameter is accessible via EL in the `contentDefault.xhtml` page as shown in the following code:

```
<ui:composition>
  #{playernamesurname} (passed through ui:param)
</ui:composition>
```

Moreover, `headertext` and `footertext` are accessible via EL in the `topDefault.xhtml` and `bottomDefault.xhtml` pages. Now, the result of using `<ui:param>` will be as shown in the following screenshot:

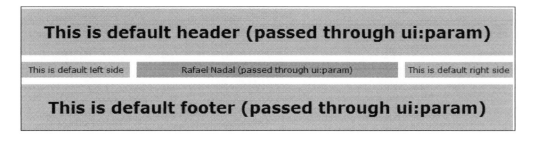

The complete application is called `ch12_11`.

# Passing bean properties and action methods via <ui:param>

In the previous example, you saw how to exploit <ui:param> for sending literal strings to a template or included page, but <ui:param> can be used for more than this. Let's suppose that we have the following code of the bean, TemplatesBean:

```
@Named
@ViewScoped
public class TemplatesBean implements Serializable {

  private String msgTopDefault="";
  private String msgBottomDefault="";
  private String msgCenterDefault="No center content ...
    press the below button!";

  //getters and setters

  public void topAction(String msg){
    this.msgTopDefault = msg;
  }

  public void bottomAction(String msg){
    this.msgBottomDefault = msg;
  }

  public void centerAction(){
    this.msgCenterDefault="This is default content";
  }
}
```

Further, we want to display the value of the msgCenterDefault property in contentDefault.xhtml. Of course, this is very easy to accomplish using the following line of code:

```
<h:outputText value=#{templatesBean.msgCenterDefault} />
```

But we want to pass the name of the bean and the name of the property via <ui:param>. This can be accomplished using the following code:

```
<ui:insert name="content">
  <ui:include src="/template/default/contentDefault.xhtml">
    <ui:param name="templatesBeanName" value="#{templatesBean}"/>
    <ui:param name="contentPropertyName"
      value="msgCenterDefault"/>
  </ui:include>
</ui:insert>
```

Next, in `contentDefault.xhtml`, you can display the value of the `msgCenterDefault` property as shown in the following line of code:

```
<h:outputText value="#{templatesBeanName[contentPropertyName]}"/>
```

Well, that was easy! But how about calling the `centerAction` method, which modifies the value of the `msgCenterDefault` property? For this, we add the method name between single quotes, in square brackets, followed by a pair of parentheses indicating a method without arguments, as shown in the following code:

```
<h:form>
  <h:commandButton value="Center Button"
    action="#{templatesBeanName['centerAction']()}"/>
</h:form>
```

Finally, we want to call the `topAction` (or `bottomAction`) method. This time, we want to pass via `<ui:param>` the bean name, action method name, and the argument value. For this, we will write the following code:

```
<ui:insert name="top">
  <ui:include src="/template/default/topDefault.xhtml">
    <ui:param name="templatesBeanName" value="#{templatesBean}"/>
    <ui:param name="topActionName" value="topAction"/>
    <ui:param name="arg" value="Hello from topDefault.xhtml .."/>
  </ui:include>
</ui:insert>
```

In `topDefault.xhtml`, we can exploit the information passed through these three parameters, as shown in the following code:

```
<h:form>
  <h:commandButton value="Top Button"
    action="#{templatesBeanName[topActionName](arg)}"/>
</h:form>
```

In the following screenshot, you can see that everything worked as expected:

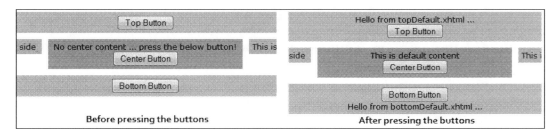

The complete application is named `ch12_13`.

A `<ui:param>` value can be accessed from a managed bean, as shown in the following code:

```
FaceletContext faceletContext = (FaceletContext)
  FacesContext.getCurrentInstance().getAttributes().
    get(FaceletContext.FACELET_CONTEXT_KEY);
String paramValue = (String) faceletContext.getAttribute("param");
```

# Exploiting the <ui:decorate> and <ui:fragment> tags

First, let's talk about the `<ui:decorate>` tag. As its name suggests, this tag is used for decorating pieces of a page. Unlike `<ui:composition>`, this tag doesn't ignore the content that is not enclosed in it, which may be an added advantage sometimes. Well, a simple example is shown in the following code (the `template` attribute is mandatory):

```
<?xml version='1.0' encoding='UTF-8' ?>
<!DOCTYPE html PUBLIC "-//W3C//DTD XHTML 1.0 Transitional//EN"
"http://www.w3.org/TR/xhtml1/DTD/xhtml1-transitional.dtd">
<html xmlns="http://www.w3.org/1999/xhtml"
  xmlns:h="http://xmlns.jcp.org/jsf/html"
  xmlns:ui="http://xmlns.jcp.org/jsf/facelets">

  <h:head>
    <title></title>
  </h:head>
  <h:body>
    <h:outputText value="You can see this header text
      thanks to ui:decorate!"/>
      <ui:decorate template="template/layout.xhtml">
        <ui:define name="content">
          Rafael Nadal Website
        </ui:define>
      </ui:decorate>
    <h:outputText value="You can see this footer text
      thanks to ui:decorate!"/>
  </h:body>
</html>
```

The preceding snippet produces the following screenshot:

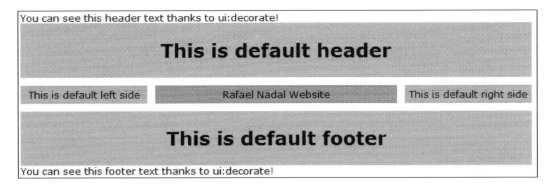

The complete example is named ch12_10. Basically, this example decorates a page with a template and proves the effect of the <ui:decorate> tag against the <ui:composition> tag. However, let's see a better example of decorating a part of a page.

In this example, we will decorate a <div> element with an <ul> list. The items of list <li> come from two separated pages, and the technique for accomplishing this is based on nested <ui:decorate> tags. The template client, index.xhtml, uses <ui:decorate> to decorate the <div> element with a template that contains the <ul> list, as shown in the following code:

```
<h:body>
  <div style="border:2px solid; border-radius:25px;width:180px;">
    <ui:decorate template="/files/ul.xhtml"/>
  </div>
</h:body>
```

Furthermore, the ul.xhtml template provides the <ul> list and a part of <li> items, but also uses the <ui:decorate> tag to decorate the <ul> list with the remaining <li> items, which are available via the li.xhtml template, as shown in the following code:

```
<ul>
  <li style="color: red;">Andy Murray</li>
    <ui:decorate template="/files/li.xhtml"/>
  <li style="color: red;">Stanislas Wawrinka</li>
</ul>
```

The li.xhtml template uses the <ui:fragment> tag to provide the rest of the <li> list. But since <ui:fragment> doesn't block the unclosed content, we can slip some <li> items outside of it as well, as shown in the following code:

```
<li style="color: green;">John Isner</li>
  <ui:fragment>
```

```
    <li>Rafael Nadal</li>
    <li>Roger Federer</li>
    <li>Novak Djokovic</li>
  </ui:fragment>
<li style="color: green;">Fabio Fognini</li>
```

Done! We have especially used different colors for `<li>` items. This is very useful, because it really helps us understand how the page is composed using the `<ui:decorate>` tag. Please refer to the following screenshot:

The complete application is named `ch12_24`.

The same result can be obtained using different kinds of approaches. But, another one that can be used as a templating technique consists in replacing the `<ui:decorate>` tag from the `ul.xhtml` template with a combination of the `<ui:insert>`, `<ui:define>`, and `<ui:include>` tags. In order to do that, we change the `ul.xhtml` template using the following code:

```
<ul>
  <li style="color: red;">Andy Murray</li>
    <ui:insert name="content"/>
  <li style="color: red;">Stanislas Wawrinka</li>
</ul>
```

This will change the code for the template client to the following:

```
<h:body>
  <div style="border:2px solid; border-radius:25px;width:180px;">
    <ui:decorate template="/files/ul.xhtml">
      <ui:define name="content">
        <ui:include src="/files/li.xhtml"/>
      </ui:define>
    </ui:decorate>
  </div>
</h:body>
```

The complete application is named `ch12_23`.

# Iterating with <ui:repeat>

The <ui:repeat> tag is a component handler that is capable of iterating over a collection, and at each iteration, it adds a copy of its child elements in the component tree. We can say that <ui:repeat> acts as a <h:dataTable> tag without rendering an HTML table. Of course, you can do that explicitly, by wrapping its mechanism in a <table>, <tr>, and <td> suite (you will see an example in the upcoming section, *Using the jsfc attribute*).

It contains a set of very handy attributes that deserve to be mentioned before an example. Besides the well known attributes, value (representing the collection to iterate as java.lang.Object) and var (representing the iterator as java.lang. Object), we have--all the following attributes that are optional:

- step: This attribute allows us to indicate, as an int value, the number of items that will be skipped for each iteration. By default, the <ui:repeat> tag iterates over each item of the collection, which indicates a step attribute equal to 1, and indicates that the process starts with the first one item.

- size: This is the size of the collection over which to iterate; it has to be evaluated to an int value.

- offset: By default, <ui:repeat> begins the iteration process from the first item of the collection. This attribute allows us to jump over a number of items, by telling Facelets to start the iteration process for a certain offset. This offset is settled before the iteration process begins; it has to be evaluated to an int value.

- varStatus: This attribute reveals the status of the current item via a POJO object. An explicit example of using it will follow shortly, but for now let's have several examples of iterating different kinds of Java collections.

A simple example of iterating an ArrayList collection looks like the following code (the same approach can be applied to any java.util.List package):

```
<ui:repeat value="#{myBean.dataArrayList}" var="t">
  <h:outputText value="#{t}" />
</ui:repeat>
```

However, <ui:repeat> can also iterate over a HashSet collection using the toArray method, as follows (the same approach can be applied to TreeSet and LinkedHashSet):

```
<ui:repeat value="#{myBean.dataHashSet.toArray()}" var="t">
  <h:outputText value="#{t}" />
</ui:repeat>
```

Or, even more, `<ui:repeat>` can also iterate over a `Map` collection (`HashMap`, `TreeMap`, and `LinkedHashMap`) using the following approaches:

- The following is the code for the first approach:

```
<ui:repeat
    value="#{myBean.dataHashMap.entrySet().toArray()}"
    var="t">
    <h:outputText value="key:#{t.key} value:#{t.value}" />
</ui:repeat>
```

- The following is the code for the second approach:

```
<ui:repeat value="#{myBean.dataHashMap.keySet().toArray()}"
    var="t">
    <h:outputText value="key:#{t}
        value:#{myBean.dataHashMap.get(t)}" />
</ui:repeat>
```

- The following is the code for the third approach:

```
<ui:repeat value="#{myBean.dataHashMap.values().toArray()}"
    var="t">
    <h:outputText value="#{t}" />
</ui:repeat>
```

- The following is the code for the fourth approach:

```
<ui:repeat value="#{myBean.dataHashMap.entrySet()}"
    var="t">
    <ui:repeat value="#{t.toArray()}" var="q">
        <h:outputText value="key:#{q.key} value:#{q.value}" />
    </ui:repeat>
</ui:repeat>
```

The preceding examples iterate the entire collection. But if you want to iterate only the items from even positions, then we can bring the `step` attribute into the scene, as shown in the following code:

```
<ui:repeat value="#{myBean.dataArrayList}" var="t" step="2">
    <h:outputText value="#{t}"/>
</ui:repeat>
```

For odd items, you may want to combine the powers of the `step` and `offset` attributes, using the following code:

```
<ui:repeat value="#{myBean.dataArrayList}" var="t" step="2"
    offset="1">
    <h:outputText value="#{t}"/>
</ui:repeat>
```

Another common approach for displaying even/odd items consists of using the `varStatus` attribute. The POJO object, representing the value of this attribute, contains several read-only JavaBeans properties. Between these properties, we have the even and odd properties, which can be easily used in combination with `<ui:fragment>`, as follows:

- For the even properties, the code is given as follows:

```
<ui:repeat value="#{myBean.dataArrayList}" var="t"
  varStatus="vs">
  <ui:fragment rendered="#{vs.even}">
    <h:outputText value="#{vs.index}. #{t.player}"/>
  </ui:fragment>
</ui:repeat>
```

- For the odd properties, the code is given as follows:

```
<ui:repeat value="#{myBean.dataArrayList}" var="t"
  varStatus="vs">
  <ui:fragment rendered="#{vs.odd}">
    <h:outputText value="#{vs.index}. #{t.player}"/>
  </ui:fragment>
</ui:repeat>
```

The entire set of properties is exposed in the following snippet of code:

```
<ui:repeat value="#{myBean.dataArrayList}" var="t" varStatus="vs">
  Index: #{vs.index}
  First: #{vs.first}
  Last: #{vs.last}
  Begin: #{vs.begin}
  End: #{vs.end}
  Step: #{vs.step}
  Current: #{vs.current}
  Even: #{vs.even}
  Odd: #{vs.odd}
</ui:repeat>
```

All the preceding examples presented are united under the complete application named `ch12_6`.

# Working with <ui:include> and <f:viewParam>

You may think that combining <ui:include> with <f:viewParam> is a strange combination, and maybe it is. But, as you know, <ui:include> is able to encapsulate and reuse content from multiple pages, while <f:viewParam> can be useful for adding view parameters in links (using the GET query string). This means that we can take parameters passed on the current page via <f:viewParam> and use them in <ui:include>.

For example, in the current page, we can include a random page, or a page whose name was hardcoded as the value of a view parameter in an outcome. We can also use the includeViewParams attribute to tell other pages to include the same content as the current page. These three examples are just on open gate to more scenarios. The following example speaks for itself:

```
<h:head>
  <title></title>
  <f:metadata>
    <f:viewParam name="in" value="#{randomInBean.in}"/>
  </f:metadata>
</h:head>
<h:body>
  <ui:include src="#{randomInBean.in}"/>

  <h:button value="Tell mypage.xhtml To Include The Same Page As
    You Did" outcome="mypage.xhtml" includeViewParams="true"/>
  <h:button value="Random Page" outcome="index.xhtml"
    includeViewParams="false"/>

  <h:button value="Include in_index_A.xhtml Page"
    outcome="index.xhtml?in=in_index_A.xhtml"/>
  <h:button value="Include in_index_B.xhtml Page"
    outcome="index.xhtml?in=in_index_B.xhtml"/>
  <h:button value="Include in_index_C.xhtml Page"
    outcome="index.xhtml?in=in_index_C.xhtml"/>
</h:body>
```

The code for `RandomInBean` is as follows:

```
@Named
@RequestScoped
public class RandomInBean {

   private String in = "";

   public RandomInBean() {
      int in_rnd = new Random().nextInt(3);
      if (in_rnd == 0) {
         in = "in_index_A.xhtml";
      } else if (in_rnd == 1) {
         in = "in_index_B.xhtml";
      } else if (in_rnd == 2) {
         in = "in_index_C.xhtml";
      }
   }

   public String getIn() {
      return in;
   }

   public void setIn(String in) {
      this.in = in;
   }
}
```

So, we have several buttons to prove the symbiosis between the `<ui:include>` and `<f:viewParam>` tags. First, we have three buttons labeled **Include in_index_A.xhtml Page**, **Include in_index_B.xhtml Page**, and **Include in_index_C.xhtml Page**. All three act the same way; they pass a view parameter named `in`. The value of the view parameter is a string literal, and represents the page that should be included. This will generate a URL of the following type:

```
http://localhost:8080/ch12_12/faces/index.xhtml?in=in_index_B.xhtml
```

So, conforming to this URL, the `<ui:include>` tag will include the `in_index_B.xhtml` page.

Further, we have a button labeled **Random Page**. This button will randomly choose between those three pages. In order to obtain this, we need to add `includeViewParams="false"`, as shown in the following code:

```
<h:button value="Random Page" outcome="index.xhtml"
   includeViewParams="false"/>
```

Finally, we can tell other pages to include the same content as the current page. When you click on the button labeled **Tell mypage.xhtml To Include The Same Page As You Did,** the mypage.xhtml page will include the same page as the current page. For this, we need to add includeViewParams="true".

The complete application is named ch12_12.

# Working with <ui:include> and <ui:param>

The <ui:include> and <ui:param> tags are two tag handlers that can be used for accomplishing many kinds of tasks; as long as we keep in mind that tag handlers are efficient only when the view tree is built, we can exploit them for our benefit. For example, we can use them to generate a tree node structure as shown in the following screenshot:

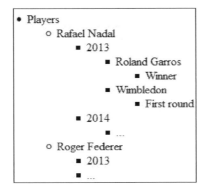

In order to accomplish this task, we will spice up the <ui:include> and <ui:param> tags with a dash of JSTL (the <c:if> and <c:forEach> tag handlers) and recursivity.

First, we need a class that represents the abstractization of the tree node concept. Basically, a tree node representation is a hierarchical structure of labels that can be recursively traversed. Based on this, we can write a generic tree node class as shown in the following code:

```
public class GenericTreeNode {

    private final List<GenericTreeNode> descendants;
    private final String label;

    public GenericTreeNode(String label, GenericTreeNode...
       descendants) {
```

```
      this.label = label;
      this.descendants = Arrays.asList(descendants);
    }

    public boolean isHasDescendants() {
      return !descendants.isEmpty();
    }

    public List<GenericTreeNode> getDescendants() {
      return descendants;
    }

    public String getLabel() {
      return label;
    }
}
```

This class can serve a bean capable of defining a particular tree node, as follows:

```
@Named
@RequestScoped
public class TreeNodeBean {

    private GenericTreeNode root = new GenericTreeNode("Players",
      new GenericTreeNode("Rafael Nadal",
      new GenericTreeNode("2013",
      new GenericTreeNode("Roland Garros",
      new GenericTreeNode("Winner")),
      new GenericTreeNode("Wimbledon",
      new GenericTreeNode("First round"))),
      new GenericTreeNode("2014", new GenericTreeNode("...")))),
      new GenericTreeNode("Roger Federer",
      new GenericTreeNode("2013"), new GenericTreeNode("...")));

    public GenericTreeNode getRoot() {
      return root;
    }
}
```

The interesting part is how to display this structure as a tree node. HTML provides the `<ul>` and `<li>` tags that are able to represent data as a list. Moreover, nested `<ul>` tags output a hierarchical structure, which is very useful since it spears us for finding a custom representation. In order to reflect the tree node defined in `TreeNodeBean`, we write a page named `node.xhtml` capable of autoinclusion in an iterative-recursive process using the `<ui:include>` tag, as follows:

```
<h:body>
  <ui:composition>
    <li>#{node.label}
      <c:if test="#{node.hasDescendants}">
        <ul>
          <c:forEach items="#{node.descendants}" var="node">
            <ui:include src="node.xhtml" />
          </c:forEach>
        </ul>
      </c:if>
    </li>
  </ui:composition>
</h:body>
```

The `node` parameter is passed via `<ui:param>` from the main page named `index. xhtml`. From the main page, we pass the tree node root. Furthermore, in `node.xhtml`, we iterate the descendants of the root in a recursive approach and display each node as shown in the following code:

```
<h:body>
  <ul>
    <ui:include src="node.xhtml">
      <ui:param name="node" value="#{treeNodeBean.root}" />
    </ui:include>
  </ul>
</h:body>
```

If you didn't find this example useful, at least keep in mind that `<ui:include>` can be used in a recursive process. The complete application is named `ch12_14`.

# Debugging with <ui:debug>

The `<ui:debug>` tag (`ComponentHandler`) defines a debug component in the component tree that is capable of capturing debugging information such as component tree, scoped variables, and view state. For example, you can add the `<ui:debug>` tag into a template using the following code:

```
<ui:debug hotkey="q" rendered="true"/>
```

Now, when you press *Ctrl + Shift + Q*, you will see something like the following screenshot:

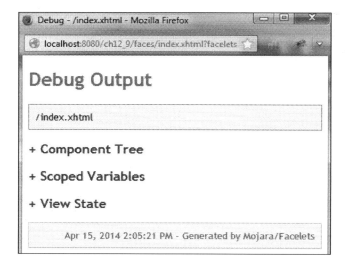

The complete application is named `ch12_9`. The `<ui:debug>` tag was added in `layout.xhtml`.

# Removing the content with <ui:remove>

The `<ui:remove>` tag is used for removing the content. This tag is rarely used, but a perfect example of this is removing comments of type `<!-- -->`. You probably thought of something like the following line:

```
<!-- <h:outputText value="I am a comment!"/> -->
```

It doesn't have any side effects on the HTML rendered code. Well, that isn't true, because in the HTML source code, you will see something similar to the following screenshot:

```
<body>

    <!-- &lt;h:outputText value="I am a comment!"/&gt; -->

</body>
```

But if we encapsulate this in `<ui:remove>`, then the preceding client side effect will not be produced anymore, which has the following code.

```
<ui:remove>
   <!-- <h:outputText value="I am a comment!"/> -->
</ui:remove>
```

The same effect will have the following code:

```
<ui:remove>
   <h:outputText value="I am a comment!"/>
</ui:remove>
```

In order to remove comments from the generated HTML code, you add the `context` parameter in `web.xml`, as shown in the following code:

```
<context-param>
   <param-name>javax.faces.FACELETS_SKIP_COMMENTS</param-name>
   <param-value>true</param-value>
</context-param>
```

Alternatively, for backwards compatibility with existing Facelets tag libraries, the code is given as follows:

```
<context-param>
   <param-name>facelets.SKIP_COMMENTS</param-name>
   <param-value>true</param-value>
</context-param>
```

The complete application is named `ch12_8`.

# Using the jsfc attribute

Facelets comes with an attribute named `jsfc`. Its main goal consists in converting HTML elements in JSF components (the HTML prototype in the JSF page). For example, in the following code, we have an HTML form converted into a JSF form:

```
<form jsfc="h:form">
  <input type="text" jsfc="h:inputText"
    value="#{nameBean.name}" />
  <input type="submit" jsfc="h:commandButton" value="Send"/>
</form>
```

This attribute stands for fast prototyping and is easy to use. The following is another example—this time the `jsfc` attribute is combined with `<ui:repeat>` for generating a `<table>` tag:

```
<table>
  <thead>
    <tr>
      <th>Ranking</th>
      <th>Player</th>
      <th>Age</th>
      <th>Coach</th>
    </tr>
  </thead>
  <tbody>
    <tr jsfc="ui:repeat" value="#{playersBean.dataArrayList}"
      var="t">
      <td>#{t.ranking}</td>
      <td>#{t.player}</td>
      <td>#{t.age}</td>
      <td>#{t.coach}</td>
    </tr>
  </tbody>
</table>
```

The first example is named `ch12_7` and the second one is named `ch12_25`.

# Extending the PageLayout template

Remember the `PageLayout` template developed at the beginning of this chapter? Well, that is a decent template, but let's extend it so it becomes a bit more realistic. Usually, a web template contains the sections title, login, search, logo, header, menu, left, center, right, and footer over and above the five sections that we have used. It would also be nice to have a template that allows us to do the following:

- Remove sections without side effects and without manually removing orphan CSS code (usually, you can remove a section by writing an empty `<ui:define>` tag, but this will not remove the corresponding CSS code for that section). Moreover, an empty `<ui:define>` tag will still have a side effect of type the empty `<div>` tag or the empty `<span>` or `<td>` tag. This happens because, usually, `<ui:define>` is wrapped in a `<div>`, `<span>`, or `<td>` tag.

- Set the width of the template, that is, the left and right panels without altering CSS. These are common adjustments; therefore we can expose them via `<ui:param>` and spear the page author to scroll through CSS files.

- Add a menu section. We can provide support for adding it via `<ui:include>` as a separate file or having a convention mechanism that allows the page author to add it much easily.

At the end, the template will look like the following screenshot:

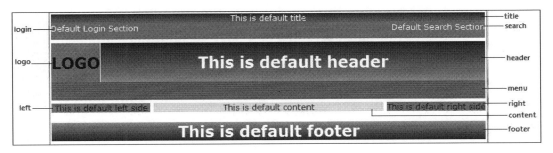

There is no secret that most websites place the content in multiple columns, which are created using the `<div>` or `<table>` elements. Afterwards, these elements are positioned in the page using CSS. Basically, this is the main idea behind most templates, and this one is no exception. In the following diagram, you can see the layout of our template, which is based on the `<div>` elements (in the diagram, you can see each `<div>` ID):

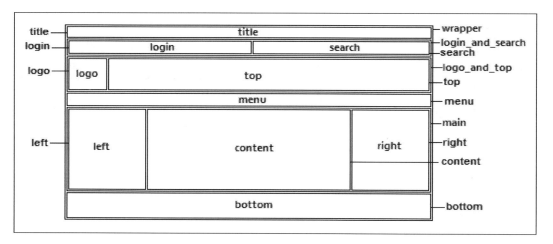

Well, since each section is wrapped in a `<div>` element, we can easily remove it using the `<ui:fragment>` tag and its `rendered` attribute. We can wrap each section in a `<ui:fragment>` tag and remove it by setting the value of the `rendered` attribute to `false` via a `<ui:param>` tag. This will remove the section without any side effects. When a section is removed, we need to skip loading the corresponding CSS code. For this, we can split the CSS files into the following three categories:

- A CSS file that holds general styles for templates (usually this is a small file)
- A CSS file that holds styles for positioning each section on a page (usually this is a small file)
- A CSS file per section, which holds styles specific to each section (these can be pretty large files)

Having this structure, we can easily decide not to load the CSS code for the sections that have been removed. This can be accomplished in the `<h:outputStylesheet>` tag with a simple condition based on the same parameters passed for removing the sections. When a section is removed, we load an empty CSS file named `dummy.css` for it.

So, the template file (`layout.xhtml`) may be changed to the following:

```
<h:head>
  <meta http-equiv="Content-Type" content="text/html;
    charset=UTF-8" />
  <h:outputStylesheet name="css/default.css"/>
  <h:outputStylesheet name="css/cssLayout.css"/>
  <h:outputStylesheet name="#{title eq false ?
    'css/dummy.css' : 'css/titleStyle.css'}"/>
  <h:outputStylesheet name="#{loginsearch eq false ?
    'css/dummy.css' : 'css/login_and_searchStyle.css'}"/>
  <h:outputStylesheet name="#{top eq false ?
    'css/dummy.css' : 'css/topStyle.css'}"/>
...
</h:head>

<h:body>
  <div id="wrapper"
    style="width: #{empty wrapperWidth ? '100%' : wrapperWidth}">
    <ui:fragment rendered="#{empty title ? true : title}">
      <div id="title">
        <ui:insert name="title">
          <ui:include src="/template/default/titleDefault.xhtml"/>
        </ui:insert>
      </div>
    </ui:fragment>
  ...
    <ui:fragment rendered="#{empty bottom ? true : bottom}">
      <div id="bottom">
        <ui:insert name="bottom">
          <ui:include src="/template/default/bottomDefault.xhtml"/>
        </ui:insert>
      </div>
    </ui:fragment>
  </div>
</h:body>
```

So, in the template client, we can easily remove a section (for example, the title section), using the following line of code:

```
<ui:param name="title" value="false"/>
```

At this moment, in the template client, we can easily use `<ui:define>` to provide our content to the template, and `<ui:param>` for the following settings:

- Remove the title section: This sets the `title` parameter to `false`
- Remove the login and search sections: This sets the `loginsearch` parameter to `false`
- Remove only login section: This sets the `login` parameter to `false`
- Remove only search section: This sets the `search` parameter to `false`
- Remove the logo section: This sets the `logo` parameter to `false`
- Remove the top section: This sets the `top` parameter to `false`
- Remove the menu section: This sets the `menu` parameter to `false`
- Remove the left section: This sets the `left` parameter to `false`
- Remove the right section: This sets the `right` parameter to `false`
- Remove the bottom section: This sets the `bottom` parameter to `false`
- Set template fixed width: This sets the `wrapperWidth` parameter to *widthpx*
- Set left panel fixed width: This sets the `leftWidth` parameter to *widthpx* (default 150px)
- Set right fixed width: This sets the `rightWidth` parameter to *widthpx* (default 150px)

Now, let's focus on adding a menu. The template user can define a menu in a separate file, as long as it respects the following simple convention of writing:

```
<h:body>
  <ui:composition>
    <ul>
      <li>
        <h:link value="..." outcome="..."/>
      </li>
      <li>
        <h:link value="..." outcome="..."/>
      </li>
    ...
    </ul>
  </ui:composition>
</h:body>
```

This file can be included as follows:

```
<ui:define name="menu">
  <ui:include src="myMenu.xhtml"/>
</ui:define>
```

Another approach consists of passing menu items via `<ui:param>` using the following code:

```
<ui:param name="items" value="item#outcome,item#outcome,..."/>
```

This will work because the `menuDefault.xhtml` page provides a default implementation that looks like the following code:

```
<ui:composition>
  <c:if test="${not empty items}">
   <ul>
    <ui:repeat value="${fn:split(items, ',')}" var="t">
      <li>
        <h:link value="${fn:substringBefore(t, '#')}"
          outcome="${fn:substringAfter(t, '#')}"/>
      </li>
    </ui:repeat>
   </ul>
  </c:if>
</ui:composition>
```

The complete application is named `ch12_18`. In the application `ch12_19`, you can see a usage example of this template, which looks similar to the following screenshot:

Notice that we have dropped the search and right panel sections.

# Facelets' programmatic aspects

In the second part of this chapter, we will focus more on several programmatic aspects of Facelets. We will start with a new feature of JSF 2.2 regarding `FaceletFactory`, which produces Facelets relative to the context of the underlying implementation.

## FaceletFactory considerations

In JSF 2.0, the `FaceletFactory` class was not accessible via the standard API for accessing factories, `FactoryFinder`. This means that something like the following line was not working:

```
FaceletFactory faceletFactory = (FaceletFactory)
FactoryFinder.getFactory
  (javax.faces.view.facelets.FaceletFactory);
```

But starting with JSF 2.2, the preceding snippet of code should work. At least this is what the list of JSF 2.2 features said. Unfortunately, it doesn't work because the specification doesn't contain a class named `javax.faces.view.facelets. FaceletFactory`. In Mojarra 2.2.6 implementation, the `FaceletFactory` class doesn't even exist; there is a public class named `com.sun.faces.facelets.impl. DefaultFaceletFactory`. On the other hand, in MyFaces 2.2.2, we have the abstract class, `org.apache.myfaces.view.facelets.FaceletFactory`. So, keep these aspects in mind when you decide to use, decorate, or write a new `FaceletFactory` class.

In the near future, we may have the ability to programmatically create a Facelet and call the `apply` method in order to build a component tree.

## Working with FaceletCache

Starting with JSF 2.1, Facelets are created and cached via the `FaceletCache` API. The cache handles two different kinds of Facelets: **View Facelets** and **View Metadata Facelets**. For each type, the `FaceletCache` API provides a method that returns/creates a cached instance based on the URL that is passed (`getFacelet`/`getViewMetadataFacelet`) and a method capable of determining whether a cached Facelet instance exists for the given URL (`isFaceletCached`/ `isViewMetadataFaceletCached`).

 **View Metadata Facelets** is a special kind of Facelet that corresponds to `ViewDeclarationLanguage.getViewMetadata(javax.faces. context.FacesContext, java.lang.String)`.

Facelets instances are created in the `getFacelet`/`getViewMetadataFacelet` method using the public static interface, `FaceletCache.MemberFactory`; this interface is responsible for the creation of Facelet or View Metadata Facelet instances using a method named `newInstance(URL key)`. The `getFacelet` method has access to `FaceletCache.MemberFactory` via the protected method, `getMemberFactory`. The `getViewMetadataFacelet` method has access to the same interface via the protected method, `getMetadataMemberFactory`.

The `FaceletCache` API's instances are obtained from `FaceletCacheFactory`. This is a factory class that provides two methods: `getFaceletCache` and `getWrapped`. The first one returns a `FaceletCache` instance, the latter one returns an instance of the class being wrapped.

In order to return a custom `FaceletCache` instance, we can start with a custom implementation of `FaceletCacheFactory`, as shown in the following code:

```
public class CustomFaceletCacheFactory extends FaceletCacheFactory {

  private FaceletCacheFactory faceletCacheFactory;

  public CustomFaceletCacheFactory() {}

  public CustomFaceletCacheFactory(FaceletCacheFactory
    faceletCacheFactory) {
    this.faceletCacheFactory = faceletCacheFactory;
  }

  @Override
  public FaceletCache getFaceletCache() {
    return new CustomFaceletCache();
  }

  @Override
  public FaceletCacheFactory getWrapped() {
    return this.faceletCacheFactory;
  }
}
```

This factory has to be configured in `faces-config.xml` using the following code:

```
<factory>
  <facelet-cache-factory>
    book.beans.CustomFaceletCacheFactory
  </facelet-cache-factory>
</factory>
```

Now, our `CustomFaceletCache` class will override the `getFacelet` and `getViewMetadataFacelet` methods for disabling the cache mechanism; our implementation will not cache Facelets. The code of the `CustomFaceletCache` class is as follows:

```java
public class CustomFaceletCache extends FaceletCache<Facelet> {

  public CustomFaceletCache() {}

  @Override
  public Facelet getFacelet(URL url) throws IOException {
    MemberFactory<Facelet> memberFactory = getMemberFactory();
    Facelet facelet = memberFactory.newInstance(url);

    return facelet;
  }

  @Override
  public boolean isFaceletCached(URL url) {
    return false;
  }

  @Override
  public Facelet getViewMetadataFacelet(URL url) throws
    IOException {
    MemberFactory<Facelet> metadataMemberFactory =
      getMetadataMemberFactory();
    Facelet facelet = metadataMemberFactory.newInstance(url);

    return facelet;
  }

  @Override
  public boolean isViewMetadataFaceletCached(URL url) {
    return false;
  }

  public FaceletCache<Facelet> getWrapped() {
    return this;
  }
}
```

The complete application is named `ch12_15`.

In order to update the cache, JSF performs periodic checks of Facelets views changes. In the development stage, you may need to perform this check much often than in production. For this, you can set the `javax.faces.FACELETS_REFRESH_PERIOD` context parameter as shown in the following example (the value represents the number of seconds between two consecutive checks):

```
<context-param>
  <param-name> javax.faces.FACELETS_REFRESH_PERIOD</param-name>
  <param-value>2</param-value>
</context-param>
```

Alternatively, for backwards compatibility with existing Facelets tag libraries, the following is the code:

```
<context-param>
  <param-name>facelets.REFRESH_PERIOD</param-name>
  <param-value>2</param-value>
</context-param>
```

If you want to disable these checks, then set the `javax.faces.FACELETS_REFRESH_PERIOD` (or `facelets.REFRESH_PERIOD`) parameter to `-1`.

# ResourceResolver swallowed by ResourceHandler

JSF 2.0 promotes the `ResourceResolver` class as the custom approach for loading Facelets views from other locations beside the application web root (like a hook that allows us to alter the way that the Facelets loads template files). Custom locations represent any location for which we can write a URL.

For example, let's suppose that the Facelets views of our `PageLayout` template are stored on the local machine, in the `facelets` folder in `D:`. A custom `ResourceResolver` class can load the Facelets views from this location—just override the `resolveUrl` method, as shown in the following code:

```
public class CustomResourceResolver extends ResourceResolver {

  private ResourceResolver resourceResolver;

  public CustomResourceResolver(){}

  public CustomResourceResolver(ResourceResolver
    resourceResolver){
```

```
      this.resourceResolver = resourceResolver;
   }

   @Override
   public URL resolveUrl(String path) {

      URL result = null;
      if (path.startsWith("/template")) {
         try {
            result = new URL("file:///D:/facelets/" + path);
         } catch (MalformedURLException ex) {
            Logger.getLogger(CustomResourceResolver.class.getName()).
               log(Level.SEVERE, null, ex);
         }
      } else {
         result = resourceResolver.resolveUrl(path);
      }

   return result;
   }
}
```

A custom `ResourceResolver` class is recognized by JSF if we configure it properly in the `web.xml` file, as shown in the following code:

```
<context-param>
   <param-name>javax.faces.FACELETS_RESOURCE_RESOLVER</param-name>
   <param-value>book.beans.CustomResourceResolver</param-value>
</context-param>
```

However, starting with JSF 2.2, we can skip this configuration and use the `@FaceletsResourceResolver` annotation as follows:

```
@FaceletsResourceResolver
public class CustomResourceResolver extends ResourceResolver {
...
```

The complete application using the `web.xml` configuration is named `ch12_2`. The same application, using the `@FaceletsResourceResolver` annotation, is named `ch12_5`.

On the other hand, the `ResourceHandler` class is recommended to be used for serving different kinds of resources to the client, such as CSS, JS, and images; see the *Configuring resource handlers* section in *Chapter 5, JSF Configurations Using XML Files and Annotations – Part 2*. By default, the preferred location of `ResourceHandler` is the `/resources` folder (or `META-INF/resources` on the `CLASSPATH`). A custom `ResourceHandler` class is recognized by JSF if we configure it properly in the `faces-config.xml file`, as follows:

```
<application>
  <resource-handler>fully_qualified_class_name</resource-handler>
</application>
```

Since this was a pretty awkward approach, JSF 2.2 unifies these classes into a single one. More exactly, the functionality of the `ResourceResolver` class has been merged into the `ResourceHandler` class, and the `ResourceResolver` class itself has been deprecated. The main result of this action was a new method in `ResourceHandler` named `createViewResource`. The purpose of this method is to replace the `resolveUrl` method. So, instead of loading Facelets views from custom locations via `ResourceResolver`, we can use a custom `ResourceHandler` class and a `createViewResource` method, as shown in the following code:

```java
public class CustomResourceHandler extends ResourceHandlerWrapper {

  private ResourceHandler resourceHandler;

  public CustomResourceHandler() {}

  public CustomResourceHandler(ResourceHandler resourceHandler) {
    this.resourceHandler = resourceHandler;
  }

  @Override
  public Resource createResource(String resourceName,
    String libraryOrContractName) {

    //other kinds of resources, such as scripts and stylesheets
    return getWrapped().createResource(resourceName,
      libraryOrContractName);
  }

  @Override
  public ViewResource createViewResource(FacesContext context,
    String resourceName) {
```

```
    ViewResource viewResource;
    if (resourceName.startsWith("/template")) {
      viewResource = new CustomViewResource(resourceName);
    } else {
      viewResource = getWrapped().
      createViewResource(context, resourceName);
    }

    return viewResource;
  }

  @Override
  public ResourceHandler getWrapped() {
    return this.resourceHandler;
  }
}
```

When the `ResourceResolver` class was deprecated, the existing type `javax.faces.application.Resource` class has been given a base class named `javax.faces.application.ViewResource`. This class contains a single method named `getURL`. So, when a Facelets view should be loaded from a custom location, we tell JSF to use our `CustomViewResource` class as follows:

```
public class CustomViewResource extends ViewResource {

  private String resourceName;

  public CustomViewResource(String resourceName) {
    this.resourceName = resourceName;
  }

  @Override
  public URL getURL() {
    URL url = null;
    try {
      url = new URL("file:///D:/facelets/" + resourceName);
    } catch (MalformedURLException ex) {
      Logger.getLogger(CustomViewResource.class.getName()).
        log(Level.SEVERE, null, ex);
    }
  return url;
  }
}
```

The `createViewResource` method provides several advantages, because it *is applicable to general view resources and by default is functional equivalent to the existing* `createResource` *method. Besides being much more consistent, this means it's now also possible to load Facelets from a JAR file without needing to provide a custom resolver.*

The complete application is named `ch12_3`.

For backward compatibility, JSF will let the default resolver to call the new `createViewResource` method as shown in the following code:

```
public class CustomResourceResolver extends ResourceResolver {
...
  @Override
  public URL resolveUrl(String path) {

    URL result;
    if (path.startsWith("/template")) {
      ViewResource viewResource = new CustomViewResource(path);
      result = viewResource.getURL();
    } else {
      FacesContext facesContext =
        FacesContext.getCurrentInstance();
      ResourceHandler resourceHandler =
        facesContext.getApplication().getResourceHandler();
      result = resourceHandler.createViewResource
        (facesContext, path).getURL();
    }

  return result;
  }
}
```

The complete application is named `ch12_4`.

# Include Facelets programmatically

You already know how to include Facelets using the `<ui:include>` tag. But, sometimes you may need to programmatically reproduce something like the following code:

```
<ui:include src="/files/fileA.xhtml">
  <ui:param name="bparam" value="string_literal"/>
</ui:include>
<ui:include src="/files/fileB.xhtml">
```

```
    <ui:param name="cparam" value="#{managed_bean_property}"/>
</ui:include>
<ui:include src="/files/fileC.xhtml"/>
```

Programmatically speaking, the same thing can be accomplished if you know: how to obtain access to `FaceletContext`, how to use the `FaceletContext.includeFacelet` method, and how to set attributes using `FaceletContext.setAttribute`. For example, the programmatic version of the preceding snippet of code is:

```
public void addFaceletAction() throws IOException {

    FacesContext context = FacesContext.getCurrentInstance();
    FaceletContext faceletContext = (FaceletContext)
      context.getAttributes().
      get(FaceletContext.FACELET_CONTEXT_KEY);

    faceletContext.includeFacelet(context.getViewRoot(),
      "/files/fileA.xhtml");
    faceletContext.setAttribute("bparam",
      "file B - text as ui:param via string literal...");
    faceletContext.includeFacelet(context.getViewRoot(),
      "/files/fileB.xhtml");
    faceletContext.setAttribute("cparam", cfiletext);
    faceletContext.includeFacelet(context.getViewRoot(),
      "/files/fileC.xhtml");
}
```

The complete application is named `ch12_22`.

# Creating a TagHandler class

You already know that several Facelets tags are tag handlers, while the others are component handlers—in *Chapter 10, JSF Custom Components*, you saw how to write a `ComponentHandler` class for a custom component. In this section, you will see how to write a `TagHandler` class.

 Tag handlers are efficient only when the view tree is built.

In order to write a `TagHandler` class, you need to perform the following steps:

1. Extend the `TagHandler` class and override the `apply` method; this method process changes on a particular `UIComponent` class. Access the tag attributes via the `getAttribute` and `getRequiredAttribute` methods, which returns a `TagAttribute` instance that exposes the attribute value, namespace, local name, tag (the latter is new in JSF 2.2, see the `getTag`/`setTag` documentation), and so on. Moreover, use the `tag` and `tagId` fields to refer to the `Tag` instance corresponding to this `TagHandler` instance. Delegate control to the next tag handler using the `nextHandler` field.

2. Write a `*taglib.xml` file to configure the tag namespace, name, and handler class.

3. Indicate the location of the `*taglib.xml` file using the `javax.faces.FACELETS_LIBRARIES` context parameter in the `web.xml` file.

For example, let's suppose that we need the following functionality: we provide a piece of text, the number of times it should be displayed, and the possibility to be displayed in uppercase. We may think of a tag as follows:

```
<t:textrepeat text="Vamos Rafa!" repeat="10" uppercase="yes"/>
```

A `TagHandler` class can be the response to our need. First, we extend the `TagHandler` class, as shown in the following code:

```
public class CustomTagHandler extends TagHandler {

    protected final TagAttribute text;
    protected final TagAttribute repeat;
    protected final TagAttribute uppercase;

    public CustomTagHandler(TagConfig config) {
        super(config);
        this.text = this.getRequiredAttribute("text");
        this.repeat = this.getRequiredAttribute("repeat");
        this.uppercase = this.getAttribute("uppercase");
    }

    @Override
    public void apply(FaceletContext ctx, UIComponent parent)
        throws IOException {
        String s = "";
        UIOutput child = new HtmlOutputText();
```

```
for (int i = 0; i < Integer.valueOf(repeat.getValue()); i++) {
  s = s + text.getValue() + " ";
}

if (uppercase != null) {
  if (uppercase.getValue().equals("yes")) {
    s = s.toUpperCase();
  } else {
    s = s.toLowerCase();
  }
}

child.setValue(s);
parent.getChildren().add(child);

nextHandler.apply(ctx, parent);
    }
}
```

Furthermore, you need to write the *taglib.xml file and configure it in the web.xml file. The complete application is named ch12_17.

# Writing custom Facelets taglib functions

When you need a value to be evaluated directly in EL, then Facelets taglib functions (or expression functions) are a great solution. For example, let's say that we want to encrypt/decrypt text and the result to be placed directly into an EL expression. In order to do this, you need to perform the following general steps of writing a function:

1. Write a Java public final class.

2. In this class, implement the desired functionality using public static methods.

3. Write a *taglib.xml file for linking the public static methods (functions) with JSF pages. For each static method, you need to specify the name (<function-name>), the fully qualified class name that contains the static method (<function-class>), and the declaration of the static method (<function-signature>).

4. Indicate the location of the *taglib.xml file using the javax.faces. FACELETS_LIBRARIES context parameter in the web.xml file.

So, based on these steps, we can write a class that contains two functions, one for encryption and one for decryption, as shown in the following code:

```
public final class DESFunction {

  ...

  public static String encrypt(String str) {
  ...
  }

  public static String decrypt(String str) {
  ...
  }
}
```

The *taglib.xml file is straightforward as can be seen in the following snippet:

```
<?xml version="1.0" encoding="UTF-8"?>
<facelet-taglib
  xmlns="http://java.sun.com/xml/ns/javaee"
  xmlns:xsi="http://www.w3.org/2001/XMLSchema-instance"
  xsi:schemaLocation="http://java.sun.com/xml/ns/javaee
  http://java.sun.com/xml/ns/javaee/web-facelettaglibrary_2_0.xsd"
  version="2.0">

  <namespace>http://packt.com/encrypts</namespace>

  <function>
    <function-name>encrypt</function-name>
    <function-class>book.beans.DESFunction</function-class>
    <function-signature>String encrypt(java.lang.String)
    </function-signature>
  </function>

  <function>
    <function-name>decrypt</function-name>
    <function-class>book.beans.DESFunction</function-class>
    <function-signature>String decrypt(java.lang.String)
    </function-signature>
  </function>
</facelet-taglib>
```

After you configure the preceding `*taglib.xml` file in `web.xml`, you can try to call the encrypt/decrypt functions, as follows:

```
<h:outputText value="#{des:encrypt('Rafael Nadal')}"/>
<h:outputText value="#{des:decrypt('9QnQL04/hGbJj/PqukPb9A==')}"/>
```

The complete application is named `ch12_16`.

# Facelets pitfalls

It is a well-known fact that JSF pitfalls are not easy to understand and fix. This is mostly because their roots originate in: JSF life cycle, bad practices of using listeners and events, misunderstandings regarding EL processing and evaluation, conflicting combinations of tag handlers with components, and so on.

In this section, we will focus on three common Facelets pitfalls.

## AJAX and <ui:repeat>

There is a common scenario to use AJAX for re-rendering the content of an `<ui:repeat>` tag. It is absolutely intuitive to write something like the following code:

```
<h:form>
  <ui:repeat id="playersId" value="#{playersBean.dataArrayList}"
    var="t">
    <h:outputText value="#{t.player}" />
  </ui:repeat>
  <h:commandButton value="Half It"
    action="#{playersBean.halfAction()}">
    <f:ajax execute="@form" render="playersId" />
  </h:commandButton>
</h:form>
```

So, initially, there is a list of *n* players and when we click on the button labeled **Half It**, we want to remove half of the players and re-render the list. The problem is that the preceding snippet of code will not work as expected, because the `<ui:repeat>` tag doesn't render HTML code; therefore, there will be no HTML element with the ID, `playersId`. Instead of seeing a list with only five players, we will get a `malformedXML` error.

 This more of a pitfall of using JSF AJAX with components that do not get rendered as expected.

A simple workaround will be to enclose the `<ui:repeat>` tag inside a `<div>` tag, as shown in the following code:

```
<h:form>
  <h:panelGroup id="playersId" layout="block">
    <ui:repeat value="#{playersBean.dataArrayList}" var="t">
      <h:outputText value="#{t.player}" />
    </ui:repeat>
  </h:panelGroup>
  <h:commandButton value="Half It"
    action="#{playersBean.halfAction()}">
    <f:ajax execute="@form" render="playersId" />
  </h:commandButton>
</h:form>
```

The complete application is named `ch12_26`.

# Exemplifying <c:if> versus <ui:fragment>

Another common scenario is to render a table data based on a `<c:if>` condition, as follows:

```
<h:dataTable value="#{playersBean.dataArrayList}" var="t">
  <h:column>
    <c:if test="#{t.age gt 26}">
      <h:outputText value="#{t.player}, #{t.age}"/>
    </c:if>
  </h:column>
</h:dataTable>
```

Again, the result will not be as expected. The problem is that `<c:if>` is a tag handler; therefore, it is efficiently reflected when the tree is built. A perfect workaround will be to replace `<c:if>` with the `<ui:fragment>` tag, which is a component handler. The rendered attribute of `<ui:fragment>` can successfully replace the `<c:if>` test using the following code:

```
<h:dataTable value="#{playersBean.dataArrayList}" var="t">
  <h:column>
    <ui:fragment rendered="#{t.age gt 26}">
      <h:outputText value="#{t.player}, #{t.age}"/>
    </ui:fragment>
  </h:column>
</h:dataTable>
```

Alternatively, in an even simpler way, use the `rendered` attribute of `<h:outputText>`; this approach is particular to this example:

```
<h:dataTable value="#{playersBean.dataArrayList}" var="t">
  <h:column>
    <h:outputText value="#{t.player}, #{t.age}"
      rendered="#{t.age gt 26}"/>
  </h:column>
</h:dataTable>
```

Instead, even cooler, using a lambda expression (EL 3.0), you can write the following code:

```
<h:dataTable value="#{(playersBean.dataArrayList.stream().
  filter((p)->p.age gt 26 )).toList()}" var="t">
  <h:column>
    <h:outputText value="#{t.player}, #{t.age}"/>
  </h:column>
</h:dataTable>
```

The complete application is named `ch12_20`.

# Exemplifying <c:forEach> versus <ui:repeat>

Apparently, you may think that the `<ui:repeat>`/`<ui:include>` pair is the perfect choice for including a list of Facelets pages using the following code:

```
<ui:repeat value="#{filesBean.filesList}" var="t">
  <ui:include src="#{t}"/>
</ui:repeat>
```

Well, the `<ui:include>` tag is a tag handler; therefore it will be available when the view is built, while the `<ui:repeat>` tag is a component handler available during the rendering process. In other words, when `<ui:include>` needs the t variable, `<ui:repeat>` is not available. Therefore, `<ui:repeat>` should be replaced by a tag handler, as `<c:forEach>`, as shown in the following code:

```
<c:forEach items="#{filesBean.filesList}" var="t">
  <ui:include src="#{t}"/>
</c:forEach>
```

The complete application is named `ch12_21`.

# Summary

Facelets is a large subject with many interesting aspects which are pretty hard to cover in a few chapters of a book. As you know, there are books entirely dedicated to Facelets, but I hope that in the final three chapters I managed to cover a decent part of the JSF 2.2 default VDL. Probably, the most used part of Facelets is templating; therefore, I have tried to cover some handy techniques for writing flexible and cool templates. Of course, besides skills and techniques, writing templates is also a test of the imagination. Once we master the Facelets tags and choose the right techniques, we are ready to start writing templates. If we choose some naming conventions as well, then we can easily share our templates with the JSF world, like Mamadou Lamine Ba tried in a Java.Net project at `https://weblogs.java.net/blog/lamineba/archive/2011/10/03/conventional-ui-design-facelets-and-jsf-22`. In addition, if we spice up our template files with some Facelets programmatic tricks, then we can really rock the world of JSF templating!

# The JSF Life Cycle

The initial and postback requests in JSF go through a JSF life cycle. When an initial request is processed, it only executes the *Restore View* and *Render Response* phases, because there is no user input or actions to process. On the other hand, when the life cycle handles a postback request, it executes all of the phases.

Moreover, JSF supports AJAX requests. An AJAX request consists of two parts: partial processing (the `execute` attribute) and partial rendering (the `render` attribute).

In the following diagram, you can have a look at the different phases of the JSF life cycle:

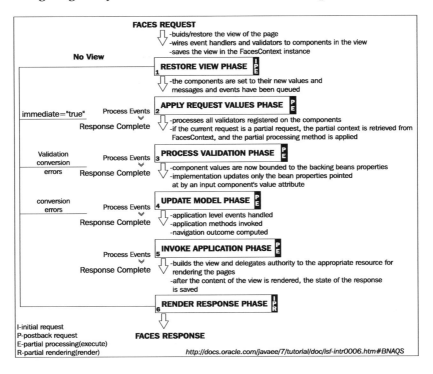

The symbols from the preceding diagram **I**, **P**, **E**, and **R** stand for:

- **I**: This is the phase executed for the initial request
- **P**: This is the phase executed for the postback request
- **E**: This is the phase executed at partial processing
- **R**: This is the phase executed at partial rendering

# Index

# A

Facelets, including programmatically 531
ResourceResolver and ResourceHandler
classes 527-531
TagHandler class, creating 532-534
**Facelets taglib functions**
writing 534-536
**Facelets tags**
<ui:component> tag 497
<ui:composition> tag 495
<ui:debug> tag 497
<ui:decorate> tag 497
<ui:define> tag 496
<ui:fragment> tag 497
<ui:include> tag 496
<ui:insert> tag 496
<ui:param> tag 496
<ui:remove> tag 498
<ui:repeat> tag 497
about 495
URL 498
**Facelets Templating namespace 148**
**Facelet templates 467**
**Faces Core namespace 148**
**Faces Servlet class 404**
**finalizer**
using 120-123
**first property 288**
**Flash**
configuring 239, 240
**Flash scope**
used, for passing parameters 64-69
**FlowBuilder API**
used, for configuring flows 114
**FlowBuilder.finalizer method**
using 120
**FlowBuilder.initializer method**
using 120
**flow scope**
about 100
and AJAX, mixing 329-333
and navigation cases 116-119
beans 107-109
finalizer, using 120-122
flow definition 102
flow switch, using 123-125

inbound parameters 102
initializer, using 120-122
navigation cases, inspecting 119, 120
nested flow 110-114
outbound parameters 102
packaging 125, 126
parameters implementation 129
programmatic access 126-129
programmatic configuration 114-116
return node 100
simple flow 104-107
start node 100
using 102
using, benefits 101
using, example 102, 103
**flow switch**
using 123-125
**forClass attribute**
used, for configuring converters 166
**FullVisitContext method 297**

# G

**generateCredentials method 331**
**getCommonPropertyType method**
implementing 29
**getFacelet method 525**
**getFeatureDescriptors method**
implementing 29
**getInitParameter method**
context parameters, accessing via 42
**getPhaseId method**
using 193
**GET requests**
actions, calling on 53-58
**getReturnValue method 330**
**getSinglesRankings method 30**
**getState() method 396, 397**
**getter method, Map collection**
about 265
table code 265
**getType method**
implementing 27
**getValue method**
implementing 26

resetFile method 372
resetValues attribute
  about 325
  AJAX request, using with 324
resource bundle
  about 158
  configuring 158
ResourceHandler class
  versus ResourceResolver class 527-531
resource handlers
  configuring 200-207
Resource Library Contracts 467
ResourceResolver class
  versus ResourceHandler class 527-531
responseCode property 318
ResponseStateManager class 396
ResponseStateManager.writeState()
    method 396
responseText property 318
ResponseWriter object 420
responseXML property 318
restore view phase 541
right parameter 522
rightWidth parameter 522
rowclasses attribute
  used, for coloring alternate
      table rows 306, 307
rowCount property 288
row numbers
  displaying 282
rows property 288
rvalue 10

# S

saveFileToDisk method 375
schedule-flow.xml file
  programmatic translation 115, 116
search parameter 522
semicolon operator
  working with 36
server-state serialization, session 406, 407
session map
  programmatic access 91

used, for communication between managed
    beans 78-80
session scope
  about 90
  invalidating 92
  using 90-92
setPropertyResolved method 30
setRowIndex method
  overriding 274
setValue method
  implementing 27, 28
showHideRacquetPicture method 25
showSelectedPlayer method 283
showSelectedPlayers method 286
simple flow
  confirm.xhtml page 106
  defining 104-106
  done.xhtml page 106
  faces-config.xml file 107
  registration-flow.xml file 106
  registration.xhtml page 105
single row, table
  selecting 283-285
size attribute 508
source 38
source parameter 342
source property 318
SQL injection 412
StateHelper.put method
  using 422
stateless view
  programmatic detection 411
StateManager.writeState() method 396
status property 318
step attribute 508
streams 38
string concatenation operator
  working with 36
Submit button
  value submission, to request scoped
      managed bean 328
  value submission, to view scoped managed
      bean 326